The Human Rights Breakthrough of the 1970s

The Human Rights Breakthrough of the 1970s

The European Community and International Relations

Edited by
Sara Lorenzini, Umberto Tulli and
Ilaria Zamburlini

BLOOMSBURY ACADEMIC
LONDON · NEW YORK · OXFORD · NEW DELHI · SYDNEY

BLOOMSBURY ACADEMIC
Bloomsbury Publishing Plc
50 Bedford Square, London, WC1B 3DP, UK
1385 Broadway, New York, NY 10018, USA
29 Earlsfort Terrace, Dublin 2, Ireland

BLOOMSBURY, BLOOMSBURY ACADEMIC and the Diana logo are trademarks of
Bloomsbury Publishing Plc

First published in Great Britain 2022
This paperback edition published 2023

Copyright © Sara Lorenzini, Umberto Tulli and Ilaria Zamburlini, 2022

Sara Lorenzini, Umberto Tulli and Ilaria Zamburlini have asserted their right under the
Copyright, Designs and Patents Act, 1988, to be identified as Editors of this work.

For legal purposes the Acknowledgements on p. xi constitute an extension
of this copyright page.

Cover design: Terry Woodley
Cover image © January 01, 1977, Foreign Ministers of the European Community
meet at Lancaster House in London. Keystone Press/Alamy Stock Photo

All rights reserved. No part of this publication may be reproduced or transmitted
in any form or by any means, electronic or mechanical, including photocopying,
recording, or any information storage or retrieval system, without prior
permission in writing from the publishers.

Bloomsbury Publishing Plc does not have any control over, or responsibility for, any
third-party websites referred to or in this book. All internet addresses given in
this book were correct at the time of going to press. The author and publisher
regret any inconvenience caused if addresses have changed or sites have
ceased to exist, but can accept no responsibility for any such changes.

A catalogue record for this book is available from the British Library.

Library of Congress Cataloging-in-Publication Data
Names: Lorenzini, Sara, editor. | Tulli, Umberto, editor. | Zamburlini, Ilaria, editor.
Title: The human rights breakthrough of the 1970s : the European community and
international relations / edited by Sara Lorenzini, Umberto Tulli & Ilaria Zamburlini.
Description: London ; New York : Bloomsbury Academic, 2022. | Includes bibliographical
references and index.
Identifiers: LCCN 2021029045 (print) | LCCN 2021029046 (ebook) | ISBN 9781350203129
(hardback) | ISBN 9781350203136 (pdf) | ISBN 9781350203143 (ebook)
Subjects: LCSH: Human rights—Europe—History—20th century. | International economic
relations—History—20th century. | Convention for the Protection of Human Rights and
Fundamental Freedoms (1950 November 5) | Europe—Foreign relations—1945-
Classification: LCC JC599.E9 H846 2022 (print) | LCC JC599.E9 (ebook) |
DDC 323.094—dc23/eng/20211004
LC record available at https://lccn.loc.gov/2021029045
LC ebook record available at https://lccn.loc.gov/2021029046

ISBN: HB: 978-1-3502-0312-9
PB: 978-1-3502-1067-7
ePDF: 978-1-3502-0313-6
eBook: 978-1-3502-0314-3

Typeset by Deanta Global Publishing Services, Chennai, India

To find out more about our authors and books visit www.bloomsbury.com and
sign up for our newsletters.

Contents

List of illustrations — vii
Notes on editors and contributors — viii
Acknowledgements — xi
List of abbreviations — xii

Introduction: The place of human rights in European integration
Sara Lorenzini, Umberto Tulli and Ilaria Zamburlini — 1

Part 1 The European community and human rights violations in the world

1 Knocking on Europe's doors: Community Europe and human rights after dictatorial rule in Southern Europe (1974–7) *Víctor Fernández Soriano* — 13
2 Introducing human rights within development cooperation policies: The European Community between the United States and the Soviet Union (1968–79) *Ilaria Zamburlini* — 30
3 A reluctant promoter: The EC, CSCE and human rights in East–West relations *Umberto Tulli* — 45
4 EC member states' stance on human rights issues: The perspective from the UN General Assembly, 1970–9 *Lorenzo Ferrari* — 63

Part 2 Member states, supranational institutions, European parties

5 The European Union of Christian Democrats and the controversy regarding the Spanish accession to the EC in the 1970s: The human rights problem *Marialuisa Lucia Sergio* — 81
6 The Socialist Group of the European Parliament and human rights in the second half of the 1970s *Christian Salm* — 100
7 An awkward partner?: Britain's human rights policy and EC relations, 1977–9 *David Grealy* — 120
8 Between restrictiveness and humanitarianism: EC institutions and the asylum policies of the 1980s *Gaia Lott* — 139

Part 3 Other Europes

9 Human rights NGOs in Western Europe and the intervention of the Council of Europe in the Nigerian Civil War *Oluchukwu Ignatus Onianwa* — 157

10 Beyond victims of communism?: Austria and the human rights question in the 1970s *Maximilian Graf* 178

Part 4 After the breakthrough: The European Union and human rights

11 The Twelve and the 1993 World Conference on Human Rights *Elena Calandri* 199
12 The European Union's influence on the Dutch position in the United Nations Human Rights Commission, 1995–2003 *Peter Malcontent* 216

References 235
Index 262

Illustrations

Figures

1.1	Mikis Theodorakis and Melina Mercouri at a press conference in Paris on 29 April 1970	18
2.1	Ex-Officer in the Ugandan Army and alleged 'guerrilla' Tom Masaba is stripped of his clothes and tied to a tree before his execution at Mbale	37
3.1	Opening speech at the first Sakharov Hearings	53
3.2	Soviet writer and dissident Andrei Amalrik in front of the Elysee Palace in Paris on 23 February 1977	54
5.1	Don Carlos Arias Navarro, the Prime Minister of Spain between 1973 and 1976	86
5.2	Italian Christian-Democrat leader Mariano Rumor	87
6.1	Protesters in Paris	111
6.2	German Social-Democrat Willy Brandt and German Chancellor Helmut Schmidt in a meeting of the German Social Democratic Party during the campaign for the European elections in 1979	113
7.1	British Prime Minister James Callaghan, Foreign Secretary David Owen and US Secretary of State Cyrus Vance seated together at a Council meeting at Lancaster House, London, 10 May 1977	130
9.1	Women and children receiving food at refugee camp during the Biafra war	160

Table

4.1	Index of Agreement among EC Member States Values	67

Chart

4.1	Cohesion of EC member states in the roll-call votes on human rights at the UN General Assembly	69

Editors and Contributors

Editors

Sara Lorenzini is Professor of Contemporary History at the Department of Humanities and at the School of International Studies, University of Trento. She holds a Jean Monnet Chair on the global history of European integration. She participates in several national and international projects, such as the recent 'Inventing the Global Environment: Science, Politics, Advocacy and the Environment-Development Nexus in the Cold War and Beyond'. Her latest book, *Global Development* (Princeton, 2019), analyses development aid as Cold War political and ideological project.

Umberto Tulli is Assistant Professor of Contemporary History at the Department of Humanities and at the School of International Studies, University of Trento. His recent publications include *A Precarious Equilibrium. Human Rights and Détente in Jimmy Carter's Soviet Policy* (Manchester, 2020) and 'The European Parliament in EC External Relations, from the Inception of European Political Cooperation to the Single European Act,' *Journal of European Integration History* (Baden-Baden, 2021).

Ilaria Zamburlini received her PhD in Contemporary History at the University of Trieste in 2018, with a dissertation on the EEC, human rights and development. She is the author of several essays, including 'Calling on European Responsibility to Shape the Vision of Europe? Human Rights, Development Assistance and European Identity in the 1970s,' in *Visions and Revisions of Europe*, ed. by K. Czerka-Shaw, M. Galent and B. Gierat-Bieroń (Göttingen, 2018); and 'Human Rights and Foreign Aid. Three NGOs Influencing the European Community (1974-1979),' in *The Informal Construction of Europe*, ed. by Mechthild Roos and Lennaert van Heumen (Abingdon and New York, 2019).

Contributors

Elena Calandri is Professor of International History at the University of Padua. Her recent publications include 'EEC and the Mediterranean: Hitting the Glass Ceiling' in U. Krotz, K.K.Patel, F.Romero, ed., *Europe's Cold War Relations: The EC toward a Global Role* (London, 2019) and *L'Europa adulta. Attori, ragioni e sfide all'Atto Unico alla Brexit* (Bologna, 2020) (together with Simone Paoli and Giuliana Laschi).

Lorenzo Ferrari received a PhD in political history at the IMT Institute for Advanced Studies, Lucca (Italy) in 2014, and was a visiting fellow at the University of Turku

(Finland) in 2016. His publications include *Sometimes Speaking with a Single Voice* (Brussels, 2016) as well as journal articles on the EC's international activity, human rights and decolonization. Since 2017 he has been working at the Center for International Cooperation, Trento (Italy).

Maximilian Graf is Research Fellow in the ERC project 'Unlikely refuge? Refugees and Citizens in East-Central Europe in the 20th Century' at the Masaryk Institute and Archives of the Czech Academy of Sciences. Previously he held positions and fellowships at the Austrian Academy of Sciences, the University of Vienna, the Centre Marc Bloch in Berlin, the European University Institute in Florence, the Austrian Historical Institute in Rome and Stanford University.

David Grealy received his PhD from the University of Liverpool in 2020 ('Human Rights and British Foreign Policy, c.1977-97: An Intellectual Biography of David Owen') and is currently teaching at Lancaster University. He has participated in the Global Humanitarianism Research Academy at the Leibniz Institute of European History, and studied at the Library of Congress in Washington, D.C., as an AHRC Fellow at the John W. Kluge Center.

Gaia Lott is visiting fellow at the European University Institute. She also works for the Italian Ministry of the Interior, as official responsible for the examination of asylum applications, specialized in Human Trafficking. She holds a PhD in History of International Relations from the University of Florence. She was postdoctoral research fellow at the Fondazione Luigi Einaudi (Torino), visiting fellow at the Wilson Center (Washington DC) and Max Weber Fellow at the European University Institute. Her research interests include History of International Relations, History of European Integration, African History, Asylum Policies and Policies to contrast human trafficking.

Peter Malcontent is Assistant Professor at the History of International Relations Department of Utrecht University (The Netherlands). He has published many books and articles, including *Facing the Past. Amending Historical Injustices through Instruments of Transitional Justice* (Cambridge, 2016) and *Een open zenuw. Nederland, Israël and Palestina* [An Open Nerve. The Netherlands, Israel & Palestine] (Amsterdam, 2018).

Oluchukwu Ignatus Onianwa is a diplomatic historian specializing in transnational, diplomatic and military history of the Nigerian Civil War and Biafran Studies. He received his PhD from the University of Ibadan in 2020. He is the author of several articles and books, such as *Britain's Injurious Peace Games in the Nigerian Civil War* (Washington and London, 2019) and *Once Upon a Time in Biafra: Memories, Foreign Visitations, and Life Experiences in the Nigerian Civil War, 1967-1970* (Washington and London, 2019).

Christian Salm is a historian at the European Parliamentary Research Service of the European Parliament. He obtained a PhD from the European Centre for European and International Studies Research at the University of Portsmouth. He has published on several issues pertaining to European transnational history, political parties in European integration, EU policy-making and the history of the European Parliament; among these: *Transnational Socialist Networks in the 1970s: European Community Development Aid and Southern Enlargement* (London, 2016).

Marialuisa Lucia Sergio is Associate Professor of Contemporary History at Roma Tre University. Her research interests focus on the history of political institutions, parties and movements and on the relationship between political-cultural dynamics and the religious dimension. Her recent publications include *La Convenzione ONU sui diritti dell'infanzia e dell'adolescenza tra storia e futuro* (Rome, 2020); 'Bonaventura Cerretti and the Impossible Missions,' in A. Melloni, G. Cavagnini, G. Grossi (ed.), *Benedict XV: A Pope in the World of the 'Useless Slaughter' (1914-1918)* (Brepols, 2020); and *Diario di Alcide De Gasperi 1930-1943* (Bologna, 2018).

Víctor Fernández Soriano holds a PhD in Contemporary History at the Université Libre de Bruxelles. His research revolves around human rights activism and European integration in the long 1970s. He has been a research fellow at the ULB Institute for European Studies, the Luxembourgish Centre for Contemporary and Digital History and Berlin Humboldt University. He also teaches at ESPOL Lille. He is the author of the book *Le fusil et l'olivier. Les droits de l'Homme en Europe face aux dictatures méditerranéennes (1947-1977)* (Brussels, 2015).

Acknowledgements

This book is one of the scientific outcomes of the Jean Monnet Chair in European Integration History 'Globalizing Europe/Europeanizing the World' supported by the European Commission.

The editors of the volume want to express their gratitude to the European Commission, whose support for the production of this publication does not constitute an endorsement of the contents, which reflect the views only of the authors, and the Commission cannot be held responsible for any use which may be made of the information contained therein.

Abbreviations

ACP	African Caribbean Pacific countries
ACS	Archivio Centrale dello Stato (Italian State Archive)
ADSA	Andrei D. Sakarov Archives
AEI	Archive of European Integration
AI	Amnesty International
AMA	Aldo Moro Archive
AMAE	Archives du Ministère des Affaires Étrangères (Archives of the french Foreign Ministry)
ASEAN	Association of Southeast Asian Nations
ASSR	Archivio Storico del Senato della Repubblica (Historical Archive of the Italian Senate)
BOE	*Boletín Oficial del Estado*
CAHAR	Ad Hoc Committee of Experts on the Legal Aspect of Territorial Asylum, Refugees and Stateless Persons
CDU	Christlich Demokratische Union
CFDT	Confèdèration Française Dèmocratique du Travail
CFSP	Common Foreign and Security Policy
CHR	Commission on Human Rights
CIJ	Commission Internationale de Juristes
CoE	Council of Europe
COPO	Political Committee
COREPER	Committee of Permanent Representatives
COREU	Correspondance Européenne
CSCE	Conference on Security and Cooperation in Europe
CSU	Christlich-Soziale Union
CVP	Christelijke Volkspartij
DAFM	Dutch Archive Foreign Ministry
DAO	Foreign Ministry's Asia and Oceania Department
DC	Democrazia Cristiana
DFB	Deutscher Fußball Bund

DHR	Dutch House of Representatives
DIO	Dutch Foreign Ministry's Department of International Organisations
DLMLA	Danish Labour Movement's Library and Archives
DMD	Dutch Foreign Ministry's Human Rights, Good Governance and Democratisation Department
DOP	David Owen Papers
EC	European Communities
ECHR	European Convention on Human Rights
ECSC	European Coal and Steel Community
EDU	European Democratic Union
EEC	European Economic Community
EFTA	European Free Trade Association
EMU	European Monetary Union
EP	European Parliament
EPC	European Political Cooperation
ETA	Euskadi Ta Askatasuna
EUCD	European Union of Christian Democrats
FCO	Foreign and Commonwealth Office
FIFA	Féderation Internationale de Football Association
FRG	Federal Republic of Germany
GPSE	Group du Parti socialiste européen du Parlement européen
HACEU	Historical Archives of the Council of the European Union
HAEC	Historical Archives of the European Commission
HAEP	Historical Archives of the European Parliament
HAEU	Historical Archives of the European Union
HRC	Human Rights Collection
ICRC	International Committee of Red Cross
IISH	International Institute of Social History
IUCW	International Union for Child Welfare
IYHR	International Year for Human Rights
JCPL	Jimmy Carter Presidential Library
LSFC	Swiss League of Catholic Women
MEP	Member of the European Parliament
MRF	Mariano Rumor Fonds

NATO	North Atlantic Treaty Organization
NGO	Non-Governmental Organization
NUOI	Nations Unies et Organisations Internationales
N+N	Neutral and Non-aligned Countries
OJ	*Official Journal of the European Communities*
ÖStA	Österreichisches Staatsarchiv (Austrian State Archive)
OUA	Organisation of African Unity
PACE	Parliamentary Assembly of the Council of Europe
PCE	Partido Comunista de España
SALT	Strategic Arms Limitation Talks
SAPMO	Stiftung Archiv der Parteien und Massenorganisationen der DDR im Bundesarchiv
SI	Socialist International
SIA	International Institute for Social History
TNA	The National Archives
UCD	Unión de Centro Democrático
UK	United Kingdom
UN	United Nations
UNGA	United Nations General Assembly
UNHCR	United Nations High Commissioner for Refugees
UNICEF	United Nations Children Fund
USSR	Union of Socialist Soviet Republics
WEOG	Western European and Others Group
YMCA	Young Men's Christian Association

Introduction

The place of human rights in European integration

Sara Lorenzini, Umberto Tulli and Ilaria Zamburlini

Human rights 'belong to the common background of our civilisation, they are part of our democratic structures and are one of the most authentic and measurable values of our society', announced the president of the European Commission François-Xavier Ortoli to the European Parliament, on the 15th of October 1975. He was confronting Francisco Franco's regime by condemning the execution of three members of the Revolutionary Antifascist Patriotic Front, in violation of basic human rights. Spain was not the only target of this human rights criticism. By 1975, the European Community (EC) was discussing the place of human rights in East–West relations, as embodied by the Conference on Cooperation and Security in Europe (CSCE), and debating how to sanction some African, Caribbean and Pacific Countries for their blatant violations of human rights.

The Human Rights Breakthrough of the 1970s is about the EC and the dramatic reappearance of human rights as a crucial element of global politics during the 1970s. It argues that the EC reacted to the new prominence of human rights by radically transforming its role in the world and adopting the protection of human rights as a distinctive feature of its nascent foreign policy. Human rights became crucial to the self-proclaimed European identity and surged to one of the fundamental principles governing its external relations. But translating principles into diplomatic action was not an easy task, and the place of human rights in the EC external relations mechanism remained a contested one. The specific tensions mixed up with the dynamics of the global reshaping of the decade.

Of course, the history of human rights in Western Europe began way before the 1970s. Human rights were an early concern for Europeans in the aftermath of the Second World War, when the protection of freedom and human rights was a topic that entered public discourse. Speeches of all European leaders across the political spectrum featured concerns around human rights. Similarly, human rights in postwar Europe were enshrined in new constitutions. In France, Italy and West Germany, for example, constitutions protected 'inalienable and sacred' human rights, as the French Constitution declares. Internationally, the Council of Europe took the lead in the writing of the European Convention on Human Rights (ECHR). Signed in 1950, it served as basis for the establishment of the European Court of human rights in 1959.[1] Building on the aftermath of the Second World War, the Cold War, European federalist ambitions and the attempt to preserve the British and the French empires, the Council of Europe worked with a definition of human rights that was different from the one included in the 1948 Universal Declaration of Human Rights. The right of self-determination did not figure in the ECHR's catalogue of rights, nor did economic and social rights. The ECHR became an anti-communist manifesto that defined the coordinates of a 'Europe of rights', in opposition to the Soviet-controlled Central and Eastern Europe, which did not respect individuals' rights or fundamental freedoms. It was a 'conservative revolution'[2]. To British and French conservatives, not only was the ECHR supposed to protect individuals' freedoms and rights from the Soviet threat, but also it had to counter the threatening moves of governments that were determined to empower the state and implement left-wing policies. To others, including European federalists, such as Belgian socialist Fernand Dehousse or the French republican Pierre Henri Teitgen, the ECHR was to become the first step in an integration process based on international law.[3]

The EC was quite a different kind of project to the Council of Europe and the ECHR. Culture, freedom and rights were not the primary concerns of the EC. Although growing out of the same glob of movements and ideas, the EC was based on a 'functionalist' vision that sought to promote peace and economic development by transferring resources and decision power to supranational institutions. It was mainly about building a common market and developing specific trade and economic policies. Both the 1952 Treaty of Paris that established the European Coal and Steel Community (ECSC) and the 1957 Treaty of Rome establishing the European Economic Community were silent on human rights and democracy, apart from a vague reference to freedom in the Treaty of Rome's Preamble. The protection of human rights was not in the European Commission's mandate. As an executive body and the engine of integration, its first task was to come up with practical solutions to implement the treaties' objectives. It entailed political divisions within the council and among member states, in a moment in which France had no hesitation in violating human rights in its colonial war in Algeria. For its part, the European Court of Justice was determined to define the primacy of European law over national law. Even the European Parliament, which eventually played an important role in the promotion of human rights during the 1970s, was rather inconsequential during the 1950s and 1960s. Indeed, it is hard to find an official statement or document discussing human rights before the early 1970s. A major exception was the Birkelbach Report. Approved by the European Parliament in 1962 to prevent Francoist Spain's accession to the EC, it claimed that candidate member states should meet geographic, economic and political criteria, such as the respect for human rights, democracy and the rule of law.[4]

At the time of the Birkelbach Report, human rights were confined to academic discussions among international lawyers, United Nations diplomats and interested experts. These debates revolved around the political meaning and hierarchy of rights. Absorbed by Cold War logics and dichotomies, many in the West began perceiving individual freedoms as the sole and quintessential expression of human rights. It was clearly a self-serving understanding with a patently anti-communist bias. Nevertheless, it was also deeply rooted in the history of human rights – civil and political rights came first, economic and social rights came after – and in their own nature: unlike individual freedoms, economic and social rights required state intervention that could not be universally assured soon after the war. Conversely, the Soviets overturned such concepts to point out that material equality was a prerequisite of fundamental freedoms. Economic and social rights were the more modern and intrinsically superior rights, they claimed. The confrontation between civil and political rights and economic and social rights became a continuous leitmotiv in mutual accusations between the East and the West.

The ideological reconceptualization of human rights produced by the Cold War had relevant consequences. In 1952, the UN General Assembly approved the drafting of two separate covenants: the International Covenant on Civil and Political Rights and the International Covenant on Economic, Social and Cultural Rights supplemented the Universal Declaration of Human Rights. Both were adopted in 1966. Among Western NGOs, the Cold War led to a similar dynamic with many organizations focusing almost exclusively on individual freedoms, pointing their finger against Communist Europe. This was, for example, the case of European sections of the International League for the Rights of Man; the Paris-based *Fédération internationale des droits de l'homme*; the *Commission Internationale contre le Régime Concentrationnaire*, established by the former Buchenwald inmate and French intellectual David Rousset; the long-standing British Anti-Slavery Society; or the more recent International Commission of Jurists.

The founding of Amnesty International, an NGO established in 1961 by British lawyer Peter Benenson, brought a renewed push for human rights. It began to conduct international campaigns in favour of political prisoners in Western, Eastern and less developed countries. Despite its universalist orientation, Amnesty International's centre of gravity 'settled in [the] northern latitudes' of Europe (in its founder's words), while the principal focus of its initial energy was on human rights violations within Europe – Communist Europe but also Spain, Portugal and Greece – and its colonies.[5]

Amnesty International was the prototype of those NGOs that transformed international politics in the 1970s, fostering ideas about global interconnectedness and interdependence. Following its lead, new human rights groups were formed and their transnational action contributed to making human rights the central concern of the 1970s. They emerged 'seemingly from nowhere' as a new utopian ideology to replace previous exhausted utopianisms, offering a new vision of the world community based on the respect of individuals' rights. Yet, as ubiquitous as the language of human rights was, it was also highly divisive and contested. For many activists around the world, human rights offered a universal ideal to transform international politics. To governments in the 'Global South', the language of human rights was a new way to promote the right to self-determination. Socialist countries, which were confronted with their abuses, reacted by reaffirming the primacy of economic and social rights over political and civil liberties. The United States found in the new universalism of human rights a strategy to cope with the crisis of containment and wage a new kind of Cold War by wielding human rights as an ideological weapon. In Western Europe, the European Communities developed a special vision, which was supposed to be free of Cold War schemes, and made the promotion of human rights in the world one of their main political pillars.[6]

The EC entered the 1970s with a renewed sense of political direction and purpose. In 1970, EC member states inaugurated the so-called European Political Cooperation (EPC). This harmonization of EC member states' foreign policies was intended to be a first step of a political union based on 'a common heritage of respect for the liberty and rights of man' that would bring 'together democratic States with freely elected parliaments'. This purpose was strengthened in 1973 by the adoption of a Solemn Declaration on European Identity by EC heads of state and government, which asserted the existence of a specific EC political identity, one based on shared norms of representative democracy, the rule of law, social justice and human rights and the common will to achieve 'an active role of European foreign policy in world politics'.[7] The link between the internal construction of a European polity and the definition of the EC in relation to the 'other' developed in the tumultuous transatlantic relations of the 1970s. Affirming a new political identity for the EC was meant to present the world with an autonomous European voice, different from that of the United States. Concerns about human rights in the world entered the European agenda as a political area where Europe was different from Richard Nixon and Henry Kissinger's America. Human rights became a distinctive feature of the EC's self-perception, something that allowed the Community to describe itself as different from both the 'other Europe' and the American ally. It is not by coincidence that by 1972, political scientist and long-time associate of Jean Monnet, François Duchêne, began referring to the EC's role in the world as a 'civilian power', pointing to a possible EC's unique role in international relations and manifesting an early and vague notion of 'Euroexceptionalism'. To Duchêne, the EC should internationally project its 'inner characteristics', which were: 'civilian ends and means, and a built-in sense of collective action, which in turn express, however imperfectly, social values of equality, justice and tolerance'. It should become 'a force for the international diffusion of civilian and democratic standards'.[8] While Duchêne's analysis did not tackle human rights specifically, it contributed to directing greater attention to the role of norms and values in international relations and to the ambitious willingness of the EC to play a significant role in them, thus creating a framework which was conductive to more attention towards human rights in the world. In addition, with a series of decisions between 1969 and 1974, the European Court of Justice recalled the fundamental rights accepted by the international community and member states' constitutions. By doing so, it meant to invite the EC to introduce human rights in its legal order. In the same years, the European Commission pondered the opportunity to adhere to the ECHR.[9] The collapse of authoritarian regimes in Portugal, Spain and Greece fuelled further discussions on democracy and human rights, and created enough room for European initiatives to strengthen their democratic transitions.[10]

Transnational human rights groups made EC governments and institutions more sensitive to human rights issues. Each government, they contended, was to be held accountable for its human rights abuses and violations. This was particularly true for the Soviet Union and Eastern European governments, which were under the scrutiny of the so-called Helsinki transnational network, which formed in connection to the CSCE. Born of a Soviet initiative to secure the division of Europe in order to preserve Moscow's stranglehold over Central and Eastern Europe, the CSCE became a multilateral forum in which human rights became quite unexpectedly the main focus.

Adding to a genuine interest in responding to the pressures from European citizens, members of the European Parliament appropriated the human rights jargon of the decade to affirm the role of their assembly as a guardian of democratic values and a mechanism to challenge national governments' quasi-monopoly over international affairs. Beginning in the early 1970s, MEPs regularly debated how EC institutions and member states, as well as foreign ministers convening in EPC, should approach human rights violations in the world. Between 1979 and 1984, human rights were the subject of at least 120 parliamentary resolutions, 230 oral questions, almost 300 written questions, and 80 petitions signed by its presidents, Simone Veil and Piet Dankert. In addition, over the same period, the EP organized at least three public hearings on human rights violations across the globe, established a permanent working group on human rights, and introduced a yearly report on the global respect for human rights.[11]

The search for a specific political identity, political ambitions, pressures from citizens and NGOs, EC institutional dynamics, and external transformations contributed to fuelling the EC's growing interest in human rights. Yet, this was not immediately translated into effective political initiatives. EPC was shaped almost exclusively by EC member states, each one with its own priorities and agenda: this prevented shared action for the promotion of human rights in the world and allowed governments to resist parliamentary initiatives. The EC as a whole lacked a clear political vision to make human rights a fundamental pillar of its external relations, fearing that human rights could endanger its networks worldwide.[12] As a consequence, during the 1970s and most of the 1980s, EC's policies were fairly disastrous. While the EC as a whole assumed a firm stance vis-à-vis many human rights violations during the democratic transitions in Spain, Portugal and Greece, until the late 1970s it avoided protesting the violations of human rights in Eastern Europe, fearing that too firm an approach could endanger détente. Equally, it avoided drastic criticism against the less developed countries bound to the EC by the Lomé Convention. A timid attempt to introduce human rights conditionality arrived in 1977, with the adoption of the so-called Uganda Guidelines, which stated that assistance provided by the Community should not lead to the denial of basic human rights in Uganda or other receiving countries. Yet, after being vaguely recalled in the preamble of the Third Lomé Convention (1984), the respect for human rights became relevant for EC development aid only with the Fourth Lomé Convention in 1989. The end of the Cold War, the empowerment of the now directly elected European Parliament by the Single European Act (1987), and French president François Mitterand's decision to make French aid conditional on the establishment of democracy and the respect of human rights put individuals' rights at the centre of the Lomé Convention.[13]

The Human Rights Breakthrough explains how the EC came to appropriate the human rights language of the 1970s and participate in the human rights revolution of the decade. The chapters gathered here reflect and advance many of these conceptual insights, linking together transnational movements, European institutions, national governments and political ambitions of the Community. These essays collected here do not cover the EC action (or inaction) for the protection and promotion of human rights in every corner of the world. Human rights violations in Latin America, for example, are not the primary focus of any of the chapters. It is not an oversight. While grass-roots activism across European countries spotlighted on Latin American authoritarian regimes' abuses and violations, and the European Parliament approved numerous resolutions censuring human rights violations in Chile, Brazil, Argentina and many other Latin American countries, the EC as a whole did not go beyond some symbolic gestures to condemn these regimes, such as moving its offices from Santiago de Chile to Caracas, Venezuela. Indeed, the EC had limited official contacts with South American governments, thus had no concrete leverage to discuss their violations of human rights.[14]

The chapters included here, with a variety of approaches, perspectives, arguments and topics, focus on the complex and often conflicted developments produced by the growing importance for the EC of championing human rights in the world. From different vantage points, the chapters place the European emphasis on human rights within the larger context of the construction of Europe.

Part I traces the ways in which the EC discussed and acted on human rights within broader contexts. The first relevant EC demonstration of attention and action in the promotion of human rights coincided with the democratic transition of the Iberian Peninsula and of Greece, as Víctor Fernández Soriano clearly shows. Indeed, in this context, the EC succeeded in making the respect for human rights a central pillar of its projection towards Spain, Portugal and Greece, and a precondition for their subsequent adhesion to the Community. Ilaria Zamburlini describes a different trajectory for human rights in the EC action towards African, Caribbean and Pacific countries. Human rights concerns emerged early in connection to these areas. Yet, it was not until the end of the 1970s that an initial and lukewarm commitment to human rights became a reality. Umberto Tulli's chapter tackles the role of the EC in introducing some human rights principles and language into the CSCE Final Act and its subsequent actions. It points out that the EC was lacking a clear strategy for the promotion of human rights in East–West relations and that it was reluctant to pursue a firm stance on human rights violations in the East, for fear that doing so could endanger détente. Focusing on the UN, Lorenzo Ferrari's chapter shows how, far from being cohesive on human rights issues, EC member states split several times on human rights votes at the UN General Assembly.

Part II focuses on key EC players. In their chapters, Christian Salm and Marialuisa Sergio focus on the intricate web of formal and informal contacts that the two major political families of the European Parliament – the European socialists and the European Christian democrats, respectively – developed for the promotion of human rights abroad. Their chapters show how informal actors, such as human rights NGOs and transnational political parties, assumed an important role in socializing European institutions to the international jargon of human rights and in fostering certain EC initiatives. David Grealy's focus on the British government explains the enlargement-related dynamics of the EC's major worldwide commitment to human rights protection.

Part III of the book deals with 'other' Europes, namely the Council of Europe and neutral countries. While the EC tried to assert itself as the main supranational institution within Western Europe, it was hardly alone. Indeed, by the late 1960s, the EC was increasingly interested in discussions taking place at the Council of Europe. An important moment for the convergence between these two supranational organizations was the Greek coup in 1967, when the junta's human rights violations drew international attention, particularly given the popular conceptions of Athens as the birthplace of democracy. Western European concern with human rights in the world was further fuelled by the humanitarian crisis and human rights violations occurring in Nigeria during the Biafra war. European consideration for the crisis was partly a consequence of many NGOs' lobbying over the Council of Europe in connection to the Biafra war, as Oluchukwu Ignatus Onianwa argues in his chapter. Similarly, the EC had to cope with initiatives coming from non-aligned countries. Austria, in particular, played a major role in offering an alternative strategy for the promotion of human rights in the world and in Eastern Europe, in particular. Maximilian Graf's chapter discusses how EC member states and Austria mutually supervised each other's stances on human rights in the world.

While human rights wandered in search of home in the EC's external relations, they became associated with the constructed self-perception of the EC. For this reason, Part IV of the book looks at the EC/EU approach to human rights beyond the 1970s. By the end of the Cold War, human rights became a new principle for international relations. Once the bipolar system had definitely collapsed, many hoped the world community would view human rights as a new consensual principle. In reality, the new emphasis on human rights created new controversies over their real 'place' in international relations. Gaia Lott's chapter focuses on asylum seekers coming to Europe during the 1980s and 1990s. It highlights how EC/EU member states tended to frame this issue as a security-related problem, thus contributing to the affirmation of the idea of a 'Fortress Europe', while the European Parliament followed a human rights-based approach. In her chapter, Elena Calandri points out that the EC/EU was the driving force behind the positive conclusion of the 1993 World Conference on Human Rights sponsored by the UN. While the risk of failure was real and a clear split between 'Western' human rights and the so-called Asian values was underway, the EC/EU was crucial in forging a consensus in the final document. Peter Malcontent focuses on the EU's influence over Dutch actions in the UN Commission on Human Rights during the 1990s and early 2000s; the chapter focuses on a brand-new Europe, with more ambitions for international relations and more formal institutions to conduct a European foreign policy. While contradictions and divisions on human rights remained, the Dutch government was an outspoken proponent of a strong human rights commitment for the EU.

The history of human rights in the EC/EU's external relations still is in its formative stages. We hope that this volume will serve as a valuable introduction to students and scholars interested in pursuing research in this field. Above all we hope it will encourage readings on how the global human rights breakthrough shaped the formal and informal construction of Europe.

Notes

1 Daniel C. Thomas, 'Constitutionalization through Enlargement: The Contested Origins of the EU's Democratic Identity', *Journal of European Public Policy*, 13 (2006): 1190–210.

2 The felicitous phrase is in Marco Duranti, *The Conservative Human Rights Revolution: European Identity, Transnational Politics, and the Origins of the European Convention* (Oxford and New York: Oxford University Press, 2016).

3 Rasmus Mariager, Karl Molin and Kjersti Brathagen, eds, *Human Rights in Europe during the Cold War* (London and New York: Routledge, 2014); Mikael R. Madsen, *La genèse de l'Europe des droits de l'Homme. Enjeux juridiques et stratégies d'État* (Strasbourg: Press Universitaires de Strasbourg, 2010).

4 Víctor F. Soriano, *Le fusil et l'olivier. Les droits de l'Homme en Europe face aux dictatures méditerranéennes (1949-1977)* (Brussels: Éditions de l'Université de Bruxelles, 2015); Emma De Angelis and Eirini Karamouzi, 'Enlargment and the Historical Origins of the European Community's Democratic Identity', *Contemporary European History*, 25 (2016): 439–58.

5 Tom Buchanan, 'Human Rights, the Memory of War and the Making of a "European" Identity, 1945-75', in *Europeanization in the Twentieth Century: Historical Approaches*, ed. Martin Conway and Kiran K. Patel (Basingstoke: Palgrave Macmillan, 2010).

6 Samuel Moyn, *The Last Utopia: Human Rights in History* (Cambridge, MA: Harvard University Press, 2010), 3; Jan Eckel and Samuel Moyn, eds, *The Breakthrough: Human Rights in the 1970s* (Philadelphia: University of Pennsylvania Press, 2015); Barbara Keys, *Reclaiming American Virtue: The Human Rights Revolution of the 1970s* (Cambridge, MA: Harvard University Press, 2014); Akira Iriye, Petra Goedde and William Hitchcock, eds, *The Human Rights Revolutions: An International History* (Oxford and New York: Oxford University Press, 2012).

7 'Declaration on European Identity', *Bulletin of the European Communities*, 12 (1973): 118–22; Niall Ferguson, Charles S. Maier, Erez Manela and Daniel J. Sargent, eds, *The Shock of the Global: The 1970s in Perspective* (Cambridge, MA: Harvard University Press, 2010); Antonio Varsori and Guia Migani, eds, *Europe in the International Arena during the 1970s: Entering a Different World* (Brussels: Peter Lang, 2011).

8 François Duchêne, 'Europe's Role in World Peace', in *Europe Tomorrow: Sixteen Europeans Look Ahead*, ed. R. Mayne (London: Fontana: 1972); Id., 'The European Community and the Uncertainties of Interdependence', in *A Nation Writ Large? Foreign-Policy Problems before the European Community*, ed. M. Kohnstamm and W. Hager (London: Macmillan, 1973), 1–21.

9 Pauline Bonino, 'France against Human Rights? The Difficult Ratification of the European Convention on Human Rights (1950-1974)', *Relations Internationales*, 174 (2018): 91–108.

10 Soriano, *Le Fusil et l'olivier*; Mario Del Pero, Víctor Gavín, Fernando Guirao and Antonio Varsori, *Democrazie. L'Europa meridionale e la fine delle dittature* (Florence: Le Monnier, 2010); Antonio Varsori, 'Crisis and Stabilization in Southern Europe during the 1970s: Western Strategy, European Instruments', *Journal of European Integration History*, 15 (2009): 5–14.

11 *Official Journal of the European Communities*, No. C 172/36, 2 July 84; Aurélie Elisa Gfeller, 'Champion of Human Rights: The European Parliament and the Helsinki Process', *Journal of Contemporary History*, 49 (2014): 390–409.

12 Ilaria Zamburlini, 'Diritti umani e politica di sviluppo. Il caso della Comunità europea' (PhD Diss., University of Trieste, 2018); Lorenzo Ferrari, *Sometimes Speaking with a Single Voice: The European Community as an International Actor* (Brussels: Peter Lang, 2016).

13 Jean-Marie Palayret, 'Da Lomé I a Cotonou: morte e trasfigurazione della Convenzione Cee/Acp', in *Il primato sfuggente. L'Europa e l'intervento per lo sviluppo*

(1957-2007), ed. Elena Calandri (Milan: FrancoAngeli, 2009), 35–51; Guia Migani, 'Lomé and the North-South relations (1975-1984): from the "New International Economic Order" to a New Conditionality', in *Europe in a Globalising World: Global Challenges and European Responses in the 'long' 1970s*, ed. Claudia Hiepel (Baden-Baden: Nomos, 2014); Karin Arts, *Integrating Human Rights into Development Cooperation: The Case of the Lomé Convention* (The Hague: Kluwer Law International, 2000), 123–46.

14 Ferrari, *Sometimes Speaking with a Single Voice*, 178–80; Anna Ayso, 'La relación euro-latinoamericana a través del proceso de integración regional europea', *Afers Internacionals*, 32 (1996): 147–64.

Part I

The European community and human rights violations in the world

1

Knocking on Europe's doors

Community Europe and human rights after dictatorial rule in Southern Europe (1974–7)

Víctor Fernández Soriano

Once upon a time, Mr Roy Jenkins, there were six European countries that decided to come together, and so there was the EEC. Then three others came and joined them. Now three other more are candidates, poor and noble like the heroes of a fairy tale. In diplomatic terms, this is called 'the Community's second enlargement'. It started in 1974 and 1975 with much euphoria, with the rise of three new democracies in Europe: Greece, Portugal and Spain [. . .]. But the time went by. Now people speak of money, agriculture, industry, banking. Especially agriculture. And we ask Brussels whether an 'economic yes' will echo the so firmly pronounced 'political yes'.[1]

These words opened an article on the Greek, Portuguese and Spanish requests of accession to the European Community (EC) published in the economic magazine *Vision* in March 1977.[2] They are a good reflection of the political significance of enlargement towards Greece, Portugal and Spain, the three countries that had just escaped long periods of dictatorial rule. Rather than a 'fairy tale' about democratic ideals, economic interest overshadowed political considerations on the new democracies' quality and capacities to comply with fundamental political rights as the ones codified in the European Convention on Human Rights (ECHR).

This chapter dips into the so firmly pronounced 'political yes' mentioned in the *Vision* article. It will focus on the political dimension of EC's relations with Southern countries at the time when these countries went through processes of democratic transition after the end of dictatorial rule. It will argue that the EC did not immediately set an agenda on democratization towards these countries, but rather developed it as a reaction to political change within them. In other words, the EC did not foresee democracy promotion in these countries as a first priority, but adapted to the internal events in these countries and to the international impact that these events had. The EC did not intend at first glance Europeanization as a means of democratization. The equation 'Europeanization equal democratization' resulted a posteriori from a combination of factors such as these countries' expectations on the accession to the EC and the development of an EC democratic identity in the late 1970s.

Indeed, several factors conditioned the first EC's attitude towards Greece, Portugal and Spain after their respective ends of dictatorial rule. The EC was at the time essentially a macroeconomic organization with the potential to encompass social policies within its supranational framework and to encourage political cooperation among its nine members. However, the EC's so-called democratic deficit was facing growing criticism by the mid-1970s. In order to fill in the democratic deficit, some actors, such as the Belgian prime minister Leo Tindemans, proposed extending the EC's supranational power to new policy areas,[3] while voices in favour of a direct election of the European Parliament multiplied throughout the member states. Furthermore, in the previous years, right before the end of dictatorial rule in Greece, Portugal and Spain, the EC's somewhat friendly relations with these countries had caused some discomfort. Vis-à-vis these dictatorships, the EC was placed in a position of 'rhetorical trap' in which the EC's generic allegiance to liberty was in sharp contrast with its will to institutionalize its relations with these countries via agreements and seemingly endless negotiation processes.[4]

In the 1970s, the Council of Europe (CoE) seemed more willing to debate on democracy and political regimes. This is no surprise, as the ECHR was indeed a covenant within the CoE's legal framework and the CoE (an organization for political cooperation somewhat specialized in cultural issues), unlike the EC, officially requested rule of law compliance for accession. In this sense, a dynamic existed between the CoE and the EC, which consisted in the exchange of ideas on democracy and political principles. This dynamic is particularly interesting for the case of political transition processes in Southern Europe, as it reveals that both organizations shared similar opinions on political change in Greece, Portugal and Spain, and their respective agendas vis-à-vis these countries were strongly influenced the one by the other. Rather than a CoE or EC attitude towards political change in Southern Europe, there was to some degree a Community Europe's attitude that encompassed both organizations.

This contribution will look in particular at the notion of human rights. Historians have recently stressed that human rights came to the forefront of international policies in the long 1970s and have become ever since a leitmotiv of international relations. This 'human rights breakthrough' during the long 1970s also affected Community Europe and even its relations with Southern Europe: the Greek case at the European Commission of Human Rights was a landmark case motivated by the Greek dictatorship's noncompliance with the ECHR, for which Greece had to pay the price of its membership to the CoE. However, human rights were hardly present in the policies of the EC during this very period and only emerged sporadically as a reference to the generic democratic philosophy shared by its member states, best represented by the ECHR. Human rights seldom appeared in the EC's relations with Greece, Portugal and Spain, to evoke the democratic philosophy that candidates for accession should respect as well. However, when they did, they played a key role, as they asserted the idea that democracy was the first condition sine qua non to join the EC. In this regard, the EC took inspiration and even borrowed normative ideas from the debates at the CoE.

A *breakthrough* for Europe?

The nexus between accession to the EC and democratization in Southern Europe has inspired myriad works. The historians of enlargement processes stress that in Greece, Portugal and Spain, Europeanism encompassed a will of democratic homologation with the political systems of Northwestern Europe.[5] Some authors have assessed the impact of European integration on democratization in Southern Europe.[6] Other authors have shown that these countries' European aspirations were instrumental in the geopolitics of the Cold War's late détente: Western powers spurred these countries' integration in Community Europe not only to promote democracy but also to stabilize the geopolitical flanks of the continent.[7]

Quid pro quo, EC relations with these countries had an impact on the EC's very democratic identity. Some scholars study how the EC's external relations contributed to the EC's political assertion. Laschi has shown how the configuration of a foreign policy of its own fostered the EC's political identity as a community of democratic countries that promote human rights.[8] Hebel and Lenz have delved into this process focusing on the European Political Cooperation introduced by EC members in the 1970s.[9] Tulli has explained how the European Parliament (EP) saw in the EC's external policies new opportunities not only for the EC's democratic identity as a whole but also for itself as a key institution in a new democratic functioning.[10] Following this same logic, some scholars address enlargement to stress it as a key element in the assertion of today's political identity of the European Union (EU): its 'constitutionalization'.[11] Political scientists tend to focus on enlargement to the East in the 1990s and 2000s but usually recognize the importance of enlargement to the South in the 1970s and 1980s in paving the way to the EU's polices on democratic conditionality.[12] Thomas even tracked the origins of this constitutionalization through enlargement to the first relations established by the EC with Francoist Spain in the early 1960s.[13]

De Angelis and Karamouzi are the authors of the main study on how the second enlargement contributed to the EC's democratic identity. In a 2016 article, they traced the EC's first official statements on democracy, from the Birkelbach Report at the EP in December 1961 to the Copenhagen Council Declaration on Democracy in April 1978, and connected them to the negotiation processes with Greece, Portugal and Spain. Their study puts forward that the discursive stance on democracy taken by the EC in the late 1970s owes much to the integration of Southern countries in the EC, as these countries had just gone into a process of political transition from dictatorial rule to democracy.[14]

De Angelis and Karamouzi point out that the use the EC made of the concept of democracy in the 1970s enclosed the ideas of respect of human rights and rule of law.[15] A closer look into the EC's first official declarations on democracy proves them right. In the Document on European Identity issued at the Copenhagen European Summit of December 1973, the EC Heads of State and Government declared, right after the first enlargement, that '[the Nine] are determined to defend the principles of representative democracy, of the rule of law, of social justice and of respect for human rights'.[16] In the Declaration on Democracy issued at the Copenhagen European

Council of April 1978, the EC Heads of State and Government 'solemnly declare that respect for and maintenance of representative democracy and human rights in each member state are essential elements of membership of the European Communities'.[17] These declarations actually recaptured the post-war and then Cold War conception of democracy as a Western model based on representativeness and on the rule of law principle.[18] However, the mention of 'human rights' also reflects the boom that this concept experienced in the international politics of the long 1970s: the so-called human rights breakthrough.[19]

How did the human rights breakthrough affect European integration? This is a question still unresolved by historical research. The long 1970s also correspond to a period of increased attention for human rights issues within Community Europe. The European Commission of Human Rights and the European Court of Human Rights stepped up their activity throughout this period by delivering more and more judgements on individual petitions, although this increase was also the consequence of the fact that more countries ratified the ECHR.[20] In the framework of the EC, references to human rights multiplied at different levels during this period too. The European Court of Justice delivered a series of judgements (Stauder 1969, Nold 1974, etc.) by which it intended to embed human rights into the EC's legal order by deriving them from the member states' legal systems and their international commitments. The EP called the Council and the Commission to foster a human rights agenda in the framework of the EC's external relations.[21] Meanwhile, in the official rhetoric, the recurrent mention of a 'common ideal of peace and liberty' shifted to 'fundamental rights'[22] as the generic political background of the whole European integration project.[23] In April 1977, these ideas converged in a joint declaration by the EC Commission, the Council and the EP in which the three institutions simply stressed 'the prime importance they attach to the protection of fundamental rights, as derived in particular from the constitutions of the member states and the [ECHR]', and stated that 'in the exercise of their powers and in pursuance of the aims of the European Communities they respect and will continue to respect these rights'.[24]

The following paragraphs aim to shed some light on the nexus between the human rights breakthrough and European integration by analysing the use of the term 'human (or fundamental) rights' in the EC's relations with Greece, Portugal and Spain during the period 1974–7. The EC barely invoked this term in this context; it did so only to refer to the political philosophy shared by its member states. However, these invocations served to assert the idea of making access of other European states to the Common Market contingent on respect of these rights, identified with democracy and the rule of law. This idea had already been the object of European debates long before the end of dictatorial rule,[25] but its assertion became paramount when dictatorial rule began to disappear in Southern Europe. Through these invocations, motivated by internal events in the countries of Southern Europe and a preceding reaction by the CoE, the EC made clear that it also demanded democratization in Greece, Portugal and Spain. Through these invocations, the EC also closed the discussion and, consequently, no provisions for the assessment of the quality of democracy and human rights compliance in these countries were foreseen in the subsequent accession negotiations.

Greece, who else?

On 24 July 1974, the military junta that had imposed a stern martial law in Greece for seven years collapsed after a military fiasco in Cyprus. At that very moment, the EC's relations with Greece were poor but not inexistent: although partially frozen after the coup d'état of 1967, the Association Agreement signed between the EC and Greece in 1961 remained in force. The last meeting of the EC–Greece Association Council established by this agreement had indeed taken place on 5 July 1974.[26] However, these relations took a new vigorous pace after the end of dictatorial rule when Konstantinos Karamanlis came into office.

Karamanlis based his strategy to consolidate the new Greek democracy on Greece's full integration into Community Europe.[27] Both the EC and the CoE responded by intensifying their relations with Greece with a series of political gestures and later with the reactivation of funding from the European Investment Bank,[28] intended to mark European sponsorship of the Greek democratic transition.[29] From this perspective, the EC's unfreezing of its Association Agreement in September 1974 and its fast readmission into the CoE on 14 October 1974, even before the organization of the first democratic elections, became the symbols of the Greek return to the club of democracies.

Looking back to the historical documents of that process, mentions of democracy or human rights are rare on the part of Community Europe. Even at the CoE level, there was not much insistence on these terms during Greece's re-accession in the late summer and early autumn of 1974. In September 1974, the Parliamentary Assembly of the CoE (PACE) declared it was 'wholeheartedly welcoming and encouraging the recent efforts of the Greek Government towards the restoration of human rights and the rule of law, the installation of a democratic constitution and the announcement of free elections for November 1974'.[30] After these elections, the PACE simply declared 'that Greece thus fulfils the conditions for accession'.[31] Unlike in the past,[32] the PACE actually retained from expressing its opinion on EC's attitude towards Greece. The CoE Secretariat also recommended readmitting Greece 'without the need for any formal act on her part',[33] even though it remained formally a pre-democratic state.

On the EC side, when the Council of Ministers agreed to unfreeze the Association Agreement, it expressed its deep satisfaction to see Greece's return to the 'ideals that inspired the negotiators of the Athens [Association] Agreement'.[34] That was all, and so some months later Karamanlis could present the Greek application for membership to the EC as the culmination of Greece's transition to democracy.[35]

Commitment with democracy and human rights seemed, therefore, taken for granted in the Greek case. This idea derived from the fact that prior to dictatorial rule, Greece had already been a member of the CoE and a signatory of the ECHR, as well as the EC's main commercial partner, and that Karamanlis had been prime minister during this period too. Greek transition appeared as a process of democratic 'restoration', regarding which the European allies were more preoccupied on the geostrategic stabilization of the Eastern Mediterranean over the political quality of the new Greek regime.[36] The EC actually found itself in a comfortable position in its post-dictatorial relations with Greece. Without having to develop a policy on democracy

Figure 1.1 Mikis Theodorakis and Melina Mercouri at a press conference in Paris on 29 April 1970. They were exiled from Greece since the Colonels Putsch of 1967. Here they are giving a press conference, after the safe return of the musician who, because of his opposition to the Greek Colonels Regime, had just spent three years in prison.

promotion and while avoiding any statement on human rights, it benefited from an aura as an implicit and indirect source of democratization. This fact, along with the old stereotype of Greece as the 'cradle of democracy', helped to construct a narrative in which Greek legitimacy to become a member was incontestable. Who other than the country that had invented democracy? Who else but Greece?[37]

This narrative likely contributed to the fast opening of negotiations for Greek accession to the EC. Introduced on 12 June 1975, Greece's application for membership (already foreseen in the Association Agreement)[38] quickly led to negotiations. The EC Commission recommended the Council to do so by arguing that

> it is clear that the consolidation of Greece's democracy, which is a fundamental concern not only of the Greek people but also of the Community and its member states, is intimately related to the evolution of Greece's relationship with the Community. It is in the light of these considerations that the Commission recommends that a clear affirmative reply be given to the Greek request.[39]

A long period of technically complex talks and bargaining would follow,[40] which paved the way to the subsequent negotiations with Spain and Portugal too.[41]

During the process of negotiations with Greece, human rights made an only but symbolic quick appearance. In May 1979, the accession treaty was ready, and the EC Commission had to deliver an opinion on Greece's accession before proceeding to its signature. The Commission based its opinion on the idea that 'the principles of pluralist democracy and respect for human rights form part of the common heritage of the peoples of the States brought together in the European Communities and are therefore essential elements of membership of the said Communities'.[42] With this sentence, the Commission embedded once and for all the principle of democratic conditionality and human rights compliance into EC enlargement. This principle was in continuity with the previous declarations on democracy and fundamental rights, but rather than for the just concluded negotiations with Greece, it seemed pertinent for the just commenced negotiations with Portugal and Spain. The EC would no longer explicitly mention this principle in its further negotiations with Portugal and Spain.

Portugal: Positive but cautious

On 25 April 1974, the Carnation Revolution gave the coup de grâce to the Portuguese dictatorship, the *Estado Novo*, deathly wounded by ravaging colonial wars and economic turmoil. Portugal was then bound to the EC by a trade agreement, signed in July 1972 contemporaneously to other EFTA countries,[43] much criticized by European political actors of the socialist spectrum as a sort of 'Portuguese association'.[44] The Portuguese dictatorship had obviously not been a member of the CoE.

After almost fifty years of dictatorial rule, Portugal entered a complex process of political transition. Two models of democratization coexisted and sometimes antagonized during the Portuguese transition: a revolutionary one inspired by communist ideas, and a parliamentary one inspired by the Western democracies. The followers of the latter, namely the representatives of non-communist political parties and government members with a technocratic profile, had a European agenda that linked democratization with European integration.[45] However, at the first stages of the Portuguese transition, Portugal's accession to Community Europe did not seem a priority. These actors' European agenda had a broader sense and aimed at first to move Portugal towards the Western Bloc. One of its most prominent figures, Mário Soares (leader of the Portuguese Socialist Party), spent much of his time in office as Portuguese minister for foreign affairs (from May 1974 to March 1975) travelling around European capitals and inviting European leaders to Lisbon in search for support to the Portuguese 'democratization efforts'[46] as well as to his own party.[47] Quid pro quo, the Western allies also found that promoting Portugal's closer ties with Community Europe was a means to bind Portugal to their block against the revolutionary trends that looked to the East with more sympathy.[48]

The difficulty to predict how the political situation in Portugal would evolve after the Carnation Revolution motivated a wait-and-see attitude at the EC, described by the Commission as 'positive, but cautious'.[49] On the contrary, the CoE hastened to define a position vis-à-vis the new Portuguese authorities. On 9 May 1974, while a military National Salvation Junta was still in power in Lisbon, the PACE issued a resolution on Portugal in which it welcomed 'the initiative taken by the new authorities to restore democracy' and the abolition of censorship and political police. The PACE also appealed to the governments of member states to prepare Portugal's adherence to the CoE and 'to provide economic assistance to Portugal in view of the fact that unresolved economic problems would endanger the newly-won freedom'.[50] This resolution already encompassed the guidelines for the further attitude of Community Europe towards Portugal: encouragement for the Western model of democratization (subsequently referred as 'pluralist democracy'), promotion of Portugal's integration in Community Europe and economic assistance. These last two goals should actually serve as stimuli for the first main goal of promoting pluralist democracy in Portugal.

These three goals of pluralist democracy, European integration, and economic assistance became also apparent in the strategy deployed by the Portuguese officials who were not partisans of a revolutionary turn. Along with Soares, this was also the case of the high-ranking officials at the ministries of Economy and Finances, responsible for the negotiations with the EC. At the 27 June 1974 EC-Portugal Joint Committee held in Brussels (according to the terms of the 1972 agreement), the Portuguese delegates put on the table a demand of economic assistance to the EC stressing Portugal's link with 'the democratic principle and the fundamental objectives of the EC'.[51] In other words, they offered pluralist democracy and Europeanism in exchange of financial aid. This became the reasoning put forward by the pro-European Portuguese officials in their tours and relations (many of them informal)[52] with European leaders.[53]

The EC initially responded in favour of helping the Portuguese economy by investing through project aid over a period of several years. However, in the months that followed, the internal situation in Portugal brought the talks on EC investment to a halt. In the words of Christopher Soames (then the commissioner in charge of external relations), 'we never got any further with it because things got so chaotic in Portugal that clearly it wasn't the time to take it further'.[54] As a result, the EC kept its wait-and-see attitude and refused to change the status quo of the 1972 agreement with Portugal: 'while [. . .] we wish to establish closer links with a democratic Portugal, the question of the form of such links has deliberately been kept open'.[55] After the political turmoil in early March 1975 that led to the instauration of the Council of the Revolution, the EC Commission concluded that 'all the EEC can do for the moment seems to repeat its readiness to develop and extend relations with a democratic Portugal, and to wish the Portuguese people well on its road to democracy'.[56]

The situation shifted after the first democratic election held in Portugal on 25 April 1975. This election had the effect of polarizing even more Portuguese politics. While the revolutionary forces took the road of radicalization in the so-called Hot Summer, some pro-European ministers (including Mário Soares as a minister without portfolio) consolidated their positions in the government. In this situation, the EC decided to adopt a clear stance promoting pluralist democracy in Portugal. The Commission took the lead and, following a meeting of the EC-Portugal Joint Committee on 28 May 1975, proposed to the Council to open negotiations on an emergency aid to Portugal that should avow pluralist democracy. 'It is clear that, in the current international political context, only the Community is in a position to take initiatives which are not only wide-ranging and effective but also acceptable to an important sector of Portuguese opinion,' the Commission argued. The Commission also stressed that, in its view,

> emergency aid of this kind should be seen clearly in the perspective of the establishment in Portugal of a pluralist democracy and the Community's interest in giving her effective support to achieve this end. If Portugal were to abandon this objective or if it were to become unachievable, the reasoning in favour of aid would lose all its validity.[57]

The Council backed the Commission's initiative and the Brussels European Council of 16–17 July 1975 included a declaration on Portugal in its conclusion, in which it pointed out that the EC in accordance with 'its historical traditions, can only support a pluralist democracy'.[58]

The EC stuck to its stance and retained its economic assistance until pluralist democracy was confirmed in Portugal following the events of late 1975. On 24 September 1975, before the EP, the commissioner for regional policy, George Thomson, made it clear that financial aid was not only 'an internal affair for Portugal, but also an internal affair for Europe as such. The survival and enlargement of a free society in Western Europe will be influenced by events in Portugal and by the type of aid that the Community gives'.[59] In 1976, the EC agreed on a vast financial programme to Portugal that amounted for up to 175 million dollars in loans allocated by the European Investment Bank (actually the first time that this bank operated in a country that was neither a member nor an associate to the EC).[60] In September 1976, Portugal became a member of the CoE. This was also a means to endorse the Portuguese pluralist democracy, from that moment on ready for accession to the EC, without further political considerations.

Spain, the *desired* democratization

In the summer of 1975, the EC was ready to undertake accession negotiations with Greece and negotiations for economic assistance to Portugal on the condition that these countries committed to the principle of pluralist democracy. And so remained Spain as the last remnant of fascism in Europe and the oldest dictatorship in the Mediterranean area, under the rule of the decrepit general Francisco Franco. The EC was also negotiating at that time with Franco's Spain a protocol to the Preferential Agreement that it signed with Spain in 1970 to adapt the agreement to the newly enlarged community.[61]

By the end of the summer of 1975, state violence in Franco's Spain caused a crisis that prompted the EC to adopt a firmer stance towards Spain[62] and that also became a point of no return for Francoist Spain's foreign policy.[63] On 27 September 1975, the Spanish dictatorship executed, by fire squads, five men convicted of terrorism and sentenced to death by military tribunals. These executions had been preceded by a wave of unrest at a world scale and by appeals for clemency addressed to Franco by disparate organizations and dignitaries such as the pope.[64] On 22 September 1975, the PACE not only issued a resolution calling the EC to defend human rights in its negotiations with Spain but also expressed its desire that Spain should 'soon occupy her place among the democratic families at the Council of Europe'.[65] Three days later, the EP issued another resolution protesting against the violation of human rights in Spain and calling the EC Commission and Council to freeze the ongoing negotiations with the Spanish government.[66] The Commission even prompted the Council to issue an official statement in the name of the EC, but the news of the executions arrived before the Council could discuss on it.[67]

The executions provoked an international wave of protests. Demonstrations, rallies and even strikes took place in the days that followed. Many prominent political figures, even heads of government such as the Dutch prime minister Joop den Uyl, participated in it.[68] Some EC civil servants also manifested on 29 September 1975 to protest against Franco in front of the Commission headquarters in Brussels;[69] they also sent letters to the president of the Commission, François-Xavier Ortoli, urging to suspend the negotiations with Spain in the name of fundamental freedoms and human rights.[70] Many governments, among whom those of most of the members of both the CoE and the EC, decided to withdraw their ambassadors from Madrid. However, although the calls for a common European response conveyed by the EC persisted, the governments took these decisions individually. Among the EC members, the Irish government refused to withdraw its ambassador alleging that the Republic of Ireland was also facing problems with terrorism.[71]

Despite the fact that the first reactions against the Spanish executions were individual, the EC members soon came up with the idea of giving a common response to Franco. This common response should involve two EC policies: the ongoing negotiations between the Commission and the Spanish government, and the informal European Political Cooperation (EPC).[72] In both cases, the EC would impose mild sanctions to Spain on behalf of human rights.

The EC Commission decided indeed to suspend its negotiations with Spain without consulting the Council. Its spokesman, Bino Olivi, announced this decision to the press on 1 October 1975 with a concise declaration: 'under present circumstances, negotiations cannot be continued'.[73] *The Times* smartly remarked that 'the Commission was careful not to commit itself to a precise definition of the conditions under which it would resume negotiations with Madrid'.[74] Then Ortoli along with the president of the EP, Georges Spénale, prompted the Council to freeze the EC's diplomatic relations with Spain.[75]

In the framework of EPC, the nine EC governments tried a first common response to Spain at the General Assembly of the United Nations in New York. There, the EC delegates left the hemicycle on 30 September 1975 when the Spanish ministers for foreign affairs intervened to justify the executions.[76]

On 6 October 1975, after three hours of discussion, the EC Council finally decided to break off relations with Spain. The representatives of the member governments at the Council agreed then on a declaration in which they affirmed that 'human rights constitute the common heritage of the peoples of Europe'. In the same declaration, they condemned the Spanish executions as opposed to the principle of the rule of law, and expressed their 'desire that a democratic Spain might take its place in the assembly of European nations'.[77] In other words, the EC called for the respect of human rights in Spain and conditioned Spanish participation in European integration to its democratization.

Nevertheless, apart from this declaration, the representatives of the member governments failed to achieve a common position towards Spain in the framework of EPC because of the divisions among them. The discussion at the Council on 6 October 1975 took indeed so long because some of the delegations (the Netherlands, Britain, Italy and Denmark) demanded a severe condemnation, while others preferred a polite reprobation (Germany, Belgium and Luxembourg) or a flexible disapproval (France and Ireland). In addition, the French delegation accused the president of the Commission (also a French) of having exceeded his competences when suspending the negotiations with Spain.[78]

In the days that followed, the French government even disavowed the previous declaration and affirmed that the protests had gone too far.[79] The French government was actually the first to restore its ambassador in Madrid; the remaining six followed so that by the time of Franco's death in November 1975 all the EC members maintained normal diplomatic relations with Spain.[80]

Even the suspension of the negotiations with Spain did not last very long. This time, by decision of the Council, the embargo was lifted on 20 January 1976,[81] and the Commission resumed its talks with Spain, a country that had still a long road to drive to achieve democratization.

Nonetheless, the events of September–October 1975 left a fundamental footprint to the EC's further attitude towards Spain. They changed the course of relations with Spain, conducted up to that moment with a more permissive stance in political terms. With the background of the previous proceedings with Greece and Portugal, these events contributed to promoting human rights as the generic political philosophy behind the EC's external action. As President Ortoli put it in a speech on Spain at the EP on 15 October 1975, the Spanish freeze was the consequence of the fact that human rights 'belong to the common background of our civilisation, they are part of our democratic structures and are one of the most authentic and measurable values of our society'.[82] In the case of Spain, this philosophical principle did not apply to the relations in course, but to the relations to be. This principle translated into the idea of the 'desire that Spain shall become a democracy' expressed in resolutions and declarations of September–October 1975 and became a commonplace from that moment onwards every time the Spanish question was evoked.

Since the Spanish transition process did not really take off until the first democratic election in December 1976, no stimulus could be offered to a democratization that still had to occur. The only stimulus possible was the promise of closer relations and accession based on the fulfilment of the 'desire to see Spain join the European Community when it has evolved towards a genuinely democratic regime', as the EP put it in a resolution in May 1976.[83] As a result, after resuming relations with Spain in January 1976, the EC kept being careful not to commit itself to other form of framework than the 1970 Preferential Agreement, waiting for political change in Spain, while in the public discourses of the Spanish politicians a 'hazy' concept of Europe became associated with the promise of democratization.[84]

The Spanish transition closed the circle opened by the beginning of the Greek transition (Μεταπολύτευση) started in the summer of 1974. It was the last stone in the building of a democratic condition for membership at the EC. Greece had paved the way, Portugal had stiffened it and now the political evolution in Spain was regarded with a watchful eye within a complex context of crossed international interests: economic, political, geostrategic and so on.[85]

Conclusion

The end of dictatorial rule in Southern Europe reinforced the idea of Community Europe as it indirectly created a new nexus between the CoE and the EC. If democracy, rule of law and human rights compliance were the conditions for accession to the EC, then the conditions for entering both organizations had to be technically the same. In January 1976, at the occasion of a debate on Spain at the PACE, the German minister for foreign affairs, Hans-Dietrich Genscher, was asked about this. He answered: 'I personally would make no distinction between rapprochement with the Council of Europe and rapprochement with the European Community, for the democratic principles which unite us in both these institutions are the same.'[86] The candidacies of Greece, Portugal and Spain to the CoE and the EC at the early stages of their transitions to democracy gave legitimacy to the idea that the basic rules to join the European club were the same.

In an irony of history, there has been a shift in the incarnation of human rights from the CoE to the EU. In the 1970s, what was at stake was the recognition of democracy and human rights as a political principle of the EC, while no case was made about the CoE's legitimacy to represent them. Today, the trends seem reversed: the EU celebrates the twentieth anniversary of its charter of fundamental rights, considers triggering article 7 against Poland and Hungary for different breaches of their respective rule of law systems, and considers sanctions against Belarus. As a result of these and other measures, the EU tends to appear as a sort of 'champion' of human rights to international public opinions. On the other hand, the CoE, despite the intensive activity of the European Court of Human Rights, struggles to keep the flame of its legitimacy alive as many of its member governments (the most prominent ones being Russia and Turkey), seems to care less and less for the principle of rule of law.

Notes

1 'Trois coups frappés à la porte des Neuf', *Vision. Le magazine économique européen* 76 (March 1977).
2 *Vision, le magazine économique européen* was a Swiss monthly business magazine, published in Geneva from 1970 to 1982, which frequently published articles on the EC and the Common Market.
3 Leo Tindemans, 'Report on European Union', *Bulletin of the European Communities*, supplement 1 (1976): 11–35.
4 Víctor Fernández Soriano, *Le fusil et l'olivier: Les droits de l'Homme en Europe face aux dictatures méditerranéennes* (Brussels: Éditions de l'Université de Bruxelles, 2015).
5 António Costa Pinto and Nuno Severiano Teixeira, eds, *Southern Europe and the Making of the European Union* (New York: Columbia University Press, 2002); Antonio Varsori, 'Crisis and Stabilization in Southern Europe during the 1970s: Western Strategy, European Instruments', *Journal of European Integration History*, 15 (2009): 5–14.
6 Susannah Verney, 'Justifying the Second Enlargement: Promoting Interests, Consolidating Democracy or Returning to the Roots?', in *Questioning EU Enlargement: Europe in Search of Identity*, ed. Helene Sjursen (London and New York: Routledge, 2006), 19–43.
7 Mario Del Pero, Víctor Gavín, Fernando Guirao and Antonio Varsori, *Democrazie. L'Europa meridionale e la fine delle dittature* (Florence: Le Monnier, 2010); Kiran

Klaus Patel, 'Who Was Saving Whom? The European Community and the Cold War, 1960s-1970s', *The British Journal of Politics and International Relations*, 19 (2017): 29–47.

8 Giuliana Laschi, *L'Europa e gli altri. Le relazioni esterne della Comunità dalle origini al dialogo Nord-Sud* (Bologna: Il Mulino, 2015), 11–176.
9 Kai Hebel and Tobias Lenz, 'The Identity/Policy Nexus in European Foreign Policy', *Journal of European Public Policy*, 23 (2016): 473–91.
10 Umberto Tulli, 'Challenging Intergovermentalism and EPC: The European Parliament and Its Actions in International Relations, 1970-1979', *Journal of Contemporary European Research*, 13 (2017): 1076–89.
11 Berthold Rittberger and Frank Schimmelfenning, eds, *The Constitutionalization of the European Union* (London and New York: Routledge, 2007).
12 Sjursen, *Questioning EU Enlargement*; Martin Sajdik and Michael Schwarzinger, *European Union Enlargement: Background, Developments, Facts* (New Brunswick and London: Transaction, 2008); Jessie Hronesova, Petra Guasti and Zdenka Mansfeldová, *The Nexus between Democracy, Collective Identity Formation, and EU Enlargement* (Prague: Academy of Sciences of the Czech Republic, 2011); Eli Gateva, *European Union Enlargement Conditionality* (Basingstoke: Palgrave Macmillan, 2015); Thomas Melhausen, *European Union Enlargement: Material Interests, Community Norms and Anomie* (London and New York: Routledge, 2016).
13 Daniel C. Thomas, 'Constitutionalization through Enlargement: The Contested Origins of the EU's Democratic Identity', *Journal of European Public Policy*, 13 (2006): 1190–210.
14 Emma De Angelis and Eirini Karamouzi, 'Enlargement and the Historical Origins of the European Community's Democratic Identity', *Contemporary European History*, 25 (2016): 439–58.
15 Ibid., 440.
16 Declaration on European Identity, European Summit (Copenhagen, 14 December 1973), https://www.cvce.eu/content/publication/1999/1/1/02798dc9-9c69-4b7d-b2c9-f03a8db7da32/publishable_en.pdf (accessed July 2020).
17 Declaration on Democracy, European Council, Conclusions of the Presidency (Copenhagen, 7–8 April 1978), https://www.cvce.eu/en/obj/declaration_on_democracy_at_the_copenhagen_european_council_7_and_8_april_1978-en-c054acb7-0d62-466b-81ed-30c40f097567.html#:~:text=Twitter-,Declaration%20on%20democracy%20at%20the%20Copenhagen%20European,7%20and%208%20April%201978)&text=On%208%20April%201978%2C%20the,membership%20of%20the%20European%20Communities. (accessed July 2020).
18 Martin Conway, 'Democracy in Postwar Western Europe: The Triumph of a Political Model', *European History Quarterly*, 32 (2002): 59–84; Martin Conway and Volker Depkat, 'Towards a European History of the Discourse of Democracy: Discussing Democracy in Western Europe 1945-60', in *Europeanisation in the Twentieth Century: Historical Approaches*, ed. M. Conway and Kiran Klaus Patel (Basingstoke: Palgrave Macmillan, 2010), 132–55.
19 Samuel Moyn, *The Last Utopia: Human Rights in History* (Cambridge, MA: Harvard University Press, 2010); Jan Eckel and Samuel Moyn, eds, *The Breakthrough: Human Rights in the 1970s* (Philadelphia: University of Pennsylvania Press, 2014); Robert Brier, 'Beyond the Quest for a Breakthrough: Reflections on the Recent Historiography on Human Rights', *European History Yearbook*, 16 (2015): 155–73;

Stefan-Ludwig Hoffmann, 'Human Rights and History', *Past & Present*, 232 (2016): 279–310.

20 Birte Wassenberg, *History of the Council of Europe* (Strasbourg: Council of Europe Publishing, 2013), 95–9.

21 Aurélie É. Gfeller, 'Champion of Human Rights: The European Parliament and the Helsinki Process', *Journal of Contemporary History*, 49 (2014): 390–409.

22 Although used indistinctively, the EC and the EU today have always preferred the term *fundamental rights* to *human rights*, probably as a means to distant itself from the CoE's legal order.

23 Étienne Davignon, 'Report by the Foreign Ministers of the Member States on the Problems of Political Unification', *Bulletin of the European Communities*, 11 (November 1970): 9–14; Leo Tindemans, 'Report on European Union', https://www.cvce.eu/en/collections/unit-content/-/unit/02bb76df-d066-4c08-a58a-d4686a3e68ff/63f5fca7-54ec-4792-8723-1e626324f9e3 (accessed 20 July 2020).

24 Joint Declaration by the European Parliament, Council and the Commission concerning the protection of fundamental rights (Luxembourg, 5 April 1977), https://www.cvce.eu/en/obj/joint_declaration_by_the_european_parliament_council_and_the_commission_concerning_the_protection_of_fundamental_rights_and_the_echr_luxembourg_5_april_1977-en-9b6086c8-9763-4355-bf66-3699f1d78b79.html#:~:text=On%205%20April%201977%2C%20the,States%20and%20the%20European%20Convention (accessed July 2020).

25 Soriano, *Le fusil et l'olivier*.

26 Historical Archives of the European Union (hereinafter HAEU), BAC 50/1982 12, Meeting of the EEC–Greece Association Council, Brussels, 5 July 1974.

27 Eirini Karamouzi, *Greece, the EEC and the Cold War, 1974-1979: The Second Enlargement* (Basingstoke: Palgrave Macmillan, 2014), 14–34; Id., 'A Strategy for Greece: Democratization and European Integration, 1974-1975', *Cahiers de la Méditerranée*, 90 (2015): 11–24.

28 HAEU, BAC 66/1985 187, Meeting of the EEC–Greece Association Council (Brussels, 2 December 1974).

29 Antonio Varsori, 'L'Occidente e la Grecia: dal colpo di Stato militare alla transizione alla democrazia (1961-1976)', in *Democrazie*, ed. Del Pero, Varsori, Guirao and Gavín, 5–94.

30 Parliamentary Assembly of the Council of Europe (hereinafter PACE), Resolution 578 (1974), Situation in Greece, Strasbourg, 27 September 1974.

31 PACE, Opinion 69 (1974), Readmission of Greece, Strasbourg, 27 November 1974.

32 Víctor F. Soriano, 'Facing the Greek Junta (1967-1974): The Council of Europe, the European Community, and the Rise of Human Rights Politics', *European Review of History*, 24 (2017): 358–76.

33 Secretariat memorandum on the admission of Greece to the CoE, Strasbourg, 14 October 1974, https://www.cvce.eu/content/publication/2004/3/5/189d0510-96a6-4959-b8bd-3f82627db819/publishable_en.pdf (accessed July 2020).

34 HAEU, CM2 1974/36 EC Council of Ministers press declaration on the Association Agreement with Greece, Brussels, 17 September 1974.

35 Karamouzi, *Greece, the EEC and the Cold War*, 30–3.

36 Ibid., 35–62.

37 Víctor Fernández Soriano, 'Quel pays plus que la Grèce? La place de la Grèce dans la construction de l'Europe : une mise en perspective historique', *Histoire@Politique*, 29 (2016): 141–57.

38 Susannah Verney, 'The Greek Association with the European Community', in *Southern Europe and the Making of the European Union, 1945-1980s*, ed. António Costa Pinto and Nuno Severiano Teixeira (New York: Boulder, 2002), 109–56.
39 'Commission Opinion on Greek application for membership, 29 January 1976', *Bulletin of the European Communities*, supplement 2 (1976).
40 Karamouzi, *Greece, the EEC and the Cold War*, 63–183.
41 Sethelos Isidoros Balios, *Grecia y España de las dictaduras a la CEE: Procesos de democratización, representaciones y relaciones bilaterales* (PhD diss., Universidad Complutense, Madrid, 2019).
42 Commission Opinion on the application for accession to the European Communities by the Hellenic Republic (Brussels, 23 May 1979), https://www.cvce.eu/en/obj/commission_opinion_on_the_application_for_accession_to_the_european_communities_by_the_hellenic_republic_23_may_1979-en-3f7a93d1-1498-4de4-83ed-edb01558bcec.html (accessed 20 July 2020).
43 Portugal was then a member of the European Free Trade Association (EFTA), whose members signed respective agreements with the EC in 1972, at the occasion of the EC first enlargement, in order to create a big European free trade zone.
44 Nicolau Andresen-Leitão, *Estado Novo: Democracia e Europa, 1947-1986* (Lisbon: Impresa de Ciências Sociais, 2007); Id., 'The Reluctant European: A survey of the literature on Portugal and European integration', *e-Journal of Portuguese History*, 3 (2005): 1–12; Id., 'Portugal's European Integration Policy, 1947-72', *Journal of European Integration History*, 7 (2001): 25–35; António José Telo, 'Portugal y la integración europea (1945-1974)', *Ayer* 37, *Portugal y España contemporáneos* (2000): 287–319.
45 Alice Cunha, 'Underwriting Democracy: Portugal and European Economic Community's Accession', *Cahiers de la Méditerranée*, 90 (2015): 47–58.
46 David Castaño, 'Mário Soares e o sucesso da transição democrática', *Ler História*, 63 (2012): 9–31.
47 David Castaño, 'A Practical Test in the Détente: International Support for the Socialist Party in the Portuguese Revolution (1974-1975)', *Cold War History*, 15 (2015): 1–26.
48 Mario Del Pero, 'La transizione portoghese', in *Democrazie*, ed. Del Pero, Varsori, Guirao and Gavín, 95–171.
49 HAEU, BAC 48/1984 567, Note to Christopher Soames, vice-president of the Commission, Brussels, 17 July 1974.
50 PACE, Resolution 564 (1974), Situation in Portugal, Strasbourg, 9 May 1974.
51 HAEU, BAC 250/1980 372, Joint Committee EC-Portugal, Brussels, 27 June 1974.
52 Pedro Ponte e Sousa, 'Portugal and the EEC Accession: Informal Practices and Arrangements', *e-International Relations*, 14 May 2017.
53 Cunha, 'Underwriting Democracy'.
54 University of Pittsburgh, Archive of European Integration (hereinafter AEI), EC European Parliament Press release, Chistopher Soames interview on BBC World Service, 6 August 1975.
55 HAEU, BAC 48/1984 567, Note for the attention of Christopher Soames, Brussels, 7 February 1975.
56 HAEU, BAC 48/1984 567, Note for the attention of M. de Margerie, Brussels, 24 March 1975.
57 HAEU, COM 1975 287 Commission communication to the Council on measures to be undertaken in favour of Portugal, Brussels, 11 June 1975.
58 Summary of the conclusions adopted by the European Council held in Brussels on 16 and 17 July 1975, European Council conclusions (1975–92).

59 AEI, Commission, Information brochure: Relations between the European Community and Portugal (Brussels, 1976).
60 Financial protocol between the EC and the Portuguese Republic, Brussels, 20 September 1976, https://www.cvce.eu/content/publication/2006/10/16/f285db8c-9a91-424d-8abd-36cd96301067/publishable_en.pdf (accessed July 2020).
61 Julio Crespo MacLennan, *Spain and the Process of European Integration, 1957-85* (Basingstoke: Palgrave Macmillan, 2000), 94-120; Raimundo Bassols Jaca, *Veinte años de España en Europa* (Madrid: Política Exterior, 2007), 112-25; Matthieu Trouvé, *L'Espagne et l'Europe: De la dictature de Franco à l'Union européenne* (Brussels: Peter Lang, 2008), 115-40.
62 Antonio Moreno Juste, 'The European Economic Community and the End of the Franco Regime: The September 1975 Crisis', *Cahiers de la Méditerranée*, 90 (2015): 25-45.
63 Rosa Pardo Sanz, 'La politique extérieure espagnole de la fin du franquisme et son héritage sur la transition démocratique', *Histoire@Politique*, 29 (2016): 125-40.
64 'Le pape fait appel à la clémence du général Franco', *Le Monde*, 23 September 1975, 3.
65 PACE, Resolution 599 (1975), Situation in Spain, Strasbourg, 22 September 1975.
66 'Résolution sur la situation en Espagne', *Journal officiel des Communautés européennes* C 239/41 (20 October 1975).
67 'Les Neufs tentent toujours de s'accorder pour agir en faveur des condamnés espagnols', *Le Soir*, 26 September 1975, 3.
68 'Pays-Bas: quinze mille personnes derrière le premier ministre', *Le Monde*, 30 September 1975, 4.
69 'Eurocrats Join Protest against Spain', *Financial Times*, 30 September 1975, 6.
70 HAEU, BAC 173/1995 1263, Letters from trade union representatives and interns at the EC Commission, Brussels, 29-30 September 1975.
71 'Dix gouvernements ont appelés en consultation leur représentant', *Le Monde*, 30 September 1975, 3.
72 Moreno Juste, 'The European Economic Community and the End of the Franco Regime', 36-9.
73 'La Commission européenne s'est prononcée pour la suspension des négociations avec l'Espagne, et elle invite le Conseil à faire sienne cette position', *Europe* 1830, 2 October 1975, 4.
74 'Commission calls on EEC nations to Break off Trade Talks with Madrid', *The Times*, 2 October 1975, 6.
75 HAEU, BAC 173/1995 1263, Letter from Georges Spénale to the president of the Council, Mariano Rumor, 3 October 1975.
76 'Les évènements d'Espagne: Le boycott s'étend', *Europe* 1830, 2 October 1975, 3.
77 'Le Conseil constate que les négociations entre la CEE et l'Espagne ne peuvent pas être reprises et les ministres reprouvent les récents évènements en Espagne', *Europe* 1834, 8 October 1975, 4-5.
78 HAEU, CM2 1975/85 Verbatim of the Council of Ministers, 6 October 1975.
79 MacLennan, *Spain and the Process of European Integration*, 94-120.
80 Trouvé, *L'Espagne et l'Europe*, 169-70.
81 'La CEE est diposée à reprendre les contacts avec l'Espagne dans les limites des anciennes orientations - Aucune évolution n'est pour le moment prévue vers d'autres liens', *Europe* 1901, 21 January 1976, 4.
82 European Parliament, *Débats, 1975-1976*, 15 October 1975, 161.

83 European Parliament, Resolution on the situation in Spain (12 May 1976), *Official Journal of the European Communities*, C125 (1976): 25.
84 Carlos López Gómez, 'Europe as a Symbol: The Struggle for Democracy and the Meaning of European Integration in post-Franco Spain', *Journal of European Contemporary Research*, 10 (2014): 74–89, esp. 83.
85 Fernando Guirao and Víctor Gavín, 'La dimensione internazionale della transizione politica spagnola (1969-1982): Quale ruolo giocarono la Comunità europea e gli Stati Uniti', in *Democrazie*, ed. Del Pero, Varsori, Guirao and Gavín, 173–264.
86 PACE, *Official Report of Debates*, 27th ordinary session, 3rd part, Strasbourg, 27 January 1976, 793–4.

2

Introducing human rights within development cooperation policies

The European Community between the United States and the Soviet Union (1968–79)

Ilaria Zamburlini

The 1970s represented a decisive turning point in the history of foreign aid in the twentieth century. In that period, the process of decolonization reached its almost full accomplishment and, as a consequence, many newly independent nations emerged on the global arena and looked for their own economic development and growth. The two superpowers of the Cold War, namely the United States and the Union of the Soviet Socialist Republics (USSR), put into practice many programmes in order to deliver aid to developing countries as well as to gain control over them. However, in the same years, another actor decided to invest much energy in its relationship with such countries: the European Community (EC).

This chapter discusses whether the attempt of the EC to introduce the concept of human rights within its development assistance policies during the 1970s can be seen as a way for the EC to be recognized on the international stage by developing countries as well as by the United States and the USSR. In particular, this chapter wishes to underline how the EC tried to give its foreign aid scheme, namely the *Lomé Convention*, a specific connotation thanks to a continuous reference to human rights and therefore to differentiate its strategies from the plans put in practice by the United States and the USSR in the same period.

In the growing corpus of literature on human rights in the 1970s,[1] little attention was given to the EC. There are some relevant exceptions, such as the works by scholars Angela Romano, Umberto Tulli and Aurélie É. Gfeller,[2] yet these analyses mainly concentrate on human rights in East–West relations and do not consider the attention paid by the EC to human rights and development cooperation policies in the 1970s. At the same time, there are notable studies on the introduction of human rights within EC foreign aid policies,[3] but they either tend to consider the 1970s as 'years of inactivity'[4] or they look at the legal implications only, thus ignoring the political implications of such action. This chapter intends to fill this gap and to specifically look at the period ranging from 1968 to 1979.

Bipolar confrontation over development assistance

According to historian Federico Romero, decolonization can be described as the widest and most significant political transformation of contemporary history.[5] This process took place largely after the Second World War and the resulting demise of European empires, and saw the emergence of many newly independent nations willing to acquire their own position on the global stage.[6]

In 1955, around thirty African and Asian governments and national liberation movements met in the Indonesian city of Bandung and demonstrated to be quite a homogeneous group, which soon started to be referred to as the Third World.[7] These nations represented a non-industrialized and rural world, and were above all keen on developing and on reaching satisfactory economic growth, prosperity and autonomy vis-à-vis the wealthiest northern nations. Moreover, all these countries were determined to affirm a wide anti-colonial discourse, and many of them decided to refrain from assuming a specific political position and to remain non-aligned with regards to the Cold War confrontation existing since the end of the 1940s between the United States and the USSR. However, the logic of the Cold War was soon expanded to extra-European areas,[8] and the so-called Third World became a new target of attention of the two blocs and played a decisive role in that context. Consequently, the nature of the North–South relationship transformed and acquired much more importance than in past decades,[9] and this also contributed to change East–West balance.

The presence of new actors on the international stage during the Cold War caused what historian Sara Lorenzini defines as 'a strange Cold War',[10] meaning an additional side of the conflict that arose between the two superpowers. Both blocs understood that what developing countries desired most was to reach economic development, and they hence started a race around the allocation of development assistance and economic aid to those nations in order to be able to count them within their respective influence.[11]

The practice of delivering aid had largely emerged after the Second World War, but helping poor countries had become the main scope of rich countries mostly after the Bandung conference. Indeed, in 1961 the United Nations (UN) launched the so-called First Development Decade, through which it aimed at addressing the issue of underdevelopment worldwide.[12] Later on, the UN looked at the problems arising from the unequal distribution of wealth as well as at poverty, while specific attention was also given to the wrong administration of aid programmes, since two reports had pointed out both the inadequacies of the management of aid (and this was pointed out in the *Jackson Report* – elaborated by UN official Robert Jackson in order to underline various problems of the UN aiding schemes) and the direct responsibilities of donor and recipient actors to this respect (as outlined in the *Pearson Report* – a document issued by the Commission on International Development of the World Bank led by former prime minister of Canada, Lester Pearson). The UN Second Development Decade was opened in 1971 and underlined the role of both developed and developing countries in reaching out to specific objectives.[13] Thus, development assistance was considered as a fundamental tool on various levels, and as such acquired a prominent relevance even in front of international public opinion.

Although both the United States and the USSR presented development aid as a way to help independent nations to foster their economic and social advancement, what they (more or less openly) intended to do was to include those nations under their respective sphere of control and to steal them from the other power's influence. The so-called Third World represented at that point an enormous potential of people, resources, and energy, and could not be left aside neither ideologically nor geopolitically. The United States, whose history of donations to recover poor economies in the twentieth century had the European Recovery Plan, also known as Marshall Plan, at its core, highlighted its role in promoting economic growth, and mainly spoke the language of technological advancement. In 1971, for instance, President Richard Nixon launched a reform of foreign aid policies and underlined how development assistance was central to US foreign policy.

On the other hand, only after Joseph Stalin's death did the USSR start looking with true interest at developing countries as well as at their willingness to emancipate. It promised to export the triumph of the Soviet economic model to promote progress and modernity, and sponsored socialism as a way to overcome capitalism and hence imperialism.[14] The Soviet Union was aware that it had more appeal than the United States had, for it did not recall to developing interlocutors any colonial past,[15] and this of course brought about anxiety for the United States.

Providing assistance thus ended up being another way for the two blocs to compete and to fight, and to impose different models of society around the world. However, this ideological contrast over developing assistance partially decreased during the 1970s, when the two blocs demonstrated their willingness to cooperate and thus opened the way to détente, a period of relaxation that lasted until the end of the decade. Many reasons can be put forward to explain why the United States and the USSR decided to initiate a dialogue during that period. Historiography used to describe the 1970s as a moment of great crisis, and indeed the economic and oil crises had a role in making world powers rethink their relations. Although Hobsbawm's famous elaboration on the history of the twentieth century[16] interpreted those years as the end of the golden age that had begun after the Second World War, this negative connotation stopped being used in recent times. More neutral explanations, like Tony Judt's definition of the 1970s as a 'post-everything' era,[17] gained increasing attention and are useful to understand that various innovative factors contributed to calm the bipolar confrontation down, such as the understanding of world connections as interdependent and interrelated.

The EC and its development assistance policies

It was exactly in the 1970s, though, that another actor specifically affirmed its intention to invest into the economic development of Southern countries and decided to acquire a visible position on the global arena, precisely in front of newly independent nations[18]: the EC.

Development assistance was not a recent scope for the EC. Many developing nations being former colonies of some of the EC member states, the EC felt that it wanted to keep those historical ties in place. Therefore, it started its development assistance programme already at the end of the 1950s, when the 1957 Treaty of Rome set up a series of bilateral relations between the EC and a very limited group of developing countries that obtained to be recognized as associated to the Community. Part IV of the Treaty of Rome was precisely devoted to the 'association of overseas countries and territories', with articles 131 to 133 establishing special linkages between the EC member states and their associated territories, and aiming at promoting economic and social development.[19] This first step was seen as an occasion for the EC to undertake political expansion, in order to promote 'the great civilizing mission of Europe all over the world', as Joseph Luns, foreign minister of the Netherlands, declared in Rome.[20]

However, in the early 1960s the EC had to rethink its relations with the so-called Third World[21] and in 1963 decided to approve a new kind of agreement that was structured around eighteen partners. The Yaoundé Convention, as it was known, did not lose the regional intentions that the EC had been pursuing since the beginning of development assistance policies, for France was again the main intermediary between the EC and many African countries and opposed other EC countries' will to expand links of association to other developing nations.[22] The agreement expired in 1969, but was then renewed for another five years.

It was mainly in the 1970s, yet, that the EC emerged as one of the main actors devoting aid to Southern countries. A true turning point took place between 1971 and 1972. In 1971, the European Commission published a memorandum in which it suggested to open EC development policies also to countries that were not former colonies of EC member states.[23] This position was then officially undertaken during the 1972 Paris Summit, when the EC decided to adopt 'an overall policy of development cooperation on a world-wide scale', and affirmed 'its determination within the framework of a world-wide policy towards the developing countries, to increase its effort in aid and technical assistance to the least favoured people' and to take 'particular account of the concerns of those countries towards which, through geography, history',[24] it had specific responsibilities. It was the first time that the EC used development cooperation as a way to obtain a place within international relations, and that presented itself as a power able to act and influence the world through its normative capacity.[25]

In 1975 a new development assistance scheme was created with the Lomé Convention. This new association agreement lasted for almost thirty years, with renovations every five years, and involved up to seventy partners, known as African Caribbean and Pacific (ACP) countries, that put together French sensibility with British demands after EC 1973 enlargement.[26] Lomé was welcomed as the most advanced tool for North–South cooperation,[27] given that it was based on the principles of equality and dialogue among the partners, and it provided the EC with the means to appear as an international actor willing to promote democracy through social and economic advancement.[28]

The EC in between: Strategies to stand out

Promoting human rights

During the 1970s, once it had defined its development programmes, the EC was eager to acquire a specific position on the international stage. One first strategy that the EC put in practice to reach that goal was to give its policies a precise connotation: creating a link with human rights.

Although human rights had already been exposed to public interest before, it was mainly after 1968 that they gained a new and unexpected global relevance. During the 1970s, they obtained an importance that they had hardly experienced before and they almost became a 'popular'[29] subject that was discussed not only in the conference rooms of international organizations but also in the media as well as in the speeches of pop stars, actors and musicians.[30] Human rights became a prominent topic on the international scene and they also represented, as Ignatieff puts it,[31] the 'lingua franca' of the global moral thought, as well as a 'global imagination'.[32] Many reasons could be put forward to explain why the 1970s saw this outbreak of human rights. In 1966, for instance, the UN approved two covenants, the International Covenant on Civil and Political Rights and the International Covenant on Economic, Social and Cultural Rights, that renovated the global attention on human rights. Moreover, just a few years later, 1968 activism called worldwide for fundamental rights and freedom,[33] and an International Conference on Human Rights took place in Teheran. Some historians, like Paul Gordon Lauren,[34] claim that the 1970s represented the peak of the evolution of human sensitivity towards the Other. Conversely, Samuel Moyn[35] affirms that human rights exploded in the 1970s as an alternative to all prior universalistic schemes and utopias that eventually collapsed. Mark P. Bradley[36] states, however, that human rights were not an alternative to other systems, yet a further addition to all the stances that were embraced by the global social mobilization that took place in the 1970s.

The respect for human rights was among the purposes of European Political Cooperation (EPC),[37] a system that the EC approved in 1970 with the aim of coordinating its foreign policy as well as expressing common intensions with a single voice. Indeed, the founding document stated that 'a united Europe should be based on a common heritage of respect for the liberty and the rights of men'.[38] Moreover, human rights were proclaimed as an official part of the EC policies in the 1973 Copenhagen Declaration on European Identity,[39] a document that the EC produced to underline that its member states were 'determined to defend the principles of representative democracy, of the rule of law or social justice [. . .] and of respect for human rights'.[40] By asserting human rights, the EC wanted to make it clear that it had its own specific identity to defend and promote, not only within the European context only, but also worldwide. A sample of this commitment was openly shown at the Conference for Security and Cooperation in Europe, which produced in 1975 the Helsinki Final Act, a document in which human rights obtained a relevant place among the principles governing international relations.

It was around 1976 that the EC started thinking about connecting human rights to its development assistance. Linking human rights to foreign aid could have two different connotations: first, to promote human rights through foreign aid, for example, to orient part of the aid to specific projects fostering human rights;[41] second, to avoid the transfer of development assistance to those countries not respecting or violating human rights. Although both cases realized, it was almost the second connotation that was mostly referred to by the EC. Indeed, at the end of the 1970s, when the EC institutions started preparing the first renovation of the Lomé Convention with fifty-eight ACP countries,[42] appeals were made to link development assistance to a country's performance on human rights.[43] During the renewal negotiations, the EC pointed out that it wanted 'more than a casual reference to basic UN principles inserted in the new convention [...] [and] to be able to suspend concessions to any ACP government which seriously violated human rights'.[44] Hence, the EC officially asserted the importance of human rights for its foreign aid in front of the ACPs as it had never done before. This represented, with no doubt, a true political change if compared to previous versions of association agreements.

The institution that was, above all, active in promoting the integration of human rights within foreign aid policies in the 1970s was the European Parliament (EP). The main reasons behind this action lay on the political ambitions of this institution, as scholar Umberto Tulli explains,[45] as well as on the pressure put by several NGOs, among which Amnesty International, on the European parliamentarians.[46] Already in 1975, when considering whether to expand the relations of the EC with the Association of Southeast Asian Nations (ASEAN), the EP argued that it was not in accordance with European identity to deliver development assistance to countries that were not respecting human rights, as it was the case for Indonesia[47] and Thailand.[48] Human rights in Ethiopia,[49] Uganda[50] and Latin America[51] soon began to be one of the concerns of the EP, too. At the beginning of 1977, one member of the European Parliament (MEP), on behalf of the Christian Democrat group, invited the Council to reflect on what the EC had proclaimed in the 1973 Copenhagen Declaration and in the 1976 Common Declaration on the Respect for Human Rights,[52] and to consequently think about the actions to be carried out with those partner countries that were violating certain basic democratic principles.[53] Later on, another MEP asked the Commission whether violations of human rights in many countries with which the EC had relations were compatible with the existing partnership.[54] MEP Alfred Bertrand asked his fellow colleagues how the EC intended to act in front of the recurrent violations of human rights, considered as the 'common basis of European cultural heritage'.[55] MEP Hector Rivierez (European Progressive Democrats) stated that it would have been 'a good thing that in the future, in our relations with countries to which we are linked by association agreement or to which we grant aid, we shall be able to stipulate that they must respect human rights', and this was supported during the same session by MEP Nicholas Bethell (Conservative and Unionist Party), who affirmed that 'human rights provide us with a basis for a philosophy which we can develop and use to great advantage in winning the hearts of the Third World and in convincing them that we feel for freedom and democracy'.[56] MEP Geoffrey de Freitas stressed that 'in view of the Community's direct association with many countries in the Lomé Convention, surely before [EC] money is spent in countries indicted by Amnesty International, [the EC] should at least make the most careful investigations to see that we are subsidising oppression'.[57] Later in 1978 the debate within the EP focused on the necessity to include the principle of respect for human rights in the renewal of the Lomé Convention, to be signed in 1979. The inclusion of the concept of human rights in the EC's development assistance programme became one of the main topics on the agenda of the EP with regards the relations with the Third World, and was soon taken into consideration by the European Commission, too.[58]

Only between 1977 and 1978 did the Commission start changing its attitude towards the link between human rights and development assistance. In 1977, the Commission affirmed that it was willing to help with regard to human rights violations in case of specific requests coming from non-governmental organizations.[59] Moreover, at the beginning of 1978, it sent the Council a memorandum on the negotiations for the renewal of the Lomé Convention, in which it proposed 'the insertion in the preamble to the new convention of a precise and explicit reference to the signatories' obligation to observe the most fundamental human rights' and stressed that it reserved 'the right to voice publicly its condemnation of infringement of any of the principles or objectives laid down in the preamble to the convention'.[60] Moreover, the Commission started preparing for the meeting that was about to renew the Lomé Convention with ACP countries, and elaborated a document in which it tried to foresee possible objections to the inclusion of human rights in the agreement, as well as tentative answers in defence of such addition. Also, Émile Noël, secretary-general of the Commission, underlined that both the Commission and the Parliament had a true interest for human rights and pointed out that the Commission wanted to insert human rights within Lomé II, notwithstanding the difficulties in convincing the Council about this.[61]

The Council, indeed, was the slowest EC institution in accepting the link between human rights and foreign aid. In 1976, for instance, it said that the EC should raise this concern only on a general and broad level, without addressing certain countries particularly.[62] Only in 1977, because of the severe violations of human rights occurring in Uganda, did it take a position, yet not a definitive one. It generally affirmed that more attention was needed when distributing foreign aid within the Lomé framework.[63] However, later in 1978, the Council started considering the issue of human rights with reference to Lomé II. In 1979, together with the Parliament and the Commission, it finally accepted the idea of pronouncing a common declaration on the problem of human rights in ACP countries, which was put forward during the negotiations but was not accepted by the counterpart and had to wait until the mid-1980s to be eventually realized.[64]

The EC's emphasis on human rights within its development assistance policy gave the EC the possibility to specifically connote its identity as well as its political and ideological profile in front of the other actors that were active in granting aid to developing countries. The concept of responsibility[65] was also much employed by the EC as a way to explain its role in helping poor nations to reach economic stability. For instance, the EC continuously stressed that providing assistance to developing countries represented something like a moral necessity[66] as well as an expression of the vocation of Europe to speak out to defend certain values.[67]

Addressing critiques to the superpowers

Attaching a moral connotation to development assistance let the EC acquire a specific profile on the international scene. And this profile was particularly helpful for the EC in underlining the differences of its aid programmes and behaviours from the two blocs of the Cold War, as well as in highlighting its superiority and in addressing various critiques to both the United States and the USSR.

Human Rights within Cooperation Policies   37

Figure 2.1 Ex-Officer in the Ugandan Army and alleged 'guerrilla' Tom Masaba is stripped of his clothes and tied to a tree before his execution at Mbale. The cruelty of Idi Amin repressive regime in Uganda pushed the EC to discuss human rights in its development aid policy and to adopt the so-called Uganda Guidelines in 1977.

Already in 1970, during the joint meetings between the EP and the Consultative Assembly of the Council of Europe, the Community stressed that the best contribution that it could give to global development assistance policy was to go on with its own action.[68] This concept was then also proposed by Franco Maria Malfatti, president of the European Commission, when he affirmed that Europe needed to change its attitude from spectator to actor with regards to the relations with the Third World[69] and hence to precisely take stance within the international arena. Helping poor nations was presented as an 'historically inescapable task'[70] to 'support peace in the world'.[71] As the Italian newspaper *Il Sole 24 Ore* affirmed, indeed, the future of Africa was tightly tied to the EC.⁷² The EC felt that it had to have a leading role with regards to the various interests related to development issues⁷³ and presented itself as the only actor that was ready to grant aid to developing countries with no intentions of receiving anything back, neither influence nor money, as it was instead the case for the two superpowers. According to the Belgian newspaper *Le Soir*, indeed, 'seule l'Europe offre au pays du Tiers Monde une coopération sans dépendance.'⁷⁴

The Communist bloc was blamed for helping the Third World less than the other rich countries around the world did.⁷⁵ Indeed, the EC accused the Soviet Union of providing very little help to poor countries, and to be more interested in commercial exchanges rather than into improving the economic situation of the Third World. Journalist Theo Sommer wrote in *Die Zeit* in 1977 that the Soviet Union was an 'absent partner', only able to foster ideological propaganda.⁷⁶ This was also what the EC thought: the USSR was seen as incapable of aiding peoples willing to reach economic growth.⁷⁷ The EC criticized the policies put in practice by the USSR, for this bloc was only willing to reach its own economic advancement and to promote the ideas of communism around the world. That is why the EP started considering the idea of helping certain underdeveloped areas in order to reduce the negative impact that cooperating with the USSR might have had. Consequently, it asked the Commission whether it was possible for the EC to expand relations outside current association agreements, in order to avoid leaving certain poor countries with the only choice of accepting the discriminatory commercial links proposed by Eastern Europe.⁷⁸ The USSR was labelled as 'hardly disinterested'⁷⁹ and continuously blamed by the EC (and by the EP above all). However, critiques were mutual. The USSR accused the EC of its kind of cooperation with the Third World, defining it as a sort of collective colonialism with regional intentions, and affirming that there was no difference between Yaoundé and Lomé.

Although the USSR was the main target of EC's accusations, even the United States did receive some critiques for its development schemes. These negative judgements came already at the beginning of the decade, when for instance *The Guardian* underlined that the EC should not wait for the United States to negotiate its help for the Third World.⁸⁰ The EC pointed out that the United States was only focused on promoting anti-communist policies, as well as on fighting the USSR on the territory of granting aid to developing nations, rather than on promoting true economic growth.⁸¹ Moreover, the EC underlined that, for the United States had diminished aid, it was almost a moral commitment for the EC itself to take care of poor Southern countries that would have been otherwise left abandoned.⁸² More interestingly, it expressed that it did not have any lesson to learn from the United States, given that it felt that Europe was, in front of the United States, as ancient Greece in comparison to ancient Rome.⁸³ As *Le Monde* put it in an article entitled 'Un plan Marshall européen pour l'Afrique et le proche Orient',⁸⁴ the EC was keen on establishing with poor countries the same link that the United States had established with Europe after the Second World War and was ready to take this commitment notwithstanding what the United States decided to do. Also, it felt that it had closer ties with those countries than the United States did.⁸⁵ This approach remained in place almost until the end of the 1970s, with a peak after 1973, when Secretary of State Henry Kissinger proclaimed the Year of Europe and made way for a deep transatlantic crisis. When President Carter was elected, though, the EC started considering the United States as an example with regards to promoting human rights, and this had a repercussion on foreign aid programmes, too.[86] The EC started looking at the transatlantic partner as a model and argued that the world was divided into two sections: one bloc believing in human rights and moral values; the other bloc perpetrating injustices and exploitation. That is why it was necessary to put common plans into practice between the United States and the EC, and this is what the EC increasingly did after the end of 1970s.[87]

Conclusion

Following the process of decolonization, the emergence of new independent countries willing to reach their own economic and social advancement and the decision of the two superpowers of the Cold War, the United States and the USSR, to deliver money to those nations in order to gain influence, the 1970s saw the gradual appearance of the EC on the global arena as well as its intention to acquire a prominent role in addressing aid to the so-called Third World. The EC, whose development assistance policies had started already in 1957, decided to invest much energy in its foreign aid programmes in the 1970s and sought to become a well-recognized actor in front of both the two blocs and the developing countries. To do so, it put in practice two parallel yet different strategies. First, it gave a strong moral connotation to its policies, by presenting human rights as one of the most important issues at the core of its aid programmes. Linking human rights to foreign aid meant, for the EC, that continuous attention was paid to the violations of human rights within countries that were recipient of EC assistance. Second, the EC tried to underline its moral superiority with respect to the two superpowers and their foreign aid schemes. Indeed, it highlighted that it was the only actor willing to help without having any other intentions, such as gaining influence or exporting a precise model of society and ideology, and it moved specific accusations against the USSR, which was the main target of critiques, and the United States.

In conclusion, some further considerations can be outlined concerning the behaviour of the EC as well as its position in the framework of the Cold War. First, it can be affirmed that the emphasis put by the EC on its identity and values as well as on its differences from the other actors was necessary for the EC in order to construct its own specific image, and to obtain an autonomous space on the international stage. Indeed, the EC wanted to stand out and to be seen as an alternative to the United States and the USSR and their purposes vis-à-vis developing countries. That is why throughout the 1970s it sought to shape a precise profile of its actions and underlined that it did not aim at subjugating developing countries, neither politically nor economically. However, the scheme of development put in practice by the EC was not really different from those of the two blocs, for also the EC wanted to obtain something from aiding Southern countries, like being recognized as a relevant international player. Moreover, the accent on human rights was almost unilateral and univocal, as the EC paid great attention to the violations of human rights perpetrated within developing nations yet did not listen to the requests coming from them with regards to the promotion of human rights such as the right to development and the application of reciprocity. In fact, 'the ACP argued that reciprocity would have to apply, giving them the right to inquire into legal and administrative abuses in Europe',[88] but the EC did not accept, and this led to the lacking insertion of human rights within the renewal of the Lomé Convention, as well as to the suspect that the EC was perpetrating some sort of civilizing neo-colonial mission and a Eurocentric vision of moral values.

During the 1970s, the EC feared to be left aside on the fringes of détente. However, while it can be said that the EC found its autonomy in the context of the bipolar confrontation, it is not possible to state that this was the case also for its relations with the so-called Third World. Indeed, although the EC sought to obtain its space within the North–South dialogue, its behaviour was not seen, by developing countries, as radically different from that of the other actors, and this left no true room for the EC in that sector.

Notes

1 Samuel Moyn, *The Last Utopia: Human Rights in History* (Cambridge, MA: Harvard University Press, 2010); Jan Eckel, 'The Rebirth of Politics from the Spirit of Morality: Explaining the Human Rights Revolution of the 1970s', in *The Breakthrough: Human Rights in the 1970s*, ed. Jan Eckel and Samuel Moyn (Philadelphia: University of Pennsylvania Press, 2014), 226–60; Barbara Keys, *Reclaiming American Virtue: The Human Rights Revolution of the 1970s* (Cambridge, MA: Harvard University Press, 2014).
2 Angela Romano, *From Détente in Europe to European Détente: How the West Shaped the Helsinki CSCE* (Brussels: Peter Lang, 2009); Umberto Tulli, 'Challenging Intergovermentalism and EPC: The European Parliament and Its Actions in International Relations, 1970-1979', *Journal of Contemporary European Research*, 13 (2017): 1076–89; Aurélie É. Gfeller, 'Champion of Human Rights: The European Parliament and the Helsinki Process', *Journal of Contemporary History*, 49 (2014): 392.
3 Marjorie Lister, *The European Community and the Developing World: The Role of the Lomé Convention* (Adershot: Avebury, 1988), 186–223; Lorenzo Ferrari, *Sometimes Speaking with a Single Voice: The European Community as an International Actor* (Brussels: Peter Lang, 2016), 171–98; Lorand Bartels, *Human Rights Conditionality in the EU's International Agreements* (Oxford: Oxford University Press, 2005); Karin Arts, *Integrating Human Rights into Development Cooperation: The Case of the Lomé Convention* (The Hague: Kluwer Law International, 2000).
4 Toby King, 'Human Rights in the Development Policy of the European Community: Towards a European World Order?', *Netherlands Yearbook of International Law*, 28 (December 1997): 51–99.
5 Federico Romero, *Storia internazionale dell'età contemporanea* (Roma: Carocci, 2012), 80.
6 Raymond F. Betts, *Decolonization* (London: Routledge, 1998); Frederick Cooper, *Colonialism in Question: Theory, Knowledge, History* (Berkeley and Los Angeles: University of California Press, 2005), 91–112.
7 This expression was formulated by French demographer Alfred Sauvy in 1952 and elaborated within his essay *Trois mondes, une planéte*, where he explained that all

subdued people would soon awake and rebel like the *Tiers état* did during French revolution.

8 Elena Calandri, *Prima della globalizzazione. L'Italia, la cooperazione allo sviluppo e la guerra fredda* (Padova: Cedam, 2013).

9 Romero, *Storia internazionale*, 81–4.

10 Sara Lorenzini, *Una strana guerra fredda. Lo sviluppo e le relazioni Nord-Sud* (Bologna: il Mulino, 2017).

11 The term *development assistance* is used to indicate the international transfer of aid (goods, capital, services) from a donor – and richer – country to a recipient – and poorer – country with the aim of helping the receiver with its development.

12 Among various other purposes, the UN wanted to 'accelerate progress towards self-sustaining growth of the economy of the individual nations and their social advancement so as to attain in each under-developed country a substantial increase in the rate of growth'. United Nations 1084th Plenary Meeting of 19 December 1961 on *United Nations Development Decade. A Programme for International Economic Cooperation (I)*, number 1710 (XVI).

13 United Nations, 1912th Plenary Meeting of 19 November 1970 on *International Development Strategy for the Second United Nations Development Decade*, number 2626 (XXV).

14 Lorenzini, *Una strana guerra fredda*, 71–80.

15 Giuliano Garavini, 'Il confronto Nord-Sud allo specchio: l'impatto del Terzo mondo sull'Europa occidentale (1968-1975)', in *Alle origini del presente. L'Europa occidentale nella crisi degli anni Settanta*, ed. Antonio Varsori (Milano: Franco Angeli, 2007), 67–95.

16 Eric J. Hobsbawm, *Age of Extremes: The Short Twentieth Century, 1914-1991* (London: Random House, 1994).

17 Tony Judt, *Postwar: A History of Europe since 1945* (New York: The Penguin Press, 2005), 478.

18 Mario Del Pero and Federico Romero, eds, *Le crisi transatlantiche. Continuità e trasformazioni* (Roma: Edizioni di storia e letteratura, 2007).

19 Treaty of Rome, https://www.cvce.eu/en/obj/treaty_establishing_the_european_econo mic_community_rome_25_march_1957-en-cca6ba28-0bf3-4ce6-8a76-6b0b3252696e .html (accessed 7 December 2020).

20 Quoted in Lorenzini, *Una strana guerra fredda*, 239.

21 Martin Holland, *The European Union and the Third World* (Houndmills: Palgrave, 2002).

22 Guia Migani, 'Strategie nazionali ed istituzionali alle origini dell'assistenza comunitaria allo sviluppo: la Cee, la Francia e l'Africa negli anni sessanta', in *Il primato sfuggente. L'Europa e l'intervento per lo sviluppo (1957-2007)*, ed. Elena Calandri (Milano: Franco Angeli, 2009), 17–34.

23 Giuliana Laschi, *L'Europa e gli altri. Le relazioni esterne della Comunità dalle origini al dialogo Nord-Sud* (Bologna: il Mulino, 2015).

24 Final Statement of the 1972 Paris Summit, http://www.cvce.eu/obj/statement_from _the_paris_summit_19_to_21_october_1972-en-b1dd3d57-5f31-4796-85c3-cfd221 0d6901.html (accessed 7 December 2020).

25 The concept of Europe as a civilian power was formulated by François Duchêne, one of Jean Monnet's most strict collaborators, in 1972.

26 Holland, *The European Union and the Third World*.

27 Calandri, *Prima della globalizzazione*, 210–26.

28 Karin Arts and Anna K. Dickinson, eds, *EU Development Cooperation: From Model to Symbol* (Manchester: Manchester University Press, 2004). It must be recalled that Lomé also got some critiques. According to John Ravenhill, the Lomé Conventions represented a sort of collective clientelism, still regional and completely centred on technicalities and bureaucracy. John Ravenhill, *Collective Clientelism: The Lomé Conventions and North-South Relations* (New York: Columbia University Press, 1985).
29 Stefan-Ludwig Hoffmann, 'Introduction. Genealogies of Human Rights', in *Human Rights in the Twentieth Century*, ed. Stefan-Ludwig Hoffmann (New York: Cambridge University Press, 2010), 20.
30 Eckel and Moyn, *The Breakthrough*.
31 Michael Ignatieff, *Human Rights as Politics and Idolatry* (Princeton: Princeton University Press, 2001).
32 Poul Villaume, Rasmus Mariager and Helle Porsdam, eds, *The 'Long 1970s'. Human Rights, East- West Détente and Transnational Relations* (Copenhagen: Museum Tusculanum Press, 2010).
33 Marcello Flores and Giovanni Gozzini, *1968. Un anno spartiacque* (Bologna: il Mulino, 2018), 119–46.
34 Paul Gordon Lauren, *The Evolution of International Human Rights: Visions Seen* (Philadelphia: University of Pennsylvania Press, 2011).
35 Moyn, *The Last Utopia*.
36 Mark Philip Bradley, 'The Origins of the 1970s Global Human Rights Imagination', in *The 'Long 1970s'*, ed. Villaume, Mariager and Porsdam, 15–32.
37 On EPC see David Allen, Reinhardt Rummel e Wolfgang Wessels, eds, *European Political Cooperation: Towards a Foreign Policy for Western Europe* (London: Butterworth Scientific, 1982); Federiga Bindi, *The Foreign Policy of the European Union: Asserting Europe's Role in the World* (Washington: Brookings Institution Press, 2012), 13–40; Leon Hurwitz, *The European Community and the Management of International Cooperation* (Santa Barbara: Greenwood Press, 1987), 207–19.
38 European Communities, *First Report of the Foreign Ministers to the Heads of State and Government of the member states of the European Community* (Luxembourg: European Communities, 1970).
39 Ian Manners, 'The Constitutive Nature of Values, Images and Principles in the European Union', in *Values and Principles in European Union Foreign Policy*, ed. Sonia Lucarelli and Ian Manners (Abingdon: Routledge, 2006), 19–41.
40 'Declaration on European Identity', *Bulletin of the European Communities*, 12 (1973): 118–22.
41 Bethany Barratt, *Human Rights and Foreign Aid: For Love or for Money?* (Abingdon: Routledge, 2008), 1–32.
42 Bruno Simma, Jo Beatrix Aschenbrenner and Constanze Schulte, 'Human Rights Considerations in the Development Co-operation Activities of the EC', in *The EU and Human Rights*, ed. Philip Alston, Mara Bustelo and James Heenan (Oxford: Oxford University Press, 1999), 571–626.
43 Lorenzo Ferrari, 'The European Community as a Promoter of Human Rights in Africa and Latin America, 1970-80', *Journal of European Integration History*, 21 (2015): 217–30.
44 Overseas Development Institute, 'Briefing Paper', *ODI Briefing Papers*, 1 (1980), www.odi.org/sites/odi.org.uk/files/odi-assets/publications-opinion-files/6636.pdf (accessed December 2020).
45 Tulli, 'Challenging Intergovernmentalism and EPC'.

46   Ilaria Zamburlini, 'Human Rights and Foreign Aid: Three NGOs Influencing the European Community (1974-1979)', in *The Informal Construction of Europe*, ed. Lennaert Van Heumen and Mechthild Roos (Abingdon: Routledge, 2019), 129–42.
47   Historical Archives of the European Union (HAEU), PE0 14290, Question écrite de Madame Marie-Thérèse Goutmann à la Commission – Object: développement des relations avec les pays ASEAN et défense des droits de l'homme, 24 October 1975.
48   Historical Archives of the European Commission (HAEC), BAC 131/1983, N. 486, Question écrite n. 636/77 à la Commission des Communautés européennes – Object: Atteinte aux droits de l'homme en Thaïlande et en Indonésie, 30 September 1977.
49   HAEC, BAC 131/1983, N. 486, Question orale n. 0-22/77 de MM Granelli, Scelba, Bertrand et Pison au nom du groupe démocrate-chrétienne à la Commission des Communautés européennes – Object: Actions à entreprendre pour la sauvegarde des droits de l'homme en Ethiopie, 31 May 1977; HAEU, PE0 5626, Interrogazione orale (0-22/77) – Oggetto: azioni da intraprendere per la tutela dei diritti umani in Etiopia, 31 May 1977; HAEU, PE0 16077, Question écrite n. 426/77 –Object: Convention de Lomé et violation des droits de l'homme, 29 July 1977.
50   HAEC, BAC 131/1983, N. 486, Question écrite n. 941/76 – Object: Les droits de l'homme en Ouganda, 1 March 1977.
51   Historical Archives of the European Parliament (HAEP), PE 45.750, Mémorandum sur la désagrégation des institutions démocratiques dans le Sud de l'Amérique Latine, 19 September 1976.
52   HAEC, BAC 131/1983, N. 486, Déclaration commune du Parlement Européen, du Conseil et de la Commission concernant le respect des droits de l'homme, 14 July 1976.
53   HAEC, BAC 131/1983, N. 486, Question orale n. 0-111/76, avec débat, posée au Conseil par M. Alfred Betrand au nom du groupe démocrate-chrétienne de l'Assemblée, 23 February 1977.
54   HAEC, BAC 131/1983, N. 486, Question écrite n. 151/76 de Mme Goutmann à la Commission des Communautés européennes – Object: Parlementaires détenus or disparus, 9 May 1976.
55   HAEU, PE0 5599, Question orale 110/76 – Object: Défense des droits de l'homme dans le monde, 01 April 1977.
56   HAEP, PE0 AP DE 1977 DE 19770511049900 EN, Debates of the European Parliament, 11 May 1977.
57   HAEP, PE0 AP QP QH_H-0432/77, Debates of the European Parliament – Question 52, 15 March 1978.
58   HAEP, PE 53.355, 13th Inter-parliamentary Meeting, 28–31 March 1978. MEP Colette Flesch affirmed that it was necessary to intervene to safeguard at least basic human rights and hence to insert a clause to that regard.
59   HAEP, PE0 AP QP QE E-0298/77, Question écrite n. 289/77 de M. Maigaard à la Commission des Communautés Européennes (15 juin 1977), *OJ* C 259, 27 October 1977, 11–12. It is important to underline that during the 1970s NGOs acquired a relevant position within world affairs, and specifically with regards to foreign aid deliverance: Simone Dietrich and Amanda Murdie, 'Human Rights Shaming through INGOs and Foreign Aid Delivery', *The Review of International Organizations*, 12 (2016): 1–26.
60   HAEC, BAC 39/1986, n. 535, Extract from the Commission memorandum of 16 February 1978 on negotiations for the renewal of the *Lomé Convention*, undated.

61 HAEC, BAC 381/1995, n. 141, Letter from Émile Noël to Amnesty International, undated.
62 HAEC, BAC 19/2001, n. 59, Extrait de la relève des décisions du Conseil des 26/27 Juin 1976, undated.
63 HAEC, BAC 39/1986, n. 535, Council press release of 21 June 1977 – statement on Uganda, undated.
64 HAEC, BAC 39/1986, n. 535, Note de dossier – Object: Relations ACP/CEE et problème du respect des droits de l'homme, 26 July 1979.
65 HAEU, PE0 1594, Documenti di seduta, n. 87/73 – Oggetto: Relazione presentata a nome della Commissione per lo sviluppo e la cooperazione sui risultati della nona riunione annuale della Conferenza parlamentare dell'associazione CEE-SAMA, 6 June 1973.
66 HAEU, BAC 25/1980 n. 1623, Humanitarian assistance, 23 April 1971.
67 HAEU, FMM n. 33, Discours prononcés par le Président Franco Maria Malfatti en 1971, February–September 1971. Speech pronounced by Franco Maria Malfatti on the occasion of the European Day, Brussels, 5 June 1971: 'The respect of human rights and fundamental values of our society is an indispensable condition for any European action. Without the respect of these principles the construction of the European Communities would have been unthinkable'.
68 HAEU, AP-RJ, PE0 5149, 'Resoconto della sessione', 17 September 1970.
69 HAEU, AP-RJ, PE0 5150, 'Resoconto della sessione', 27 September 1971.
70 HAEU, UWK NS/46, The enlarged community and the Third World, undated.
71 HAEC, BAC 154/1980 n. 888, *Le Soir*, 21 May 1975, 3.
72 HAEC, BAC 154/1980 n. 944, *Il Sole 24 Ore*, 23 April 1972, 10.
73 HAEC, BAC 130/1983 n. 254, Progetto di risoluzione sui risultati della XVII sessione delle Nazioni Unite sul tema dello sviluppo – New York, 16 Settembre 1975, 6 January 1976.
74 HAEC, BAC 154/1980 n. 944, *Le Soir*, 3–4 April 1972, 13.
75 HAEC, BAC 154/1980 n. 943, *Il Popolo*, 1 August 1974.
76 HAEC, BAC 154/1980 n. 924, *Die Zeit*, 20 June 1977.
77 Lorenzini, *Una strana guerra fredda*, 233–66.
78 HAEU, AP-RJ, PE0 5154, 'Resoconto della sessione', 14 September 1976.
79 Ibid.
80 HAEC, BAC 154/1980 n. 944, *The Guardian*, 4 July 1972.
81 HAEP, AP PE D-US 19760919, '10th Working Session – Interparliamentary Meeting', 19–25 September 1976.
82 HAEU, PE0 19871, 1971.
83 HAEU, AP-RJ, PE0 5154, 'Resoconto della sessione – European Responsibilities in the World', 14 September 1976.
84 HAEC, BAC 154/1980 n.924, *Le Monde*, 11 September 1978, 2.
85 Lorenzini, *Una strana guerra fredda*, 125–58.
86 HAEP, PE0 AP DE 1977 DE 19770706059900 IT, 'Discussioni del Parlamento europeo', 6 July 1977, 232.
87 HAEP, PE 45.662, 'Délégation du Parlement Européen pour les relations avec les Etats Unis – Object: Soutien de la démocratie et des droits de l'homme', 25 August 1976.
88 Overseas Development Institute, 'Briefing Paper'.

3

A reluctant promoter

The EC, CSCE and human rights in East–West relations

Umberto Tulli

The elevation of human rights to a central concern in East–West relations was an unexpected effect of the negotiations leading to the Conference on Security and Cooperation in Europe (CSCE) and the signing of its Final Act in Helsinki in August 1975. Such a document was a solemn but non-legally binding agreement, which was composed of three main sets of recommendations known as 'baskets': (1) questions relating to security in Europe; (2) cooperation in the fields of economics, of science and technology, and of the environment; and (3) cooperation in humanitarian and other fields. These baskets were followed by a concluding section, a sort of fourth basket that called for a review conference within two years to be held in Belgrade.

Human rights did not figure prominently in the Helsinki Final Act. They were mentioned in Basket I as one of the fundamental principles governing international relations in Europe and in some articles of Basket III, as a way to enhance cooperation across the blocs. When the CSCE Final Act was signed, it was criticized for not focusing more on human rights. While it was generally greeted as a grandiose event and even as the 'formal conclusion' of the Second World War,[1] a few voices pointed out that it enshrined Soviet dominance over enslaved Eastern Europe and that its human rights provisions represented a window-dressing for repressive communist regimes. As the *New York Times* wrote, 'nothing signed at Helsinki will in any way save courageous free thinkers in the Soviet empire from the prospect of incarceration'.[2] Yet, the Final Act developed a life of its own almost immediately. Benefiting from the growing transnational movement for human rights in the world, the vague provisions on human rights and humanitarian affairs became the essence of the CSCE. The Final Act, which at the beginning seemed like a conservative process aimed at freezing the Cold War division of Europe, became an unpredicted transformative process that prioritized human rights in East–West relations and fuelled a transnational movement urging Eastern European governments to respect the human rights provisions they had agreed to. To the constellation of Western activists and Eastern dissidents that coalesced around the CSCE and formed the so-called Helsinki network, these human norms were both a source of legitimacy and a sounding box for their demands.³

Scholars tend to consider the introduction of human rights provisions in the CSCE Final Act as a Western success, specifically an action embraced by the European Community (EC). Daniel Thomas, for example, has argued that the human rights provisions were a deliberate instrument of Western states. They were used as a sort of price the Soviets had to pay for the conference. For Richard Davy, EC countries were determined to push the human rights agenda forward.⁴ However, as scholar Angela Romano has argued, EC member states and supranational institutions never identified human rights as a high priority for their CSCE agenda and feared that a too-firm approach to Soviet abuses of human rights could endanger the positive conclusion, and later continuation, of détente. They had other priorities, ranging from the international recognition of the EC as a diplomatic player to the multiplication of trade and human contacts between the East and the West.⁵

Sharing much of this analysis, this chapter will argue that the EC had no clear and well-defined strategy for human rights, neither in negotiations leading to the 1975 Final Act nor in its follow-up meetings. On the contrary, the EC followed an unplanned and mostly reactive approach to human rights in Eastern Europe. Specifically, between 1972 and 1978, the EC was determined to favour human contacts across the blocs and a 'people first' détente, more than fuelling human rights polemics between the East and the West. Although there were some divisions among EC countries on the role of human rights in these negotiations, EC member states were quite united in proposing an approach that should prioritize human contacts across the blocs. After 1978, and far beyond EC members' control, human rights took an unprecedented importance in international relations. The human rights breakthrough hit the EC like a tornado in a moment in which the EC was proposing a new reflection on the existence of a specific European political identity in international relations, as well as the introduction of direct elections to the European Parliament transformed it. To a community that found in representative democracy, human rights and the respect of the rule of law the pillars of its identity and under the impulse of the directly elected European Parliament, the prioritization of human rights could no longer be resisted.

Promoting contacts across the blocs: The EC and the CSCE Final Act

Early proposals for a conference on European security emerged from Soviet leaders in the mid-1950s as a tool to secure the post-war order and Soviet territorial expansion. Since the invitation was addressed exclusively to European states, thus excluding the United States, it was rejected immediately by Western countries. Nevertheless, the Soviets were persistent in this proposal. In March 1969, Warsaw Pact countries circulated a new appeal for the summoning of an international conference in which all participant states would address issues relating to European security. Two differences made this appeal more convincing. First, it did not exclude the United States, thus it could not be used as a wedge to separate Western allies. Second, it was considered in the context of a broader effort at reducing Cold War tensions and at fostering a dialogue between East and West. On one side, the newly elected US President Richard Nixon inaugurated an era of superpower negotiations. Known as détente, it led to international summits, expanded economic exchanges, and an intricate web of agreements and treaties between the United States and the Soviet Union, ranging from those limiting strategic nuclear arms to those fostering scientific cooperation. On the other side, the West German government, now led by social-democrat Willy Brandt, developed its own détente process. Known as *Ostpolitik*, it deliberately aimed at defining a less conflictual way of experiencing the Cold War, developing a dialogue with socialist countries and paving the way for a future rapprochement with the East and, eventually, East Germany. Bipolar détente and German *Ostpolitik* gave the necessary framework for the conference. By December 1969 NATO countries accepted the Warsaw Pact proposal. They connected the summoning of the conference to the positive conclusion of the Federal Republic of Germany's treaties with the USSR and Poland, a quadripartite agreement on Berlin, a positive development of inner-German talks, and an agreement to open negotiations on mutual and balanced force reduction (MBFR). Binding the conference together with these conditions, NATO countries aimed at avoiding the risk that the conference might end with exclusively Soviet benefits and leave the main European problems unsolved.[6]

Preparatory negotiations officially opened in Helsinki in 1972, involving thirty-five countries. It was soon clear that participants had different priorities. For the Soviets, the conference created an opportunity for the formal recognition of post-war boundaries, including their domination over half Europe.[7] The American President Richard Nixon and his National Security Advisor Henry Kissinger considered the entire negotiations a marginal process. Kissinger's interest in the conference was so limited that he confessed to his staff: 'They can write it in Swahili for all I care.'[8] The US delegation had no written instructions from the Secretary of State when negotiations begun. Despite this dismissive attitude, the United States participated in the CSCE negotiations because, as Kissinger later explained, 'we didn't want to break with our allies or confront the Soviets on it.'[9] Thus, the American presence in CSCE negotiations was consistent with Kissinger's understanding of détente as a bipolar process and with the idea that cooperation with the Soviets on these negotiations would have assured the United States Soviets' cooperative attitude in other more important areas. In addition, it could help the United States improve transatlantic relations and affirm its leadership within the Atlantic community in a moment in which transatlantic relations were strained.[10] After all, Kissinger explained, Western Europeans considered CSCE negotiations 'as their equivalent to SALT – as the vehicle by which Western European governments can engage visibly in negotiations with the East on issues relating to their security'.[11]

The American dismissive attitude created room for an autonomous EC initiative. Given the American disregard towards the conference, EC countries took front stage in negotiations with the Warsaw Pact. Moreover, their actions became an important test for European Political Cooperation (EPC). Introduced by the Davignon Report in 1970, EPC represented the first attempt to define an embryonic European foreign policy. Although it was an intergovernmental mechanism, with no formal link to EC supranational institutions, EPC assumed a fundamental importance for EC members, as an attempt to foster political integration and enable all member states to exercise more influence on the world stage than any single member could have done acting alone. Moreover, EC heads of state and government's adoption of a solemn declaration on the existence of a specific European political identity based on democracy and human rights further contributed to the development of EPC as a cornerstone of a nascent 'European polity' and as a tool to achieve 'an active role [...] in world politics'.[12]

The nexus between EPC and European identity found in CSCE negotiations was an important test. Acting as a unitary player, the EC spoke effectively with a single voice during CSCE negotiations, thus reflecting the existence of its political identity in this diplomatic forum. By the same token, this growing harmonization among EC member states' foreign policy fostered the socialization to the notion of European identity among EC member states. Moreover, CSCE negotiations allowed the EC to foster its own vision and priorities for détente. The strong sense of purpose resulting from EPC and the Declaration on European Identity led EC member states to seize the initiative in CSCE negotiations, advancing their own priorities. By early 1973, EC member states identified two main aims for the conference.

First, they were determined to gain diplomatic recognition for the EC from the USSR and communist countries. Soviet bloc countries had never recognized the EC and insisted on concluding bilateral agreements and treaties with single EC member states. This attitude was inconsistent with both EPC aims and ambitions and with the EC commercial policy, which entitled the European Commission to negotiate trade agreements with third-world countries on behalf of all member states.[13] The EC was able to contain and minimize Soviet protests over the community's role in the negotiations and to assure the involvement of representatives from the European Commission. EC's almost official role was confirmed during the closing ceremony in 1975 when Italian Prime Minister Aldo Moro signed the Final Act in his dual role as head of the Italian government and President of the European Council, explicitly recalling the EC and its commitment to the full implementation of the Final Act. This was an important symbol towards the international recognition of the EC.[14]

Second, EC members were able to shape the agenda of negotiations. Acting as a single entity, the EC was also aiming at transforming détente and loosening Cold War constraints in Europe. As conceived by the EC, CSCE negotiations would serve the purpose of bringing détente to European citizens and peoples, instead of limiting it to a diplomatic state-to-state process. In this sense, contrary to Kissinger's definition of détente as a conservative policy, Western European countries began to consider détente as a dynamic process, whose aims were to promote and reinforce economic, cultural and social interconnections and exchanges across the blocs, to make frontiers more permeable, and, eventually, to overcome the Cold War in Europe. As French President Georges Pompidou explained to German Chancellor Brandt, 'we could dissolve the blocs, a little bit [...] and bring together all nations, East and West'.[15] EC member states succeeded in promoting their vision of détente as a people-based process in making the Final Act endorse Principle VII, which defined the respect of fundamental freedoms and basic human rights as 'an essential factor for the peace, justice and well-being' of

Europe. Similarly, under the EC's impulse, Basket III of the Final Act listed measures to foster cultural cooperation (opening movie theatres and reading rooms as well as eliminating barriers that prevented the circulation of cultural objects and artists), science and education (enhancing scientific exchange), the diffusion of information (improving journalists' working conditions as well as distributing the press) and human contacts (reunifying families as well as facilitating bi-national marriages and tourism). As such, Basket III identified the promotion of a freer movement of people, ideas and information as a fundamental aim of CSCE. To assure the general approval of these points, EC member states slowed down discussions of other themes and even threatened to interrupt negotiations should the Soviets refuse to accept Basket III provisions.[16]

Beyond this unitary stance, there were some divisions on the place human rights should have in CSCE. According to Sara Lamberti-Moneta, the Dutch government assumed a firm stance on introducing human rights in CSCE negotiations as a weapon to perforate the Iron Curtain and denounce Soviet repression. Such an approach was responsive to domestic pressures and to the evolution of the Dutch political debate. Moreover, after the 1967 Six-Day War, the Dutch embassy in Moscow began serving as the diplomatic representative of Israel because the Soviet Union had broken off its diplomatic ties with Israel. As a consequence, Dutch diplomats, politicians and even NGOs became increasingly familiar with the plight of Soviet Jews and *refuseniks*, as Soviet citizens who were denied permission by their government to emigrate were known. However, such an approach left the Dutch government isolated within the EC. Only the Dutch were willing to use human rights as an ideological weapon to challenge the Soviets. Most EC member states were determined to discuss humanitarian affairs in a non-confrontational language in order to foster cooperative measures, as those listed in Basket III, rather than scoring propaganda points against the Soviets.[17]

Moreover, the attention to human rights was part of a global wave of activism for human rights in the world, as many historians have illustrated over the last few years.[18] Specific attention to human rights in East–West relations was fuelled by the expulsion of writer Aleksandr Solzhenitsyn from the Soviet Union and the American debate over the free emigration of Soviet Jews. The campaign was global and transnational, with thousands of people demonstrating in public rallies across Western Europe and the United States, hundreds of Western correspondents in Moscow covering the stories of well-known dissidents, and scientists and academicians signing petitions demanding more freedom for their Soviet colleagues. This transnational movement in solidarity with Soviet dissidents had also an impact on CSCE negotiations. In 1974, for example, a Dutch proposal on free correspondence, social aspects of culture, and access to foreign books and literature was renamed the 'Solzhenitsyn proposal' by Dutch diplomats in their correspondence to their Foreign Ministry.[19]

Unfortunately, these appeals fell on deaf ears. Basket III provisions could favour some advancements, but it could not overturn the relationship between Soviet bloc countries and their citizens. Moreover, the human rights commitment contained in Principle VII was balanced by an explicit recognition of the principle of non-interference in each state's domestic affairs. As such, the Final Act was an ill-mixed cocktail of national priorities, transnational pressures, ideological positions and EC ambitions. There was no clear strategy to highlight human rights in East–West relations when the CSCE Final Act was signed, especially from the EC. On the contrary, the EC urged some respect for human rights and humanitarian contacts both to consolidate its ongoing discussions on the distinctiveness of its identity and to favour a rapprochement between the two halves of Europe. A new era of intra-European relations, as the EC had hoped for, could now begin.

Avoiding polemics: The EC at the Belgrade Conference

In September 1975, just one month after the signing of the Final Act, EC member states identified future CSCE negotiations as a permanent feature of EPC and began to work almost immediately for a strong and cohesive EC stance towards the first CSCE Review Conference, which opened in Belgrade in 1977.[20] Over the following months, discussions on CSCE issues intensified both within EC institutions and among EC member states. A general agreement was easily reached. It recognized détente as a global, evolutionary and dynamic process. Similarly, it called for ensuring visibility to the EC during the conference and for the involvement of the European Commission in discussions relating to Basket II and economic cooperation.[21]

Differences among EC members emerged in the definition of their specific aims for the Belgrade Conference and on the place human rights issues would assume in the EC's strategy. An agreement was made difficult by the prominence human rights were assuming. After August 1975, Helsinki monitoring groups, the spontaneous groups established in Eastern Europe and demanding compliance with CSCE humanitarian provisions, were flourishing in the East. In 1976, their influence led the American Congress to establish the CSCE Commission. Moreover, in 1977, when Amnesty International was awarded the Nobel Peace Prize, Jimmy Carter entered the White House promising a foreign policy based on the promotion of human rights. As part of this global surge for human rights, Western European public opinion, national parliaments and the European Parliament were generally supportive of the American firm stance on human rights. The European Parliament, in particular, passed a number of resolutions inviting EC institutions and member states to consider human rights and the fate of political dissidents in all their contacts with Eastern Europe and the Soviet Union.[22] The European Parliament's emphasis on human rights was also a consequence of the thousands of petitions and letters addressed by Western European human rights activists, dissidents in Eastern Europe or political prisoners in Latin America. Moreover, Members of the European Parliament (MEPs) appropriated human rights jargon to demonstrate the institutional limits of EPC and to demand their association with it.[23] Accordingly, MEPs began to scrutinize EC preparatory works towards the Belgrade Conference. In April 1977, on behalf of the Parliament's Political Affairs Committee, Mr Radoux presented a 23-page document on the implementation of the Helsinki Final Act and a resolution, which called the EC to play a major role during the Belgrade Conference in order to assure that human rights and all the fundamental principles of the Final Act were respected by all participant states.[24]

Parliamentary pressures contributed to fuel divisions among EC member states. In negotiations leading to the Final Act, the Dutch government proposed a firm stance challenging the Soviets on their limited implementation of the humanitarian provisions of the Final Act. This time it was joined by the British government. Assuming the EC presidency in January 1977, British officials debated in detail the role human rights should assume in preparation of the Belgrade Conference: 'As representative of the EC Presidency', the British government should be 'prepared to take the initiative this year in coordinating the Nine's support' and favour a harmonization of EC's stance on human rights with the 'strategy and tactics of the United States'.[25]

Most of EC member states were less enthusiastic about the rising emphasis on human rights. From their perspective, a too-firm stance on human rights would endanger the continuation of the CSCE process and, eventually, of their intra-European détente. The German and the French governments, in particular, repeatedly expressed their doubts, thundered against the American overemphasis on human rights and invited European partners to follow a different path during the Belgrade Conference. French President Giscard d'Estaing did not hesitate to show his personal doubts. After avoiding an official meeting with Soviet émigré Andrei Amalrik, who had been expelled from the USSR in late 1976, he celebrated the success of quiet diplomacy and reciprocal accommodation, as opposed to the negative reactions open diplomacy and interference in domestic affairs could elicit.[26] German chancellor Schmidt was even firmer. He dismissed Carter's human rights campaign as inconsistent with détente and the CSCE, as well as a threat to German *Ostpolitik*.[27] From an economic perspective, Germany was the European country that was benefiting the most from the dialogue with Eastern countries and the one that had most direct interest in stabilizing détente.[28] In addition, Carter's firm stance threatened the constant increase in the number of ethnic Germans and GDR citizens emigrating to the Bundesrepublik (reaching over 60,000 each year between 1974 and 1977), as well as the multiplication of contacts. During the two-year period between 1976 and 1977, nearly 8 million West Germans were allowed to cross the boundary and meet their relatives and friends living in the East.[29] Finally, Schmidt's scepticism towards Carter's human rights policy was also a consequence of the German domestic debate where the CDU/CSU, the Christian Democrat opposition party, urged Schmidt to take a firm stance towards the GDR and its human rights violations. From Schmidt's perspective, a European cooperative approach to CSCE could assist the chancellor in containing domestic criticism.[30] German and French doubts were echoed in Rome, Brussels and other European capitals. Many Western European governments had to face growing domestic opposition, which repeatedly questioned their governments on the lack of action in criticizing the persecution and the imprisonment of political dissidents in the Soviet Union.[31]

Bringing together the transformations occurring at the international, Community and domestic levels, it is clear that EC members were divided over the role human rights should have in the Belgrade Conference. For these reasons, the EC developed a minimalist approach to the Belgrade Conference, which called for prioritizing cooperation over confrontation. Their approach to achieve their basic aims, namely the continuation of détente and the strengthening of the economic, cultural and human ties with Eastern Europe, was that EC members would avoid any direct polemics on human rights. Belgrade should not become a tribunal on communist compliance with human rights provisions of the Helsinki Final Act. Based on such concerns, the British government partially reversed its original stance and began working for a moderate EC common position. The British initiative seemed to produce a concrete outcome in April 1977 when EC foreign ministers agreed on a common declaration that recalled the importance of human rights in East–West relations and that EC members attributed great importance to respect for all CSCE principles, thus satisfying both of those governments that were advocating a firm stance on human rights and those who wanted to prioritize cooperation with the East over confrontation.[32]

On the eve of the official opening of the Belgrade Conference there was a clear sense of purpose and priorities among the EC members, which included that each member state would negotiate on behalf of its government and the EC, positive and cooperative measures should take precedence, and the EC should pay attention to human rights without being demagogic. Yet, almost immediately, such a strategy encountered numerous difficulties. First, American emphasis on human rights in East–West relations worsened the international climate and threatened the EC's moderate stance. EC strategy was further endangered by Soviet actions. In the weeks preceding the opening of the conference, the Soviets cracked down on dissidents with a new wave of arrests that were supposed to curb contacts with Western activists.[33] Yet, they could not prevent information from circulating between East and West. A documented report prepared by the Moscow-based Commission to Investigate the Misuse of Psychiatry for Political Purposes, for example, was released in the West by the *Chronicle of Human Rights in the USSR* and became the basis for a motion adopted by the British Royal College of Psychiatry condemning Soviet misuse of psychiatry that was then sent to all signatories of the CSCE.[34] Western networks for the promotion of the Helsinki Accords echoed dissidents' activities through petitions to their national governments, public demonstrations, conferences and some specific initiatives, such as the second 'International Sakharov Hearings,' a non-governmental tribunal that denounced Soviet repression or the 1977 Venice Biennale, where Soviet and Czechoslovak dissidents' paintings were exhibited.[35]

Similarly, the European Parliament passed a number of resolutions inviting EC institutions and member states to consider human rights and the fate of political dissidents in all their contacts with Eastern Europe and the Soviet Union, as well as to prioritize Basket III during the Belgrade Conference.[36]

On 4 October 1977, the conference officially opened. For two weeks, American ambassador Goldberg avoided any direct polemics with Eastern European countries. Diplomats from EC countries welcomed this attitude, which allowed them to pursue their cooperative aims.[37] For this reason, EC member states focused immediately on Basket II. Cooperation in the fields of the economy, the environment, science and technology were particularly important to the EC. Not only did these topics represent areas in which the Commission could play a clear role, given its formal competencies in these areas, but also because they represented areas in which it was possible to foster cooperation and contacts with Eastern Europe.[38]

Despite the cooperative stance on these issues, an agreement on Basket II-related measures was made impossible by discussions on Soviet and Eastern European

Figure 3.1 Opening speech at the first Sakharov Hearings. The first Sakharov Hearing opened in Copenhagen, 17–19 October 1975, and focused on the respect of the Helsinki Accords signed that year. Soviet scientist and human rights activist Andrei D. Sakharov became a quintessential symbol for human rights activists in the Soviet Union and inspired dozens of demonstrations, exhibitions and parliamentary resolutions, such as the 1975 'Sakharov hearings'.

compliance with norms relating to human rights and human cooperation. After a few weeks from the opening of the conference, a confrontation between the United States and the Soviet Union came to dominate the summit.

By late 1977, a consensus on a final document was far from being reached and fears about a failure of the conference multiplied. In November, FRG ambassador Per Fischer warned against the American firm approach on human rights, which was poisoning

Figure 3.2 Soviet writer and dissident Andrei Amalrik in front of the Elysee Palace in Paris on 23 February 1977. On the eve of the opening of the CSCE Review Conference in Belgrade, Soviet dissidents and human rights activists urged EC member states to require the Soviets the respect of CSCE human rights provisions.

the atmosphere at Belgrade.[39] Moreover, British delegates perceived this confrontation on human rights as a choice between their commitment to European integration or to their special relationship with the United States. In an early November telegram to its mission in Belgrade, the British government suggested to the ambassador to follow the American lead. This triggered a controversy within the British bureaucracy and government. Both the ambassador and the CSCE group within the British government objected and argued that this would represent a breach in EC cohesion. The opposition worked, and, in a following telegram, the government invited the ambassador to abstain from major initiatives on the Soviet record on human rights in order to keep a strong EC cohesion.[40] On 22 November 1977, EC foreign ministers met in Brussels and decided 'not to put the Belgrade negotiations at risk even in the case of new human rights court cases' in communist countries. The 'human rights prioritization' was a false move for the EC.[41] This implied that EC member states should continue differentiating between general human rights issues and criticism and more specific humanitarian issues, such as fostering human contacts, cultural exchanges and the flow of information, or the reunification of families divided by the Cold War. Not only would such a pragmatic approach promote some versions of human rights in Eastern Europe but it would also avoid provoking the Soviets and, potentially, the failure of the conference. It was also consistent with the general aim of the EC, namely the continuation of a multilateral intra-European détente based on improving living conditions of European citizens.

Negotiations continued until March 1978. Between December and February, the Secretariat of the conference received more than 100 draft proposals for a final document. Yet, American delegates rejected any proposal that was not focused on human rights, while the Soviets and other Eastern European delegations were uncompromising on drafts focusing on human rights. From the EC's perspective, the stalemate at the conference was matched by the fear that the United States was preparing a spectacular breakdown of the conference by wielding the human rights weapon against the Soviets. For this reason, EC diplomats urged the Soviets to strengthen their proposed concluding documents and, at the same time, invited the United States not to focus exclusively on human rights because this would endanger the positive conclusion of the conference. In the end, a meagre document that admitted that 'consensus was not reached on a number of proposals' was approved. With high expectations from the 'Helsinki network' and on the EC's ability to impose its agenda, the Belgrade Conference was perceived as a setback for the development of the Helsinki process of imposing the respect of human rights to the Soviet bloc and even for the EC's capability to act as an international player. However, when placed in the contexts of the crisis of détente, the global surge for human rights, and the difficulties the EC was experiencing at that time, the experience of the Belgrade Conference is quite different. Belgrade was the first step of a follow-up process that could not be taken for granted, and the EC succeeded in acting as a unitary player. Criticism over human rights, at times harsh, did not reach the threshold for which communist countries would leave negotiations, thus sanctioning the end of the Helsinki process and the failure of EC's strategy to advance a 'people first' détente.

Nevertheless, many criticized the lack of a radical human rights advancement and pointed to the lack of a clear EC strategy for this scope. According to Italian MEP Michele Cifarelli, for example, the failure of the Belgrade Conference depended on EC member states' 'lack of coordination and inadequate preparation'.[42] Other MEPs believed that diplomats from EC member states were not addressing CSCE humanitarian norms properly, thus betraying European citizens' expectations and those values that the heads of state and government had identified as the main pillars of the European identity. For this reason, in May 1978, the European Parliament adopted a resolution in which it regretted that 'certain of the preoccupations [. . .] concerning the human dimension of the Final Act were not reflected in the final document as they should have been, notably as regards respect for human rights and fundamental freedoms, including freedom of thought, of conscience, of religion or conviction'.[43]

Prioritizing human rights: The EC and the Madrid CSCE Conference

After the conclusion of the Belgrade Conference, contradictory tendencies shaped EC discussions on the preparations for the second CSCE Review Conference, which opened in Madrid in 1980. EC member states were determined to follow their traditional commitment to a 'people first détente', which was building economic, cultural and human bridges across the blocs. Refusing to conceive the CSCE as a confrontational forum in which the West could score propaganda points, early discussions on the new CSCE stage were based on the political will to avoid a too-firm approach on human rights to ensure its continuation. To the EC, the failure of the Belgrade meeting because of the confrontational attitude followed by the United States on human rights was a further demonstration of the soundness of their balanced and concrete approach.[44] In addition, increasing economic relations across the blocs strengthened EC members' preference for a policy of economic interdependence. Trade across the bloc was expanding constantly, and in 1982, even after the crisis in Afghanistan and Poland, the EC heads of state and government 'recognised the role which economic and commercial contacts and cooperation have played in the stabilisation and the development of East-West relations as a whole and which they wish to see continue on the basis of a genuine mutual interest'. As a consequence, EC foreign ministers reached an early agreement to ensure that détente would remain an ongoing process, requesting the participating countries to act according to the Helsinki principles and that the Madrid Conference would provide for a full and balanced review of the implementation of the Final Act.[45]

The worsening of bipolar détente and the growing international attention towards human rights threatened the continuation of détente and EC's cohesion towards the Madrid Conference. A new wave of repression in the USSR poisoned the international climate. Between June and July 1978, Soviet authorities concluded the trials against prominent dissidents Ida Nudel, Vladimir Slepak, Aleksandr Ginzburg, Nathan Sharansky and Ivan Filatov. Western reaction was immediate. Many organizations of the 'Helsinki lobby' began to criticize the Western soft approach to Soviet violations of human rights and proposed some retaliatory measures, such as interrupting all cultural programmes or even boycotting the 1980 Olympic Games. All Western capitals hosted protest demonstrations and rallies. Although reluctantly, most EC governments were forced to protest against the sentences.[46] The European Parliament joined the protest. This time, however, it could claim a stronger role since, by 1979, its 410 members were directly elected by universal suffrage. As such, they could and did claim to speak for European citizens, who were urging EC national governments to assume a firmer stance vis-à-vis Soviet violations of human rights. According to former Italian prime minister and now Christian Democrat MEP Mariano Rumor: 'the very nature of our Parliament, which is the direct expression of EC peoples will give us the responsibility of a direct participation in the preparation and development of the Madrid meeting'.[47]

Even more than during the Belgrade Conference, the European Parliament approved a number of resolutions censoring human rights violations in the Soviet bloc, discussed the lack of adherence to the human rights and humanitarian provisions of the CSCE or other human rights issues not directly addressed by the CSCE, such as restrictions on Jewish emigration from the Soviet Union, the violation of citizens' civil and political liberties in all Soviet bloc countries, and the detention of political prisoners in psychiatric hospitals.[48] In addition, MEPs took the initiative of discussing specific cases or 'naming the names' of victims of Soviet abuses, such as prominent dissidents like Yuri Orlov, Nathan Sharansky and Andrei Sakharov, and lesser-known individuals, such as Soviet writers Alexander Paritsky, Sonja Krachmalnikowa and Josif Begun, Soviet psychiatrist Semion Glouzman, and DDR philosopher Rudolf Bahro.[49] Under the direction of its new president, French Holocaust survivor Simone Veil, the European Parliament developed a constructive dialogue with individual human rights activists, generally former Eastern European émigrés in Western Europe and numerous NGOs. In an unprecedented action, in July 1979, the Institutional Affairs Committee decided to involve some human rights NGOs in the organization of public hearings on communist countries' respect of the Helsinki Accords and, later, a specific demonstration to protest Andrei Sakharov's exile to Gorki. Even more important, the EP's Political Affairs Committee decided to establish a specific working group on the CSCE meeting, which began scrutinizing both the respect of human rights and humanitarian provisions in all signatory countries and ECP and EC national governments' preparations for the Madrid Conference.[50] The Commission was short-lived since the following year it was absorbed by a brand-new EP's Working Group on Human Rights, which in an unprecedented decision authorized a European Parliament's mission to the Madrid CSCE Review Conference to communicate the European Parliament's demand for greater attention to human rights by EC diplomats.[51] As a consequence, by early 1980, human rights were now high on the EC agenda for the Madrid Conference.

The Madrid Conference took place in a new international climate. Bipolar détente was finally over and doubts remained over the possibility to continue with intra-European détente. As a consequence of these transformations, discussions in Madrid were centred on human rights. Western countries (the EC and the United States) were aligned in censoring Soviet actions and in prioritizing human rights and Basket III over the rest of the CSCE. By 'naming the names' of dissidents and victims of repression, the EC and the United States galvanized the Helsinki lobby, kept a strong cohesion and succeeded in forcing the Soviets to accept a full review of their adhesion to human rights and humanitarian provisions.[52] After three years, the Madrid concluding document explicitly reconfirmed existing provisions on human rights and humanitarian affairs and contained some new commitments in this area, such as the right of workers to freely establish and join trade unions, more detailed rules concerning the freedom of religion, and improved procedures for family reunification.[53]

Conclusion

It was only after the Belgrade Conference of 1977/78 that human rights took front stage in the EC's strategy towards Eastern Europe and the USSR, a policy that was embodied in, and developed through, the CSCE framework. To EC members, the early

CSCE process was about shaping détente and assuring a prominent and internationally recognized role for the Community that favoured economic, cultural, humanitarian contacts across the blocs. As such, there was no room for a polemic stance on human rights abuses taking place in communist countries. Of course, fostering human contacts and the free flow of information was part and parcel of a growing awareness about human rights. Yet, EC priorities were not about confronting the Soviets, nor about interfering in Soviet domestic affairs. They were aiming at creating links between East and West, in order to make the Iron Curtain more permeable and loosening the Cold War constraints on peoples.

In negating the Helsinki Final Act and, later, during the Belgrade Conference, the EC was reluctant to wield the human rights weapon, favouring a constructive and cooperative attitude. It was not immune from the human rights breakthrough of the 1970s. Yet, its institutional features and willingness to bring a 'people first' détente with different priorities among its member states prevented the EC's full endorsement of human rights.[54] Although discussions on the 'place' of human rights in both the definition of a specific EC identity and in EPC intensified over the years, there was no consensus on prioritizing them. The only EC institution that constantly lobbied for more emphasis on human rights was the European Parliament. Beyond a genuine interest in the promotion of human rights, the EP was using human rights as a weapon to advance its role in the EC.

By the late 1970s, however, things began to change and the EC's attentions within the CSCE process began to shift towards human rights. The transnational attention to human rights violations constantly grew. NGOs, scientific associations, journalists and single personalities began lobbying both EC national governments and EC institution to focus on human rights violations occurring in the Communist bloc. Also, the introduction of direct elections to the European Parliament in 1979 made the European Parliament more determined to have a say in the EC's external relations, forcing other EC institutions to be more responsive to its pressure. As the first directly elected supranational assembly and the only EC institution that could claim direct democratic legitimacy, the EP was searching for new powers both within the Community and EPC. In this scheme, the European Parliament became a sounding box for human rights, NGOs and activists, and pushed EC member states towards a firmer stance at the second CSCE Review Conference, which opened in Madrid in 1980. The fact that the Madrid Review Conference opened in the shadow of both the Soviet invasion of Afghanistan and the Polish crisis removed further obstacles towards a firmer stance on Soviet violations of human rights.

Notes

1 John Maresca, *To Helsinki: The Conference on Security and Cooperation in Europe, 1973-1975* (Durham: Duke University Press, 1987), 3.
2 'Brezhnev at Helsinki', *New York Times*, 1 August 1975.
3 Daniel C. Thomas, *The Helsinki Effect: International Norms, Human Rights and the Demise of Communism* (Princeton: Princeton University Press, 2001); Sarah B. Snyder,

Human Rights Activism and the End of the Cold War (New York and Cambridge: Cambridge University Press, 2012); Jeremi Suri, 'Détente and Human Rights: American and West European Perspectives on International Change', *Cold War History*, 8 (2008): 527–45.
4. Thomas, *The Helsinki Effect*, Richard Davy, 'Helsinki Myths: Setting the Record Straight on the Final Act of the CSCE', *Cold War History*, 9 (2009): 1–22; Floribert Baudet, '"It Was Cold War and We Wanted to Win": Human Rights, Détente, and the CSCE', in *Origins of the European Security System: The Helsinki Process Revisited, 1965-75*, ed. Andreas Wenger, Vojtech Mastny and Christian Nuenlist (London: Routledge 2008), 184–91.
5. Angela Romano, *From Détente in Europe to European Détente: How the West Shaped the Helsinki CSCE* (Brussels: Peter Lang, 2009).
6. Raymond L. Garthoff, *Detente and Confrontation: American-Soviet Relations from Nixon to Reagan* (Washington: The Brookings Institution, 1985); Angela Romano, 'The EC and the Socialist World', in *Europe's Cold War Relations: The EC Towards a Global Role*, ed. Ulrich Krotz, Kiran Klaus Patel and Federico Romero (London: Bloomsbury, 2019).
7. Snyder, *Human Rights Activism*, 15–37.
8. Jussi Hanhimäki, '"They Can Write It in Swahili". Kissinger, the Soviets and the Helsinki Accords', *Journal of Transatlantic Studies*, 1 (2003): 37–58.
9. Memorandum, Cabinet Meeting, 8 August 1975, http://cdn.geraldrfordfoundation.org/memcons/1553206.pdf (accessed 19 November 2012).
10. Matthias Schulz and Thomas A. Schwartz, eds, *The Strained Alliance: U.S.-European Relations from Nixon to Carter* (Cambridge: Cambridge University Press, 2010).
11. Rogers to the President, 'United States and Allied Approaches to the Current Issues of European Security', 31 October 1969, http://history.state.gov/historicaldocuments/frus1969-76v39/d10 (accessed 19 November 2012).
12. 'Declaration on European Identity', *Bulletin of the European Communities*, 12 (1973): 118–22.
13. Historical Archives of the European Union (HAEU), FMM 36, Réunion des Ministres des affaires étrangères, discussion sur la CSCE, Paris, 14 May 1971; EN 1985 Note à l'attention des Messieurs Ortoli et Sir Christopher Soames, 5 July 1973.
14. HAEU, KM 50, Note à l'attention de Messieurs les membres de la Commission, objet: CSCE, 14 February 1974.
15. Romano, *Détente*, 219–28; Federico Romero and Silvio Pons, 'Europe between the Superpowers, 1968-1981', in *Europe in the International Arena during the 1970s*, ed. Antonio Varsori and Guia Migani (Brussels: Peter Lang, 2011), 85–98.
16. Walden to Tickell, 'Human Contacts', 14 April 1973, in *Documents on British Policy Overseas*, Series III, Vol. II (London: The Stationery Office, 1987).
17. Piet Buwalda, *They Did Not Dwell Alone: Jewish Emigration from the Soviet Union 1967-1990* (Baltimore and London: Johns Hopkins University Press, 1997), 75; Romano, *Détente*; Sara Lamberti-Moneta, 'Helsinki Disentangled (1973-75): West Germany, the Netherlands, the EPC and the Principle of the Protection of Human Rights' (PhD diss., University of Trento, Trento, 2012).
18. S. Moyn, *The Last Utopia: Human Rights in History* (Cambridge, MA: Harvard University Press, 2010); J. Eckel and S. Moyn, eds, *The Breakthrough: Human Rights in the 1970s* (Philadelphia: University of Pennsylvania Press, 2014); Mark Ph. Bradley, *The World Reimagined: Americans and Human Rights in the Twentieth Century* (New York: Cambridge University Press, 2016).

19 Lamberti-Moneta, 'Helsinki'; U. Tulli, *A Precarious Equilibrium. Human Rights and Détente in Jimmy Carter's Soviet Policy* (Manchester: Manchester University Press, 2020), 27–38; B. Boel, 'Western Journalism in the Soviet bloc during the Cold War: Themes, Approaches, Theses', *Cold War History*, 19 (2019): 593–614; Nicolas Badalassi and Sarah B. Snyder, eds, *The CSCE and the End of the Cold War: Diplomacy, Societies and Human Rights, 1972-1990* (New York: Berghahn Books, 2019).

20 Archives du Ministère des Affaires Etrangères (AMAE), Europe 1971-76, 3820, Réunion du Comité Politique (3–4 septembre): CSCE, 9 September 1975; HAEU, EN 1090, Document de Travail de la Commission – Préparation de la Réunion de Belgrade.

21 AMAE, Europe 1971–76, 4208: Rapport aux Ministres sur l'état de préparation de la réunion de Belgrade, 7 December 1976; Réunion du Comité Politique, 8/9 November 1976; Document sur une définition de la détente préparé par le groupe de travail des Neuf, 14 February 1977; TNA, FCO 28/3227, Telegram: East European Experts Working Group, 16 February 1977; TNA, FCO 49/668, Planning Paper: East/West Relations and the Future of Détente; HAEU, EN 1989, CSCE: Représentation de la Communauté à la Conférence de Belgrade, 23 May 1977.

22 HAEP (Historical Archives of the European Parliament), Document 60/77, Motion for a Resolution tabled by Mr Fellermaier and Mr Sieglerschmidt on the protection of human rights, 20 April 1977; Document 62/77, Motion for a Resolution tabled by Mr A. Bertrand, Mr Bangemann, Mr Rivierez, Lord Reay on the protection of human rights throughout the world, 20 April 1977; HAEU, PE0 2572: Résolution sur le recours abusif à la médecine psychiatrique en Union Soviétique, 16 November 1977; PE0 2574 Résolution sur le respect des engagements contractés aux termes de l'Acte final de la Conférence d'Helsinki, 12 December 1977.

23 Aurélie É. Gfeller, 'Champion of Human Rights: The European Parliament and the Helsinki Process', *Journal of Contemporary History*, 2 (2014): 390–409.

24 HAEU, PE0 2567: Report on the Preparatory Meeting of 15 June 1977 in Belgrade as Provided for by the Final Act of the Helsinki Conference on Security and Cooperation in Europe, 11 May 1977.

25 TNA, FCO 30/3641, '33rd Session of Commission on Human Rights, Human Rights: Steering Brief', 4 February 1977.

26 Jimmy Carter Presidential Library (JCPL), NLC-1-2-5-18-4, 'Giscard Press Conference', 23 June 1977; 'Giscard, Schmidt on Détente', *Washington Post*, 19 July 1977.

27 JCPL, NSA–CF, Box 22, F. 2; Memorandum, 'Concern Expressed by Chancellor Schmidt over RFE/ RI', 29 June 1977; H. Schmidt, *Men and Power: A Political Retrospective* (New York: Random House, 1989), 182.

28 Juhana Aunesluoma, 'Finlandisation in Reverse: The CSCE and the Rise and Fall of Economic Détente, 1968–1975', in *Helsinki 1975 and the Transformation of Europe*, ed. Oliver Bange and Gottfried Niedhart (New York: Berghahn Books, 2008), 98–113.

29 Joe Renouard, 'No Relief for a Troubled Alliance: Human Rights and Transatlantic Relations in the 1970s', in *Transatlantic Conflict and Consensus: Culture, History and Politics*, ed. R. Haar and N. Wynn (Cambridge: Cambridge Academic, 2009), 145–62; O. Bange, 'The Greatest Happiness of the Greatest Numbers … The FRG and the GDR and the Belgrade CSCE Conference (1977– 1978)', in *From Helsinki to Belgrade: The First CSCE Follow-Up Meeting in Belgrade*, ed. V. Bilandžić, D. Dahlmnn and M. Kosanović (Bonn: Bonn University Press, 2012), 225–53.

30 JCPL, NLC-128-12-6-15-4, Cyrus Vance to the President, 'Christopher Meeting with Biedenkopf', 16 March 1977; CDU/CSU Group in the Bundestag, *White Paper on the Human Rights Situation in Germany and of the German in Eastern Europe* (Bonn, October 1977).
31 TNA, FCO 28/3002, Parliamentary Question by Mr Stephen Hastings MP: Persecution of Political Dissenters in the USSR and Other Communist Countries, 10 March 1977; Valentine Lomellini, *L'appuntamento mancato. La sinistra italiana e il dissenso nei regimi comunisti, 1968–1989* (Florence: Le Monnier, 2010).
32 TNA, FCO 28/3002, 'President Carter and Human Rights in Europe' and 'Telegram, Foreign Office to Washington', 20 February 1977; FCO 28/3237, 'Telegram 1005', 7 March 1977; FCO 58/1159, European Political Cooperation: Ministerial Meeting, 'Eastern Europe: Dissent and Human Rights', 18 April 1977.
33 Tulli, *Precarious Equilibrium*, 95–110.
34 *Chronicle of Human Rights in the Soviet Union*, March 1977.
35 JCPL, NSA – President's Daily Report Files, Box 1, F. '2/ 15/ 77– 2/ 28/ 77', Brzezinski to the President, 'Information Items: CSCE: Soviets and East Europeans Feel Pressure as Belgrade Conference Approaches', 15 March 1977. On the Biennale and the International Sakharov Hearings, see Andrei D. Sakarov Archives at Harvard (ADSA), HRC, Box 4, Folder 48, F. Janouch and P. Zaccaria to A. Sakharov, 29 September 1977, and P. Flores D'Arcais to E. and T. Yankelevich, 11 November 1977.
36 HAEU, PE0 2572, Résolution sur le recours abusif à la médecine psychiatrique en Union Soviétique, 16 November 1977; PE0-2573: Résolution sur le Prix Nobel de la Paix 1977, 17 November 1977; PE0-2574, Résolution sur le respect des engagements contractés aux termes de l'Acte final de la Conférence d'Helsinki, 12 December 1977.
37 Tulli, *Precarious Equilibrium*, 107–8.
38 A. Romano, 'The European Community and the Belgrade CSCE', in *From Helsinki to Belgrade*, ed. Bilandžić, Dahlmnn and Kosanović, 205–25.
39 Bange, 'The Greatest Happiness', 225–53.
40 TNA, FCO 28/3652, P. L. Hunt, 'East-West Governments at the Belgrade CSCE Follow Up and HMG', 14 December 1977. I wish to thank Dr Paul Leighton for sharing this document with me.
41 Quoted in Bange, 'The Greatest Happiness', 225–53.
42 HAEP, PE0 APQP/QE E-1348/770010, Written Question no. 1348/77 by Mr Cifarelli.
43 HAEU, PE0 2829, Résolution et Rapport sur les Résultats de la rencontre de Belgrade prescrite par l'Acte final de la conférence d'Helsinki sur la sécurité et la coopération en Europe (Lucien Radoux), 10 May 1978.
44 HAEU, EN 1905, Commission, Secrétariat Général, Note à l'attention de M. Ortoli, Vice-Président, 'Session du Conseil Européen, 7 and 8 April 1978 – Sujets de la Coopération politique européenne', 6 April 1978, AMAE, Europe 1976–1980, 4211 bis, 'Consultations franco-américaines sur la CSCE et la CDE', 27 May 1980.
45 Angela Romano, 'G7 Summits, European Councils and East-West Economic Relations (1975-1982)', in *International Summitry and Global Governance: The Rise of the G7 and the European Council*, ed. Emmanuel Mourlon Druol and Federico Romero (London and New York: Routledge, 2014), 198–222.
46 HAEP, PE0 AP PR B0–0030/780010, Working Document 30/78, Motion for a Resolution tabled by Mr Hamilton on the Holding of the Olympic Games in 1980 in the Union of Soviet Socialist Republics; and PE0 AP PR B0–0030/780030 Working Document Presented by Mr Berkhouwer, 8 November 1978.
47 M. Rumor, *Débats du PE*, 15 October 1980, 130.

48 'Resolution on the Situation of the Jewish community in the Soviet Union', *OJEC*, 11 December 1978, no. C296, 'Resolution on Human Rights in the Soviet Union', *OJEC*, no. C61, 20 June 1983; 'Resolution on the Respect for Human Rights in Czechoslovakia', *OJEC*, 12 April 1980, no. C117; 'Resolution on Human Rights in Poland', *OJEC*, 13 October 1980, no. C265.
49 HAEP, PE1 AP PR B1-033482 0010, Motion for a resolution tabled by Mrs Theobald-Paoli on the right of Semion Glouzman to leave the USSR, 14 June 1982; PE1 AP PR B1-091782 0010, Motion for a resolution tabled by Mrs van Hemeldonck, Mrs Fuillet and Mr Saby on emigration problems for manual workers of the Jewish faith in the USSR, 24 November 1982; Resolution on human rights in the Soviet Union, 1983; 'Resolution on the trial of Mr J. Sabata', *OJEC*, 5 June 1983, no. C140.
50 HAEU, PE1 1104 Réunion du 19 décembre 1979; PE1-1106 Réunion du 15 janvier 1980; PE1 1109 Réunion du 22 janvier 1980; PE1 1113 Réunion du 30 janvier 1980; PE1 1116 Réunion du 19 février 1980.
51 HAEU, PE1-1092 Réunion du 21 janvier 1981.
52 HAEU, EN-1994, Rencontre avec M. Ospal, 24 May 1982; and Rencontre avec M. Ospral, 13 October 1982.
53 Snyder, *Human Rights Activism*, 136–57.
54 HAEU, PE1 17477, Report drawn up on behalf of the Political Affairs Committee on European Political Cooperation and the role of the European Parliament by lady Elles, 30 June 1981, 32.

4

EC member states' stance on human rights issues

The perspective from the UN General Assembly, 1970–9

Lorenzo Ferrari

In the 1970–9 period, the members of the UN General Assembly were asked to vote 258 times on resolutions focusing on human rights issues.[1] An analysis of the voting behaviour of the member states of the European Community (EC) in that arena can shed light on their positioning vis-à-vis the question of human rights, which rapidly gained salience in the international arena during the 1970s. The UN General Assembly constitutes an interesting vantage point in this respect, because of its salience and nearly universal membership. Debates taking place in it and their outcomes both reflected and contributed to shape the international agenda. Even if the expression 'human rights' became widely popular throughout the decade, the UN General Assembly dealt with the problem of violations of individuals' and groups' basic rights from early on – well before the time when EC institutions and member states decided to turn the promotion of human rights into an item on the agenda of their own international activity.

EC member states started their attempt at coordinating in the foreign policy realm starting from 1970, following the decision to establish a system of European Political Cooperation (EPC), which was adopted by EC leaders at The Hague summit in 1969. In the first years of operation of EPC, EC member states essentially dealt with human rights matters in a reactive manner. They felt pressured to take a stance on some of the most repelling instances of human rights violations, either by sectors of their own public opinions or by foreign countries. It was only in the late 1970s that EC member states started to sketch a more proactive strategy in this field, discussing, for instance, the introduction of negative conditionality in their development cooperation policy. To observe EC member states' stance on human rights issues at the UN General Assembly over the 1970s means to observe them as they struggled to gradually shape a common position on those issues, weighing questions of consistency, double standards, geopolitics and even the EC's own international identity.

This chapter focuses on the voting decisions made by EC member states in the roll-call votes on human rights issues at the UN General Assembly, looking at them from both a quantitative and a qualitative perspective. This focus makes it possible to account for the positions adopted by all EC member states on the different issues at stake,[2] as well as to measure their degree of cohesion and observe their tendency to break into sub-groups, identifying the human rights issues which proved to be the least and the most divisive for EC countries during the 1970s.[3] The UN General Assembly did not debate all aspects of human rights violations taking place in the world, but it rather tended to focus on the violations that were committed by some countries tied to the West, such as Portugal, South Africa or Israel. Precisely because of such ties, EC member states had no easy path and had to weigh different considerations in making their voting choices. As the analysis shows, some EC member states ended up expressing a stronger attachment to human rights – at least in the way they were framed at the UN – compared to others.

Being based on the voting choices of national delegations at the UN General Assembly, the chapter focuses essentially on EC member states and on their intergovernmental forms of coordination, such as EPC. This is not to downplay the role that the EC Commission or the European Parliament played in putting human rights on the EC's agenda during the 1970s but, due to the delimitation of their competences, they did not have much chance to influence the voting behaviour of member states' delegations in New York.

EC member states' voting patterns on human rights issues at the UN General Assembly

During the 1970s, 258 roll-call votes on human rights issues took place at the UN General Assembly, addressing issues such as the rights of prisoners of war or freedom of the press, as well as instances of discrimination against some individuals based on their gender, ethnic profile or political ideas.[4] On average, the UN member states voted on resolutions devoted to human rights matters twenty-six times per session in the 1970–9 period, ranging from a minimum of fifteen resolutions in 1974 to a maximum of forty-one resolutions in 1979 (when human rights-related topics made 35% of all the resolutions voted upon during that session). About 75 per cent of the votes on human rights issues at the UN General Assembly related either to the rights of Africans suffering because of apartheid and oppression in the austral region of the continent (i.e. Portuguese territories, South Africa, Namibia, Rhodesia) or to the rights of Palestinians, and especially Palestinian refugees. The other roll-call votes concerned a variety of subjects, such as women's rights, racism, religious intolerance, death penalty, the respect of the 1949 Geneva conventions, rights violations in Pinochet's Chile and so on.

EC member states managed to show a notable degree of cohesion on human rights issues at the UN General Assembly. If we set aside the resolutions approved by consensus and eight resolutions unanimously approved by the entire Assembly,

EC member states voted unanimously in 125 of the 250 remaining votes during the 1970s – that is exactly half of the time. Their voting cohesion tended to increase over time, with unanimity rising from 29 per cent in 1970–1 to 53 per cent of votes in 1978–9, despite the parallel increase in the number of EC member states.[5] Unanimity between EC member states even reached two-thirds of the votes on human rights issues in some sessions of the UN General Assembly (1972, 1974, 1977). In fact, this figure underestimates the degree of EC cohesion to some extent, as most of the time its member states were asked to vote on the topic that was the most divisive for them, that is, human rights violations in Austral Africa. EC countries managed to present a united front in this field only 32 per cent of the time. If the share of votes on other human rights issues were higher, it is reasonable to expect that the voting cohesion of EC member states would have occurred more frequently.

Unanimity on human rights matters was not always the case for EC member states at the UN General Assembly – half of the time, disagreement was the case instead. If one compares the voting choices of each EC member state to the ones made by its partners, it turns out that Italy, West Germany and the Benelux countries formed a relatively cohesive core, while France, the United Kingdom, Ireland, and Denmark tended to break more often from the rest of the EC countries. This was particularly evident in the case of Austral African issues. Cohesion tended to be higher on other issues – on both Palestine and racism, France tended to break more often from the EC consensus compared to the other member states; in the roll-call votes on global human rights issues, it was Ireland which broke away the most often. Of course, each EC member state was ready to go its own way when it felt that some of its national interests were at stake.

Why were France, the United Kingdom, Ireland and Denmark more likely to go their own way and make voting decisions different from their EC partners? In a way, they were all in a special position. France and the United Kingdom were permanent members of the UN Security Council, and from the outset of EPC up until the twenty-first century, they were eager to stress their difference in status compared to the other EC member states. On some occasions and on some topics, they were reluctant to let the EC 'speak with a single voice' and they rather preferred to mark their distinctive position. The French government was also wary of an increasing EC coordination on human rights issues in Africa, because it was afraid that coordination in this field could lead to an increasing harmonization of EC member states' African policies as a whole – a development that it strongly opposed.[6] Ireland was also eager to stress its distinctive position, being the only EC member state that was not part of NATO and that considered itself as a formerly colonized country – so it was readier to side with the developing countries rather than with the West, at least on some issues.[7] Finally, Denmark was both a very recent member of the EC and a member of the Nordic Council, wherein the five Nordic countries (Denmark, Sweden, Norway, Finland and Iceland) sought a coordination in foreign policy matters, including in human rights issues. For this reason, Denmark had to cope with its double allegiance, and on some occasions cohesion with the Nordic partners proved to be more important than cohesion with the EC partners for the government in Copenhagen.

By looking at the voting decisions of EC member states on each resolution that underwent a roll-call vote at the UN General Assembly, it is possible to quantify the degree of agreement of each pair of states and build an index of agreement. Every instance of agreement between two EC member states is assigned a 100 value, every instance of mild disagreement (i.e. one votes 'Yes' or 'No' while the other abstains) is assigned a 0 value and sharp disagreement (i.e. one votes 'Yes' and the other 'No') is worth −100. If one calculates an average of these values, it is possible to quantify the average degree of agreement between any pair of EC member states in a given session of the UN General Assembly, or in the votes on some human rights issues throughout the 1970s. By performing such an analysis on the 250 roll-call votes on human rights issues that were held during the 1970s, it turns out that the pairs of member states that tended to be in agreement with each other the most often were Belgium–Luxembourg, West Germany–United Kingdom and Ireland–Denmark. The members of each of these pairs tended to vote in the same way 90–92 per cent of the time. To the contrary, the pairs of EC member states that tended to be in disagreement with each other the most often were the United Kingdom–Ireland and France–Denmark, as they tended to vote in the same way only 58–60 per cent of the time when human rights issues were at stake.

In the 1973–9 period, that is, when the EC was present with 9 member states at the UN General Assembly, 188 votes on human rights issues took place in New York. EC member states voted unanimously ninety-nine times and split eighty-nine times. How did they split? The variety of voting patterns is remarkable, as it is possible to trace thirty-one different voting coalitions. In some cases, it was one member-state voting differently from all the EC partners – but this happened only a handful of times, mostly as a result of France's divergence on Palestine in the late 1970s. In the vast majority of cases, the minority coalition breaking away from the predominant position among EC member states was formed of two, three, or even four members. Even if a large variety of such voting coalitions can be traced, a few recurrent patterns can actually be identified. For instance, in twelve votes out of eighty-nine the split divided Ireland and Denmark on one side from all the other EC member states on the other side. Those were all votes on Austral African issues, where the two countries took a position which was closer to the developing countries' one compared to the other EC member states. In ten more cases, Italy and the Netherlands joined Ireland and Denmark in adopting a more progressive position compared to the rest of the EC. Conversely, in several other votes on Austral African issues the majority of EC member states sided with the developing countries while a coalition made of France and the United Kingdom (as well as West Germany most of the time) adopted a more conservative position. To some extent, the thirty-one different detectable voting coalitions were in fact variations of these two main clusters, determined by occasional shifts or by their expansion to include, for instance, Belgium and Luxembourg, which featured very seldom in a coalition breaking away from the predominant position among the EC member states.

Even if half of the time EC member states failed to display unanimity on human rights issues at the UN General Assembly, they usually managed to keep under control and virtually eliminate the starkest form of division, that is, when at least one of them voted 'Yes' to a given resolution and at least another one voted 'No' to it. Disagreements between the member states tended to take milder and less embarrassing forms: for

Table 4.1 Index of Agreement among EC Member States Values refer to the average level of agreement between any couple of EC member states in the roll-call votes on human rights at the UN General Assembly, 1970–9, whereas complete agreement = 100 and complete disagreement = -100. © Lorenzo Ferrari.

	France	West Germany	Italy	The Netherlands	Belgium	Luxembourg	United Kingdom	Ireland	Denmark
France	-	86	69	62	75	74	85	55	52
West Germany	86	-	79	76	88	87	91	62	65
Italy	69	79	-	81	82	82	64	79	78
The Netherlands	62	76	81	-	81	82	64	78	84
Belgium	75	88	82	81	-	92	73	68	72
Luxembourg	74	87	82	82	92	-	74	69	72
United Kingdom	85	91	64	64	73	74	-	49	52
Ireland	55	62	79	78	68	69	49	-	90
Denmark	52	65	78	84	72	72	52	90	-
Average level of agreement with the EC partners	**69**	**79**	**77**	**76**	**78**	**78**	**68**	**69**	**71**

instance, it could be the case that some member states voted 'Yes' or 'No' to a given resolution while others decided to abstain on it or not to take part in the roll-call vote at all.

Instances of stark division among EC member states occurred only 15 times out of 250 roll-call votes on human rights during the 1970s. All of them concerned Austral African issues, except for a vote on Palestine in 1970 and a vote on the legal status of the so-called 'freedom fighters' in 1973. Many instances of such a split form took place at the end of the decade, in 1979, on a stretch of resolutions concerning the adoption of an array of sanctions against the South African government, including an oil embargo and the end of all military and nuclear collaboration. In almost all instances of stark division between EC member states, the split took a complex form: it did not consist in a binary opposition between one or more member states and all the others, but it typically took the form of a three-way split, whereas some EC countries would vote 'Yes' on a given resolution, others would vote 'No' and others would abstain. In a couple of occasions EC member states even managed to make four different voting decisions, since some of them chose not to take part in the vote. Once more, the fault lines tended to see France and the United Kingdom on one end of the spectrum, often joined by West Germany – while the Netherlands, Ireland and Denmark were on the other end, and all the other member states occupied an intermediate position and tended to abstain on these controversial resolutions. The three- or even four-way splits that took place constituted outright failures of the attempt at coordinating the member states' foreign policy positions. Such splits took place in a tiny number of occasions, but they often concerned issues on top of the international agenda, such as sanctions against the apartheid regime in South Africa.

It is worth noting that in many cases where the EC member states managed to agree on a common voting decision, their position did not imply an agreement with the United States, the EC's main ally and partner. In fact, in 47 out of the 125 times in which the EC member states voted unanimously, their voting decision differed from the one adopted by the US delegation. This means that the EC member states were compact on a position different from the one of the United States in about one-fifth of all the votes on human rights issues held at the UN General Assembly during the 1970s. In almost the entirety of such cases, the EC settled for a milder, opener position vis-à-vis the views on human rights that were held by the developing and socialist countries – which enjoyed the majority within the UN General Assembly – while the United States went for a sharper opposition to them. Indeed, in seventeen instances of transatlantic division the EC member states joined the winning majority at the Assembly, while the United States rather abstained; in twenty-seven cases both the EC member states and the United States ended up in the minority opposing the adoption of a resolution, but while the former decided to abstain the latter went for a 'No' vote. However, transatlantic divisions never went as far as to have the EC compact on a 'Yes' vote and the United States choose a 'No' vote, or the other way round. Unsurprisingly, the level of disagreement between the EC and the United States reached its maximum during the heated 1972 session, when the EC started to raise its political ambitions on the international stage, in parallel with the outcome of the EC Paris Summit, which took place in the same weeks as the yearly session of the UN General Assembly. In

Paris, the leaders of EC member states decided that 'Europe must be able to make its voice heard in world affairs [. . .] and to establish its position in world affairs as a distinct entity'.[8]

Over the entire decade, transatlantic disagreement at the UN General Assembly was particularly visible not only on the resolutions concerning the Palestinians' rights but also on the resolutions on racism and on the dictatorship in Chile. The EC member states that ended up the most often in expressing a divergent position from the one of the United States were Ireland and Denmark, while the United Kingdom and West Germany proved to be the member states the closest to the United States on human rights matters at the General Assembly. Still, their level of agreement with the United States was not exceptionally high, compared to their level of agreement with the other EC member states: the United Kingdom voted in keeping with the United States in 77 per cent of the cases, while West Germany did so 71 per cent of the time.

EC member states' cohesion on human rights issues

Unanimity among EC member states at the UN General Assembly occurred in over 75 per cent of the time, especially when resolutions on human rights in Chile and on racism were at stake, as well on some global aspects of human rights, including for instance the resolutions on women's rights, on the protection of those detained on the grounds of mental illness, on the creation of the UN High Commissioner for Human Rights, on the death penalty, on religious intolerance and on war crimes. EC member states' voting cohesion was higher than average in the case of Palestinians' rights as well.

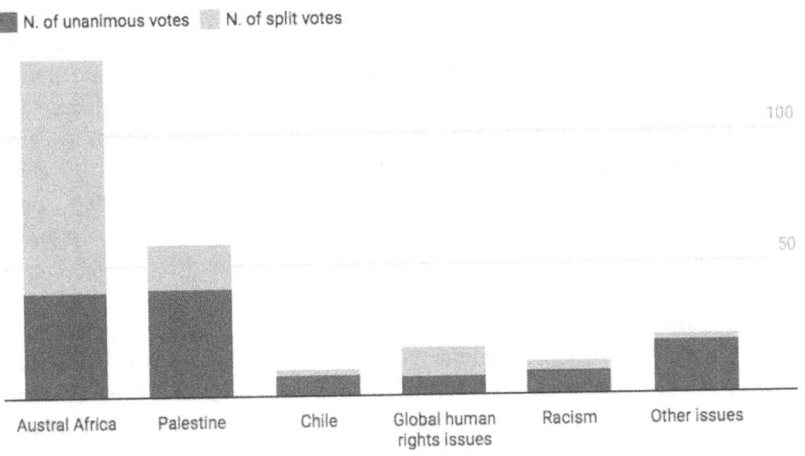

Chart 4.1 Cohesion of EC member states in the roll-call votes on human rights at the UN General Assembly, 1970–9, per topic. © Lorenzo Ferrari.

When EC member states managed to present a common front at the UN General Assembly, they sometimes tended to align with the majority of the Assembly's members in supporting a winning resolution, while other times they tried to oppose the approval of some resolutions (which passed anyway, typically thanks to the support of the developing and socialist countries). In the 125 cases where EC member states voted unanimously on human rights matters in the 1970-9 period, 54 times they chose to support the resolution at stake, 51 times they preferred to abstain, and 20 times they decided to go for an outright opposition to the proposed resolution. This was the case for instance of resolution A/RES/32/122, which expressed 'solidarity with the fighters for national independence and social progress of their people', or of the infamous resolution A/RES/3379 that stated that 'zionism is a form of racism and racial discrimination'. Throughout this period, EC member states were also united in rejecting resolutions proclaiming that the regime of South Africa was illegitimate or finger-pointing at some countries for collaborating with it.

The mere fact that unanimity between the EC member states took place half of the times when they were called to vote on some human rights issue indicates that to reach cohesion was possible or even likely, but it was not obvious at all, at least on some issues. In some cases, cohesion resulted from a natural convergence of political views, interests and sensitivities between these Western European countries – or at least from a similar assessment of the statements that were put to vote at the UN General Assembly. In many such occasions, convergence went beyond the EC's borders, involving other European countries, such as Austria, the Nordic countries, as well as Spain and Portugal in the second half of the 1970s. However, in many cases cohesion between the EC member states required a deliberate, sustained effort at coordinating EC governments' foreign policy positions – an activity which was gradually tested and fine-tuned.

As long as human rights matters were concerned, this harmonization effort was carried out in the framework of EPC, a structure that was created in order to favour a convergence between EC member states' foreign policy positions. EPC functioned as an intergovernmental forum for cooperation, wherein EC member states would jointly discuss issues of their choice and possibly reach common positions; the system was deliberately conceived as lightly structured and based on consensus. As part of EPC, EC governments created a group of experts specifically dealing with UN matters, and their delegations at the UN convened regularly in order to jointly discuss political issues since 1971.[9] Starting from the 1972 session, the president of the Council of the EC regularly intervened on behalf of the Community in the plenary session of the General Assembly. EPC coordination procedures were streamlined once West Germany had become a full member of the UN and the EC had undergone its enlargement in 1973.[10] An additional factor favouring an increasing cohesion of the EC member states at the UN was the admission of the EC as such as an observer member of the General Assembly on a permanent basis, which was approved on 11 October 1974.[11] Either through Community mechanisms or EPC, by the end of 1974 the EC was able to express common positions on almost all issues discussed at the UN, including human rights. EPC coordination was used in a growing number of fields and with increasing success, largely becoming standard practice – even if some EC member states continued to object to coordination with the partners in a few areas that they regarded as *domains reservés*.

Voting cohesion at the UN was one of the most effective means for EC member states to signal a common stance on international issues, to the extent that West German officials regarded it as 'the ultimate manifestation of European identity'.[12] To increase their consistency in voting at the UN, Community and EPC institutions devoted much energy to coordinate member-state positions: their delegations in New York could hold as many as a few hundred meetings during a single session of the General Assembly.[13] Coordination did not concern only the final votes in the plenary sessions but also discussions in the General Assembly's committees, where delegations could influence the object and wording of new resolutions.[14] In 1975 the representatives of EC governments decided that a systematic effort at achieving voting cohesion should occur for any new session of the General Assembly and that EC member states should never vote against each other, that is, whereas one of them would vote 'Yes' to an item while another one would vote 'No'. Two years later an 'early warning' system was introduced in the framework of EPC, meant at making it easier for the EC governments to detect and address divisive issues on time. For a comprehensive and balanced assessment of the human rights situation around the world, starting from 1977 the EC member states required their ambassadors to regularly report on the situation in their host countries.[15]

In order to explain their voting decisions on human rights and other issues, EC member states frequently made common statements at the UN General Assembly. This development was part of a more general tendency of the EC and of its member states to release a large number of common statements on international issues starting from the mid-1970s. For instance, joint EPC statements at the General Assembly increased from two declarations in 1973 to sixty-one in 1977.[16] From 1975 onwards, it became customary for EPC president to make a statement at the opening of each session of the General Assembly, expressing the common view of the EC countries on the overall international situation and on the main issues at stake, including human rights.[17] Such a comprehensive statement was regarded as 'an ideal opportunity to show the profile of the [Nine]' in international affairs.[18] EC member states sometimes released joint voting declarations at the UN General Assembly even when they did not actually have a common voting position. This activity was meant at showing that despite some differences, the EC member states did share a common basic stance on the subject at stake. Thanks to these and other efforts, by the mid-1970s EC member states' delegations to the United Nations were able to report that they had become 'a recognizable group'[19] at the United Nations, and even that 'Western delegations as a whole now look to the Nine for a lead on the entire range of human rights questions'.[20]

It must be noted that unanimity on a resolution debated at the UN General Assembly did not necessarily imply substantial political agreement between EC member states on the best way to address human rights violations in a given country. Just as it was possible that different voting choices hid a substantial convergence of political views on some issues, common voting choices sometimes hid some substantial divergences.

The debates on the ongoing violations in Pinochet's Chile are a good case in point. At the UN General Assembly, the EC countries were united in supporting resolutions that expressed concern and indignation regarding the constant, flagrant violations of human rights in the country. At the same time, however, they failed to agree on the deployment of actual measures to put political pressure on the Chilean regime. To be sure, the EC countries and institutions released a series of declarations and statements, exerted some pressure through confidential diplomatic contacts, met with leaders of the Chilean opposition, and diverted some aid to the country.[21] In a symbolic move, the headquarters of the EC Commission's representation office in Latin America were moved from Santiago del Chile to Caracas. However, words, symbols and votes were not matched by subsequent substantial political initiatives, as they lacked the necessary consensus within the EC. In fact, the situation in Chile was not even thoroughly discussed within EPC system in those years, except for specific occasions such as when a resolution about it was to be debated at the UN General Assembly.

The case of Chile illustrates the fact that it was often easier for EC member states to harmonize their voting behaviour at the UN General Assembly – or to release a joint statement – than to agree on the adoption of sanctions or on the deployment of serious political pressure on regimes violating human rights. However, it was remarkable that EC member states did manage to show a high degree of cohesion on most occasions where human rights issues were discussed at the UN General Assembly, despite the fact that they sometimes had different underlying positions and EPC coordination mechanisms were quite new. Among other factors, EC member states' display of cohesion in the human rights field at the UN General Assembly was also favoured by the fact that this image was in line with the more general goal of presenting the EC as 'force for good' on the international stage. Especially after the defeat of the EC's attempt at affirming its political autonomy from the United States in 1973-4,[22] it became crucial for the EC member states to find some niches where they could still cultivate and highlight their specificity and their distinctive approach to international matters, which was meant to be more attentive to considerations of justice and to the developing countries' agenda compared to the US line. Throughout the entire decade, debates on human rights at the UN General Assembly proved to constitute a good opportunity for the EC to highlight its distinctive approach.

EC member states' divisions on human rights issues

During the 1970s, EC member states failed to reach unanimous voting choice in 125 out of 250 votes on human rights matters at the UN General Assembly. Violations of rights in Austral Africa were the topic at stake in 71 per cent of the roll-call votes where a split among EC countries occurred, even if they made just 52 per cent of all the resolutions on human rights issues that UN members were asked to vote on during the 1970s. No other area related to human rights proved to be so divisive for EC member states, at least at the UN. The vast majority of resolutions addressing human rights violations in Austral Africa concerned the fight against apartheid and the proposed adoption of sanctions against the South African regime; some of those resolutions also targeted Bantustans, called for majority rule in Southern Rhodesia or condemned acts of aggression carried out by the Portuguese army. As a way to express international solidarity towards the victims of those violations and towards the promoters of human rights in the region, some of these resolutions were presented and approved at every session of the UN General Assembly, usually with minor changes.

Why did these issues – and South Africa's apartheid policy – prove to be so tough for the EC's political cohesion? One reason was the fact that human rights violations in Austral Africa gained a notable prominence on the international agenda during the 1970s. The EC governments' actions and positions on those issues were closely scrutinized and exposed to multiple pressures, which sometimes made it more costly for them to bow to the compromises that were necessary to agree on common voting decisions at the UN General Assembly. In particular, many EC governments had significant economic ties with South Africa, as well as with Rhodesia and the Portuguese empire, and in some cases they even had political and military ties with them. This made them a natural target of pressure. For instance, EC member states started to be criticized more and more often by the developing and Soviet countries for their alleged support to the Austral African white regimes. Through its engagement in development cooperation, the EC had gained a capital of credibility among the African countries – so it could not present itself as a committed partner of African peoples on the one hand, and support white regimes oppressing them on the other hand.[23] Starting from the early 1970s, the mobilization of pressure groups expressing solidarity with oppressed individuals and groups in Austral Africa also increased throughout Western Europe. This development was particularly visible in the United Kingdom, West Germany and the Netherlands, but it also invested the EC as such.[24]

In order to respond to the pressures asking EC countries for a more forceful defence of human rights in Austral Africa, EC member states and institutions resorted to the release of joint statements criticizing apartheid and other gross violations in the region, which were sometimes followed by confidential diplomatic contacts with some of the actors involved. They could also agree on mostly symbolic initiatives, such as the provision of humanitarian aid to the victims of apartheid, the freezing of sporting and cultural contacts with South Africa, and the introduction of a code of conduct for EC companies that were active in the country, whose implementation was quite limited in fact.[25] It is possible to expand this list of mostly verbal or symbolic measures adopted by the EC member states to address human rights violations in Austral Africa by adding their support to many resolutions denouncing such violations at the UN General Assembly.

The divisions that repeatedly surfaced at the UN reflected an underlying split between the EC member states that deemed the adopted measures insufficient, and those that deemed it undesirable to expand, strengthen or combine them with sharper words or tougher sanctions. Countries such as Denmark or Ireland did not have significant material interests in Austral Africa, while they had influential domestic pressure groups calling for the adoption of a clearer stance against human rights violations. For these reasons, those governments proposed that the EC exerted public pressures on South Africa, introduced comprehensive trade sanctions against it, provided liberation movements with stronger support – and adopted a sharper voting position at the UN

General Assembly.[26] According to their EC partners, these governments were more interested in improving their own image than in effectively bringing about real change in Austral Africa:

> Pour les Irlandais et les Danois, soutenus par les Italiens et les Hollandais, il faut que les Neuf prennent à l'égard de l'Afrique du Sud des initiatives dans le seul but d'afficher leur hostilité à l'apartheid, et cela indépendamment des évènements qui peuvent survenir. [. . .] Il s'agit de leur part d'une attitude de principe qui, du reste, se justifie plus par le désir de manifester leur intérêt pour la défense des droits de l'homme et d'afficher des positions 'anticolonialistes' que par le souci de provoquer des changements réels.[27]

To the contrary, France, West Germany and the United Kingdom argued that confidential pressures would be much more effective than the adoption of public positions.[28] Their cautious attitude was clearly reflected in their voting behaviour at the UN General Assembly. It was due to both geopolitical concerns and economic interests – concern with human rights could enter the picture, but it had to be balanced with other foreign policy considerations.[29] Geopolitical concerns were closely linked to confrontation with the Soviet bloc, as evolutions in Austral Africa in any way should not endanger stability and the preservation of Western influence in the region. France, West Germany and the United Kingdom also had strong material interests in South Africa, which was both a supplier of commodities and a significant market for them. According to British estimates, a universal trade embargo against South Africa could cost the United Kingdom 1 per cent of its GDP.[30] As a result of these different considerations, the EC's line on human rights violations in the region was not always clear and consistent. Criticism was balanced with the prosecution of some forms of ties and dialogue with rogue regimes. As a result, even when EC member states could agree on common positions or political initiatives, they often turned out 'insufficiently robust in substance and insipid in tone', as a British official recognized in 1976.[31] Because of their ambivalent character, no member state was ready to strongly defend such compromise positions, and many of them rather preferred to advance their own distinctive views or interests – for instance by aligning with the developing countries at the UN General Assembly in the case of Denmark and Ireland, or by opposing their demands more openly in the case of France and the United Kingdom.

Conclusion

As soon as EC member states sought to harmonize their foreign policy positions through EPC, they had to respond to the increasing salience that human rights issues were gaining at the UN General Assembly. UN scrutiny was instrumental in putting human rights violations taking place in Africa, Asia and Latin America on the common agenda of the EC member states. Throughout the 1970s, debates on such issues typically resulted in dozens of roll-call votes in a single session of the General Assembly. Those votes constituted an interesting test for EC member states' cohesion in foreign policy matters, but they were also an occasion for them to highlight the specificity of the EC as an emerging political actor on the international stage, and its attention to human rights issues both within Europe and outside it. Voting decisions and attempts – as well as failures – at coordination on those issues at the UN General Assembly accompanied the shaping of the EC member states' positions and initiatives in the human rights field, resulting in the exertion of a lasting influence on their character. Roll-call votes at the UN General Assembly forced EC member states to express a stance on some of the most delicate human rights matters of the time, and they encouraged the harmonization of EC member states' views and positions, by pressing them to show that the EC could express cohesion in international political issues and was concerned with human rights violations around the world.[32] Votes at the UN General Assembly also lead to highlight some of the most controversial issues for EC member states, inviting to address them to some extent.

The analysis of the voting behaviour of EC member states at the UN during the 1970s indicates that they managed to display quite an impressive degree of cohesion for such a supposedly fragmented group of countries, achieving unanimity in half of the votes, also thanks to the remarkable efforts at coordination that were carried out in EPC framework. On many occasions, they even managed to agree on a common position that was different from the one of the United States, contributing in this way of pursuing the EC leaders' goal of asserting the EC as an international actor with its own distinctive profile. EC member states managed to display both a significant cohesion and an international profile that presented them as quite attentive to the developing countries' demands and positions and open to the dialogue with them.

However, the analysis of roll-call votes also shows that cohesion was hard to achieve in some fields, notably in addressing human rights violations in Austral Africa, and apartheid in South Africa in particular. Even if attempts at coordination did manage to avoid stark voting splits in almost all the occasions, it was frequent for EC member states to divide themselves and make different voting decisions. Data on voting records clearly shows that three main clusters existed: largest EC member states (United Kingdom, France and West Germany) were typically on a rather conservative position; the Netherlands, Denmark and Ireland on a more progressive or even radical position; all other member states in an intermediate position between these two clusters, sometimes joining the one or the other. Part of the reasons why those groups of countries tended to make different voting decisions on Austral Africa at the UN General Assembly lie in their willingness to stand out and not to coordinate with EC partners on some human rights matters, as well as in the different weight that their government assigned to the promotion of human rights compared to other foreign policy goals. Internal and external political pressures did play a significant role in these weighty decisions.

Notes

1 UN voting data are drawn from Erik Voeten, Anton Strezhnev and Michael Bailey, United Nations General Assembly Voting Data, Harvard Dataverse (2019), https://doi.org/10.7910/DVN/LEJUQZ (accessed 20 October 2020). The classification of

the resolutions on human rights issues was made by the author, based on the main subject of the resolution. The resolutions considered in this chapter do not include the resolutions concerning the rights of entire peoples or states, such as those concerning self-determination or the economic rights of the states. Roll-call votes on single paragraphs or amendments are not included in the analysis.

2 West Germany was an observer member to the UN General Assembly until 1972. It became a full member of it starting from the 1973 session, along with East Germany.

3 For more general analyses of the EC member states' voting patterns at the UN General Assembly, see Leon Hurwitz, 'The EEC in the United Nations: The Voting Behaviour of Eight Countries, 1948-1973', *Journal of Common Market Studies*, 13 (1975): 224–43; Albert C. Maes, 'The European Community and the United Nations General Assembly', *Journal of European Integration*, 3 (1979): 73–83; Rosemary Foot, 'The EC's voting Behaviour at the UN General Assembly', *Journal of Common Market Studies*, 17 (1979): 350–60. Most studies on European cohesion and initiatives at the UN, including on human rights, focus on the European Union phase: see for instance Paul Luif, 'EU Cohesion in the UN General Assembly', Occasional paper n. 49 (European Union Institute for Security Studies, Paris, 2003); Elisabeth Johansson-Nogués, 'The Voting Practice of the Fifteen in the UN General Assembly: Convergence and Divergence', Working Papers OBS n. 54 (Institut Universitari d'Estudis Europeus, 2004); Karen E. Smith, 'Speaking with One Voice? European Union Co-ordination on Human Rights Issues at the United Nations', *Journal of Common Market Studies*, 44 (2006): 113–37; Gabriele Birnberg, 'The Voting Behaviour of the European Union Member States in the United Nations General Assembly' (PhD diss., LSE, London, 2009); Madeleine O. Hosli, Evelyn van Kampen, Frits Meijerink and Katherine Tennis, 'Voting Cohesion in the United Nations General Assembly: The Case of the European Union', Paper presented at the 5th ECPR Pan-European Conference, 24–26 June 2010.

4 During the period considered, roll-call votes took place for about half of the resolutions adopted by the UN General Assembly, the rest of the resolutions were adopted by consensus.

5 For any session, the analysis refers to the voting behaviour of the European countries that were part of both the EC and the UN at that time.

6 The National Archives (hereinafter TNA), FCO 98/6, Report on EPC meeting on Angola, 25 February 1976; FCO 58/973, Note on Southern Africa by the British embassy in Paris, 04 May 1976; Archives du Ministère des Affaires Étrangères (hereinafter AMAE), Aff. politiques, CE 4149, Martin to De Guiringaud, 03 October 1977.

7 Christophe Gillissen, 'Her Place among the Nations of the Earth: Irish Votes at the UN General Assembly, 1955-2005', *Estudios Irlandeses*, 2 (2007): 68–77.

8 'Statement from the Paris Summit', *Bulletin of the European Communities*, 10 (1972).

9 Maria Gainar, *Aux origines de la diplomatie européenne: Les Neuf et la Coopération politique européenne de 1973 à 1980* (Brussells: Peter Lang, 2012), 353.

10 Paul Brückner, 'The European Community and the United Nations', *European Journal of International Law*, 1 (1990): 177.

11 On this process, see Lorenzo Ferrari, 'How the European Community Entered the United Nations, 1969-1976, and What It Meant for European Political Integration', *Diplomacy & Statecraft*, 29 (2018): 237–54.

12 German delegation to EPC reported in AMAE, BAC 48/1984 128, Phanvan Phi, 'Réunion du groupe des Nations Unies', 10 June 1975.

13 Luciano Tosi reports 250 meetings during the 1977 session of the General Assembly ('Europe, the United Nations and Dialogue with the Third World', in *Europe in the International Arena during the 1970s: Entering a Different World*, ed. Antonio Varsori and Guia Migani (Brussels: Peter Lang, 2011), 164). In 1984, Bernard R. Bot was reporting around 250–300 meetings per session ('Cooperation between the Diplomatic Missions of the Ten in Third Countries and International Organisations', *Legal Issues of Economic Integration*, 11 (1984): 160.
14 Beate Lindemann, 'Europe and the Third World: The Nine at the United Nations', *World Today*, 32 (1976): 262–3. The influence of EC coordination on the unfolding of the debates was already noticed in AMAE, BAC 48/1984 115, Hijzen, 'Coordination des positions des États membres', 5 December 1973.
15 TNA, FCO 58/1146, Note by Simpson-Orlebar on human rights, 19 September 1977; FCO 58/1146, Note by Simpson-Orlebar on human rights and foreign policy, 7 December 1977.
16 Beate Lindemann, 'European Political Cooperation at the UN: A Challenge for the Nine', in *European Political Cooperation*, ed. David Allen, Reinhardt Rummel and Wolfgang Wessels (London and Boston: Butterworth Scientific, 1982), 119.
17 Tosi, 'Europe', 163. For an analysis of the EC statements at the UN General Assembly, see Id., 'L'Europa all'Assemblea Generale delle Nazioni Unite (1974-1991). Non solo parole', in *L'Europa nel sistema internazionale. Sfide, ostacoli e dilemmi nello sviluppo di una potenza civile*, ed. Giuliana Laschi and Mario Telò (Bologna: il Mulino, 2009), 184–203.
18 Bot, 'Cooperation', 163.
19 TNA, FCO 58/894, Thomas, 'Cooperation between the Nine', 4 March 1975; AMAE, Aff. politiques, CE 3794, Comité politique de la CPE, 'Coopération politique des Neuf', 26 May 1976.
20 TNA, FCO 58/1009, Note of the UN British delegation on human rights at the UN, 3 May 1976.
21 Lorenzo Ferrari, 'The European Community as a Promoter of Human Rights in Africa and Latin America, 1970-80', *Journal of European Integration History*, 21 (2015): 218–20.
22 EC member states had to consent to the establishment of a system of consultation with the United States on foreign policy matters in April 1974.
23 AMAE, Aff. politiques, CE 3775, EPC presidency on the political implications of aid to Austral African countries, 31 March 1976.
24 Ferrari, 'The European Community as a Promoter', 220–1, 225–6.
25 Ibid., 222.
26 AMAE, Aff. politiques, CE, EPC, Groups of experts for Africa, Report by the EPC presidency on a joint meeting of the groups of experts for Africa and the United Nations, 28 June 1976; TNA, FCO 58/977, Dalton to Reith on the Community coordination on Namibia, 21 December 1976; FCO 98/400, Report on the EPC meeting on South Africa, 17 March 1978. See also H. Kvale Svenbalrud, 'Apartheid and NATO: Britain, Scandinavia, and the Southern Africa Question in the 1970s', *Diplomacy & Statecraft*, 23 (2012): 753.
27 AMAE, Aff. politiques, CE 4150, Note on measures to be taken against South Africa, 17 May 1978. See also TNA, FCO 58/977, Dalton to Reith on Community coordination on Namibia, 21 December 1976.
28 TNA, FCO 98/400, Brief on Southern Africa, 30 March 1978; AMAE, Aff. politiques, CE 4150, Note on measures to be taken against South Africa, 17 May 1978.

29 However, according to the British Foreign Secretary David Owen, 'A Concern for Human Rights should Permeate Our Whole Foreign Policy', in id., *Human Rights* (London: Jonathan Cape, 1978), 2.
30 TNA, FCO 49/727, Paper on the future British policy towards South Africa, 29 March 1977; AMAE, Aff. politiques, CE 4150, Note on measures against South Africa, 17 May 1978. On trade flows between South Africa and the EC member states, see Martin Holland, *The European Community and South Africa: European Political Cooperation under Strain* (London and New York: Pinter, 1985), 53.
31 TNA, FCO 58/977, Dalton to Reith on Community coordination on Namibia, 21 December 1976.
32 As Elisabeth Johansson-Nogués argues, the UN General Assembly was 'a vital vehicle for the EPC agenda setting and coagulation of EPC measures' (id., 'The Voting Practice', 3).

Part II

Member states, supranational institutions, European parties

5

The European Union of Christian Democrats and the controversy regarding the Spanish accession to the EC in the 1970s

The human rights problem

Marialuisa Lucia Sergio

This chapter focuses on how the European Union of Christian Democrats (EUCD), as the coordination among European Christian-Democratic parties was known, discussed human rights concerns in Spain during the democratic transition and at the inception of the adhesion process to the European Community.

The analysis of this topic allows a critical reinterpretation of the 'peaceful transition myth'[1] which has dominated the historiographical literature concerning Iberian democratization and European integration for a long time. At least up to the beginning of the millennium, in fact, historiography about contemporary Spain emphasized the gradual and agreement-based nature of this transition. The view is that of a 'negotiated break' between the regime's elite and the players of political change,[2] or even of a 'concession' of democracy,[3] managed with moderation by the Francoist ruling class and by the monarchic component with a secondary involvement of the opposition.[4]

From this perspective, the enlargement of the European Community to include Iberian countries has been mainly described as a negotiation process concerning the totality of the juridical and economic accession conditions, the so-called *acquis communautaire* (opening up of goods markets, freedom of movement, budget transfer systems etc.),[5] excluding the role of the political players, in particular transnational ones.[6]

This chapter aims instead to reconstruct the complex action of the EUCD, which acted within the EC as an institutional actor and, at the same time, as an informal network of Catholic-inspired, anti-Francoist and pro-European movements. By highlighting the violation of human rights and the spread of political violence characterizing the Spanish political context during the 1970s, this chapter also takes into consideration the political-ideological magma of Spanish Catholicism, torn between a longing for renewal and a realpolitik keen to keep compromises with the Francoist ruling class seeking for international legitimacy. For this purpose, it is above all necessary to understand the features of European politics in Spain at that time of transition and to identify the main players of the complex universe that was Spanish political Catholicism.

Spain's accession to the EC had been a fundamental goal of the second Francoism's ruling class, the so-called technocrats, the government's elite that was close to the Opus Dei and that, from the eighth government of the Francoist era (1957–62) onward, had reduced the old Falangist guard and arranged a series of new measures regarding juridical and economic liberalization known as the *Plan de Estabilización y Liberalización económicas*.[7] The technical and financial support of institutes such as the International Monetary Fund and the World Bank was crucial for the passing of such measures, even though their implementation risked being impossible without a European 'rehabilitation' of Francoist Spain.

On 9 February 1962, the decision was made to initiate EC talks. This responded to the aim of re-launching the international importance of the Francoist regime,[8] which was very skilful at inserting itself in the Franco-German cooperation[9] using effective economic arguments.[10] But when, in 1964, the FRG minister for foreign affairs Gerard Schröder presented a proposal for Spanish 'association' to the Common Market,[11] the Italian government strongly opposed it. In fact, during the 4 May European Union's Council of Ministers, Italy had circulated a memorandum, which was drawn up by Minister for Foreign Affairs Giuseppe Saragat, that underlined the observance of the democratic standards needed to adhere to the EC as enshrined in the 1962 Birkelbach Report: respect for human rights and for political pluralism.[12]

But the human rights issue was not present on the political horizon of the technocratic Catholic right wing in power that had succeeded, through modernization of administrative organization[13] and industrial growth (the *Desarrollo* or 'Spanish miracle' of the 1960s), in progressively integrating Spain in the Western capitalistic system without mining the authoritarian structure of the regime.[14]

The diplomatic proposal that Spain addressed to Community institutions was thus aimed at promoting European integration more in the interest of a political survival of the Francoist ruling class than in the perspective of a rupture and a breakaway from the regime. It was based on the assumption that economy ruled over politics, following the idea that market development was sufficient for modernizing the state, even without political pluralism. This emerges from the *spunti di conversazione* (conversation cues) – drawn up by Italian diplomacy in view of the 27 January 1970 Roman meeting between Aldo Moro, minister for foreign affairs under Mariano Rumor's second government, and the Spanish minister for foreign affairs Gregorio López-Bravo.

> The first objective – declared Lòpez Rodò [Ministry for the Development Plan] – is to obtain an income of 1000 dollars per-capita a year; everything else, social and political, will naturally follow. The absolute supremacy given to the economical element is clear from these words; an orientation that can perhaps be partially explained by the 'forma mentis' of the Opus Dei's followers and partially by the lack of contacts that this institution has with the working class. [. . .] After all, it is a widespread opinion that Opus Dei will certainly not sacrifice the country's economic development for political freedom. And recalling that economic

progress is generally linked with stronger and more widespread aspirations of democracy, many see a possible source of great problems in this orientation.[15]

This contradiction between economic liberalism and political authoritarianism derived from the full trust the technocrats had in economic well-being as a factor of social consent, capable of assuring the passive participation of the middle class birthed from the *Disarrollo*.[16] However, starting from 1970, the high social costs of their liberalist politics, which were against equitable measures of wealth distribution and diminishment of regional unbalance, produced an unstoppable wave of strikes in the working class, which was sustained by the Catholic world's solidarity and by the anti-Francoist clergy, united with Catalan and Basque[17] separatists in opposing the regime.

The action in favour of the Spanish democratization, promoted by the EUCD, which was headed by the Italian leader Mariano Rumor between 1966 and 1873 and from the German Kai-Uwe von Hassel between 1973 and 1976, is placed in this context.

With Mariano Rumor as president, the EUCD looked for its Spanish interlocutors among those opposed to the regime: that is, among the Catholics who were not colluding with the government and the Movimiento Nacional, wanting to favour a convergence of Catholic anti-Francoist movements into a Unitarian party, following the model of the Italian Christian democracy (DC), which could possibly become the central axis of the democratic transition and guide the Spanish integration process.

A long 1968 report about Spain's political situation addressed to President Rumor in fact identified the goal 'of realizing a vast, long-term, Catholic movement comparable to the Italian DC', 'cross-classist' and simultaneously 'anti-Communist and anti-Francoist', able to go beyond the social and ideological fractures inherited from the civil war.[18] This report did, however, observe two important obstacles for the success of this project. The power and consent were still relished by the regime's Catholics: on the one hand, the Opus Dei, which had however started a political evolution in terms of liberalism, and the antagonist Catholic Association of Propagandists, represented by 'one of its most dynamic and unscrupulous exponents in the Government, the Minister for Public Works [Federico] Silva Muñoz', whose followers 'are undoubtedly Francoists and try to monopolize the vast, potentially clerical, electorate, which has been the base of the anti-communist "crusade" and that, still today, continues to support Franco and the public order'; on the other hand, the Marxist Catholics, defined as 'irrational idealists'. The presence of 'a belligerent and discredited plethora of small personal and local movements' that had 'contributed to discrediting the Catholic opposition movements as a whole and to confusing the ideas of the many moderate elements'[19] was underlined between these two extremes.

To get out of the impasse, the report suggested the EUCD to bet on a figure comparable to Aldo Moro, the 'undisputed and charming' Joaquín Ruiz-Giménez, a lawyer, the only person able to 'broaden his political audience towards the left and in the centre' going beyond 'ideological sectarianism' and promoting 'a vast moderate and responsible, Catholic centre' through experimenting an 'ingenious formula', that of a 'federation of movements [. . .] that share generic centre-left politics'. According to the report, the international Christian Democracy could do a lot to sustain and help the success of this initiative, both directly (moral and financial support) and indirectly (e.g. by encouraging the renewal of ecclesiastic hierarchies). Above all, by recognizing Ruiz-Giménez's leadership on an international level as soon as possible and allowing only his unified group to participate in the meetings of the European and worldly CD parties, EUCD would have given a political support of ample resonance, which would certainly help the positive development of the whole operation, especially in regards to the vast Spanish Catholic world that is still partially depoliticized.

The EUCD intervention in Spain had to avoid appearing like an attempt of 'ideological colonization from the outside' so as to 'assure a peaceful and orderly progress of social and economic life, which would allow Spain's full return into the European family', which constitutes 'one of the essential goals that the regime itself constantly asserts it wants to reach'.[20]

For their part, the Spanish Christian-democrat movements, federated into Equipo democrático cristiano del Estado Español (Federación Popular Democrática, Izquierda Democrática, Partido Nacionalista Vasco, Union Democrática de Catalunia e Union Democrática del Páis Vanciano), asked the EUCD to oppose the Spanish accession to the European Community before the country's actual democratization, so as to avoid the agreements being exploited by the regime as a form of international validation and thus of internal strengthening.

For this reason, the Spanish Catholics belonging to the anti-Francoist opposition considered the 29 June 1970 Luxembourg signing of the Acuerdo Preferencial between Spain and EC, in front of the Ministry for Foreign Affairs Gregorio López-Bravo, the President of the EC Council Pierre Harmel and the President of the Commission Jean Rey,[21] as a betrayal by Italy, which had factually contributed to the preliminary negotiations.[22]

In October 1970, the members of the Equipo democrático cristiano wrote to Mariano Rumor denouncing the triumphant tones used by the Francoist government after the signing of the commercial agreement:

> The Equipo, that is presenting this memo, is composed by groups that have complained more than once about how difficult it is to harmonize doctrinal purity with practical convenience and want Christian-democrat parties not to sacrifice the first within their relations with totalitarian regimes. We will not highlight examples, as they are not necessary. Sadly they are as frequent as they are painful. [. . .] There is the risk of sacrificing the fundamental principles of an ideology for the practical needs of the government that often protects private economic interests, which can be perfectly licit in themselves, in the guise of public interest.[23]

Denouncing the regime's authoritarian character, as it was still void of a democratically elected parliamentary delegation, the Spanish Christian democrats also asked to be formally allowed into the EUCD so as to have an international platform from where to fight Francoism.[24]

In the end, in 1972, the European Christian democrats granted the Equipo admission to the EUCD, thus officializing a strong and significant political investiture in the leadership of Ruiz-Giménez, identifying him as the Spanish Christian democrats' guide in the transition and in the perspective of Spain's entry to the European Community.

As stated in a resolution signed by Dutch vice-president of the EUCD Pieter Hendrik Kooijmans and by German deputy secretary general Karl Josef Hahn, the Spanish Christian democrats have found in Ruiz-Giménez a leader of national and international prestige, who is able to openly defend the thesis of a legal and democratic opposition, void of revolutionary aspirations or subversive intentions, and offer an alternative to the regime's frozen situation. According to the Kooijmans-Hahn's resolution, a moral or political weakening of this action, a formal exclusion from the EUCD team, would have had immediate consequences: it would have eliminated any future justification of the idea of a Christian-democrat movement, and youth groups, intellectuals and the young clergy would automatically move towards more extremist circles, as well as generating a profound sense of frustration in its leaders. This would have been that more deplorable and would have constituted a mistake of almost historical importance in the moment in which Spain realized the urgent need to strengthen its ties with the European Community.[25] This EUCD decision surely reflected the position of President Rumor, to whom Ruiz-Giménez wrote directly to express his gratitude,[26] and at the same time established the common strategy of not collaborating with Catholic groups that were near to the regime.

In the same year, 1972, Franco's regime had in fact once again shown its repressive side through the arrest of the trade union leader Marcellino Camacho and of other Comisiones Obreras' directors, who were held captive in the Pozuelo de Alarcón Oblate convent in Madrid, where they had gathered for a secret meeting. The detention lasted for more than a year, notwithstanding the complaints coming from Sicco Mansholt,[27] President of the European Commission; the protests of Georges Aronstein's Ligue des droits humains; and the several solidarity messages from all over Europe addressed to the defence attorneys, Joaquín Ruiz-Giménez and the socialist, Enrique Tierno Galván.[28] The outcome of the so-called Proceso 1001 and the drastic sentences pronounced against the trade union leaders on 30 December 1973 (including a ten-year sentence for Marcelino Camacho) brought the international public opinion's attention back to the dramatic human rights situation in Spain, which had further deteriorated after the death of admiral Luis Carrero Blanco, Franco's successor as government leader, in an ETA attack.

On 26 August 1975, Carlos Arias Navarro's government, which had followed Carrero Blanco's, approved a very strict 'antiterrorist law' (Decreto-Ley 10/1975) that widened the use of the death sentence and aimed at repressing any propaganda and ideological support in favour of groups of communist, anarchist or separatist[29] origin, through extensive and general legal wording. Signed by Franco and Arias, this law in fact imposed the death penalty to anyone who attacked – 'kidnapping' was considered a form of attack – members of the armed forces, security officers and government officials. It authorized the closure of newspapers and media and condemned to detention even those who simply showed solidarity towards the defendants of the urgent Consejos de guerra lawsuits, the military court's hasty legal actions for terrorism repression.[30]

Based on this law, between 28 August and 19 September the war councils prosecuted eleven young activists accused of having tried to kill members of the police in Bugos, Barcelona and Madrid; five were shot in front of a firing squad the morning of 27 September 1975 (Ramón García Sanz, twenty-seven; José Luis Sánchez Bravo,

Figure 5.1 Don Carlos Arias Navarro, the Prime Minister of Spain between 1973 and 1976. In August 1975, his government approved a repressive antiterrorist law that widened the use of the death sentence (Photo by: Photo 12/Universal Images Group via Getty Images).

twenty-one; José Humberto Baena Alonso, twenty-four; Juan Paredes Manot, twenty-one; and Ángel Otaegui, thirty-three).

A few days before the execution of the five defendants, which took place on 27 September in the midst of European Community and Holy See protests, the EUCD adopted a resolution that firmly condemned the human rights violations in Spain, reaffirmed its solidarity to the Spanish Christian-democrat forces and asked all Christian Democratic-inspired parties to translate such international support in a tangible and coherent testimony of Francoist opposition:

> The European Christian democrats forcefully protest against the renewed civil rights restrictions and human rights violations that follow the implementing of the new Spanish law with the excuse of fighting terrorism. [. . .] They remain profoundly convinced that only the full recognition of democratic freedom and the respect for human rights can guarantee Spain the peace the country needs to reach freedom. [. . .] They express their full solidarity to Spanish Christian democrats, who are members of the EUCD, and they appeal to all Christian-democrat parties to give this solidarity a concrete and effective expression.[31]

Figure 5.2 Italian Christian-Democrat leader Mariano Rumor was a strong advocate of a stable cooperation between the European Union of Christian Democrats and Spanish moderate forces in order to stabilize democracy and promote human rights in the Iberian Country.

Given that at the time the rotating presidency of European Political Cooperation (EPC) was in the hands of the Italian Minister for Foreign Affairs Mariano Rumor, Italian Christian democrats held the historical responsibility of the politics of European cooperation; and for them defending human rights in Spain symbolized a decisive benchmark for the ideals of a political and supportive Europe.

The idea of a European foreign policy cooperation, discussed during The Hague summit of 1–2 December 1969, had been outlined by the Davignon Report, which was adopted by the ministers for foreign affairs gathered in Luxembourg on 27 October 1970 and which established a recurring and regular information and consultation system among the ministers for foreign affairs of member states. On 19 November 1970, during the first EPC meeting in Munich, which put the Conference regarding European safety and cooperation on the agenda, a shared position was taken up regarding the need to safeguard Europe's common culture founded on democratic precepts.[32] In the case of third countries, like Spain and Portugal, the cooperation procedures were dealt with by the diplomatic representations in the form of regular meetings, information exchanges and communication with the Madrid and Lisbon governments and the respective opposition groups.[33] This was especially true after the 12 September 1975 session in Venice, during which Holland asked to take on a common European position regarding the Spanish human rights situation.[34]

Two weeks later, the Community ministers moved to New York, for the opening session of the UN General Assembly. There, they agreed to send the Spanish government an appeal for the suspension of capital sentences. A confidential telegram from Rumor to Ambassador Piero Vinci, Italy's permanent UN representative, reads:

> Based on the decision taken today in New York by the Ministers for Foreign Affairs of the Nine [member States of the European Community], Y.E. is requested to quickly take an adequate step toward such a government [Madrid's] in relation to the death sentences pronounced in Spain, and pointing out that such a step is taken on by the Italian Presidency on behalf of the nine governments of the European Community. Given that the initiative is inspired by humanitarian considerations and has no intention of constituting any interference in Spanish internal affairs, Y.E. will express it as a concern regarding the execution of such capital sentences.[35]

Franco continued relentlessly to execute death sentences, notwithstanding the international mobilization and the intervention of Pope Paul VI himself. For the Spanish Christian democrats, united in the EUCD, this clearly demonstrated the authoritarian character of the conservative political class called upon to manage the end of Francoism, which was still willing to use past instruments of repression. The only possible road for democracy had to pass through a clear choice of discontinuity and rupture with the regime's apparatus. The Equipo Demócrata Cristiano del Estado Español's 30 September 1975 resolution expressed gratitude for the European Christian-democrat family and leaders' solidarity by declaring:

> We restate our determination to continue our fight for radical change in structures that should actually guarantee the exercise of human rights and the immediate abolishment of the death penalty. We reiterate our firm conviction that in Spain only the establishment of authentic democratic relationships can resolve the problems that our society has to deal with. These cannot be resolved through the use of violence, which we condemn, or solely through sanctions, as the decree and executions are a sad and educational example of. We have been supported by the open and efficient solidarity of international Christian-democrat parties and organizations and by personal and direct interventions of their most prominent personalities.[36]

On 6 October 1975, EPC adopted two texts that eliminated any chance of the immediate recovery of negotiations between Madrid's government and the EC[37] and underlined the conviction that only a truly democratic Spain could find place within the Community. Following the principles stated in the Copenhagen Declaration of 14–15 December 1973, this was the first communitarian act to veer away from a functionalist formulation, which was linked to economic interests, and to recognize representative democracy, the rule of law, social justice, and the respect for human rights as the ethical and political foundations of 'European identity'.[38]

However, these declarations of moral and political disapproval were totally void of practical efficiency and of any tangible prevision of intervention tools to use on the Francoist government. Their final formulation in fact did not contain neither Denmark's and Holland's request of revoking the 1970 economical agreement nor the proposal of pulling the nine ambassadors from Madrid at the same time, which had been drawn up by EPC political committee based on an initiative of the Italian presidency.[39] Worried that the EC's direct interference in internal Spanish matters might have a counteractive effect and so an ulterior escalation of violence and a strengthening of the regime in power,[40] France's opportunist position had prevailed.

These different perspectives really hid both the discrepancy between national interests and pro-European visions and the duty conflict between EPC's intergovernmental strategy and the EC Commission's work.[41]

On 20 October, Rumor wrote to the socialist leader Francesco De Martino to explain the reasons that were pushing the Italian government to send the ambassador Ettore Staderini back to Madrid. In the same letter Rumor was worried about clearing his own position as president of EPC. He underlined his firm condemnation of the human rights violation and the priority defence of European culture values, which were to prevail over the ever so important commercial and productive interests of Italian economy in Spain:

I give you due notice that we have verified the binding need and urgency to send Ambassador Staderini back to Madrid.

In the fulfilment of the responsibilities accruing to the Political Cooperation Presidency of the Nine communitarian Countries, our Ambassador to Spain has the task and duty to coordinate his colleagues in a unitary sense, considering each common action and, in particular, those action that the Nine Ministers for Foreign Affairs and the Political Committee decide upon, specifically in regards to the Spanish events. The common step taken by the Nine, and brought forth by Ambassador Staderini, against the execution of the recent death sentences belongs to this setting. All other communitarian Ambassadors are now present in Madrid again with the objective of trying to impede other Spanish Authorities' decisions which go against the European heritage of civil concepts and of freedom. If our Ambassador's absence had been prolonged, we would have found it impossible, both as Italy and as European Presidency, to assure the carrying out of the action all democratic political forces ask us for.

This is regardless of the considerable Italian interests, for which we have serious concerns. These interests, as you know, affect the production, and thus the occupation, of many companies in Italy or refer to the situation of our workers in Spain. Naturally Ambassador Staderini has received appropriate instructions on the behaviour and the language to keep towards Spanish governors, so that our permanent condemnation of hasty trials, death sentences and executions be expressed there on every occasion and at the highest levels. He will furthermore participate in any initiative that could contribute to the evolution of the Spanish situation towards what we all hope for. A road that would allow democratic Spain to occupy its place in Europe, as specified in the recent Luxembourg declarations by the Nine's Ministers for Foreign Affairs.[42]

Franco's death on 20 November 1975, the proclamation of Juan Carlos de Borbón as king of Spain by the Spanish Cortes on 22 November 1975 and his coronation on 27

November seemed to indicate a decisive turn in the transition towards democracy. The proclamation of Don Juan Carlos was in fact accompanied by a gesture of national reconciliation, the emission of the general pardon decree, which allowed the release of hundreds of political prisoners.[43]

In reality, notwithstanding the liberation of many political prisoners, the efficiency of the decree was practically null, because the measure did not decriminalize the so-called propaganda crimes, nor those related to being member of associations, groups or organizations included in the late-Francoist antiterrorist legislation.[44]

Carlos Arias Navarro's new government was formed in December under the king's initiative. It promised a comprehensive reform of political representation aimed at broadening the base of the institutional system on the model of Western democracies and entrusted the Foreign Affairs and Internal Ministries respectively to José María de Areilza and Manuel Fraga Iribarne, both coming from the top of the Movimiento Nacional but counted in the ranks of the *aperturistas*, that is, the exponents of the Francoist ruling class in favour of a gradual evolution of the regime towards the liberal state. On 14 January 1976 – following a report regarding the Spanish situation by the Italian Christian-democrat Giuseppe Reale – the European Council implemented a resolution that favourably welcomed the reform programme announced by the Arias government, but also demanded the reinstatement of human rights and fundamental freedom, starting from a real amnesty for political prisoners and exiles as a prerequisite of an authentic reconciliation of the Spanish people.[45] The human rights issue remained in fact of absolute topicality in Spanish society, which was still characterized by a great deal of political violence and ideological conflict.

On 3 March 1976, during a strike in the city of Vitoria in the Basque region – having used tear gas to disperse the workers gathered in the San Francisco de Vitoria Church, in the working-class neighbourhood of Zamanranga – the Policia Armada (the so-called grey ones, part of the Francoist police established in 1939) killed 5 fleeing protesters and wounded more than 150. Far from being an isolated episode, the massacre displayed the intimidating and violent atmosphere by which the Francoist ruling class still managed the political process that opened up after the death of Caudillo.[46] The violence of Spanish police, together with systematic torture in prison and other 'brutal and degrading' coercive forms, which was denounced by Amnesty International in its annual report,[47] could not but call into question the image of the reformed and European country that Fraga Iribarne and Areilza were presenting to the international forum.[48]

Despite evidence about the seriousness of the human rights situation in Spain, and notwithstanding the significant continuity the ministers of the Arias government had with the political praxis and mentality of the 'second Francoism' governments, Heinrich Böx, the man in charge of the CDU office for foreign relations, in close relationship with the president of the EUCD, Kai-Uwe von Hassel, identified the group connected to Ministro de la Presidencia Alfonso Osorio, Franga Iribarne and Areilza as 'a strong, quite pragmatic, democratic centre', ready to 'guide liberal Spain'.[49]

The report itself seemed to sympathize with Federico Silva Muñoz and criticized the Spanish Christian-Democrats' programme because of its federalist and autonomist instances and for its persistent request to legalize the Partido Comunista de España (PCE):

> there are two main issues, that, in the long run, separate the government's liberal forces from the equipe's Christian democrats [...]. The federal state is rejected, not only by the government, but also by the centre forces – among them Silva Muñoz. They support regionalism, as an extended provincial constitution, because – given Spanish history and the national character – they fear that federalism could degenerate into separatism. The acceptance of the communist party is the other controversial issue. The government rigorously refuses its legalisation. The same goes for all other centre forces. On the other hand, the equipe believes that the new democracy would not be credible without this step.[50]

Requesting the legalization of the Partido Comunista de España (PCE) was in fact coherent with the orientation of Izquierda Democrática, a party headed by Ruiz-Giménez, who, in the June of 1975, had contributed, together with socialists and communists, to the foundation of the Plataforma de Convergencia Democrática, the coalition of anti-Francoist opposition forces that tried promoting a constituent process, which was to be shared and autonomous from the old regime's establishment.[51]

Silva Muñoz's perspective was quite the opposite. Around the same time, he had brought to life to a right-wing Catholic formation that wanted to reconcile social Catholicism with the principles of the Movimiento national[52] and to be recognized on the international stage as a conservative alternative to Christian democracy. During a meeting with the American ambassador Wells Stabler in April of 1976, Silva Muñoz had in fact reaffirmed his aversion to recognizing the communist party, which was reclaimed by socialists and left-wing Catholics based on what he considered to be a 'foolish historical compromise'. He had also mentioned the contacts he had undertaken with the CDU, and especially with Franz Josef Strauß's CSU, notwithstanding his group's difficulty getting international consideration among the European Christian-Democratic parties, given its 'connection to the regime'.[53]

Essentially, in 1976 different orientations regarding the Spanish transition and the involved political forces started to emerge within the European galaxy of democratic-Christian parties. These leanings reflected the political equilibriums present in the various national contexts and in the field of the European cross-party cooperation itself. In Germany, the time before the federal election of 1976 had been characterized by the competition for leadership between Helmut Kohl, president of the CDU, and Franz Josef Strauß, president of the CSU. After the vote, the conflict culminated in the CSU' decision, taken during a Landesgruppe meeting in Wilbad Kreuth on 19 November 1976, to not adhere to the unitary parliamentary group with the CDU during the VIII legislation and to expand itself on a national level as a strongly conservative party, competing with and antagonistic to the Christian-democrats (this project was withdrawn following a 12 December 1976 agreement between the two parties).[54]

The two German parties also competed against each other in Europe. While the CDU worked with conviction towards the construction of the European People's Party, which was founded in Brussels in July 1976, and expressed all the sensibilities of the moderate universe (Catholics and Protestants of reformist, conservative and liberal inspiration), the CSU, together with the Österreichische Volkspartei, participated in the formation of the European Democratic Union (EDU), in April 1978 at Schloss Klessheim, near Salzburg, a platform for European right wing.[55] In Spain the CSU, through Hanns-Seidel-Stiftung loans, actively sustained Fraga Iribarne e Silva Muñoz, who, in October 1976, had started Alianza Popular, a party that, when compared to the Spanish Christian democracy, was heavily anti-communist and conservative, to the point that in March 1977 *Der Spiegel* wrote that the CDU was scared of an 'international Kreuth'.[56]

In this scenario, Helmut Kohl allowed the Konrad-Adenauer-Stiftung and the former General Secretary of the CDU Bruno Heck to support Fernando Álvarez de Miranda,[57] a former leader of Izquierda Democrática who, in disagreement with Ruiz-Giménez and his adhesion to the Plataforma next to communists and socialists, had guided the April 1976 split of the more moderate elements, which in May 1977 subsequently merged into the Unión de Centro Democrático (UCD), a party led by the new Spanish prime minister Adolfo Suárez (in power from July 1976 to February 1981).

Though steering clear of conflicts and radicalization at home and in Europe, Kohl avoided compromising himself with the Spanish right wing and with Alianza Popular. On the one hand, he did not want to alienate his consensus among progressive Catholics like Norbert Blüm and youth organizations such as the Ring Christlich-Demokratischer Studenten, whose president, Friedbert Pflüger, had asked the Christian-democrat heads in 1977 to distance themselves from Strauß and his relations with Francoists.[58] On the other hand, he did not want to jeopardize connections between the CDU and Italian and Belgian centre parties, which were fundamental for a positive start of the PPE.

In January 1977, the entire High Command of the European centre parties, including Aldo Moro, Mariano Rumor, Kai-Uwe von Hassel and Leo Tindemans (Belgian president of the PPE), attended the Madrid meeting of the Equipo Demócrata Cristiano del Estado Español *Con nosotros, a Europa*,[59] confirming their support to Spanish Christian-Democrats.

In February of the same year, European Christian democrats restated their solidarity to members of the Equipo by condemning the extreme-right terrorist attacks which were covering Spanish society[60] in blood, and by recalling the EC accession as a worthy conclusion of the transition. In particular, European Christian democrats condemned 'all acts of violence committed by small extremist groups that cannot obstruct the construction of a democracy' and reiterated their support and their full solidarity to the Equipo Demócrata Cristiano del Estado Español that, 'loyal to its long tradition in defence of human and people's rights, is conducting Spain towards a truly democratic structure'.[61]

Despite such an endorsement, in May 1977, the month before Spain's first free elections, Kohl met Suárez publicly[62] and started a tighter cooperation with the UCD. At the end of the year, with the help of the Konrad-Adenauer-Stiftung, this actually resulted in the creation of the Fundación Humanismo y Democracia,[63] the UCD's foundation.

The CDU's convergence towards Álvarez de Miranda and Suárez reflected both a choice of political pragmatism and a general divergence regarding the Italian Christian democrats' shift towards the left; they were working on the 'historical compromise' in those years and thus looked favourably at a Catholic–Communist dialogue even in Spain.[64]

Though Suárez stemmed from the Movimiento National; his government was able to immediately carry out a programme of swift democratic reforms. The Cortes (parliament) universal suffrage direct election was approved in November 1976 and voted in a referendum by the vast majority of the Spanish people in December of the same year. Around the same time, the Tribunal de Orden Público for political crimes was abolished, while the communist party and independent trade unions were legalized. In April 1977, the International Covenant on Economic, Social and Cultural Rights and the International Covenant on Civil and Political Rights[65] were ratified.

Suárez's political party ultimately took over the political space generally represented by the Equipo, considering that at the June 1977 elections the Equipo only got 215.841 votes (1.18% of the national voting), whereas the UCD got 34.44 per cent, becoming the country's first party. This electoral disaster could be explained with the political disengagement of ecclesiastic hierarchies, which had decided, within the Episcopal Conference, to stand aside so as to separate their responsibilities from Francoist national-Catholicism.[66]

In the aftermath of the election, the Equipo sent the EUCD a memo containing a lucid self-critique about the limitations of the electoral campaign of the Spanish Christian-Democrats, namely, their less efficient representation of 'the winding-up of Francoism' in terms of 'security' and 'moderate change', when compared to Suárez, and their indecisiveness, dictated by the fear of being assimilated with the socialist party,[67] regarding proposals of social politics.

In addition, many socio-economic interpretations on the transition, which linger on the economic liberalization, the development of capitalism and the rise of a moderate middle class,[68] highlight how this middle class, though conscious of the need for a readjustment of the institutional structure to the democratic rules, was in reality generally disinterested in politics and rather concerned with their own private material progress.[69] This contributes to explaining the ease with which the myth of the peaceful and bloodless 'inmaculata transición'[70] was strengthened in the Spanish collective memory. This founding myth of contemporary Spain was functional to the narrative of national reconciliation. The price to pay was the removal of any memory regarding political violence or human rights violations during the dictatorship's long epilogue.[71]

But the human rights ordeal accompanied the Spanish process of political and social transformation and influenced the stages of this country's integration in communitarian institutions. The debate regarding human rights was undoubtedly of central interest for the European democratic-Christian political family, which saw in Spain the first misalignment between centre-left parties (like the Italian DC and the Belgian CVP) and German moderate parties, that were by then on the road to leading the bipolarization of the European political framework between the conservative centre-right forces and the left-wing parties.

Italian and Belgian Christian-Democrats did not believe that the 1977 elections protected Spain from the risk of an authoritarian involution (and the 1981 coup attempt would prove them right). In September 1977, during a London study seminar of the European Parliament democratic-Christian Group, the Belgian party whip Alfred Bertrand warned against 'favouring an artificial feeling of euphoria regarding the possibility for communitarian Europe to extend itself as soon as possible to applicant countries, thus giving a swift formal approval to their reacquired democratic dignity, naturally at the cost of their own truer needs and with all due respect of the European Union':

> Our European Christian democrats' conscience clearly refuses this second perspective that would mean escaping our true responsibilities towards the countries of Mediterranean Europe and, at the same time, the defeat of the ideals of integration, for the triumph of which we've persistently fought.[72]

Notes

1 Ferran Gallego, *El mito de la Transición* (Barcelona: Crítica, 2008); Sophie Baby, *Le mythe de la transition pacifique: Violence et politique en Espagne (1975-1982)* (Madrid: Casa de Velázquez, 2013).
2 The so-called *ruptura pactada*, cfr. Juan J. Linz and Alfred Stepan, *Problems of Democratic Transition and Consolidation. Southern Europe, South America and Post-communist Europe* (Baltimore and London: Johns Hopkins University Press, 1996), 87ff.
3 Guy Hermet, 'Espagne: changement de la société, modernisation autoritaire et démocratie octroyée', *Revue française de science politique*, 27 (1977): 582–600.
4 D. Gilmour, *The Transformation of Spain from Franco to the Constitutional monarchy* (London: Quartet Books, 1985); Charles Powell, *El piloto del cambio: el rey, la monarquía y la transición a la democracia* (Barcelona: Planeta, 1991).
5 F. Guirao, 'The European Community's Role in Promoting Democracy in Franco's Spain, 1970-1975', in *Beyond the Customs Union: The European Community's Quest for Deepening, Widening and Completion, 1969–1975*, ed. Jan van der Harst (Baden Baden and Brussels: Nomos Verlag - Bruylant, 2007), 163–93.
6 The role of other transnational players, like European political parties and their respective cultural foundations has only been examined in more recent years; W. Kaiser and Christian Salm, 'Transition und Europäisierung in Spanien und Portugal Sozial- und christdemokratische Netzwerke im Übergang von der Diktatur zur parlamentarischen Demokratie', *Archiv für Sozialgeschichte*, 49 (2009): 259–82; Marialuisa L. Sergio, '"Abbiamo la responsabilità del dire certi sì e certi no". Aldo Moro e le transizioni democratiche nell'Europa Mediterranea (Grecia, Spagna, Portogallo)', in *Una vita, un Paese: Aldo Moro e l'Italia del Novecento*, ed. R. Moro and D. Mezzana (Soveria Mannelli: Rubbettino, 2014), 559–82; Id., *La diplomazia delle due sponde del Tevere: Aggiornamento conciliare e democrazia nelle transizioni internazionali (1965-1975)* (Rome: Studium, 2018), 149–93.
7 José Luis García Delgado, 'La economía', in *Franquismo. El juicio de la historia*, ed. José Luis García Delgado (Madrid: Temas de Hoy, 2000), 115–70, 145.

8   Julio Crespo MacLennan, *Spain and the Process of European Integration, 1957-85* (New York: Palgrave Macmillan, 2000), 55–65.
9   Birgit Aschmann, 'Partner in der Protektion: Die deutsch-französische Kooperation zugunsten einer EWG-Integration Spaniens in den 60er Jahren', *Historische Mitteilungen der Ranke-Gesellschaft*, 2 (1999): 262–74.
10 Germany was one of the main importers of Spanish products. The EC external rate made Spanish products more expensive for German consumers, because EC external rates were higher than the rates that had previously been bilaterally negotiated. Moreover, a decrease in Spanish profits would have weakened the peseta and reduced its purchasing power to the detriment of European imports, particularly those of German industrial products, thus also reflecting negatively on German economy, Birgit Aschmann, 'The Reliable Ally: Germany Supports Spain's European Integration Efforts, 1957-67', *Journal of European Integration History*, 7 (2001): 37–51. A similar reflection can also apply to France, which had several economic interests to salvage: its industrial giants (Renault, Saint Gobin and Électricité de France) had outsourced many companies to Spain. Spain itself depended on France, both on the technical level (25% of all sales contracts concerning facilities) and on the financial one (France was one of its five main investors). Moreover, Spain's growth perspectives made its domestic market a palatable terrain for commercial expansion; see Esther M. Sánchez, *Rumbo Al Sur: Francia y la España Del Desarrollo, 1958-1969* (Madrid: CSIC, 2006), 257–70, 336 ff.
11 Cf. B. Aschmann, 'Die deutsch-spanische Kooperation in der Europapolitik nach 1945', in *Zeiten im Wandel: Deutschland im Europa des 20. Jahrhunderts*, ed. Jürgen Elvert and Syvain Schirmann (Bern: Peter Lang, 2008), 103–17.
12 The situation was reconstructed in Sergio, 'Abbiamo la responsabilità', 599–70.
13 See the Ley orgánica del Estado proclamation, which prospectively set up Juan Carlos's succession to Franco. This law was promulgated by the Cortes on the 28th of November 1966 and approved through referendum the 14th of December of the same year, regardless of the Falangist opposition; see Julio Montero Díaz, 'El franquismo: del *esplendor* a la crisis final (1959-1975)', in *Historia contemporánea de España*, II, *Siglo XX*, ed. Javier Paredes (Barcelona: Editorial Ariel, 2004), 720–1.
14 Feliciano Montero, 'Las derechas y el catolicismo español: Del integrismo al socialcristianismo', *Historia y Política*, 18 (2007): 101–28, esp. 113.
15 Archivio Centrale dello Stato (ACS henceforth), Aldo Moro Archive (hereinafter AMA), b. 127, f. 13, Appunto. Oggetto: Spagna – Situazione politica interna.
16 Julià Santos, 'Orígenes sociales de la democracia en España', *Ayer*, 15 (1994); 165–88, 184.
17 Paul Preston, *The Triumph of Democracy in Spain* (London: Routledge, 2004), 15, 19–21.
18 Archivio Storico del Senato della Repubblica (Historical Archives of the Italian Senate, hereinafter ASSR), Mariano Rumor Fond (hereinafter MRF), b. 126, f. 128, Movimenti cattolici spagnoli. Tendenze e prospettive nella primavera 1968.
19 Ibid.
20 Ibid.
21 This agreement established a reduction in rates between Spain and the EC; on the Spanish side, a 25 per cent reduction for agricultural products and a 53 per cent reduction for industrial products, while on the European side, a reduction of 13 per cent and 22 per cent, respectively. This agreement was settled on 29 January 1973, with the addition of a protocol. Bruno Aguilera Barchet, 'España y Europa veinte años

después', in *Veinte años de España en Europa: actas de las Jornadas de Conmemoración del XX Aniversario de la Adhesión de España a la Unión Europea*, ed. Cristina J. Gortázar Rotaeche and María José Castaño Reyero (Madrid: Universidad Pontificia Comillas, 2008), 91–107, here 97, 102.

22 ACS, AMA, b. 129, f. 31, Luxembourg, Monday 29 June 1970, Elements of a conversation [between Aldo Moro and López-Bravo]: 'Regarding Italy's attitude during the longstanding six-way examination of Spain's requests, – from the point of view of the agreement's commercial content – it had always been among the most favourable [. . .]; and for fishing products – though partial – the concessions obtained by Spain are to be attributed to our delegation's action, that wanted to satisfy Spanish requests to a greater extent.'

23 ASSR, MRF, b. 119, f. 51, Equipo democrático cristiano's to Mariano Rumor, 8 November 1970.

24 ASSR, MRF, b. 116, f. 21, Resolución de l'Equipo democrático cristiano in Anton Cañellas' letter to Mariano Rumor, 22 September 1971.

25 ASSR, MRF, b. 117 f. 28, Réunion du Bureau politique, Paris 10 Novembre 1972, Rapport sur la position de l'Équipe dans l'EUDC de Pieter Hendrik Kooijmans et Karl Josef Hahn, 26 June 1972.

26 ASSR, MRF, b. 126 f. 32, letter from Joaquín Ruiz-Giménez to Mariano Rumor, 29 July 1972: 'With humane simplicity we believe that the decision is correct and that whatever other decision would have caused deep sadness; but this does not at all diminish our joy and gratefulness. We know to what extent this happy outcome results from what Your Excellency intelligent comprehension has represented.'

27 Raimundo Bassols, *España en Europa, historia de la adhesión a la CE, 1957–85* (Madrid: Política Exterior, 1992), 86.

28 Marcelino Camacho, *Memorias: confieso que he luchado* (Madrid: Temas de Hoy, 1993), 334.

29 The law mentioned 'communists, anarchists, separatist groups or organizations and others who endorse or use violence as instruments of political and social action [. . .] and that, in any case carry out propaganda for the aforementioned groups or organizations aiming at promoting or broadcasting their activities' as well as 'those who, publicly, explicitly or in secret, defend or encourage such ideologies', in Decreto-ley 2/1976 de 18 de febrero, por el que se revisa el de Prevención del Terrorismo 10/1975 de 26 de agosto, y se regula la competencia para el enjuiciamiento de tales delitos, preámbulo et art. 1°; cf. Baby, *Le mythe de la transition pacifique*, 295.

30 'Decreto-ley 10/1975', in *Boletín Oficial del Estado*, 26 August 1975 (regarding the prevention of terrorism in BOE-A-1975-18072), 1–5.

31 'Entschließung der EUCD zur Situation in Portugal, 18.9.1975 [Archiv Karl von Vogelsang-Institut (KvVI), Wien, 2861/2, Bestand Franz Karasek]', in *Transnationale Parteienkooperation der europäischen Christdemokraten und Konservativen. Dokumente 1965-1979*, I, ed. Michael Gehler, Marcus Gonschor, Hinnerk Meyer and Hannes Schönner (Berlin-Boston: de Gruyter GmbH, 2018), 887.

32 David Allen, Reinhardt Rummel and Wolfgang Wessels, eds, *European Political Cooperation: Towards a Foreign Policy for Western Europe* (Boston: Butterworth Scientific, 1982), 63.

33 Esther Barbé, 'Spain: The Uses of Foreign Policy Cooperation', in *The Actors in Europe's Foreign Policy*, ed. Christopher Hill (London: Routledge, 1996), 108–29.

34 *Bulletin des Communautés européennes*, 9 (1975): 108.

35 ASSR, MRF, b. 145, f. 168 Telegram to Piero Vinci, 25 September 1975.

36 'Entschliessung der Christlich-Demokratischen Gruppe Spaniens vom 30. September 1975 [Archiv KvVI, 0509]', in *Transnationale Parteienkooperation der europäischen Christdemokraten und Konservativen*, 927.
37 *Bulletin des Communautés européennes*, 10 (1975): 81.
38 'La «identità europea» (Copenaghen, 14 dicembre e 1973)' and 'Comunicato congiunto al termine del vertice di Copenaghen (Copenaghen, 15 dicembre 1973)', *Rivista di Studi Politici Internazionali*, 41 (1974): 123–7 and 127–9.
39 *Bulletin of the European Communities*, 10 (1975); Simon Nuttall, *European Political Cooperation* (Oxford: Clarendon, 1990), 126–7.
40 Antonio Moreno Juste, 'The European Economic Community and the End of the Franco Regime: The September 1975 Crisis', *Cahiers de la Méditerranée*, 90 (2015): 25–45.
41 Martín de la Guardia, 'In Search of Lost Europe: Spain', in *European Union Enlargement: A Comparative History*, ed. Wolfram Kaiser and Jürgen Elvert (London: Routledge, 2004), 70–91.
42 ASSR, Francesco De Martino Fond, b. 796, f. 2, Letter from Mariano Rumor to Francesco De Martino, 20 October 1975.
43 Jacinto Soriano, *Diccionario de la España franquista (1936-1975)*, ad vocem (*Amnistía, ley de*) (Paris: L'Harmattan, 2018), 29.
44 Paloma Aguilar Fernández, *Memoria y olvido de la Guerra Civil española* (Madrid: Alianza, 1996), 64; Santos Juliá, 'Presencia de la guerra y combate por la amnistía en la transición a la democracia', in *Identidades y memoria imaginada*, ed. Justo Beramendi and Maria J. Baz Vicente (Valencia: Universitat de València, 2008), 85–107.
45 Parliamentary Assembly of the Council of Europe, *Resolution on the Situation in Spain*, 14 January 1976, Doc. 3714.
46 A *L'Espresso* news story observed as follows: 'the situation has remained fundamentally unaltered on all essential things, arbitrary and intimidating arrests have continued at a sustained pace and prisons are as full as they were in the months prior to Franco's death. [. . .] In the meantime the wave of violence has extended to the whole country, fed by the vicious circle *police repression-terrorism-new police repression*'; in A. Gambino, 'Madrid: dopo Franco come Franco', *L'Espresso*, 18 April 1976, 32.
47 'Amnesty International has continued to receive persistent well-attested reports of treatment of detained people which, compared with previous years, did not amount to systematic torture but could better be described as systematically brutal and degrading. [. . .] To sum up – the most disturbing and inconsistent aspect of the human rights situation in Spain during the past year has been the Government's failure to exercise control over the police force, as regards either its dealings with crowds and demonstrations or with individuals who have been arrested and are maltreated, then released without being charged'; Amnesty International, *The Amnesty International Annual Report 1977* (London, 1977), 270.
48 Fabrizio Dentice, 'Il tempo del bastone e della garrota', *La tortura dopo Franco: L'Espresso Documenti*, 25 April 1976, 50.
49 'Heinrich Böx, Bericht zur Lage Spaniens nach dem Tode Francos', 2 March 1976 [Archiv fur christlich-demokratische Politik, Nachlass Kai-Uwe von Hassel, I-157-158-1], in *Transnationale Parteienkooperation der europäischen Christdemokraten und Konservativen*, 994.
50 Ibid., 993.

51 Plataforma de Convergencia Democrática was founded on 11 June 1975. In March 1976 it became Coordinación Democrática (Platajunta) by joining forces with the Junta Democrática de España, born in Paris on 29 July 1974, thanks to the initiative of exiled opposition representatives, mainly communists and independent thinkers connected to Don Juan De Borbón; Preston, *The Triumph of Democracy*, 56. The Italian Christian Democracy considered Izquierda Democrática's participation to the Plataforma de Convergencia Democrática positively; Pasqualino Spadafora, *La Democrazia cristiana per una Spagna democratica* (Roma: Cinque lune, 1976), 48.

52 José L. Orella Martínez and José Díaz Nieva, 'La derecha franquista en la transición', in *Actas del III Simposio de Historia Actual. Logroño, 26-28 de octubre de 2000*, ed. Carlos Navajas Zubeldía (Logroño: Instituto de Estudios Riojanos, 2002), 549–66, 552.

53 National Archives and Records Administration (NARA), Record Group 59, Telegram, American embassy in Madrid to Secretary of State, 2 April 1976: 'He [Silva] confessed to his obvious difficulties in getting international Christian democratic recognition for his conservative, regime-linked group. Silva laid considerable stress, however, on his contacts with the CDU/CSU and Strauss in particular. [. . .] On grounds of both principle and pragmatism, there was no sense in making the PCE legal, although this posed difficulties with the left wind Christian democrats (who sought a foolish "historic compromise") and the socialists. Legalization of the PCE would destabilise the whole political process.'

54 Yvonne Hempel, 'Die Staatskanzlei als heimliche Parteizentrale?', in *Die CSU: Strukturwandel, Modernisierung und Herausforderungen einer Volkspartei*, ed. Gerhard Hopp, Martin Sebaldt and Benjamin Zeitler (Wiesbaden: Springer-Verlag, 2010), 287–308, 294.

55 T. Jansen, 'The Dilemma for Christian Democracy: Historical Identity and/or the Political Expediency: Opening the Door at the Conservatism', in *Christian Democracy in the European Union 1945/1995*, ed. E. Lamberts (Leuven: Leuven University Press, 1997), 459–72, particularly 463ff.

56 'Kreuth International', *Der Spiegel*, 21 March 1977, 60–2.

57 Kaiser and Salm, 'Transition und Europäisierung in Spanien', 274–5.

58 Ibid., 275.

59 MacLennan, *Spain and the Process of European Integration*, 145.

60 Among the many episodes one must remember the 9 May 1976 Montejurra massacre in Navarra, perpetrated by the *Guerrilleros de Cristo Rey* during a religious ceremony of Carlist royalists, and the 24 January 1977 Atocha massacre, executed in a law firm dealing with employment rights, the lawyers were slaughtered by a terrorist formation connected to Blas Piñar's *Fuerza Nueva*.

61 ASSR, MRF, b. 145, f. 163, Réunion du bureau politique, Madrid, 1–2 February 1977.

62 Gerlinde Freia Niehus, *Außenpolitik im Wandel. Die Außenpolitik Spaniens von der Diktatur Francos zur parlamentarischen Demokratie* (Frankfurt am Main: Vervuert, 1989), 516.

63 See *Deutschlands neue Außenpolitik, IV, Institutionen und Ressourcen* (München: Oldenbourg, 1994), 196.

64 A reconstruction of the Italian DC and German CDU disagreement regarding the relationship with communist parties and, in general, the distension dynamics, in Marialuisa L. Sergio, 'Détente and Its Effects on Italian and German Political Systems (1963–1972)', *Rivista di Studi Politici Internazionali*, 82 (2015): 411–30.

65 Amnesty International, *Annual Report 1977*, 271–2.

66 Regarding the fundamental role of the Church and the Holy See in the transition process, see Sergio, *La diplomazia delle due sponde*, 149ff.
67 ASSR, MRF, b. 145, f. 169, Le elezioni Spagna. Nota del Equipo democrático cristiano del Estado español, 28 June 1977.
68 Michel Dobry, 'Les voies incertaines de la transitologie. Choix stratégique, séquences historiques, bifurcations et processus de path dependence', *Revue française de science politique*, 50 (2000): 585–613.
69 J. Cayo Sastre García, *Transición y desmovilización política en España (1975-1982)* (Valladolid: Universidad de Valladolid, 1997); Francisco A. Orizo, *España, entre la apatía y el cambio social. Una encuesta sobre el sistema europeo de valores: el caso español* (Madrid: Mapfre, 1983); Santos Juliá and José Carlos Mainer, *El aprendizaje de la libertad. 1973-1986: la cultura de la transición* (Madrid: Alianza, 2000).
70 José Vidal-Beneyto, *Memoria democrática* (Madrid: Foca, 2007), 164.
71 Carme Molinero, *La Transición, treinta años después* (Barcelona: Península, 2006); Josefina Cuesta Bustillo, *La Odisea de la memoria, Historia de la memoria en España Siglo XX* (Madrid: Alianza Editorial, 2008); Bénédicte André-Bazzana, *Mitos y mentiras de la transición* (Barcelona: El Viejo Topo, 2006).
72 ASSR, MRF, b. 120, f. 81, London Study Days 1-2-3 September 1977 Gli aspetti politico-istituzionali dell'allargamento della comunità ai paesi della Unione Europea.

6

The Socialist Group of the European Parliament and human rights in the second half of the 1970s

Christian Salm

The right to life is the most basic right of all human rights. If we test this apparent commonplace against reality we shall be shocked to learn what our world is really like. [. . .] And yet, if the human rights did not exist, at least as a goal, as a hope, darkness would befall us. Resignation would mean surrender to injustice and despair.[1]

These were the words of Willy Brandt when delivering his inaugural speech as president of the Socialist International (SI) in November 1976. In the mid-1970s, many high-ranking Western European socialist politicians desired a powerful president for the SI, who would prepare the global network of socialist parties to face pressing political challenges.[2] Regarded as a moral authority and a leading politician with a high international standing,[3] Willy Brandt, German Chancellor from 1969 to 1974 and acting chairman of the Social Democratic Party of Germany, seemed to be the ideal candidate.[4] In his inaugural speech at the SI congress in November 1976, Brandt highlighted three SI main working areas under his leadership: promoting peace in the world, improving relations between the North and the South, and protecting human rights. By doing so, Brandt intended to place the protection of human rights more prominently on the agenda of socialist parties and their transnational organizations than had been the case so far.

In line with their internationalist origins and traditions, Western European socialists claimed a special responsibility for the situation of human rights worldwide even before the mid-1970s. Such sentiments were clearly reflected in the human rights agendas of various Western European socialist parties at the time. For example, the protection of human rights occupied a special place on the international agenda of the progressive government of Joop den Uyl from the Dutch Labour Party. Likewise, even during the first period of the Swedish social democratic government under Olof Palme from 1969 to 1976, the protection of human rights was a high priority on the government's agenda for international relations. In contrast, the German social-democratic-led government, for example, took a rather reactive approach to human rights in its foreign policy. Moreover, as Jan Eckel has argued, Western European socialist parties did not share a common approach for human right policies.[5] As a consequence, their impact in developing human rights agendas at the international and the European level was limited. Especially at the European level, at which the European Community (EC) was increasingly perceived as an important actor in global governance,[6] Western European socialist parties' common political activities did not yet meet with their aspirations for human rights protection. Given that the SI had a strong Eurocentric character in the 1970s and that its political activities were very much directed towards the EC, Brandt's intentions from his inaugural speech can thus be read as an impetus to strengthening the Western European socialists' role in shaping and influencing EC human rights policies.

At the EC level, the Socialist Group in the European Parliament (EP) was the most institutionally developed transnational organization of Western European socialists. In the mid-1970s, it consisted of socialist parties from nine Western European countries, just in line with the number of EC member states at the time. Besides the Christian-Democratic Group, the socialists formed the biggest EP group and became the strongest political force in the EC in the first direct election to the EP in 1979.[7]

Clearly, human rights issues were an important topic of the Socialist Group's work long before Brandt's appeal in 1976. For example, when in 1967 a far-right military junta was installed in Greece, the Socialist Group, together with the other EP political groups, pointed to the violation of human rights as enshrined in the European Convention of Human Rights in the Southern European country. For this reason, as for the dismantling of the country's democratic system, the Socialist Group strongly demanded the suspension of the existing EC–Greece association agreement.[8] Nevertheless, the Socialist Group's political activities in the area of human rights extended into the second half of the 1970s. Brandt's appeal might have contributed to this development. More importantly, it was in line with the 'breakthrough of human rights' at the European level, triggered especially by the Final Act of the Conference on Security and Cooperation in Europe (CSCE) in Helsinki in 1975, which demanded the signing countries to respect human rights.[9]

Against this background, the aim of this chapter is to reconstruct the Socialist Group's activities in human rights in the second half of the 1970s. In particular, it explores how and to what extent the Socialist Group was able to shape debates and policies of human rights in the EP, but also beyond. By doing so, it investigates the Socialist Group's contribution to developing the EP as a champion of human rights, as Aurélie É. Gfeller has described it.[10] By the 1970s, the EP was already breaking the rules of parliamentary diplomacy by raising human rights problems with delegations from various non-EC countries and by adopting resolutions denouncing human rights abuses. This chapter will argue that the Socialist Group was a driving force behind the EP's engagements in human rights policies.

In order to substantiate this argument, we will zoom in on two special cases. First, we will examine the Socialist Group's activities for including human rights into the Lomé Conventions. Signed between the EC and sixty-six states in Africa, the Caribbean, and the Pacific States (ACP States) in 1975, the first Lomé Convention did not include specific provisions to terminate or suspend the convention in the case of human rights violations in a particular country. During negotiations for the Lomé II Convention to start in 1978, the inclusion of such provisions was up for debate after human rights problems in the context of the first Lomé Convention had come up in 1977.[11] Second, the chapter will analyse the Socialist Group's activities to address human rights violations in Argentina as the host of the International Federation of Association Football (Fédération Internationale de Football Association, FIFA) World Cup in 1978. Two years after its coup d'état in 1976 and its violent repression of critics, the Argentinian military regime aimed to make propagandistic use of the World Cup to polish up its image abroad. Before turning to the two special cases, however, the chapter will sketch the Socialist Group's history and its more general approach to human rights.

Finally, by exploring the Socialist Group's activities in the human rights arena, the chapter contributes to bringing the *transnational* into history writing on human rights, as called for by Sarah Snyder.[12] It does so, however, not only by making use of a transnational approach but also by looking at a transnational actor itself.

The Socialist Group's 'breakthrough of human rights'

For socialist parties in Western Europe, membership in the SI formed the basis for institutionalizing the first organized transnational cooperation structures within the emerging context of European integration. In the Common Assembly of the European Coal and Steel Community (ECSC), the forerunner of the today's EP, the socialist parties formed a Socialist Group in 1951–2, as they had already done in the assembly of the Council of Europe in 1949.[13] A common bureau and a permanent secretariat in Luxembourg were set up to coordinate the activities of the socialist parties in the ECSC assembly. As European integration progressed, the Socialist Group and its working organization grew and professionalized. Over the years, for example, the group's secretariat extended its administrative structure. Nevertheless, the group's structures remained quite small until the 1970s.

However, this was about to change over the course of subsequent years. The decision taken by the heads of state and government at the EC summit in The Hague in December 1969 in favour of direct EP elections provided a new impetus to extend and strengthen the group's organizational structure. In addition, the EC's northern enlargement in 1973 with the arrival of new group members from Britain, Denmark and Ireland required changes in the group's organizational structure and working procedures. As a result, the group's secretariat grew immensely in size, especially in the years from 1976 to 1978, and a second office was set up in Brussels. Furthermore, over the course of the 1970s the group's secretariat developed various units for supporting its members' parliamentary work. Specifically, by the end of the 1970s, the group's secretariat had set up twenty units, most of them correlating with the EP's committees.[14] Moreover, the group's professionalization increased through the establishment of various working parties to consider specific political questions and topics. Above all, these working parties were responsible for preparing the group's opinion.[15]

The working party on cooperation and development was one of these working parties. Among its main tasks was analysing problems of EC development aid policies and the economic cooperation of the EC with the associated developing countries in the form of the Lomé Convention.[16] With several members from the Dutch Labour Party, whose den Uyl government had made human rights an important element of its foreign policy, human rights problems were often discussed. Furthermore, human rights violations in the context of the Lomé Convention were increasingly evident from 1977 on, and discussions about these and other human rights issues in non-associated countries were often high on the working party's agenda.

Throughout the 1970s, however, no working party specifically tailored for working on human rights existed. The group agreed only in September 1979 to set up a small working party to consider human rights issues.[17] Given the developments in human rights in the 1970s, especially with the so-called Helsinki process triggered by the CSCE conference, the Socialist Group reacted rather late with the creation of such a working party.[18] Thus, although the Socialist Group was independent from the SI, the SI was an important guidance for the Socialist Group's human rights policies.

After Brandt had introduced human rights as one of three SI main working areas in November 1976, the SI party leaders recorded their common understanding on the importance of human rights in December 1977. Although the SI party leaders' conferences did not usually issue statements or declarations, an exemption was made at the party leaders' conference in Japan that year. The SI's Tokyo Declaration addressed especially human rights. It stated:

- We reaffirm that freedom from any kind of oppression and discrimination is a fundamental right granted to each human being.
- Deeply concerned over the fact that in some areas freedom and human rights are repressed, we express our solidarity to those who are committed to the struggle for human rights and freedom.
- Poverty and social injustice are great threats to peace, and should be fought as a prerequisite for the fulfilment of the ideas of human rights.[19]

The declaration was like a call for socialists worldwide to make their presence felt everywhere human rights were being flouted.

Heeding this call, the Socialist Group put the protection of human rights, within and outside the EC, on the top of its work programme of 1978.[20] Moreover, the group started to discuss the term and concept of human rights. For doing so, a written draft on the definition of human rights by the groups' member John Prescott, a British member of the European Parliament (MEP), served as a basis for exchange. Prescott's written draft followed the commonly used distinction between fundamental rights and fundamental freedoms. It listed personal and public freedoms and categorized human rights into economic, social, cultural, civil and political rights. As absolute human rights in the highest sense of the word, it named the right to life, the right to freedom and the right to security.[21] Although the group's concerns for human rights reach back to the 1960s,[22] its discussion of the definition of human rights as well as its prioritization of human rights atop of its working agenda demonstrate that the group began to prioritize human rights issues in the second half of the 1970s. Moreover, this is also evident in the groups' various engagements for strengthening human rights, such as its advocacy for the EC's accession to the European Convention of Human Rights in that period.[23]

From its outset, the Socialist Group paid close attention to the developments of the CSCE conference, taking place mainly in Helsinki and starting two years before the Final Acts in mid-1975. In May 1972, the group assigned its member Lucien Radoux, a Belgian MEP, to participate in the conference.[24] In the Parliament's Committee for Political Affairs, the group succeeded in securing Radoux as the EP's rapporteur on the CSCE conference negotiations. Radoux's report and the corresponding resolution on the CSCE conference outcome did not specifically address human rights.[25] This was quite different, however, in Radoux's report and motion for a resolution on the CSCE follow-up conference, taking place mainly in Belgrade from 1977 to 1979. This time Radoux made human rights central to his report.[26] The report's corresponding motion for a resolution from May 1978, which the EP plenary adopted without any changes, stated that the EP

> Notes with deep concerns that certain of the preoccupations expressed by the Governments of the nine member states of the European Community concerning the human dimension of the Final Act were not reflected in the final document as they should have been, notably as regards respect for human rights and fundamental freedoms, including freedom of thought, of conscience, of religion or conviction.[27]

One year earlier, in April 1977, the Socialist Group's German chairman Ludwig Fellermaier and Helmut Sieglerschmidt, another German socialist MEP, had tabled a motion for a resolution on the protection of human rights. Referring to the CSCE Final Act, their text demanded that 'it is essential to achieve a real improvement in the position of those whose basic rights and basic freedoms are being violated'.[28] With Radoux's second CSCE report and the motion for a resolution by Fellermaier and Sieglerschmidt, the Socialist Group significantly contributed to keeping the issue of human rights protection in Europe high on the EP's agenda. On Fellermaier and Sieglerschmidt's motion for a resolution, the Christian-Democratic Group, the Liberal Group, the European Conservative Group and the Group of European Progressive Democrats jointly reacted with their own resolution on the protection of human rights in Europe.[29] However, the Socialist Group did not achieve the appointment of a socialist MEP for drafting a report on the protection and defence of human rights. This important report, following the two motions for a resolution, was written by the British liberal MEP, Russel Johnston.[30]

Outside Europe, the Socialist Group was preoccupied with human rights issues in Latin America. In January 1976, for example, group member Ole Espersen, a Danish MEP, visited Chile to explore the imprisonment and torture of opponents by the military junta of General Augusto Pinochet.[31] Furthermore, the group addressed human rights violations of the civic-military regime in Uruguay. Just before the regime's coup d'etat in June 1973, the EC had signed a trade agreement with the southern American country. Therefore, the Socialist Group put pressure on the European Commission to take action by tabling an oral question to it in May 1976 on the EC/Uruguay relations and pointing to the high numbers of political prisoners mistreated by the Uruguayan police.[32] Likewise, following atrocities of the Idi Amin regime in Uganda, a signatory to the Lomé Convention, the Socialist Group's member Schelto Patijn, a Dutch MEP, addressed an oral question to the Commission in March 1977, asking what steps it is considering as a reaction to the happenings in the East African country.[33] In fact, cases of human rights violations in Uruguay and in Uganda, as countries contractually bound with the EC, were an important push for debates on the introduction of human rights provisions into EC trade agreements, such as the Lomé II Convention, which will be the centre of the next section.

Shaping the negotiations on the Lomé II Convention

The first Lomé Convention of 1975 between the EC and the ACP states marked an important step towards a more coherent EC development cooperation policy vis-à-vis a part of the world's developing countries.[34] Central provisions of the Lomé Convention covered free access for ACP products to the European markets without reciprocity, financial aid for the ACP from the European Development Fund and the European Investment Bank, and a system to stabilize export earnings (STABEX, from French Système de Stabilisation des Recettes d'Exportation) of the ACP states. The Lomé Convention was perceived as a revolutionary accomplishment at the time.[35] However, as mentioned earlier, it did not include specific provisions to terminate or suspend the convention in the case of human right violations.

The question of human rights in the countries of the Lomé Convention climbed higher and higher on the Socialist Group's agenda in the first half of 1977 due to a number of recent, serious violations of human rights in Lomé signatory countries like Uganda and Ethiopia. The Socialist Group did not have to discuss its position at length. In its view, provisions to ensure the respect for human rights in the ACP countries were an indispensable component for the new Lomé II Convention.[36] As the EP was not involved in any direct way in the negotiations, which were largely conducted by the EC and ACP ambassadors, the Socialist Group tried to enforce its position by making use of various policy-making channels and platforms.

When the group's bureau discussed the question of human rights in the ACP countries at its meeting in June 1977, it decided to refer the matter to the group's working party on cooperation and development.[37] The working group frequently invited guests to its informal meetings with the purpose of discussing issues of EC development aid policy and building up transnational network links with socialist politicians in middle- or high-ranking positions in the European Commission, in national governments or in the socialist opposition in other EC member states. In the working group, there was a particular interest in cooperating with the European Commissioner for Development and Cooperation, Claude Cheysson. Non-partisan but socialist-leaning, Cheysson became European Commissioner in April 1973. For the nomination of the new members of the European Commission, which took office in January 1977, François Mitterrand, party leader of the French Socialist Party, demanded the reappointment of Cheysson as European Commissioner. Cheysson had actually been a member of the French PS since 1974. Because of Mitterrand's support, he felt committed to work more closely with the French PS and its partners in the EC.[38] The networking of the working group on cooperation and development did not lead to a continuous informal contact with Cheysson. Nevertheless, it was sufficient to exchange views and to coordinate approaches and positions on the issue of introducing human rights provisions in the new Lomé Convention. Cheysson shared the Socialist Group's position, although he communicated somewhat more cautiously as European Commissioner and recommended in a memorandum to the EC that a reference to human rights should be introduced in the new convention.[39]

Two important platforms for the Socialist Group to shape the debate on the new Lomé Convention were the annual meetings of the ACP-EC Consultative Assembly and the Joint Committee meetings of the ACP-EC Consultative Assembly. Both platforms allowed the introduction of new policy issues into the debate and the establishment and maintenance of informal contacts with ACP representatives. At the annual meeting of the Consultative Assembly in Luxembourg in June 1977, for example, the Socialist Group's speaker, John Prescott, brought up the issue of human rights violation in participating states of the Lomé Convention. He set the scene by recalling the recent worldwide initiative on human rights by US President Jimmy Carter, the position taken by the EC on human rights at the CSCE Conference and the EC's refusal to consider applications for EC membership by countries in which human rights were not respected. He demanded that serious consideration should be given to include the obligation to respect human rights in the negotiations for the new convention.[40] His demand prepared the ground for further discussion of the issue at the meeting of the ACP-EC Joint Committee to take place in Maseru (Lesotho) at the end of 1977.

For this meeting, the Socialist Group's working party on development and cooperation primarily did the group's preparatory work. Of two main points of this work, one was devoted to the question of human rights in the countries of the Lomé Convention. At its meetings in October and November 1977, the working party prepared a resolution on the respect for human rights to be submitted to the ACP-EC Joint Committee's meeting. At a final preparatory meeting of all MEPs of the ACP-EC Joint Committee, however, the Christian-Democratic Group's members were critical of the submission of the Socialist Group's resolution. They argued that it would endanger the EP delegation's unity. It thus was agreed that the Socialist Group's resolution was to be submitted as a contribution to the work of the drafting group for the ACP-EC Joint Committee final declaration of the Maseru meeting.[41]

The meeting was of a more political character than former meetings of the ACP-EC Consultative Assembly. The question of human rights was brought up on the basis of the Socialist Group's resolution. Speaking on behalf of the Socialist Group, Johannes Broeksz, a Dutch MEP, emphasized that serious violations of human rights could not be accepted in any country. At the meeting, several Socialist Group members had informal exchanges with several representatives of ACP countries. Here too the question of human rights was addressed and discussed.[42] The ACP-EC Joint Committee meeting in Maseru turned out to be a success for the Socialist Group. Despite the opposition by representatives of some ACP countries, for example, Ethiopia and Uganda, the adopted declaration approved the upholding of human rights for inclusion into the new convention to be negotiated soon.[43] It stated that the respect for human rights 'must be given adequate expression in the new convention [...] in accordance with the Universal Declaration of Human Rights'.[44]

Preparing for the next ACP-EC Joint Committee meeting, taking place in Grenada from 29 May to 3 June 1978, the Socialist Group decided again to concentrate especially on the question of human rights in the convention. It was agreed that the group's members present at the meeting should adopt a position in line with the decision on human rights taken at the ACP-EC Joint Committee's meeting in Maseru. The group appointed Broeksz as spokesman on the issue.[45] At the meeting, the ACP representatives showed themselves willing to discuss further the issue of human rights obligations in the new convention. They linked human rights with migrant working conditions in the EC states.[46] Nevertheless, especially due to opposition by Ethiopia and Uganda, it was not possible to agree on repeating in the meeting's final declaration the paragraph of the Maseru meeting's Final Declaration suggesting the introduction of a reference to human rights in the new convention. The Final Declaration of the ACP-EC Joint Committee meeting in Grenada only recalled the will of the Lomé Convention partners to maintain and develop friendly relations in accordance with the principles of the United Nations Charter. In the Socialist Group's view, this was a step backwards.[47] Moreover, it was not a good omen for the formal renegotiations of the convention to start only a couple of weeks later in July 1978.

While the formal renegotiations were on-going, the Socialist Group held an exchange of views on the stage reached in the negotiations at the group's study days in Constance (Germany) in early September 1978.[48] The nine EC member states were somewhat divided on the issue of human rights. While Britain and the Netherlands were in favour of including a legally enforceable provision, Germany and France took a reluctant position on the matter.[49] Arguing that the Lomé Convention was above all an economic agreement, the ACP states were against any human rights reference in the new convention.[50] Not surprisingly, in their exchange of views, the Socialist Group's members paid special attention to human rights. The basis for their exchange was the EP's report on the negotiations for the new Lomé Convention drawn up on behalf of the Committee on Development and Cooperation.[51] As rapporteur for this report, the Socialist Group was able to secure the appointment of Broeksz. Outlining his draft at the group's study days, Broeksz 'dwelt in particular on the inclusion in the Lomé Convention of certain legal provisions authorising the use of sanctions in the event of flagrant violations of human rights'.[52] The following discussion among the group's members mirrored the positions of the EC member states. Edgar Pisani, a French MEP in 1978–9 and European Commissioner for Development Cooperation and Humanitarian Aid from 1981 to 1985, explained that the Lomé Convention should be concerned only with the possibilities of concerted planning and to foster development between the EC and ACP states, as the EC's role was not to judge on the ACP states' domestic affairs. In contrast, the British representative Prescott suggested that, in the case of human rights violations in the ACP states, aid provided for under the convention should be withheld, but this withholding should be directed at the government and not at the people of the country concerned. He furthermore said that the group had to decide whether it wished for a pure trade agreement or to give the Lomé Convention a political character by including in its text the preamble of the United Nations Declaration on Human Rights.[53]

The upcoming ACP-EC Consultative Assembly's annual meeting at the end of September 1978 was one of the last important opportunities to have a more direct influence on ACP representatives before the new convention's negotiations would go into their final phase. Therefore, the decision whether the group wanted to maintain Prescott's previous course of action was pivotal. Given that Prescott was selected as the group's spokesman at the annual meeting, it can be safely said that the group opted for continuing to strongly demand the inclusion of human rights provisions.

In fact, at the ACP-EC Consultative Assembly's annual meeting in Luxembourg from 27 to 29 September 1978, Prescott spoke at length on the issue of human rights, boldly demanding the inclusion of appropriate clauses in the new convention. He emphasized that there was a moral responsibility at every level to seek respect for human rights. In addition, he made clear that human rights provisions in the convention would apply to all participating states, the ACP and the European states.[54] However, Prescott's intervention did not help much. The ACP states' representatives maintained their opposition. Accordingly, a decision on the human rights question was adjourned,[55] and the debate was to be continued.

One of the best ways to further shape the debate was the EP's report on the renewal of the Lomé Convention, which Broeksz was appointed to draw up. When delivering his explanatory statement on the report in the EP plenary in December 1978, Broeksz addressed in particular the question on human rights. According to the Socialist Group's position, he was arguing in favour of introducing a reference to human rights in the new convention.[56] The plenary debate circled again and again around the question of human rights. However, the speakers of all groups expressed themselves rather reservedly on linking the EC's aid for the ACP states with human rights. Above all, there was a huge concern about sanctions in the case of human rights violations.[57] Finally, the adopted resolution only confirmed conformity with the report of the ACP-EC Consultative meeting of September 1978 that the question of a reference to human rights in the future convention should be approached again at a later stage.[58] The report was thus no great success for the Socialist Group in terms of influencing the debate within the EP towards the group's position that human rights should be an indispensable component for the new Lomé II Convention.

All in all, the Socialist Group's engagement in anchoring human rights in the Lomé II Convention was not a great success story. The ACP-EC Joint Committee declaration of Maseru, resting upon the Socialist Group's resolution and upholding human rights for inclusion into the new convention, was only an empty promise. The ACP-EC Joint Committee meeting's Grenada declaration greatly watered it down. In addition, a resolution of the ACP Council of Ministers from December 1977 had already emphasized that the Lomé Convention was an economic agreement and therefore provided no place for human rights.[59] The EP's report drafted by the socialist MEP Broeksz appeared at a tactically good moment in the course of the debate, shortly before the ACP-EC Consultative Assembly's meeting in February 1979 and formal renegotiations entered a more political phase. However, the report did not include a strong demand for a reference to human rights. Without much surprise, the final declaration of ACP-EC Consultative Assembly's February 1979 meeting did not entail any mention of human rights nor a statement to bring up the issue in the remaining negotiations.[60] Eventually, the formal renegotiations ended with a text for the Lomé II Convention with no reference to human rights. Despite this actual outcome, the Socialist Group's engagement cannot be called completely unsuccessful. As this section has shown, the Socialist Group kept the issue of human rights provision on the ACP/EC agenda and shaped the discourse surrounding it, thus providing the ground for the later renegotiation rounds.

'Football Yes, Torture No': The Socialist Group's public hearing on human rights violations in Argentina

The Argentinian FIFA World Cup, occurring around two years after the Argentinian military right-wing coup and its violent repression of critics, was described then by many sports and political observers as the most political in FIFA's history up to date.[61] The German journalist Erich Laser, for example, pointed out that such a broad discussion of the political situation of a country organizing a major sporting event had never previously taken place.[62] In particular, the discussion addressed human rights violations in Argentina. Numerous non-governmental organizations (NGOs) launched initiatives to inform the public in Western European countries about the human rights violations in Argentina and to counter the political propaganda the military regime was making of the World Cup.

The issue was initially a rather limited priority on the EP's agenda. In view of the upcoming World Cup in summer 1978, however, the EP's debate on human rights violations in the country became more intense in the first half of 1978. In that respect, Georg Ismar has rightly argued that European interest in news on political situations in South American countries increases with the multiplying factor of football. In that sense, football contributed to raising the issue of human rights violations in Argentina higher on the EP's agenda. Given its tendency to be preoccupied with human rights violations in Latin America, the Socialist Group had a particularly great interest in the issue.[63]

In December 1977, three MEPs from the Socialist Group and two MEPs from the Christian-Democratic Group tabled a motion for a resolution on violations of human rights in Argentina. Referring to 20,000 to 30,000 political prisoners and disappeared persons, the motion for a resolution stated that the government of the EC member states should 'propose that the World Cup Football Competition should not be held in Argentina next summer unless the government of the country gives the necessary guarantees that the physical integrity of all persons will be respected, in particular that of imprisoned because of their opinions and of those whose political beliefs have led to their disappearance'.[64] However, this motion for a resolution failed to obtain majority support in the EP.

A few weeks later, in early March 1978, the Socialist Group's bureau approved a proposal by Prescott calling the EP's Political Affair Committee for a public hearing to be held on the question of the respect for human rights in Argentina.[65] Based on the recommendations for such a public hearing by Prescott, the Political Affairs Committee agreed unanimously, with three abstentions, to hold a public hearing that should help to investigate human rights violations and the disappearance of around 100 EC citizens in Argentina. Scheduled for 25 May 1978, and thus only a couple of days before the start of the World Cup, the purpose of the public hearing was to invite international participants to speak on the Argentinean regime's record on human rights while the country was the focus of international attention as the host of this major sporting event. The idea for the public hearing followed the example of several NGOs informing the Western European public of human rights violations in Argentina by various initiatives and countering the Argentinian political propaganda about the World Cup.[66]

Crucially, the Political Affairs Committee's projected public hearing on human rights violations in Argentina was historically important, as the very first EP public hearing not dealing with an issue of EC competences. In view of the upcoming 1978 World Cup, the Political Affairs Committee considered the public hearing to be politically necessary for the following reasons: first, to uncover the details of human rights violations in Argentina; second, to draw European and international public attention to human rights violations in the South American country; third, to react to the Argentinian regime's misuse of its position as host of the World Cup to disguise its human rights violations; and fourth, to put the Argentinian authorities under pressure to stop the human rights violations.[67]

In order to pressure for a positive decision, Prescott and the Socialist Group's chairman Fellermaier tabled on behalf of the Socialist Group at the beginning of May 1978 a motion for a resolution with a request for an urgent debate. Referring to 20,000 to 30,000 political prisoners and 8,000 disappeared people, it demanded that the Political Affairs Committee hold a public hearing on 25 May 1978, as was unanimously recommended by that committee, to investigate further and in more detail the human rights violations in Argentina.[68] When the issue was up for debate in the EP's plenary only two days later, there was a discussion that such a public hearing would set a precedent for debating human rights violations worldwide, but that this would be technically impossible for the EP from the point of view of debating time.[69] Moreover, the Cold War strongly affected the dispute between the political groups on the issue. Those who condemned the right-wing Argentinian regime were criticized two years later for remaining silent on human rights violations in communist Eastern Europe and for not demanding a boycott of the Olympic Games to be held in Moscow in summer 1980.[70]

Anticipating that several other political groups would vote against the motion for a resolution, Fellermaier requested the Socialist Group's members to attend the vote on the motion for a resolution in large numbers.[71] Nevertheless, it happened, as Fellermaier had feared. The MEPs from the Christian-Democratic Group, the European Conservative Group and the Group of European Progressive Democrats blocked a positive vote for holding a public hearing. The public hearing thus not authorized by the EP's Bureau and without funding, the Socialist Group decided to use its own funds to organize a public hearing on the violations of human rights in Argentina shortly before the start of the World Cup.[72]

Figure 6.1 Protesters in Paris. Several thousands of people demonstrated on 31 May 1978 in Paris to protest against the organization of the FIFA World Cup in Argentina for the blatant violations of human rights occurring there. The European Parliament was not immune to these concerns and jumped in on the campaign linking the respect of human rights and mega sports events.

To prepare for the public hearing, the Socialist Group had already held a meeting with representatives of the NGO Amnesty International, which was awarded the Nobel Peace Prize for its work in 1977.[73] Amnesty did not call for a boycott of the World Cup, but instead requested that footballers, officials and supporters take the opportunity of the World Cup to draw attention to the political situation in Argentina. For example, Amnesty demanded the German Football Association (Deutscher Fußball Bund, DFB) to stand up against Argentinian human rights violations while participating in the World Cup.[74] The Amnesty campaign slogan was 'Football Yes, Torture No', which was also adopted by the Socialist Group as the motto for the public hearing. Furthermore, at a press conference announcing the public hearing, Fellermaier emphasized, echoing Amnesty International's policy strategy, the importance of holding a public hearing on the violations of human rights in Argentina at a time when public opinion was focused on the country as the World Cup host. Furthermore, he said, 'In a country where so many people cannot raise their voices, we feel as European politicians that it is important we should tell the people of Europe what the reverse of the sunny Argentinian coin is: it is very bloody indeed.'[75]

On the day the public hearing took place, 25 May 1978, press, radio and television correspondents were given free access to the meeting. Furthermore, representatives of all the EP's major political groups of the time were present. Talks concentrated mainly on the following topics: the disappearance of thousands of Argentinian citizens over a period of years; the imprisonment of Argentinian citizens without warrant, trial or sentence; the use of torture; and the disappearance and imprisonment of over a hundred citizens from EC member states. Evidence at the public hearing was given, for example, by Dr Solari Yrigoyen, a former Argentinian senator, and Wilson Ferreira, a former Uruguayan senator, who both suffered imprisonment and torture in Argentina, and by Father Patrick Rice, an Irish citizen, who suffered a similar fate. Lord Avebury, who led the Amnesty delegation to Argentina, and Tricia Feeney, the head of Amnesty's Latin American Research Department, spoke on their findings and experiences in Argentina. Moreover, Christopher Dodd, a member of the US Congress, called for several specific actions that parliamentarians of various countries might consider with regard to Argentina. Finally, Prescott made a specific appeal to the Argentinian regime to release the chair of the human rights movement in Argentina, who had been in prison for a considerable time.[76] The Argentinian government was not invited to participate in the public hearing because of its refusal to cooperate with Amnesty, or any other body, on the issue of human rights in the country.[77]

Obviously, the Socialist Group's public hearing did not end human rights violations in Argentina. Nevertheless, it had three pivotal effects. First, the public hearing on human rights violations in Argentina generated great media interest in Western Europe. All main daily newspapers in the core EC member states published reports on the speakers' statements. In fact, the opposition of the Christian-Democratic Group, the European Conservative Group and the Group of European Progressive Democrats to holding the public hearing had contributed to get broad media attention. Moreover, the great media presence at the public hearing helped to draw attention to the EP itself, which was then an often-ignored European institution.

Second, the Argentinian authorities reacted to the public hearing, with the Argentinian military government protesting strongly even before the hearing took place. In the course of the public hearing, Prescott and others called for the release of the leader of the Argentinian human rights movement, who was freed by the Argentinian authorities just one day after the public hearing. In addition, after the public hearing took place, the Argentinian regime confirmed the imprisonment of approximately 500 previously 'missing' persons.[78] It can therefore be argued that the EP's public hearing successfully contributed to pressuring the Argentinian regime into this release.

Third, on the basis of the declarations made during the public hearing, the EP adopted a resolution on 6 July 1978 on violations of human rights in Argentina, as well as on the procedure to be followed in the future by the EP to combat such violations throughout the world.[79] Prescott had prepared the accompanying report. A couple of days after the end of the World Cup, the resolution requested 'the Foreign Ministers of the member states meeting in political cooperation, the Commission and the Council urgently to take all appropriate measures to bring about an improvement in the situation as regards the respect of human rights and democratic freedom in Argentina'.[80] In addition, the resolution announced that the EP would 'consider the further use of public hearings in order to inform the citizens of the Community and the world about the breaches of fundamental human rights wherever they occur'. This intention consequently provided the grounds for further public hearings in the EP on human rights violations worldwide. In February 2014, for example, the EP's

Figure 6.2 German Social-Democrat Willy Brandt and German Chancellor Helmut Schmidt in a meeting of the German Social Democratic Party during the campaign for the European elections in 1979. Brandt was among the firmest proponent of a strong European voice for human rights in the world.

Subcommittee on Human Rights held a public hearing on the situation of migrant workers in the construction of football stadiums for the 2022 Qatar World Cup.[81] This and other public hearings of the EP follow a tradition that largely originated in the Socialist Group's public hearing regarding the 1978 World Cup in Argentina.

Conclusion

As this chapter demonstrates, the Socialist Group developed a strong profile in human rights protection in the second half of the 1970s. Given its challenges as a transnational actor with differing approaches to human right policies by the socialist parties and governments at the national level, the group was generally able to adopt a single line. On this basis, the Socialist Group could successfully put and keep issues of human rights protections on the EP and the EC agenda in the second half of the 1970s, as the two special cases of the public hearing on human rights violations in Argentina and the introduction of human rights provision in the Lomé II Convention clearly show. Moreover, as the latter case especially demonstrates, the Socialist Group could shape debates on human rights concerns in the EP and beyond, thereby turning issues of human rights into a central item of the debate on the convention's renegotiations in the EP, the ACP-EC Consultative Assembly and the EC, and among the EC member states.

Therefore, although the Socialist Group was not always successful in pushing through its agendas for human rights protection, it was a driving force developing the EP into a champion of human rights in the second half of the 1970s. Clearly, the Socialist

Group did not take the lead in all important EP reports with regard to human rights, which contributed to establishing this image of the EP. However, the fair distribution of reports and the cross-party support for these reports show a main characteristic of the EP in the 1970s. At this time, the EP's formal powers and official policy remits were still very limited. Topics with great attention such as human rights were an ideal playground for the EP to extend its agenda and increase its say in EC policy-making by establishing itself as a champion of human rights.[82] However, the example of the public hearing on human rights violations in Argentina, which the Socialist Group finally staged alone, shows that cross-party cooperation in the EP due to the Cold War situation was not naturally given and sometimes not possible to achieve.

Willy Brandt, with whom this chapter started, became a MEP and thus a member of the Socialist Group himself after the EP's first direct election in 1979. One of his few oral interventions in an EP plenary session concerned the second follow-up meeting of the CSCE conference, which started in Madrid in November 1980. Shortly before the start of this CSCE meeting, Brandt criticized in an EP plenary debate that some of the CSCE participating states countries were using humanitarian easing of restrictions for tactical manoeuvring.[83] In his view, human rights should not only serve as an accessory. Thus, as a MEP himself, Brandt worked on the human rights agenda he once had called out as SI president for all socialist parties and their transnational organization.

Notes

1 International Institute for Social History, Amsterdam (hereinafter IISH), Socialist International Archives (hereinafter SIA), 264, Willy Brandt, Inaugural speech, Geneva, 26 November 1976.
2 Throughout this chapter, the term 'socialist' is used for all Western European socialist and social democratic parties.
3 See, e.g. Andreas Wilkens, 'Der «Andere Deutsche» im Blick von außen. Zur Perzeption Willy Brandts zu seiner Zeit und in der heutigen Erinnerungskultur', in *Willy Brandt. Neue Fragen, neue Erkenntnisse*, ed. Berndt Rother (Bonn: Dietz, 2011), 54–84, here 54.
4 Berndt Rother and Wolfgang Schmidt, 'Einleitung. Über Europa hinaus. Dritte Welt und Sozialistische Internationale', in *Willy Brandt, Berliner Ausgabe*, vol. 8, ed. Helga Grebing, Gregor Schöllgen and Heinrich A. Winkler (Bonn: Dietz, 2006), 15–107, here 29.
5 Jan Eckel, 'The Rebirth of Politics from the Spirit of Morality: Explaining the Human Rights Revolution of the 1970s', in *The Breakthrough. Human Rights in the 1970s*, ed. Jan Eckel and Samuel Moyn (Philadelphia: University of Philadelphia Press, 2014), 235.
6 Antonio Varsori and Guia Migani, 'Introduction', in *Europe in the International Arena during the 1970s: Entering a Different World*, ed. Id. (Brussels: Peter Lang, 2011), 15–26.
7 Christian Salm, *Transnational Socialist Networks in the 1970s, European Community Development Aid and Southern Enlargement* (Basingstoke: Palgrave Macmillan, 2016), 3.
8 Víctor Fernández Soriano, 'Facing the Greek junta: The European Community, the Council of Europe and the rise of human-rights in Europe', *European Review of History: Revue européene d'histoire*, 24 (2017): 364ff.

9 Samuel Moyn, *The Last Utopia: Human Rights in History* (Cambridge, MA: Harvard University Press, 2010); Eckel and Moyn, *The Breakthrough*, 226–59, here 235; Stefan-Ludwig Hoffmann, *Geschichte der Menschenrechte – ein Rückblick* (Berlin: Suhrkamp, 2020).
10 Aurélie É. Gfeller, 'Champion of Human Rights: The European Parliament and the Helsinki Process', *Journal of Contemporary History*, 49 (2014): 390–409. On how the EP promoted human rights in order to push the EC to develop an innovative European foreign policy, see Umberto Tulli, 'The European Parliament, the Single European Act and the (partial) Institutionalization of EPC', *Journal of European Integration History*, 27 (2021): 121–38.
11 See Meno Kamminga, 'Human Rights and the Lomé Conventions', *Netherlands Quarterly of Human Rights*, 7 (1989): 28–35, here 28.
12 Sara B. Snyder, 'Bringing the Transnational In: Writing Human Rights into the International History of the Cold War', *Diplomacy & Statecraft*, 24 (2013): 100–16.
13 Andreas von Gehlen, *Europäische Parteiendemokratie? Institutionelle Voraussetzungen und Funktionsbedingungen der europäischen Parteien zur Minderung des Legitimationsdefizits der EU* (PhD diss., Berlin: Free University Berlin, 2005) 191.
14 Historical Archives of the European Union (hereinafter HAEU), Group du Parti socialiste européen du Parlement européen (hereinafter GPSE), 647, Note for the attention of members of the Socialist Group, Re: Organisation and distribution of duties of the Secretariat – Annex I. The role and functioning of the Secretariat, Luxembourg, 13 June 1979.
15 HAEU, GPSE, 643, Rules of Procedure of the Socialist Group in the European Parliament, Luxembourg, 4 March 1977.
16 HAEU, GPSE, 643, Note for the members of the Socialist Group, Subject: Item 9 of the agenda of the meeting of the Socialist Group in Paris on 2 and 3 March 1977 – Communication on the work progress of the Working Party on Development Policy Problems, Brussels, 18 February 1977.
17 HAEU, GPSE, 647, Summary of decisions taken by the Socialist Group, Brussels, 18–21 September 1979.
18 For a recent account on the CSCE and human rights, see Nicolas Badalassi and Sarah B. Snyder, eds, *The CSCE and the End of the Cold War, Diplomacy, Societies and Human Rights, 1972-1990* (New York: Berghahn, 2019).
19 The Danish Labour Movement's Library and Archives (DLMLA) Copenhagen, Socialist International, 1107, Socialist International, General Circular No. G1/78: Statement by the Socialist International Party Leaders Conference Tokyo, 17–19 December 1977, 9 January 1978.
20 HAEU, GPSE, 645, Note for the attention of members of the Socialist Group, Re: Examination of a revised and up-dated work programme of the Socialist Group, Luxembourg, 2 May 1978.
21 HAEU, GPSE, 646, Note for the attention of members of the Socialist Group, Definition of Human Rights, Luxembourg, 11 August 1978.
22 HAEU, GPSE, 646, The work of the Socialist Group in the European Parliament, Report to the 10th Congress of the Confederation of the Socialist Parties of the European Community, by Ludwig Fellermaier, Chairman of the Socialist Group of the European Parliament.
23 HAEU, GPSE, 649, Activities of the Socialist Group at the European Parliament, Report presented to the 11th Congress of the Confederation of the Socialist Parties of

the European Community, by Ernest Glinne, Chairman of the Socialist Group of the European Parliament.

24 HAEU, GPSE, 634, Projet de procès-verbal de la réunion du Bureau du Groupe socialiste du 25 mai 1972 à Pau, Luxembourg, le 32 mai 1972.

25 Historical Archives of the European Parliament (hereinafter HAEP), European Parliament (EP), Document 485/74, Report drawn up on behalf of the Political Affairs Committee on the Conference on Security and Cooperation in Europe (CSCE), Rapporteur: Mr L. Radoux, 21 February 1975.

26 HAEP, EP, Document 76/78, Report drawn up on behalf of the Political Affairs Committee on the outcome of the Belgrade meeting as provided for by Final Act of the Helsinki Conference on Security and Cooperation in Europe, Rapporteur: Mr L. Radoux, 3 May 1978.

27 Resolution on the outcome of the Belgrade meeting as provided for by the Final Act of the Helsinki Conference on Security and Cooperation in Europe, *Official Journal of the European Communities (OJ)*, No C 131/46, 5 June 1978.

28 HAEP, EP, Document 60/77, Motion for a Resolution tabled by Mr Fellermaier and Mr Sieglerschmidt on behalf of the Socialist Group pursuant to Rule 25 of the Rules of Procedure on the protection of human rights, 20 April 1977.

29 HAEP, EP, Document 62/77, Motion for a Resolution tabled by Mr A. Bertrand on behalf of the Christian-Democratic Group, Mr Bangemann on behalf of the Liberal and Democratic Group, Mr Rivierez on behalf of the Group of European Progressive Democrats, Lord Reay on behalf of the European Conservative Group pursuant to Rule 25 of the Rules of Procedure on the protection of human rights throughout the world, 20 April 1977.

30 HAEP, EP, Document 62/77, Report drawn up on behalf of the Political Affairs Committee on the protection and defence of human rights, Rapporteur: Mr R. Johnston, 10 May 1978.

31 HAEU, GPSE, 641, Confidential report by Ole Espersen to the Socialist Group of the European Parliament on a visit to Chile, 25 January to 30 January 1976.

32 HAEP, EP, Document 77/76, Question orale (0-7/76) avec débat conformément à l'article 47 du Règlement de MM. Glinne, Knud Nielsen, Broeksz et Walkhoff, au nom du Groupe Socialiste à la Commission des Communautés européennes. Object : Relations entre l'Uruguay et la Communauté, 5 May 1976.

33 HAEP, EP, Questions orales conformément à l'article 47 bis du Règlement à la Commission des Communautés européennes l'Heure des Questions du 9 et 10 mars 1977, Question de M. Patijn (H-306/76), Object: Relations CEE-Ouganda, 25 February 1977.

34 See Cosgrove Twitchett, *Europe and Africa: From Association to Partnership* (Farnborough: Saxon House, 1978), 148.

35 Lotte Drieghe and Jan Orbie, 'Revolution in Time of Eurosclerosis: The Case of the First Lomé Convention', *L' Europe en formation*, 50 (2009): 167–81.

36 HAEU, GPSE, 646, The work of the Socialist Group in the European Parliament, Report to the Xth Congress of the Confederation of the Socialist Parties of the European Community, by Ludwig Fellermaier, Chairman of the Socialist Group of the European Parliament.

37 HAEU, GPSE, 644, Draft minutes of the meeting of the Bureau of the Socialist Group on 28 June 1977 in Brussels, PE/GS/173/77.

38 DLMLA, Sammenslutningen af the socialdemokratiske partie i Europæiske Fællesskab, 1204, Vermerk Dröscher über ein Gespräch mit Mitgliedern der Europäischen Kommission am 4. Januar in Brüssel, 6 January 1977.

39 See Amy Young-Anawaty, 'Human Rights and the ACP-EEC Lomé II Convention: Business as Usual at the EEC', *New York University Journal of International Politics*, 13 (1980): 83.
40 HAEP, ACP-EEC Consultative Assembly, Second Annual Meeting, Summary Report of the Proceedings of 8, 9 and 10 June 1977.
41 HAEU, GPSE, 645, Note for the members of the Socialist Group, Report on the meeting of the Joint Committee of the Consultative Assembly of the Convention of Lomé (ACP-EEC) of 28 November–1 December 1977 in Maseru (Lesotho).
42 Ibid.
43 Karin Arts, *Integrating Human Rights into Development Cooperation: The Case of the Lomé Convention* (The Hague: Kluwer Law International, 2000), 169.
44 Cited in ibid.
45 HAEU, GPSE, 646, Record of the meeting of the members of the Socialist Group in preparation for the meeting of the ACP-EEC Joint Committee in Grenada on 29 May 1978.
46 See, e.g. Young-Anawaty, 'Human Rights', 85, 86.
47 HAEU, GPSE, 646, Note for the attention of members of the Socialist Group, Definition of Human Rights, Luxembourg, 11 August 1978.
48 HAEU, GPSE, 646, Minutes of the meeting of the Socialist Group during the study days held in Konstanz from 5 to 7 September 1978.
49 See, e.g. Lorenzo Ferrari, *Sometimes Speaking with a Single Voice: The European Community as an International Actor* (Brussels: PIE Peter Lang, 2016), 194.
50 See, e.g. Young-Anawaty, 'Human Rights', 87.
51 HAEU, GPSE, 646, Notice to Members of the Socialist Group, Subject: Item 9 on the agenda for the Socialist Group's meeting in Constance from 5 to 7 September, Draft report on the negotiations for the renewal of the Conventions of Lomé, Luxembourg, 24 July 1978.
52 HAEU, GPSE, 646, Minutes of the meeting of the Socialist Group during the study days held in Konstanz from 5 to 7 September 1978.
53 Ibid.
54 HAEP, ACP-EEC Consultative Assembly, Second Annual Meeting, Summary Report of the Proceedings of 27, 28 and 29 September.
55 See, e.g. Young-Anawaty, 'Human Rights', 88.
56 HAEP, The Committee on Development and Cooperation unanimously adopted the report and the associated motion for a resolution. European Parliament, Document 487/78, Report drawn up on behalf of the Committee on Development and Cooperation on the negotiations for a new Lomé Convention, 1 December 1978.
57 HAEP, Debate on Renewal of Lomé Convention, Sitting of Wednesday, 13 December 1978.
58 Resolution on the negotiations for the renewal of the Convention of Lomé, *OJ*, No C 6/56, 8 January 1979.
59 See, e.g. Young-Anawaty, 'Human Rights', 83.
60 Ibid., 90.
61 This section derives in parts from Christian Salm, 'Major Sporting Events versus Human Rights: Parliament's Position on the 1978 FIFA World Cup in Argentina and the 1980 Moscow Olympics', *EPRS Briefing – European Parliament History Series*, PE 563.519 (2018).
62 Erich Laaser, *Die Fußballweltmeisterschaft 1978 in der Tagespresse der Bundesrepublik Deutschland* (Berlin: Volker Spies, 1980), 62.

63 Georg Ismar, 'Der Ballsport im Dienst der eigenen Sache. Politisierung des Fußballs in Südamerika', in *Das Spiel mit dem Fußball. Interessen, Projektionen und Vereinnahmung*, ed. Jürgen Mittag and Jörg-Uwe Nieland (Essen: Klartext, 2007), 240.
64 HAEP, EP, Document 456/77, Motion for a resolution tabled by Bertrand A., Glinne E., Granneli L., Schmidt H., Zagari M., pursuant to Rule 25 of the Rules of Procedure on certain violations of human rights in Argentina, 23 December 1977.
65 HAEU, GPSE, 645, Bureau draft minutes of the meeting of the Bureau of the Socialist Group of 7 and 8 March 1978 in The Hague.
66 HAEP, EP, Minutes of the Political Affairs Committee meeting of 21 and 22 March 1978.
67 HAEP, Debates of the European Parliament, No 230, Session Report of Proceedings from 8 to 12 May 1978, 172ff.
68 HAEP, EP, Document 109/78, Motion for a resolution tabled by Mr Fellermaier and Mr Prescott on behalf of the Socialist Group with the request for urgent debate pursuant to Rule 14 of the Rules of Procedure on certain violations of human rights in Argentina, 8 May 1978.
69 HAEP, Debates of the European Parliament, No 230, Session Report of Proceedings from 8 to 12 May 1978.
70 On the political debates in Western Europe on the boycott of the 1980 Olympic Games in Moscow, see Umberto Tulli, 'Bringing Human Rights In: The Campaign Against the 1980 Moscow Olympic Games and the Origins of the Nexus Between Human Rights and the Olympic Games', *The International Journal of the History of Sports*, 33 (2017): 2026–45.
71 HAEU, GPSE, 645, Note for the attention of Members of the Socialist Group, Subject: Vote on the resolution on Argentina, 11 May 1978.
72 HAEU, GPSE, 645, Bureau draft minutes of the meeting of the Bureau of the Socialist Group held on 10 May 1978 in Strasbourg, 23 May 1978.
73 HAEU, GPSE, 645, Bureau draft minutes of the meeting of the Bureau of the Socialist Group on 12 April 1978, 13 April 1978.
74 Nils Havemann, *Samstags um halb 4 Die Geschichte der Fußballbundesliga* (Munich: Sielder, 2014), 248.
75 'Europe's Football Hooligans can Expect Heavy Penalties in Argentina, Labour MP Advices', *The Times*, 23 May 1978.
76 HAEU, GPSE, 645, Documentation for a public hearing on the violation of human rights in Argentina, 18 May 1978.
77 'Fußball-WM im Land eines Terror-Regimes. Hearing in Brüssel: In Argentinien wird gefoldert – Käsemann beschuldigt deutsche Behörden', *Süddeutsche Zeitung*, 26 May 1978.
78 HAEP, EP, Document 200/78, Report drawn up on behalf of the Political Affairs Committee on violations of human rights in Argentina (Doc. 456/77) and on the procedures to be followed in the European Parliament to combat such violations throughout the world, Rapporteur: Mr J. Prescott, 3 July 1978.
79 Resolution on violations of human rights in Argentina and on the procedure to be followed in the European Parliament to combat such violations throughout the world, *OJ*, No C 182/42, 31 July 1978.
80 Ibid.
81 EP, Subcommittee on Human Rights. Hearing on sport and human rights focusing on the situation of migrant workers in Qatar, https://www.europarl.europa.eu/cmsdata/64622/att_20140211ATT79166-3535033103333604899.pdf (accessed 2 December 2020).

82 Kiran K. Patel and Christian Salm, 'The European Parliament during the 1970s and 1980s: An Institution on the Rise?', *Journal of European Integration History*, 27 (2021): 5–20.
83 HAEP, Debate on CSCE Madrid follow-up conference, Sitting of Wednesday, 15 October 1980.

7

An awkward partner?

Britain's human rights policy and EC relations, 1977–9

David Grealy

David Owen, who was appointed as UK Foreign and Commonwealth Secretary on 21 February 1977 following the death of Anthony Crosland, wasted little time in placing a concern for human rights at the heart of British foreign policy, stating during his first major speech that Britain would take a 'stand on human rights in every corner of the globe'.[1] The elevation of the human rights dimension within British diplomacy duly became a major issue during Owen's tenure as Foreign Secretary between 1977 and 1979, shaping the response of Jim Callaghan's Labour government to a multiplicity of foreign policy dilemmas.[2] Owen was perhaps the most vocal champion of the moralistic approach to foreign affairs advanced by US President Jimmy Carter to be found in any Western capital. The pursuit of common objectives in the human rights field, moreover, served to situate the Callaghan government shoulder-to-shoulder with the Carter administration, thus facilitating the continued rapprochement between the two nations following a subtle downgrading of the so-called special relationship during the early 1970s. Within the European Community (EC), however, Owen's enthusiastic endorsement of Carter's foreign policy outlook only exacerbated the transatlantic tensions that had been developing on account of Carter's management of the human rights issue within the context of the East–West dialogue. Carter's stance on human rights caused a significant degree of consternation within the Community, with member states sensing that the President's human rights crusade – and by extension, Owen's – could disrupt détente and stymie continental cooperation between the East and the West.

By examining these triangulations, this chapter will situate hitherto neglected British diplomatic perspectives within the vast historiography on the human rights 'breakthrough' of the 1970s, further our understanding of how Carter's diplomacy was viewed within Western governments, and highlight the intricate dynamics that inhibited the development of a united European approach to international human rights promotion during this pivotal juncture.[3] It will also contribute to timely conversations concerning Britain's complex relationship with the European Union and its forebears. Indeed, the Callaghan government's attempts to reconcile its promotion of human rights internationally with its efforts to develop UK–EC relations do not sit comfortably alongside conventional narratives of British (or, for that matter, Labour Party) Euroscepticism. In some respects, the government's position on human rights served to reinforce Britain's reputation as a reluctant participant in the European project. Following David Owen's amplification of Britain's human rights policy, for instance, it is possible to observe a fundamental alteration of the UK's approach to the related issues of human rights promotion, EC relations and the Conference on Security and Cooperation in Europe (CSCE). Whereas British representatives had, both leading up to and following the signing of the Helsinki Final Act in 1975, tended to regard the human rights issue as supplementary to the more pressing objective of facilitating European cooperation within the CSCE, Owen's initiative saw to it that human rights promotion became much more identifiable as an end unto itself, irrespective of whether this stance would cause discord within the Community. The government's prolonged and ultimately unsuccessful attempts to introduce human rights provisions within the renegotiated Lomé Convention (Lomé II), however, demonstrate clearly that the EC was in fact regarded as a valuable forum within which the UK's influence in the human rights field could be augmented.

European – and British – détente

Human rights advocacy served as an edifying force within the burgeoning European Community following the negotiation of the European Convention on Human Rights (ECHR). As Tom Buchanan posits, between the entry into force of the ECHR in 1953 and the signing of the Helsinki Final Act in 1975, questions of human rights promotion and the cultivation of a European identity became 'inextricably woven'.[4] This convergence became increasingly pronounced during the 1960s as an eruption in transnational human rights activism made member states 'more sensitive to these issues', while the EC appeared 'increasingly willing to define itself in political as well as economic terms'.[5] The development of a distinctly European approach to détente, furthermore, situated human rights ideals alongside an emerging European identity as the apparatus of the CSCE was being established. Jeremi Suri, for example, has illuminated the growing divergence between West European and American conceptions of détente following the publication of the Davignon Report of October 1970 – a statement of intent which 'made the formulation of a "European" foreign policy a cornerstone of a nascent European polity', while emphasizing a 'furthering of détente across the continent' and championing the civilizational values of liberty and a respect for human rights.[6] The sense of purpose encapsulated by the Report, Suri asserts, led the European Six to seize the initiative of the CSCE process during its early stages, advancing a 'much more optimistic' approach to the linking of human rights and security negotiations than that of the Nixon administration in the United States.[7]

British policymakers were, according to Martin D. Brown, less enamoured than their continental allies by the prospect of codifying human rights provisions within the framework of the CSCE.[8] Nonetheless, following Britain's entry into the EC in 1973, Foreign and Commonwealth Office (FCO) officials began to view cooperation with their

European associates on CSCE policy as a matter of paramount importance: 'something of a test case for the development of foreign policy co-ordination among the Nine'.[9] With the imperatives of European integration in mind, British representatives working under the auspices of European Political Cooperation (EPC) would make a significant contribution towards the establishment of a 'European – and British – détente' that 'differed from, and often conflicted with' the American iteration: 'The latter aimed at stabilizing the continent and consolidating bipolarity, whereas the former had a transformative intent meant to promote a gradual overcoming of the Cold War divide in Europe.'[10] Michael Clarke suggests that, in spite of this close cooperation, Britain never approached the CSCE with the same enthusiasm as its EC partners.[11] Even so, during the two years between the signing of the Helsinki Final Act and the opening of the CSCE follow-up conference in Belgrade, Britain pursued a 'policy that effectively put EPC as a higher priority than NATO, higher than relations with the United States over these matters, and certainly higher than its pursuit of détente as such'.[12] As regards the attitudes of British representatives concerning the CSCE, then, the harmonization of a European approach, clearly informed by a perceived need to ingratiate themselves with their EC colleagues following Britain's entry into the Community, had been of the utmost importance. The pursuit of détente, and a commitment to human rights promotion therein, was seemingly incidental to this overarching ambition.

By framing human rights promotion as the raison d'etre of British foreign policy, however, David Owen served to reconceptualize the relationship between these issues.[13] The act of speaking out against human rights violations overseas, the newly appointed Foreign Secretary stated before the House of Commons on 1 March 1977, was 'not a question of interfering in other people's internal affairs'.[14] Rather, the 'United Nations Charter, the Universal Declaration of Human Rights, and the UN Covenants on Human Rights demonstrate clearly that abuses of human rights, wherever they may occur, are the legitimate subject of international concern'.[15] Owen reiterated this conviction days later while addressing the annual banquet of the Diplomatic and Commonwealth Writers Association on the subject of détente:

> In Britain we will take our stand on human rights in every corner of the globe. We will not discriminate. We will apply the same standards and judgements to communist countries as we do to Chile, Uganda and South Africa. President Carter whose obvious concern for the whole area of human rights is crucially important, has made it clear that this will also be the attitude of his administration. I am looking forward very much to seeing him and [US Secretary of State] Mr [Cyrus] Vance in Washington next week.[16]

Owen's attempts to situate human rights concerns within the East–West dialogue were certainly more measured than the US President's proclamations on the subject of human rights promotion, stressing the need to take measures which stood 'a chance of being effective' while avoiding 'counter-productive reaction'.[17] Still, as the *Washington Post* reported, Owen's address represented 'the strongest support' President Carter's human rights policy had received from abroad, and it was welcomed within the US capital accordingly.[18] It is little wonder, therefore, that some commentators were quick to interpret Owen's human rights initiative as a mere adjunct to that of the Carter administration, undertaken as a means of ingratiating the Callaghan government with the recently elected President before Owen and the Prime Minister departed for Washington.[19] After all, following a cooling of Anglo-American relations during the early 1970s, the Labour governments of Harold Wilson and Jim Callaghan appeared eager to rejuvenate the so-called special relationship between the two nations, and to repair the damage inflicted by the Conservative government of Edward Heath (1970–4), which had prioritized the cause of European integration above the vitality of UK–US axis.[20] However, regarding the extent to which statements of common purpose yielded substantive cooperation between the two governments in the human rights field, scholarly coverage has been largely sceptical, underlining the official concerns surrounding Carter's foreign policy approach, which persisted in Whitehall in spite of the Foreign Secretary's effusive public statements.[21] These anxieties, it has been contended, became particularly pronounced in relation to the Cold War implications of Carter's human rights agenda, which threatened to undermine détente and create a more unstable international environment.[22]

Certainly, the elevation of human rights concerns among Britain's diplomatic imperatives – a process which had in fact been set in motion prior to Owen's appointment, and 'before Carter had emerged as the Presidential candidate most likely to succeed' – was viewed as a problematic development within some sections of the British foreign policy establishment.[23] It is also true that Owen himself wished to maintain a degree of critical distance between his own human rights approach and that of the US President prior to his first meeting with Carter.[24] Callaghan, similarly, was initially sceptical of Carter's evangelical disposition.[25] Nonetheless, according to a despatch sent to the Foreign Secretary by the British ambassador in Washington, Peter Ramsbotham, both Owen and Callaghan returned from their US visit disabused of the notion that Carter was prone to 'shooting from the hip'.[26] The dissipation of British anxieties was subsequently underscored by Kingman Brewster, US ambassador to the UK, in his assessment of the 'British Factor in American Policy', which was submitted to the State Department in September 1977. The UK and 'other European allies', Brewster noted, 'were uncertain how candidate Carter's statements on such central issues as non-proliferation, strategic arms control, conventional arms transfers, and human rights would be affected by the realities of presidential office'.[27] After eight months, however, 'the British have been largely reassured'.[28] The UK, Brewster continued, was initially anxious 'that too much zeal for non-proliferation and human rights could be self-defeating. But it is also our impression that their concern is now largely dissipated, though they are still sometimes sceptical about our means. As long as British interests are protected, however, they are generally willing to try to help us toward our ends'.[29]

Indeed, on the formulation of major policy positions, such as the appropriate stance to take on human rights issues during the CSCE follow-up conference in Belgrade when it opened in October 1977, experts in Washington saw ample grounds for the synchronization of an Anglo-American approach based on close and candid consultation and so many shared 'assumptions and perceptions'.[30] Similar efforts to coordinate an Anglo-American approach can be observed with regard to reforming the human rights framework of the United Nations.[31] Owen also established a constructive dialogue with Patricia Derian, Assistant Secretary of State for Human Rights and Humanitarian Affairs, with a view to identifying the areas of human rights policy in which 'the USG would like British assistance or a more active British stance'.[32] Cooperation in the human rights field – buttressed by joint attempts to resolve Rhodesia's protracted constitutional crisis and bring an end to white minority rule in the former British colony – even served to mitigate US criticism of the Callaghan government over the suspension of civil liberties in Northern Ireland amid ongoing sectarian conflict in the region. According to John W. Kimball, who worked closely with the London embassy as a political officer between 1977 and 1980:

> We were able, if I may say so, to avoid meddling on human rights grounds. We were interested in having Northern Ireland come out right, that is peacefully and fairly for both [Catholic and Protestant] communities. But we were very careful not to tell the British what to do or to imply that it was a so-called humanitarian issue. For one thing, we would have been preaching to the converted about human rights.[33]

This combination of doubts regarding the perceived efficacy of interference, and a belief that the United Kingdom and the United States shared the same fundamental outlook on key human rights issues, is also clearly visible in Cyrus Vance's November 1977 assessment of British policy, accompanied in this instance by a sense of gratitude to the United Kingdom for positioning itself so clearly alongside the Carter administration on matters concerning human rights and international affairs.[34]

Following Owen's appointment as Foreign Secretary, therefore, a prevailing sense of mutual commitment to human rights promotion can be seen to reflect – and indeed expedite – the process of Anglo-American rapprochement initiated by Labour's return to power in 1974. At the very least, the British response to President Carter's human rights policy was sufficiently accommodating, making clear to the Carter administration that relations between the two countries would not be impaired by the growing human rights dimension within US foreign policy. It could even be argued that Owen's contemporaneous attempts to make human rights a central pillar of British foreign policy served to bring the United Kingdom and the United States closer together, through a rhetorical commitment to shared values that was substantiated by attempts at policy coordination pursued through bilateral meetings and multilateral fora. An analysis of the impact of the Callaghan government's human rights policy on UK–EC relations at this juncture, on the other hand, indicates that the Foreign Secretary's human rights initiative exerted a decidedly schismatic influence within the Community, which served to problematize European cooperation in the foreign policy field.

Transatlantic triangulations

In anticipation of Britain's six-month presidency of the EC, which began in January 1977, FCO officials had suggested that British representatives ought to place greater emphasis on human rights promotion and play a more active role in the cultivation of a united Community policy. A report concerning the thirty-third session of the UN Commission on Human Rights produced by the FCO's UN Department, for example, argued that, in view of the spotlight placed on human rights by the Carter administration and an 'increasing concern for human rights in Europe', the British delegation should, 'as representative of the Presidency, be prepared to take the initiative this year in coordinating the Nine's support behind a more assertive and forward-looking policy on human rights'.[35] Highlighting Britain's 'close contacts with the US', the report also emphasized the importance of ensuring that this approach was 'in harmony with the strategy and tactics of the United States'.[36] However, this was easier said than done. By the time Owen signed the EC Joint Declaration on Fundamental Rights on behalf of the European Council on 5 April, Carter's public pronouncements on human rights had already fomented a considerable degree of animosity within the Community.[37] The transatlantic dynamic that had prevailed during the early to mid-1970s had suddenly been reversed; it was now time for the European powers to call for moderation on the part of a US president, lest his assertive stance on human rights undo the progress made by the CSCE.

On 11 March, *The Times* noted that, whereas Owen's public adoption of the human rights cause was widely interpreted as a display of solidarity with President Carter's foreign policy approach, French and German appraisals of Carter administration diplomacy were conspicuous by their absence.[38] Weeks later, Chancellor of the Federal Republic of Germany (FRG), Helmut Schmidt, conveyed his reservations privately to Cyrus Vance, pointing out the potentially disastrous impact of Carter's human rights crusade on the ongoing attempts to extricate ethnic Germans from the Soviet Union.[39] French attitudes, it would appear, were no less sceptical. In preparation for an EC ministerial meeting on human rights issues scheduled for 18 April, the FCO's Reg Hibbert circulated a minute which described the concerns of French representatives regarding the recent elevation of the human rights dimension within the East–West dialogue: 'They wish to keep their hands free and not to be swept along, as they fear might happen, in a direction chosen arbitrarily by President Carter.'[40] Clearly perturbed by the growing discord, which had also been noted by a Central Intelligence Agency (CIA) report in May, Owen broached the subject with the US ambassador to the UK when the pair met to discuss a broad range of foreign policy issues on 5 July.[41] Towards the end of their lengthy discussion in the Foreign Secretary's office, 'Owen said with some sense of insistent warning that the European situation is very disquieting . . . France and Germany are quite upset by the effect of our human rights posture on détente.'[42] It was Brewster's understanding that such reservations must have been conveyed to Owen in no uncertain terms at the recent EC Summit in London.[43] Owen concluded by reiterating 'his own personal support of the US position, but seemed genuinely distressed at the growing hostility of the Germans and the French on the question of souring East-West relations'.[44] Indeed, Owen's misgivings portended a wave of European criticism directed towards the Carter administration and the destabilizing influence of its human rights agenda, with French President Valéry Giscard d'Estaing leading the charge.[45]

Owen's enthusiastic support for Carter's human rights policy, however, had hardly fostered transatlantic understanding. As the US embassy in London reported, Owen's elucidation of a human rights-based approach to British foreign policy at the annual banquet of the Diplomatic and Commonwealth Writers Association constituted a 'unilateral declaration of HMG foreign policy', that was 'not coordinated or otherwise discussed with Britain's EC partners before delivery'.[46] It follows, therefore, that during the course of Britain's EC presidency a perception began to develop among Britain's Community partners that the Callaghan government was too eager to position itself side-by-side with the Carter administration in the human rights field to take heed of European anxieties.[47] Some of Owen's public statements certainly did little to disabuse anyone of this notion, framing human rights as a distinctly *Anglophone* concept – an outgrowth of a shared philosophical inheritance which bound Britain and the United States tighter than any other Western democracies. During a July 1977 appearance on the US television programme *Face the Nation*, for instance, Owen accepted that President Carter's human rights campaign had created a 'sense of unease' within Western Europe, but encouraged viewers to recognize that every country is going to handle human rights differently:

> Britain is going to be different [than other Western European countries] because it's got, in a way, the same sort of tradition to individual freedom and moral stance in foreign policy [as the United States].... And so I find that aspect of President Carter's foreign policy deeply attractive ... France, I think has a different style on these sort of issues, it has a different attitude to civil liberties. I don't think it's a strongly felt issue in some regards as it is for instance in Britain. It seems that Italy too has a different response.[48]

By conceptualizing human rights as not so much a common theme capable of galvanizing the European Community as a multiplicity of nation-specific discourses, Owen provides an interesting counterpoint to Tom Buchanan's aforementioned framing of the EC-human rights relationship, perhaps lending support to the contention that, ultimately, the European Community 'rests upon a relatively weak sense of history and identity; partly because of the diverse historical experiences of its members'.[49]

Behind closed doors, Owen also displayed a degree of reticence when it came to the prospect of coordinating the UK's human rights policy with its European associates. In response to Michael Simpson-Orlebar's suggestion that Britain ought to discuss its ideas in the human rights field with EC members, Owen stated that 'he wanted any British initiative to be kept in British hands'.[50] It was not, in his opinion, 'necessary to do everything with the Nine', and although he was willing to countenance a collective initiative during the British presidency, he 'would not wish the Belgian Presidency to take it over'.[51] Owen's reluctance, it could be argued, was rooted in his essentially 'Churchillian' conception of Britain's overseas role, which held that Britain was not an exclusively *European* power, but was – in spite of its post-war decline – still capable of exerting a unique influence in international affairs by dint of its situation at the nexus of three interconnected relationships or 'circles': the United States, Europe and the Commonwealth.[52] In any case, the articulation of such reservations casts a harsh spotlight on the attenuated supranationalism of European cooperation in the foreign policy sphere – reflected not only in the outlook of certain member states but also within the institutional framework of the EC itself – and supports Christopher Hill's assertion that, since joining the EC, there has been 'no logical incompatibility' between support for EPC and 'another defining characteristic of the British attitude, namely, that Europe is a suitable forum for cooperation on some issues, but not all'.[53] Indeed, in December 1977, when Parliamentary Secretary Evan Luard echoed Owen's objection to the notion that the UK should coordinate its human rights policy with the rest of the EC, the debate seemingly became entangled with long-standing anxieties surrounding Britain's enduring ambivalence towards Europe, and the division between Foreign Office ministers and officials vis-à-vis the prioritization of European cooperation on foreign policy issues.[54]

Reg Hibbert warned that 'if the UK were to begin to treat the Political Cooperation process in a cavalier way others, especially France, would feel much freer to do the same and the end result would be distinctly unhelpful to the UK'.[55] As far as Hibbert was concerned, the UK should not find it too difficult to marry two propositions: the development of Political Cooperation as a central tenet of British membership of the Community, and 'advocacy of action in defence of human rights' as a 'main plank of the Government's policy'.[56] 'My own belief', Hibbert concluded,

> is that the UK can in fact achieve its aims more effectively through Political Cooperation with the partners of the Nine than through going it alone. The restraint which Political Cooperation sometimes puts on the UK's freedom of action seems to me to be on the whole more apparent than real. I hope we can be authorised to ride two horses together.[57]

This response was not only dismissed by Luard on the grounds that it had mischaracterized his position on human rights coordination with the Nine – his reply was also accompanied by the suggestion that certain parts of the Whitehall machinery had become preoccupied with the appeasement of Britain's European colleagues which, in this case, ran the risk of restricting Britain's capacity for action in the human rights field:

> I am not against consulting with the Nine and trying to get their support for our ideas if possible but, at least in the human rights field, I do not think that it should have the absolute priority that was implied by the earlier submission to me (and, like one or two other FCO Ministers, I believe (though a committed European) that the objective of keeping in step with the Nine at all costs perhaps plays an excessively dominant part in the thinking of officials here on many issues at present). I agree that our human rights policy and our European policy need not be in competition but on some issues they inevitably are . . . we should consider first what our aims are in human rights and then how far we can win support from the Nine: not vice versa.[58]

Questions regarding the appropriate degree to which the UK should consult with its EC partners on human rights issues, and the extent to which it should support the approach of the Carter administration (which had clearly antagonized some members of the EC), therefore, cannot be so easily extricated from larger debates concerning Britain's contested reorientation towards Europe. Nor, for that matter, should they be viewed in separation from the Labour Party's historic tendency towards Euroscepticism.[59] Accounts that place Britain at the 'uncooperative' end of the European foreign policy continuum, or tend to view British–EC relations through the prism of the former's distrust of the latter's supranational aspirations, however, may not tell 'the whole story'.[60] Indeed, it would certainly be unfair to suggest that Britain – an awkward partner, perhaps – was any less committed to human rights promotion within the fora of the EC than its Community partners during David Owen's tenure as Foreign Secretary. On the contrary, following its replacement as EC President by representatives of the Belgian government in July 1977 – and the Cabinet's establishment of a coherent policy regarding the development of the European project – the Callaghan government would find itself facing an uphill struggle in its attempts to ensure the codification of human rights provisions within the renegotiated Lomé Convention (Lomé II), which regulated the EC's economic relations with African, Caribbean and Pacific (ACP) countries.[61]

Renegotiating Lomé

The British desire to insert a human rights clause within the renegotiated Convention – signed initially in February 1975 and scheduled for renewal in 1980 – had developed as a response to the EC's inability to suspend aid to Uganda in 1976 in spite of the gross human rights abuses that were being perpetrated by the Idi Amin regime, and was raised explicitly as a policy objective in September 1977.[62] Following the confirmation of ministerial support for the notion in November, focus turned towards securing approval for the proposition within the Community, but this was hardly forthcoming.[63] French and German representatives had already articulated their misgivings over the insertion of a human rights element in Lomé II during an informal meeting of EC foreign ministers at Villers-le-Temple in October.[64] As the debate progressed over the course of the following year, scepticism increasingly became the consensus position within the Community. As Minister for overseas development Judith Hart reported on 13 April 1978, Claude Cheysson – the French European Commissioner who controlled the management of the development portfolio – was not as concerned about potential ACP hostility towards the prospect of a human rights provision in Lomé II as he was by the opposition which would come from EC member states, chiefly France, Denmark and Germany.[65] According to Hart, Cheysson 'believed Germany was principally opposed to a human rights provision aimed at the ACP states because they thought they would be vulnerable to strong ACP criticism over their "Gastarbeiter" policy, particularly as it affects their Turkish immigrant labour . . . Of our other EEC colleages [sic], Cheysson reported that the Belgians were sceptical on the issue'.[66]

Fearing that the Germans' reticence would be reinforced by their interactions with the French, who had made their opposition to a prospective human rights provision clear at the 13 April meeting of the Committee of Permanent Representatives (COREPER), Owen and Callaghan put their case to the FRG's Foreign Minister

Hans-Dietrich Genscher and Chancellor Schmidt.[67] Such efforts, however, were in vain, and by the time the subject was revisited during an EC 'Foreign Ministers Informal Weekend' in May, Owen was clearly struggling to contain his frustration, forcefully rejecting the suggestion that 'no differences of substance' could be found between the national positions of the Nine on this issue:

> Dr Owen ... made clear that differences did indeed exist. He had encountered a good deal of opposition from his colleagues to anything more than a general reference (perhaps drawing on the UN Declaration) to human rights in the preamble ... it was clear that he was alone in taking a tough line on human rights/ Lome.[68]

The acceptance of a preambular reference to human rights was, it seems, as far as the majority of Owen's EC colleagues were willing to go, although it must be stated that this was not for want of continued UK efforts to push for the inclusion of a more substantive human rights clause in the renegotiated Convention. At a meeting of the EC Council of Foreign Ministers on 6 June, for instance, Owen reportedly 'took the lead in pressing for some kind of language in the body of the Convention which would allow the Community to cut off aid to ACP states which violate human rights', emphasizing that its current form was 'not satisfactory in this regard, as was demonstrated last year when the Community found itself with a situation in Uganda in which its response was limited'.[69]

But even compromise solutions proved difficult to come by. As the US embassy in Brussels reported following a meeting of EC Foreign Ministers on 26–27 June, 'the UK maintained its past insistence that additional language be included in body of the Convention' linking human rights with the provision of EC aid.[70] In the face of overwhelming opposition, however, 'no serious attempt was made to settle the question, and the Council agreed only on a reference in the opening statement emphasizing the importance of human rights'.[71] UK representatives had, by this stage, been joined in this endeavour by the Netherlands, and the two governments can be seen to coordinate their attempts to modify the Community's position during the weeks and months that followed.[72] Even still, it would appear that the UK's commitment far outstripped that of its Dutch collaborators. As negotiations gathered speed in the spring of 1979, the support offered by Dutch representatives began to fade, and their acquiescence to the Community's pervasive scepticism was noted with disappointment within the FCO.[73]

In light of the lack of support behind the UK's push for the insertion of an operative human rights clause in Lomé II, the fact that the renegotiated Convention contained no such provision is hardly surprising. As such, it is also misleading to suggest, as an Overseas Development Institute briefing paper does, that the EC 'wanted more than a casual reference to basic UN principles inserted in the new convention', and that the human rights clause 'was quietly dropped during the negotiations' due to the objections of the ACP countries.[74] Rather, the Callaghan government had been swimming against the tide of EC opposition in its attempts to codify human rights considerations within Lomé II (signed on 31 October 1979). Whereas the Callaghan government's stubbornness had been a thorn in the side of the EC during its internal negotiations –

Figure 7.1 British Prime Minister James Callaghan, Foreign Secretary David Owen and US Secretary of State Cyrus Vance seated together at a Council meeting at Lancaster House, London, 10 May 1977. David Owen was crucial in making human rights a central concern for British politics.

a solitary obstacle blocking the establishment of a unanimous negotiating position with the ACP countries – the Conservative government of Margaret Thatcher, which came to power following the General Election of May 1979, would prove to be far more attentive to the concerns of its Community partners. An exchange between the Dutch embassy and the FCO's G. E. FitzHerbert, for example, reveals that Conservative ministers were keen to adopt a 'pragmatic line' on the human rights issue during negotiations with ACP representatives, although it would be 'important for the UK not to retreat too rapidly and too openly from the very strong position taken by the previous Government on human rights in Lomé'.[75]

This 'pragmatic' approach was duly adopted by Minister of State for Europe (and later Foreign Secretary) Douglas Hurd without objection.[76] It would, in fact, take until the entry into force of Lomé IV in 1989 for a human rights clause to feature in the Convention.[77] However, even the programmatic principles contained within Article 5 of Lomé IV have been criticized for lacking 'concrete human rights guarantees capable of being employed as conditions for the fulfilment of the Treaty'.[78] While the protracted development of the Convention's human rights dimension cannot be isolated from the vicissitudes of the North–South dialogue during the 1980s – the 'lost decade' of development – it ought to be noted, nonetheless, that the revival of EPC, for which the Thatcher ministries have been partially credited, apparently came at a price as far as the prioritization of human rights in the external agreements of the EC was concerned.[79]

Conclusion

David Owen's human rights initiative positioned the Callaghan government shoulder-to-shoulder with the Carter administration, and a significant degree of cooperation on human rights issues served to underscore a sense of common purpose that facilitated Anglo-American rapprochement between 1977 and 1979. Within the EC, however, the Callaghan government's assertive stance on human rights would prove to be far more problematic. This chapter has revealed that Owen's enthusiastic support for Carter's human rights policy provoked suspicion within the Community, with many members voicing their concerns over being pushed too far on human rights promotion within the context of the East–West dialogue. This was a radical departure from the transatlantic dynamic that had emerged during the early to mid-1970s when US policymakers had called for a maintenance of the status quo in Europe, and European leaders, viewing human rights as a constitutive aspect of an emerging European identity, adopted a transformative approach to détente and human rights advocacy within the CSCE. By situating Owen's public support for Carter's policy alongside this process of role reversal, this chapter has further contributed to our understanding of Britain's multifaceted relationship with its European partners, particularly in the foreign policy field. Indeed, by supporting Carter's policy, Owen can be seen to effectively subvert the British approach towards the related issues of EPC and human rights promotion as they pertained to the CSCE. Whereas British delegates had, both leading up to and following the signing of the Helsinki Final Act in 1975, tended to regard human rights promotion as a secondary issue to the more pressing objective of facilitating European cooperation within the CSCE, Owen's amplification of Britain's human rights policy was seemingly undertaken without much consideration of the schismatic influence that it could exert within the Community.

Perhaps it could be argued that Owen's promotion of human rights during his tenure as Foreign Secretary – and the response it evoked within the EC – reflected the enduring precarity of Britain's status as a *European* power, which has provided the central theme for a great deal of scholarship – *An Awkward Partner* (1990); *Reluctant Europeans* (2000); *A Stranger in Europe* (2008); *Half In, Half Out* (2018).[80] In this case, however, it would be unfair to suggest that Euroscepticism or a lack of engagement was the cause of such discord. Certainly, ministers exhibited, at times, a selective approach towards the coordination of the UK's human rights policy with EC colleagues, much to the chagrin of FCO officials. The Callaghan government's prolonged and ultimately unsuccessful attempts to secure the codification of human rights concerns within the renegotiated Lomé Convention, and Owen's concerted efforts to bring this to fruition, however, demonstrate that the Foreign Secretary was not merely focused on the pursuit of Anglo-American initiatives in the human rights field; he also clearly viewed the EC as a valuable forum through which Britain's human rights policy could be amplified in concert with its European partners. The Callaghan government was in fact far more proactive on this front than its ostensibly more pro-European Conservative successor, which was quick to adopt a 'pragmatic' position in line with the majority of the EC. Nonetheless, by investigating the Callaghan government's human rights agenda and the ways in which policies pursued served to problematize UK–EC relations, this chapter has not only attempted to situate hitherto neglected British foreign policy perspectives within the rich historiography on human rights and international relations during the 1970s – in so doing, it has also illuminated the competing visions and strategic divergences that militated against the establishment of a common European human rights policy during this pivotal breakthrough moment in human rights history.

Notes

1 University of Liverpool Special Collections & Archives, David Owen Papers (hereafter DOP), D709 2/7/2/1, 'Speech by the Rt Hon Dr David Owen MP, Secretary of State for Foreign and Commonwealth Affairs, Prepared for Delivery at the Annual Banquet of the Diplomatic and Commonwealth Writers Association, Thursday 3 March 1977'.
2 David Grealy, 'Human Rights and British Foreign Policy, c. 1977-1997: An Intellectual Biography of David Owen' (PhD Diss., University of Liverpool, September 2020).
3 For a notable exception, and by far the most in-depth examination of Owen's engagement with human rights discourse during his tenure as Foreign and Commonwealth Secretary, see Jan Eckel, *The Ambivalence of Good: Human Rights and International Politics since the 1940s*, translated by Rachel Ward (Oxford: Oxford University Press, 2019), Chapter 7: Human Rights in Western Foreign Policy. A broad overview of key developments in British human rights policy is provided by Sally Morphet, 'British Foreign Policy and Human Rights: From Low to High Politics', in *Human Rights and Comparative Foreign Policy: Foundations of Peace*, ed. David P. Forsythe (New York: UN University, 2000), 87–114. See also Grace Livingstone, *Britain and the Dictatorships of Argentina and Chile, 1973-82: Foreign Policy, Corporations and Social Movements* (Basingstoke: Palgrave Macmillan, 2018), which provides insightful analysis of emerging human rights concerns within the context of the UK's diplomatic relations with Latin American dictatorships during the late Cold War period. Regarding the significance of the 1970s in human rights history, see Jan Eckel and Samuel Moyn, eds, *The Breakthrough: Human Rights in the 1970s* (Philadelphia: University of Pennsylvania Press, 2014); Samuel Moyn, *The Last Utopia: Human Rights in History* (Cambridge, MA: The Belknap Press of Harvard University Press, 2010); Devin O. Pendas, 'Towards a New Politics? On the Recent Historiography of Human Rights', *Contemporary European History* 21, no. 1 (2012): 95–111. For a brief examination of Western responses to Carter's human rights policy during the first six months of his presidency, see Barbara Keys, '"Something to Boast About": Western Enthusiasm for Carter's Human Rights Diplomacy', in *Reasserting America in the 1970s: U.S. Public Diplomacy and the Rebuilding of America's Image Abroad*, ed. Hallvard Notaker, Giles Scott-Smith and David J. Snyder (Manchester: Manchester University Press, 2016), 229–44. On the failure of the EC and EU to establish a coherent approach to international human rights promotion, see for example Philip Alston and J. H. H. Weiler, 'An "Ever Closer Union" in Need of a Human Rights Policy: The European Union and Human Rights', in *The EU and Human Rights*, ed. Philip Alston, Mara Bustelo and James Heenan (Oxford: Oxford University Press, 1999), 3–66.

4 Tom Buchanan, 'Human Rights, the Memory of War and the Making of a "European" Identity, 1945-75', in *Europeanization in the Twentieth Century: Historical Approaches*, ed. Martin Conway and Kiran Klaus Patel (Basingstoke: Palgrave Macmillan, 2010), 157.
5 Ibid., 166. For broader coverage of the role of foreign policy cooperation in the construction of a 'European' identity, see for example Adrian Hyde-Price, 'Interests, Institutions and Identities in the Study of European Foreign Policy', in *Rethinking European Foreign Policy*, ed. Ben Tonra and Thomas Christiansen (Manchester: Manchester University Press, 2004), 99–113.
6 Jeremi Suri, 'Détente and Human Rights: American and West European Perspectives on International Change', *Cold War History*, 8, no. 4 (November 2008): 536. See also Report by the Foreign Ministers of the Member States on the Problems of Political Unification ('Davignon Report'), Luxembourg, 27 October 1970, https://www.cvce.eu/en/collections/unit-content/-/unit/02bb76df-d066-4c08-a58a-d4686a3e68ff/56b69a5e-3f16-4775-ba38-b4ef440fdccb/Resources#4176efc3-c734-41e5-bb90-d34c4d17bbb5_en&overlay (accessed 10 September 2020).
7 Suri, 'Détente and Human Rights', 538.
8 See Martin D. Brown, 'A Very British Vision of Détente: The United Kingdom's Foreign Policy during the Helsinki Process, 1969-1975', in *Visions of the End of the Cold War in Europe, 1945-1990*, ed. Frederic Bozo, Marie-Pierre Rey and N. Piers Ludlow (New York and Oxford: Berghahn, 2012), 139–56. Highlighting the relative indifference and pragmatism of successive British governments between 1969 and 1975, Brown goes so far as to suggest that British attitudes towards détente challenge 'the pre-eminence of human rights-based analyses of the CSCE' (139). See also Philip Williams, 'Britain, Détente and the Conference on Security and Cooperation in Europe', in *European Détente: Case Studies of the Politics of East-West Relations*, ed. Kenneth Dyson (London: Frances Pinter, 1986), 221–36; Sean Greenwood, *Britain and the Cold War, 1945-91* (Basingstoke: Macmillan, 2000), 175–6.
9 Mr Elliot (Helsinki) to Sir A. Douglas-Home [WDW 1/2], 13 June 1973, in G. Bennett and K. A. Hamilton, eds, *Documents on British Policy Overseas, Series III, Volume II: The Conference on Security and Cooperation in Europe, 1972-75* (London: The Stationary Office, 1997), 140. See also Steering Brief for the United Kingdom Delegation to Stage II of the CSCE [WDW 1/18], 13 September 1973, in ibid., 179–86.
10 Angela Romano, 'British Policy Towards Socialist Countries in the 1970s: Trade as a Cornerstone of Détente', in *The Foreign Office, Commerce and British Foreign Policy in the Twentieth Century*, ed. John Fisher, Effie Pedaliu and Richard Smith (Basingstoke: Palgrave Macmillan, 2016), 467.
11 See Michael Clarke, 'Britain and European Political Cooperation in the CSCE', in *European Détente*, ed. Dyson, 237–53.
12 Ibid., 249.
13 Eckel, *The Ambivalence of Good*, 192.
14 'Foreign Affairs', 1 March 1977, *Hansard: House of Commons*, Volume 927, Column 209.
15 Ibid.
16 Owen, Annual Banquet of the Diplomatic and Commonwealth Writers Association speech, 3 March 1977.
17 Ibid. See also Margaret Van Hatten, 'Owen Gives Strong Support to Carter's Human Rights Stand', *Financial Times*, 4 March 1977; Peter Jenkins, 'Delicate Balance', *Guardian*, 4 March 1977. For Carter's inaugural address of 20 January 1977 in which

he underlined his desire to infuse a sense of morality within US foreign policy, see 'Inaugural Address of President Jimmy Carter', *Public Papers of the Presidents of the United States, Jimmy Carter, 1977, Book I* (Washington, DC: United States Government Printing Office, 1977), 3. For Carter's statements on human rights and US foreign policy prior to his election, see Kristin L. Ahlberg, ed., *Foreign Relations of the United States, 1977-1980, Volume I, Foundations of Foreign Policy, 1974-1980* (Washington, DC: Government Printing Office, 2014), documents 2, 4, 6, 9.

18 Jurek Martin, 'U.S. Welcomes Owen's Human Rights Speech', *Financial Times*, 5 March 1977.

19 See for example Vincent Ryder, 'Human Rights Basic to Foreign Policy, Says Owen', *Daily Telegraph*, 4 March 1977; Bernard D. Nossiter, 'Britain Supports Carter Stand on Human Rights: Britain Backs Carter's View on Human Rights Question', *Washington Post*, 4 March 1977.

20 See David Dimbleby and David Reynolds, *An Ocean Apart: The Relationship Between Britain and America in the Twentieth Century* (London: Hodder & Stoughton, 1988), 266–87; C. J. Bartlett, *"The Special Relationship": A Political History of Anglo-American Relations since 1945* (Harlow: Longman, 1992), 130–4; Alan P. Dobson, *Anglo-American Relations in the Twentieth Century: of Friendship, Conflict and the Rise and Decline of Superpowers* (New York: Routledge, 1995), 141; John Dumbrell, *A Special Relationship: Anglo-American Relations from the Cold War to Iraq* (Basingstoke: Palgrave Macmillan, 2006), 75.

21 See for example John Dickie, *'Special' No More, Anglo-American Relations: Rhetoric and Reality* (London: Weidenfeld & Nicolson, 1994), 160–71; James E. Cronin, *Global Rules: America, Britain and a Disordered World* (New Haven and London: Yale University Press, 2014), 66–70; Thomas K. Robb, *Jimmy Carter and the Anglo-American 'Special Relationship'* (Edinburgh: Edinburgh University Press, 2017), 44–8.

22 See Brian White, *Britain, Détente and Changing East-West Relations* (London: Routledge, 1992), 136; Robb, *Jimmy Carter*, 26.

23 The National Archives, London (hereafter TNA), FCO 58/1143, M. K. O. Simpson-Orlebar to C. W. Squire, 'Human Rights', 21 April 1977. See Grealy, 'Human Rights and British Foreign Policy, c. 1977-1997', 60 –8. Official misgivings in the context of British relations with Latin American dictatorships during this period are expertly demonstrated in Livingstone, *Britain and the Dictatorships of Argentina and Chile, 1973-82*, Chapter Four: Ethical Foreign Policy? Labour Versus the Foreign Office (1974-1979).

24 'Foreign Secretary's Preview of Visit to Washington, March 10-11', 7 March 1977, https://aad.archives.gov/aad/createpdf?rid=47779&dt=2532&dl=1629 (accessed 10 September 2020).

25 Bernard Donoughue, *Downing Street Diary, Volume II: with James Callaghan in No. 10* (London: Jonathan Cape, 2008), 159.

26 TNA, FCO 73/289, Peter Ramsbotham to David Owen, 'The "Special Relationship" Revived: Visit to Washington by the Prime Minister and the Secretary of State, 9-12 March 1977', 18 March 1977. See also 'United States and Canada (Prime Minister's Visit)', 15 March 1977, *Hansard: House of Commons*, Vol. 928, Column 219.

27 'British Factor in American Policy', 23 September 1977, https://aad.archives.gov/aad/createpdf?rid=220932&dt=2532&dl=1629 (accessed 10 September 2020).

28 Ibid.

29 Ibid. On the dissipation of British anxieties, DOP, D709 2/7/15/2, 'Record of a Meeting on Berlin held at the Foreign and Commonwealth Office at 11.00 Hours on Monday 23 May 1977'.

30 'PARM – Annual Policy and Resource Assessment – Part 1', 31 March 1977, https://aad.archives.gov/aad/createpdf?rid=63575&dt=2532&dl=1629 (accessed 10 September 2020).
31 TNA, FCO 58/1145, 'Record of Second Session of Anglo-US Talks on the UN held in Mr Luard's Office on 18 July, 1977, at 3.15 PM'; 'US-UK Pre-UNGA Consultations', 19 July 1977, https://aad.archives.gov/aad/createpdf?rid=164875&dt=2532&dl=1629 (accessed 10 September 2020).
32 'Human Rights: Meeting Between Asst Secretary Derian and Foreign Secretary Owen', 12 December 1977, https://aad.archives.gov/aad/createpdf?rid=289834&dt=2532&dl=1629 (accessed 10 September 2020).
33 John W. Kimball, interview with Charles Stuart Kennedy, Association for Diplomatic Studies and Training, Foreign Affairs Oral History Project, 24 May 1999, https://www.adst.org/OH%20TOCs/Kimball,%20John%20W.toc.pdf (accessed 10 September 2020).
34 'Human Rights', 12 November 1977, https://aad.archives.gov/aad/createpdf?rid=262860&dt=2532&dl=1629: 'The UK was one of the first major countries to come out vigorously in support of the Carter Administration's human rights policy, and we should be able to continue to expect support from HMG on a broad range of human rights issues.'
35 TNA, FCO 30/3641, '33rd Session of Commission on Human Rights, Human Rights: Steering Brief', 4 February 1977.
36 Ibid.
37 TNA, FCO 30/3643, J. O'Connor Howe to Information Officer, 'Joint Community Declaration on Fundamental Rights', 11 May 1977.
38 'Handling Human Rights', *The Times*, 11 March 1977.
39 'My Meetings with German and British Leaders', 1 April 1977, https://aad.archives.gov/aad/createpdf?rid=72880&dt=2532&dl=1629 (accessed 10 September 2020). See also 'Bonn at Odds with Washington', *The Times*, 18 April 1977.
40 TNA, FCO 30/3643 R. A. Hibbert to PS/PUS, 'European Political Cooperation: Ministerial Meeting 18 April Human Rights', 5 April 1977.
41 See 'Memorandum Prepared in the Central Intelligence Agency: Impact of the US Stand on Human Rights', 11 May 1977, Document No. 42 in *Foreign Relations of the United States, 1977-1980, Volume II, Human Rights and Humanitarian Affairs*, https://history.state.gov/historicaldocuments/frus1977-80v02/d42 (accessed 10 September 2020).
42 'Luncheon Meeting with Foreign Secretary', 5 July 1977, SD 59, Electronic Telegrams, 1977, https://aad.archives.gov/aad/createpdf?rid=152259&dt=2532&dl=1629 (accessed 10 September 2020).
43 Ibid.
44 Ibid.
45 See for example Ian Murray, 'Carter Policy Attacked by President Giscard', *The Times*, 18 July 1977; 'A Bismarckian Critique', *The Times*, 19 July 1977; Anne Sington, 'Giscard "go-it-alone" policy winning support in Europe', *Daily Telegraph*, 20 July 1977.
46 'Owen Speech on Détente and Human Rights', 4 March 1977, https://aad.archives.gov/aad/createpdf?rid=45844&dt=2532&dl=1629 (accessed 10 September 2020).
47 TNA, FCO 58/1162, PUS to Mr Rowlands, 'US Foreign Policy: A European View', undated (circa August 1977): '[S]ome of our European partners consider that we have been too sensitive to American views in this field and have not taken enough account

of European sensitivities and interests, particularly over human rights in East/West relations.'

48 DOP, D709 2/7/2/2, 'Transcript of Secretary of State's Appearance on CBS Face the Nation', 24 July 1977.
49 Christopher Hill and William Wallace, 'Introduction: Actors and Actions', in *The Actors in Europe's Foreign Policy*, ed. Christopher Hill (London: Routledge, 1996), 8.
50 TNA, FCO 58/1152, 'Record of an Office Meeting held by the Secretary of State on Wednesday, 25 May 1977 at 3.30 PM'.
51 Ibid.
52 For a summary of the Churchill doctrine, see David Sanders, *Losing an Empire, Finding a Role: British Foreign Policy since 1945* (Basingstoke: Palgrave Macmillan, 1990), 1. Owen provides a positive appraisal of this diplomatic outlook in DOP, D709 2/7/2/2, David Owen, interview for BBC's *Weekend World*, 3 April 1977.
53 Christopher Hill, 'Britain: A Convenient Schizophrenia', in *National Foreign Policies and European Political Cooperation*, ed. Christopher Hill (London: George Allen & Unwin, 1983), 25. See also Jakob C. Øhrgaard, 'International Relations or European Integration: Is the CFSP Sui Generis?' in *Rethinking European Foreign Policy*, ed. Tonra and Christiansen, 26–44; Reinhardt Rummel and Jörg Wiedemann, 'Identifying Institutional Paradoxes of CFSP', in *Paradoxes of European Foreign Policy*, ed. Jan Zielonka (The Hague: Kluwer Law International, 1998), 53–66; Andrew Clapham, 'Where is the EU's Human Rights Common Foreign Policy, and How is it Manifested in Multilateral Fora?' in *The EU and Human Rights*, ed. Alston, Bustelo and Heenan, 631.
54 TNA, FCO 58/1146, M. K. O. Simpson-Orlebar to Mr Weir; PS/Mr Luard, 'Human Rights and Foreign Policy: Progress Report', 7 December 1977; and Evan Luard to Mr Simpson-Orlebar, 'Human Rights and Foreign Policy', 12 December 1977.
55 TNA, FCO 58/1146, R. A. Hibbert to PS/Mr Luard, 19 December 1977.
56 Ibid.
57 Ibid.
58 TNA, FCO 58/1146, Evan Luard to R. A. Hibbert, 20 December 1977.
59 See for example Rhiannon Vickers, *The Labour Party and the World, Volume II: Labour's Foreign Policy since 1951* (Manchester: Manchester University Press, 2011), 99: Vickers notes how Labour's historic attachment to internationalism has, at times, been a complicating factor in British–EC relations. Seen 'more in terms of having ties and commitments to the Commonwealth than Europe', Labour's internationalism, according to Vickers, has 'tended to view Britain as a world leader, not as one of many European countries'. See also Roger Broad, *Labour's European Dilemmas: From Bevin to Blair* (Basingstoke: Palgrave Macmillan, 2001).
60 Christopher Hill, 'Convergence, Divergence and Dialectics: National Foreign Policies and the CFSP', in *Paradoxes of European Foreign Policy*, ed. Zielonka, 37; Andrew Geddes, *The European Union and British Politics* (Basingstoke: Palgrave Macmillan, 2004), 20.
61 Regarding the establishment of a coherent European policy within the Cabinet, see for example David Owen, 'James Callaghan', in *Half In, Half Out: Prime Ministers on Europe*, ed. Andrew Adonis (London: Biteback, 2018), 129–30: Owen recalls how Callaghan scheduled an emergency Cabinet meeting in late July 1977 in order to resolve ongoing debates surrounding Labour's position in Europe. Owen states that the 'outcome of the all-day Cabinet meeting', which Tony Benn regarded as one of the most remarkable summits of his political career, 'was to have, at least for the rest

of our time in government, an official policy which was firmly pro-European, anti-federalist and committed to enlargement to include Greece, Portugal and Spain'.
62 TNA, FCO 58/1146, M. K. O. Simpson-Orlebar to Mr Weir; Mr Hibbert, 'Human Rights: Coordinated Approach with the Nine', 19 September 1977.
63 TNA, FCO 98/330, 'Third ACP/EEC Council of Ministers, Brussels, 13/14 March', undated (circa March 1978): 'UK Minister[s] decided in November . . . that one of our major objectives in renegotiation should be to secure a substantive human rights clause in Lome II'.
64 Ibid.
65 TNA, FCO 98/330, Judith Hart to Secretary of State for Foreign and Commonwealth Affairs, 'EDF Aid to Uganda', 13 April 1978.
66 Ibid.
67 TNA, FCO 98/330, UKREP Brussels to FCO, 'Committee of Permanent Representatives (Ambassadors): 13 April, Renegotiation of the Lome Convention: Human Rights', 13 April 1978; UKREP Brussels to FCO, 'Lome Convention: Human Rights', 19 April 1978; M. R. H. Jenkins to Mr Fretwell; Private Secretary, 'Lome Renegotiation: Human Rights', with attached brief: 'The Secretary of State's Meeting with Herr Genscher at Chequers on 24 April', 20 April 1978.
68 TNA, FCO 98/331, W. K. Prendergast to Mr Jenkins, 'EEC Foreign Ministers Informal Weekend: Lome – Human Rights', 26 May 1978.
69 'EC Foreign Ministers Council, June 6, 1978: Lome Convention Renewal', 7 June 1978, SD 59, Electronic Telegrams, 1978, https://aad.archives.gov/aad/createpdf?rid=14 1742&dt=2694&dl=2009 (accessed 10 September 2020).
70 'EC Foreign Ministers Council, June 26-27, 1978: Renewal of Lome Convention', 29 June 1978, SD 59, Electronic Telegrams, 1978, https://aad.archives.gov/aad/createpdf?rid=141258&dt=2694&dl=2009 (accessed 10 September 2020).
71 Ibid.
72 For example: TNA, FCO 98/333, European Integration Department (External), 'Lome Renegotiation: Human Rights, Meeting with Dutch Officials at 10.00 on 9 November', November 1978; and 'Summary Record of Discussion of Lome II/Human Rights between the Minister of State and the Netherlands Ambassador and Officials at the FCO on 9 November 1978 at 10.15', 14 November 1978.
73 TNA, FCO 98/614: 'Visit to London by Mr Van Gorkum on 24 April, Lome Renegotiation: Human Rights', 19 April 1979; R. B. R. Hervey to G. E. FitzHerbert, 'Lome II: Human Rights', 25 April 1979.
74 Overseas Development Institute, 'Lome II', Briefing Paper, No. 1, February 1980, https://www.odi.org/sites/odi.org.uk/files/odi-assets/publications-opinion-files/6636.pdf (accessed 10 September 2020).
75 TNA, FCO 98/615, G. E. FitzHerbert to PS/Mr Hurd, 'Lome Renegotiation: Human Rights', 23 May 1979.
76 TNA, FCO 98/615, C. T. W. Humfrey to Mr FitzHerbert, 'Lome Renegotiation: Human Rights', 29 May 1979.
77 See for example Bruno Simma, Jo Beatrix Aschenbrenner and Constanze Schulte, 'Human Rights Considerations in the Development Co-operation Activities of the EC', in *The EU and Human Rights*, ed. Alston, Bustelo and Heenan, 586–9.
78 Eibe Riedel and Martin Will, 'Human Rights Clauses in External Agreements of the EC', in *The EU and Human Rights*, ed. Alston, Bustelo and Heenan, 726.
79 Gilbert Rist, *The History of Development: From Western Origins to Global Faith*, 3rd edn (London: Zed Books, 2008), 170. For a brief exploration of the Convention's

evolution, and its relationship to broader trends within the politics of development, see Ismael Musah Montana, 'The Lomé Convention from Inception to the Dynamics of the Post-Cold War, 1957-1990s', *African and Asian Studies* 2, no. 1 (2003): 63–97. Regarding the role of the Thatcher governments in facilitating European Political Cooperation, see for example William Wallace, 'Introduction: Cooperation and Convergence in European Foreign Policy', in *National Foreign Policies and European Political Cooperation*, ed. Hill, 8.

80 Stephen George, *"An Awkward Partner": Britain in the European Community* (New York: Oxford University Press, 1990); David Gowland and Arthur Turner, *Reluctant Europeans: Britain and European Integration, 1945-1998* (Harlow: Longman, 2000); Stephen Wall, *A Stranger in Europe: Britain and the EU from Thatcher to Blair* (Oxford: Oxford University Press, 2008); Adonis, *Half In, Half Out*.

8

Between restrictiveness and humanitarianism
EC institutions and the asylum policies of the 1980s

Gaia Lott

By the mid-1980s asylum started to rank high on the political agenda of member states of the European Community and of EC institutions. Between 1985 and 1990 most of the Twelve introduced new national provisions on asylum and took part in several international discussions.[1] Among various aspects of asylum policies, the criteria to determine responsibility for asylum applications received particular attention. Starting in October 1986, member states negotiated the Dublin Convention at the intergovernmental level, the first binding agreement between the Twelve on asylum, which listed principles to establish responsibility for asylum applications.[2] In the same period, five member states drafted the Schengen Convention, which dealt with, among other migratory issues, the very same topic,[3] while the European Commission worked on a directive, again on the same issue. The European Parliament did not face the topic directly, but many of its resolutions included indirect references to the criteria to determine responsibility for asylum applications. Quite apart from the context of the EC, other international venues dealt with the same subject in the same period: worthy of mention are the Ad Hoc Committee of Experts on the Legal Aspect of Territorial Asylum, Refugees and Stateless Persons (CAHAR) of the Council of Europe and the United Nations Refugee Agency (UNHCR).[4]

Against this backdrop, this contribution aims to focus the analysis on the stated positions on asylum taken by the EC institutions (namely, the Parliament and the Commission) in the second half of the 1980s. The purpose of the reflection is to retrace the growing tensions between national governments and EC institutions, and between European institutions themselves in the field. This chapter seeks to understand whether the Parliament and the Commission can be considered autonomous and original actors, capable of influencing governments' asylum policies. The analysis takes account of the contemporary discourse on asylum developed by the intergovernmental settings mentioned earlier (Schengen and Dublin), the Council of Europe (specifically, the CAHAR) and the UNHCR in order to fully appreciate the debate from a multi-level perspective.

The chapter starts by analysing the birth of interest in asylum by EC member states in the second half of the 1980s and the role of EC institutions, the European Parliament, and the Commission, in the draft of the two main documents on the topic signed by European countries (Schengen and the Dublin Convention). It then moves on to look at the documents on asylum proposed and approved by the European Parliament and the Commission in the same period and their relations with the ongoing debate between member states.

Reflecting on the role of the Parliament and the Commission in the European asylum debate of the second half of the 1980s is a significant study for several reasons. First, the ideas and principles established in those years influenced asylum policies in Europe over the following decades. Analysing if and how European institutions were involved and participated in the exchanges at the time, whether their positions were taken into consideration or not, becomes crucial to fully understand the birth of the contemporary asylum system and its evolution. Second, even if the right of asylum is not unanimously considered a human right (differently from the right to seek asylum), it is strictly related to the human rights field, which gained a central role in the European debate of the 1970s and 1980s.[5] Retracing the involvement of EC institution in the asylum policies of the 1980s allows us to enrich the reflections on the human rights debate of the period with an original perspective. Third, the lack of historical literature on the issue makes it urgent that it is addressed: most of the existing wisdom looks at the debate on asylum in the second half of the 1980s, from the perspective of law or political science.[6] The historical dynamics that characterized that debate have remained unexplored so far: many historians have reflected on the birth of the European migratory system, looking at the role and stakes of member states and EC institutions and their mutual influences. The works of Emmanuel Comte and Simone Paoli are a cornerstone of this literature.[7] However, none of these studies looks specifically at the birth of the asylum system in Europe, which is a distinct and peculiar part of the broader migratory regime, characterized by specific norms and values. At the same time, this analysis sheds a new light on the interplay between governments and supranational institutions. By confirming the central role of governments in the establishment of the migratory and asylum system, it demonstrates that the limited role of EC institutions at the time turned out to be strategic for the following developments. Finally, the availability of unpublished primary sources guarantees the further originality of the reflection.

A topic of new interest

The increasing interest in asylum by EC member states was derived from three main factors: the growth of asylum seekers in their territories, the new characteristics of the phenomenon and the European Integration process.

Starting from the quantitative change, the number of asylum applications lodged in the territory of the Twelve passed from fewer than 80,000 at the beginning of the 1980s to more than 300,000 by the end of the decade.[8] This growth was the result of the increasing instability of various developing countries torn by civil war, economic crisis, natural disasters or a combination of the three; the technological advances in transport and communication; the closure of foreign labour recruitment by most

European countries, which made asylum with family unification the only way to enter EC territory legally; and the end of the Cold War.[9] Even if by the mid-1980s, asylum was of constant concern in only a few member states (West Germany and Denmark), this quantitative leap started to attract the attention of all of them.

At the same time, differently from previous years, most of the asylum seekers arrived from developing countries (the Middle East, India and Africa) in a spontaneous, unscheduled way.[10] Member states had the impression of losing control over the phenomenon and reacted by introducing restrictive measures at the national level, concerning entry conditions for third nationals, procedures to determine refugee status, and the rights and benefits recognized for asylum seekers and refugees.[11] The immediate effect of these first measures was to divert the flow of asylum seekers from one member state to another, urging them to start cooperating.[12]

Third, the new and lively phase of the European Integration process of the mid-1980s reinforced member states' need for negotiations on asylum. The 1985 White Paper and the 1986 Single European Act established the achievement, by 1992, of an area without internal frontiers in which the free movement of goods, persons, services and capital was ensured (article 8a of the EEC Treaty). As explicitly stated by the Political Declaration annexed to the Single European Act, the establishment of free movement of persons inside the EC urged member states to reflect on compensatory measures, such as rules of entry for third nationals (asylum seekers included).

Despite the differing interpretations of article 8a, especially concerning free movement of non-EC citizens, in the case of asylum seekers the Twelve decided to avoid paralysing discussions and followed a solution-oriented approach. They focused on the criteria to determine responsibility for the examination of asylum applications, without clarifying whether there should be an 'abolition' or an 'easing' of controls at EC internal frontiers or the extension of such measures to them.[13] An intergovernmental setting was created deliberately to deal with the issue in October 1986: the Ad Hoc Group on Immigration (hereafter Ad Hoc Group) and its asylum sub-group, which were composed of officials from the Ministries of the Interior and of Justice and included the European Commission as an observer. Interesting to stress, the five member states of the Schengen Group followed the same pragmatic approach, limiting their exchanges on asylum to the criteria to determine responsibility for applications, and so did the European Commission. The exchanges inside the CAHAR were a relevant reference point for the works of all these settings.[14]

The EC institutions and the Dublin and Schengen Convention

The European Parliament and Commission were almost excluded from the intergovernmental negotiations on asylum between member states in the mid-1980s.

Parliament was deliberately kept at the distance from the works of the Ad Hoc Group and of the Schengen Group: the plenary was never involved, nor was it informed of the proceeding of the works in the two groups. Starting from the Danish presidency (second semester 1987), updates on the work of the Ad Hoc Group were given from time to time through a letter from the president of the Group to the president of the Committee of Legal Affairs and Citizens' Right,[15] whereas, the Schengen Group gave no information on its work to Parliament, to the plenary or to its committees. The limited composition of the group, which was made up of only five member states, justified the absence of communication. The EC institution denounced the lack of involvement in the Schengen and Dublin processes several times, stressing the democratic deficit, the lack of transparency and accountability resulting from it, but this did not determine any change.[16] By virtue of its participation in the Ad Hoc Group, the EC tried to facilitate communication between the group and Parliament with little success.[17]

The EC was indeed in a different situation. Palays Berlaymont, a nickname given to the Commission and referring to its headquarters, was excluded from the Schengen Group and tried to participate in its works for years, in vain. But it participated as an observer in the works of the Ad Hoc Group, the only external actor entitled to take part in its meetings. Its participation in the Group was rather discreet, however. The Commission was not proactive: it did not promote innovative or changing ideas, and it also avoided sharing the proposals of its own draft directive with member states.[18] In the end, the participation of the Commission in the Ad Hoc Group seemed to have no specific influence on the exchanges of the Twelve; if anything, it was the other way around, it appears that it was the work of the Group that influenced the Commission's elaborations on asylum in that period (see the following section on the European Commission).

Community action

Until the adoption of the White Paper in 1985, asylum policies had never been considered a matter of Community interest and no debate on Community competence had ever arisen. The new characteristics of the phenomenon and the progress of the European Integration process shed new light on the topic, triggering an unprecedented discussion on the involvement of EC institutions in asylum policies.

Given the attribution of powers in place at the time, the European Parliament had no formal jurisdiction over the issue. However, historical evidence from the European Integration process shows that where no official competence is recognized, influence and prestige can be achieved thanks to authoritative stances.[19] The EP has exercised informal agenda-setting power in several fields from the beginning of the integration process, not least in the human rights field, which is an overlapping, even if not concomitant, area with asylum. By the mid-1980s it tried to find its own room in the European asylum debate in the same way.

Unlike the EP, the EC could aspire to a stronger and more formal role. In the 1985 White Paper, it announced the proposal of a draft directive on asylum by 1988, linking its competence to article 100 of the EEC Treaty and the implementation of the Single Market (cf. supra).[20] This interpretation was not unanimously accepted, neither by member states nor by the Commission itself, as this chapter will clearly show in the following section on the European Commission, but it did not impede

Palays Berlaymont from working on a draft directive, which focused on the criteria to determine responsibility for asylum applications.

The European Parliament

The European Parliament was the first Community institution to deal with asylum in the 1980s. Its first reflections ranged from resolutions and written questions on the granting of asylum to specific nationalities (like the Cubans, the Chileans, the Basques or the Tamils) to the enlargement of the definition of 'refugee' by the Geneva Convention.[21] Most of these stances came from single representatives and did not derive from a deep and shared study or analysis by the plenary. Specifically, propositions on human rights implications of the right to asylum tended to come from the left wing of Parliament, where the socialists were the most active, with Madame Lizin leading the motions of resolutions on the topic in this period. Whereas, when Cold War considerations were at stake, as, for instance, in the case of resolutions on people fleeing Eastern European regimes or the 'boat people of Vietnam', motions were often promoted by right-wing parties.[22] In both cases, proposals did not arouse harsh debates and tended to be approved by large bipartisan majorities.

When member states started to introduce the first restrictive measures towards asylum seekers, by the mid-1980s, the European Parliament was the unique Community institution to openly criticize the measures. Very critical motions for resolution (very often never approved) and strongly polemical written and oral questions were put forward by single representatives and parliamentary groups.[23] Some committees of Parliament started to take an interest as well: by 1984, the Political Affairs Committee included asylum policies in its annual 'Human Rights in the World' report. However, since the topic was considered 'an EC internal matter', out of the sphere of competence of the Political Affairs Committee, the debate moved to the Committee on Legal Affairs and Citizens' rights.[24]

It was in this setting that the Vetter report and the related A2-227/86/A resolution were born. The two documents can be considered the most complete picture of member states asylum policies of the mid-1980s and the most important stances of the European Parliament on asylum.[25] In June 1985, Heinz Oskar Vetter, a German representative and member of the Socialist Group, was asked by the Committee on Legal Affairs and Citizens' rights to enlarge his previous study of the Basques asylum seekers to the broader topic of member states asylum policies. Between 1985 and 1986, Vetter consulted several NGOs and visited most member states with a representative of the European Commission, Wenceslas de Lobkowicz from DG III (Internal Market). By the end of 1986 Vetter proposed a motion for a resolution, with a long and detailed explanatory statement to the Committee, which stimulated a huge debate among its members, resulting in an unusual cleavage between right and left parliamentary groups.[26] The disagreement inside the Committee concerned primarily the harsh tone of the two documents, very critical towards member states' policies. When the discussions moved to the plenary, the debate burst and the image of Europe, the link with its human rights tradition and with European identity were put on the table.

A bipartisan consensus emerged on the idea that asylum was part of European identity and tradition, but the concept was expressed with different nuances, according to the political orientation of the speaker: the reporter Vetter (Socialist Group) spoke of a 'specific historical responsibility of European people towards asylum seekers'; Fontaine (European People's Party) sustained that 'it's more than tradition, it's related to the honour of our democracies', her party-colleague Janseen Van Raay added that asylum was linked to 'our Christian tradition and European culture', while De Gucht (Liberal and Democratic Reformist Group) stated that denying the right of asylum would mean 'denying the nature, the specificity of our western culture'.[27] Since asylum can be considered an expression not only of sovereignty but also of culture, this attempt by Parliament to recognize a European culture on asylum, besides the cultures of the single member states, is of very great interest. This is especially so in light of the contemporary reflection on their own identity and distinctiveness being carried out by European countries, linking these ideas to concepts such as the defence of human rights, democracy and the rule of law.[28]

The aim of the Vetter report and resolution was to propose a different asylum system for European member states. Moving from a harsh critic of existing national systems, the resolution suggested following a 'more generous attitude': it enlarged the definition of refugee, adopting the OUA definition and including gender-based claims;[29] it introduced a series of procedural guarantees for asylum seekers; and it proposed two ground-breaking ideas: the share of asylum seekers' financial burden among member states (point 5) and the establishment of a Community spokesman on the asylum question (point 8). The resolution did not enter into detail on the criteria for determining responsibility for asylum applications, but it suggested this: 'urgently distinguish between first host country and country of asylum and to leave asylum seekers free to choose their country of asylum' (art.1h), confirming a strong sensitivity towards the individual's perspective rather than that of the state. Furthermore, during the plenary discussion, Vetter criticized the 'first entry principle' and defended the 'clause en route', but his position was not included in the resolution.[30]

Despite its harsh tone and innovative content, the Vetter report and resolution did not have much of an echo in the debate on asylum policies of the time. National discussions did not refer to the resolution, and the Ad Hoc Group on Immigration never discussed it or took its content into consideration.[31] Some member states tried to emphasize the role of the asylum seekers' intention for determining responsibility for their applications, but they did not refer to the European Parliament resolution on the point. At the same time, the president of the Ad Hoc Group responded to Parliament's stance by emphasizing the importance of the Geneva Convention and of cooperation between member states, but he did not discuss, or even refer to, the novelties the resolution tried to introduce.[32] The attitude of 'ignoring the maximalist ideas' of the European Parliament seemed to guide member states' response.[33]

Even if the EC participated in the preparatory work of the resolution and in its discussions and despite the Delors presidency's engagement in good relations with the EP, the Commission remained particularly silent on the document, avoiding any comment on its content, which 'went beyond the scope of the directive it was working on'.[34] Specifically, the Commission did not want to welcome the proposal of a

Community spokesman on the asylum question, nor the idea of sharing the financial burden between member states, because it was afraid of member states' reactions. The EP kept on asking the Palays Berlaymont to take steps to implement the Vetter resolution, expressing strong criticism of its prudent attitude. Nevertheless, its requests remained unheard.

In the end, the Vetter resolution and report remained a rather isolated move in the asylum discussions of the time. As already stressed, given the powers of the European Parliament in the mid-1980s, the document was not expected to determine any formal follow-up steps. However, even the agenda-setting power was rather unsuccessful in this case. As the paragraph on the European Commission will show, the resolution allowed Parliament to put pressure on the Commission, but in the end, even these pressures did not succeed in determining any concrete action.

In the following years (1986–90), no other agenda-setting documents on asylum were approved or discussed: Parliament limited its stance to criticizing the procedural aspects of the works of the Ad Hoc and Schengen Group, without even finding a common stance on the content of such negotiations. The two conventions were not unanimously criticized: the Left groups were more critical towards 'the securitarian character' of a number of dispositions of the agreements, whereas groups on the Right were more conciliatory on the point.[35] By the end of the 1980s, indeed, the discourse on asylum was no longer unanimous in Parliament: right-wing groups started to include security concerns in their interventions, something that rarely occurred before but that would characterize the debate in the following decade, whereas left-wing groups maintained a more human rights-oriented discourse. The result was an additional weakening of Parliament's voice, which would remain on the margin of discussions on asylum for the following years.

The European Commission

In the 1985 White Paper, the Commission announced the proposal of a draft directive on asylum by 1988. This was the first initiative on asylum in the history of Palais Berlaymont and it was strongly sustained by the European Parliament, which requested an increasing role for the Commission in the field of human rights and migration.[36]

Most member states did not support this new sphere of action for the European Commission, however. Only Italy and Portugal explicitly defended Community competence on asylum. France, the United Kingdom and Greece were strongly opposed to it: their resistance derived from jealousy over sovereignty, fear of irreversible choices and opposition to interference from the European Court of Justice.[37] West Germany's position is worthy of notice. By the mid-1980s, Bonn (and to a lesser extent Copenhagen) was the only member state to see refugees as a matter of constant concern and internal debate, given the high number of arrivals of asylum seekers into its territory and the liberalism of its constitutional provisions.[38] Against this background, it prompted a discussion on asylum in 'all possible meetings', including the Ad Hoc Group, European Political Cooperation and the Council of Europe.[39] When the Commission launched the idea of a directive, Bonn supported community competence in private meetings with Lord Cockfield (the commissioner responsible for it), but it always remained prudent in public, avoiding official support or opposition to the initiative.[40] By the end of 1987, it changed position dramatically, stating in public that article 8a assumed intergovernmental not Community competence and that a Commission initiative was out of discussion. Change in the composition of the government, hesitations of the Commission on its own competence and France's adamant refusal of Community action probably contributed to the German public reorientation.[41]

Support for a directive was not taken for granted inside the Commission either, however. The previous attempts over migration policies suggested Palays Berlaymont be particularly prudent.[42] An internal debate divided the Legal Service, 'the people of the book', whose aim was to guarantee the coherence between treaties and Commission's actions and DG III (Internal Market), the direction responsible for the directive.[43] Despite the perplexities of the Legal Service, which generally defended a conservative view, DG III started to work on the document, involving the UNHCR and the Council of Europe.[44] Consistent with this, the Commission tried to promote a 'Community dimension on asylum', submitting its candidature as a full member to the UNHCR Executive Committee and participating in academic and public debates on asylum.

By summer 1987, the draft directive was ready. The content was very similar to the Schengen and Dublin convention. This should not surprise us, given that the Commission wanted the text to be approved by member states, thus it could not propose something that had nothing to do with such discussions. Perrisich (DG III) stressed the importance of participation in the works of the Ad Hoc Group on Immigration to develop not only expertise but also awareness of member states' points of view. There were differences between the texts, however.

First, the draft directive included more liberal dispositions compared with the Schengen and Dublin documents: a broader concept of 'family union' (article 12)[45] and a stronger consideration of the asylum seeker's intention. This last point is worthy of analysis because it was strongly promoted by the European Parliament. Like the Dublin and Schengen Convention, the draft directive stated the 'First Entry principle' (article 9). However, it added the right for asylum seekers to apply to legally enter another member state of their choice within three months of their arrival, in the case of applications lodged at the border or in transit. This meant occasions when asylum seekers had not entered EC territory through a visa or a permit of stay, which were considered an indirect expression of the asylum seeker's intention.[46] The proposal would be strongly opposed by member states and the Commission would be forced to elicit the 'three months moratorium'. But the inclusion of such a disposition in the first draft can be considered an attempt to find a compromise between the Parliament's and member states' position, where the latter won over the first. Second, the draft directive tried to follow a broader approach, prompting an approximation of national procedures in abridged cases (article 20) and establishing an Advisory Committee (article 18), whose aim was to monitor national decisions and foster coherent stances. Both proposals, once again, tried to give an answer to the European Parliament's requests for a broader approach and the establishment of a Community spokesman on the asylum question. But even in this case, they did not have a long life: faced with fierce opposition of member states but bound by the need to comply with Parliament, the Commission elicited article 20 and revised the idea of the Committee, maintaining the institution but emptying it of its actual role.[47]

Despite the efforts of the Commission to comply with member states requests, resistances to Community action remained and by the end of 1988 the Commission officially shelved the directive.[48] According to 'gossipy contributions' collected by British officials, the shelving of the directive resulted from specific internal dynamics inside the Commission. The British sustained that the project did not derive from a general commitment by DG III, but was the result of pressures from the responsible commissioner and the European Parliament.[49] The personal involvement of Lord Cockfield, who tried to reshape the draft to make it acceptable to member states and defended it until the very last moment, is confirmed by archival documents. Primary sources also confirm Parliament's pressure to make the project work. Whereas the image of the commissioner isolated from the competent DG does not correspond with what emerges from the documents consulted. The gap between the interests of responsible commissioners and the stakes of DGs in charge is nothing new in the history of the European Commission, which is everything but a black box and is characterized by internal (vertical and horizontal) fragmentation. The 'scornful absence of expertise on asylum' in DG III denounced by Adrian Fortescue, Cockfield chief of Cabinet, probably did not help the commissioner promote his project, given the role of expertise in the Commission's legitimacy. Despite this, however, both Perrisich and Taschner (from DG III) are described as promoting the directive 'toughly and adamantly', presenting it as a move 'necessary as the EC progressed to becoming more than a customs union'.[50] De Lobkowicz also seemed personally engaged in the project. These officials were, perhaps, trying to take advantage of a power vacuum to shape a policy, as other colleagues were doing at the same time in other areas, but they did not succeed in their attempt.[51]

Despite the commissioner's and some officials' support for the project, by the end of 1988 the equilibrium inside the Commission was tending towards the withdrawal of the directive. With the progress of intergovernmental negotiations inside the Ad Hoc Group, resistance to Community action started to come from the Secretariat as well. Given member states' hostility to the project, David Williamson objected to the political opportunity of the directive taken at that historical juncture. Since the very beginning, Lord Cockfield had taken into consideration governments' resistance to Community competence, deliberately slating the proposal for 1988 because 'an initiative in this field at this stage would be doomed to fail'.[52] However, Williamson's reasoning went a little bit further: in order to avoid a battle of competence that would have paralyzed any progress on such a sensitive matter (which deserved a quick solution to foster the integration process), he suggested bringing forward the directive only if the work of the Twelve did not make any satisfactory progress, a reasoning coherent with the subsidiarity principle promoted by the Delors presidency in the same period.[53] Given the strong link between Williamson and Delors, such a stance could not have been taken without the president's assent. The Secretariat's pragmatic and tactical considerations were indeed referred to in July 1988 by François Lamoureux, from the Cabinet of the President: after stressing the importance of defending Community competence in public, he reiterated the need to be prudent with decisions.⁵⁴ In September 1988, the same Fortescue concluded 'this is not the right moment to be seeking confrontation with member states about competence which can only lead to a sterile distraction from the main purpose'.⁵⁵ Asylum was not a political priority for the Commission, it was perceived as an instrument for the integration process, which was the real focus of every community action. When it became clear that insisting on a directive on the topic would have worked against rather than for such process, the project was shelved. To paraphrase Delors's words, it was not worth fighting a battle of Hernani over asylum.⁵⁶

Conclusion

In the second half of the 1980s, asylum started to rank high on the political agenda of EC member states. Several fora, in the EC context and beyond, intensified discussions on asylum policies, focusing their attention on the criteria to determine responsibility for asylum applications. In June 1990, the EC member states signed the first two documents on the topic, and, broadly speaking, the first two intergovernmental agreements between European states on asylum: the Schengen and Dublin Convention.

Both agreements were the result of intergovernmental negotiations, which lasted for four to five years and did not involve the European institutions to a large extent. The European Parliament was deliberately kept at a distance from the works of the Ad Hoc and Schengen Group: regarding the first, Parliament was simply informed, in a rather synthetic way and on an ex-post basis, of the conclusions of the meetings of the Group. As far as the Schengen negotiations are concerned, it was never informed of their content, receiving only the final text of the Convention. The Commission was in a rather different position, participating as an observer in the Ad Hoc Group, but excluded from the Schengen discussions. Despite participation in the Group, the Commission followed a very cautious approach in the meetings, and its presence had no specific influence on the exchanges of the Twelve.

At the same time, the two Community institutions promoted their own initiatives on asylum in the second half of the 1980s: Parliament approved several resolutions, the most relevant one resulted from the Vetter Report, and the Commission worked on a directive on criteria to determine responsibility for asylum applications. These initiatives were rather different one from another in terms of content, because they resulted from distinct cultural and political interpretations of the asylum issue. The European Parliament looked at the topic mainly through the lens of human rights protection: it followed a broad approach, prompting original and innovative ideas and linking the right to asylum with the ongoing reflection on European identity. In these years, the Parliament anticipated many themes that would become crucial in the debate of the following decades, such as the centrality of the rights of asylum seekers, the importance of sharing the financial burden between member states and the significance of Community approach. The innovations promoted by the institution were consistent with its contemporary stances in the human rights field, epitomized by the annual 'Human Rights in the World' report, but they were particularly noteworthy because in the case of asylum they concerned an 'internal matter', where resistances to criticism and innovation were much stronger. This is probably one of the main reasons why, unlike the human rights field, the Parliament's voice remained particularly unheard and uninfluential in those years, whereas the European Commission looked at asylum mainly through the lens of European Integration and interpreted it as an instrument to prompt that process. It followed a narrower approach, looking for compromise with member states. Its attitude was more cautious than innovative: it never enlarged the reflection to take in the European identity debate; it tried to promote small liberal openings, responding to Parliament's pressures, but it gave everything up when it realized that the liberalism of its proposals and, in the end, the same project of a directive did not curry member states' favour and could penalize rather than foster the integration process.

These distinct approaches led to tensions between the two European institutions, with Parliament being particularly critical towards the cautious attitude of the Commission. This tension was exacerbated by the fact that Parliament was trying to push a Community move to gain room in the asylum field, given its lack of competence and having been completely excluded from the ongoing debates on the issue. Even if the Commission was, at least on paper, the stronger actor of the two, because it could advance a (contested) competence and was involved in the Ad Hoc Group, in the end it remained squeezed between pressures from Parliament and the wall built by member states, which were not ready to renounce their sovereign rights over asylum. The result was the withdrawal of its own project and the temporary surrender to the idea of having a voice in the asylum field.

The epilogue of the Vetter Report and resolution and of the draft directive on asylum seems to confirm Emmanuel Comte's thesis of the central role of governments, and not supranational institutions, in the formation of the European migration regime. His idea that, with the directive on asylum, the Commission was simply trying to establish a precedent for Community competence in a very contested area, as with the (failed) directive on the easing of border control, can be endorsed.[57] The importance of such an attempt should not be underestimated, however.

The withdrawal of the directive would be crucial for the following development of asylum policies in the European Community. Anticipating the Maastricht 'third pillar' approach, by the mid-1980s the Commission left 'asylum' to intergovernmental competence: a division of labour, which would only be overcome by the end of the 1990s.[58] At the same time, however, this division of labour was a way for the Commission to remain included in the debate and, when the time was ready, to establish once for all its own competence. The inclusion of the Parliament would be slower, consistent with the integration path followed in other fields, but the institution would maintain its independent and critical voice, prompting innovative ideas and reflections up to more contemporary times.[59]

Notes

1 Among others, the European Consultations on the Arrivals of Asylum-Seekers and Refugees in Europe and the exchanges inside the UNHCR and the Council of Europe.

2 Convention determining the State responsible for examining applications for asylum lodged in one of the member states of the European Communities – Dublin Convention, *Official Journal of the European Communities* (hereinafter OJ) C 254, 19 August 1997. By 'asylum' the paper means the protection granted under the 1951 Geneva Convention and the 1967 New York Protocol, despite the word referring to a broader and more complex concept. This is due to a need for synthesis and because the negotiations of the time and the Dublin and Schengen Convention defined 'asylum' in these terms.

3 Chapter VII of the Convention Implementing the Schengen Agreement of 14 June 1985, OJ L 239, 22 September 2000. The analysis of the relation between the Schengen and the Dublin Convention is beyond the scope of this article. It is enough to state that the Five of the Schengen Group came to an agreement before the Twelve and sent the same negotiators to the table of the two groups, which promoted the same core ideas. France and West Germany were particularly aligned in both fora. Archives du Ministère des Affaires Étrangères (hereafter AMAE) 101SUP8 Renouard, Note n.8329, 18 April 1989.

4 The CAHAR worked on a Convention on the criteria to determine responsibility for asylum applications from 1977 to 1989. The Convention was never signed, part of the unadopted agreement was included in Parliamentary Assembly, Recommendation 1236 (1994): 1994. Available at http://assembly.coe.int/nw/xml/XRef/Xref-XML2HTML-en.asp?fileid=15270&lang=en (accessed 2 May 2020). The UNHCR had been reflecting on criteria to determine responsibility since the 1970s, see among others UNHCR Executive Committee, Conclusion n.15 (1979), https://www.unhcr.org/excom/exconc/3ae68c960/refugees-asylum-country.html (accessed 2 May 2020).

5 To deepen the broader historical discussion on the link between the right of asylum and human rights, see Colloquy on European Law, *The Law of Asylum and Refugees. Present Tendencies and Future Perspectives: Proceedings of the Sixteenth Colloquy on European Law* (Strasbourg: Council of Europe, 1987).

6 See, among others, the works of (in alphabetical order) Christina Boswell, Matthew J. Gibney, Guy S. Goodwin-Gill, Kay Hailbronner Christian Joppke, Sandra Lavenex, Gil Loescher.

7 See, among others, Emmanuel Comte, *The History of the European Migration Regime: Germany's Strategic Hegemony* (New York: Routledge, 2018) and Simone Paoli, *Frontiera Sud: l'Italia e la nascita dell'Europa di Schengen* (Milano: Mondadori, 2018).

8 John Salt, *Current Trends in International Migration in Europe*, Council of Europe Working Paper, November 2001, https://www.coe.int/t/dg3/migration/archives/Documentation/Migration%20management/2001_Salt_report_en.pdf (accessed 20 May 2020). Statistical data on migration and asylum in these years are approximate, given the scarce reliable sources.

9 The end of the Cold War determined the growth of Eastern European asylum seekers. This flow of people reinforced a growing trend of extra-European arrivals, which started well before the fall of the Berlin Wall. For a synthetic overview of this period, see Gil Loescher, *Beyond Charity: International Cooperation and the Global Refugee Crisis* (Oxford: Oxford University Press, 1993).

10 Differently from the asylum seekers of the previous decade, called 'vote with their feet refugee', this new group of asylum seekers was defined 'jet refugees'. David A. Martin, ed., *The New Asylum Seekers: Refugee Law in the 1980's: The Ninth Sokol Colloquium on International Law* (Boston: Dordrecht, 1988), 49–51.

11 Some authors stress how the different ethnic (non-European) origin of the new asylum seekers contributed to a less favourable attitude towards them. Danièle Joly and Robin Cohen, eds, *Reluctant Hosts: Europe and Its Refugees* (Aldershot: Hants, 1989), 147.
12 Later research would show how asylum seekers' choice of destination country is linked to several factors (asylum policies, economic dynamics, presence of ethnic community, cultural and linguistic links etc.), but at that time member states were obsessed with the idea of being attractive because perceived as 'soft touch' countries or due to 'chicken game' dynamics. Tally Kritzman-Amir, 'Not In My Backyard: On the Morality of Responsibility Sharing in Refugee Law', *Brooklyn Journal of International Law*, 2 (2009): 355–94.
13 The United Kingdom, Greece, Denmark and Ireland were the most restrictive on third nationals' free movement rights. AMAE, 1914INVA5 Sauve au Ministère des Affaires Etrangères, Direction des Français à l'extérieurs et des Etrangères en France, LIB/CAB II/BJ/N.12, 6 January 1989.
14 Explicit references to the works of the CAHAR were rare both in the Ad Hoc and in the Schengen Group, such discussions were mentioned primarily as a negative example of inefficient exchanges. However, besides the fact that most delegations were composed of the same officials in the three fora, the principles and ideas expressed in the CAHAR were recalled and very often overcome by the other two fora.
15 Historical Archives of the Council of the European Union (hereafter HACEU), CM2 WGI 6 Ad Hoc Group SN/1728/88 WGI 280, 6 July 1988.
16 Parlement Européen, *Débats: Compte Rendu in extenso des séances du 13 au 16 mars 1990*; and Historical Archives of the European Union (hereafter HAEU) PE3-24386 Joint resolution replacing the previous motions by the single parliamentary groups, 14 June 1990.
17 Historical Archives of the European Commission (hereafter HAEC), BAC 321/1991 n.15 Wenceslas de Lobkowicz (European Commission, SG 1) 'Summary Coordinator Meeting', 27 March 1990.
18 The minutes of the meetings of the Ad Hoc Group and of its asylum sub-group are stored in the Historical Archives of the Council of the European Union in Brussels.
19 Before the Single European Act, the European Parliament was included in the legislation process through non-binding consultations. The Single European Act introduced the cooperation procedure and the Maastricht Treaty the co-decision system. On the European Parliament's agenda-setting power see George Tsebelis, 'The Power of the European Parliament as a Conditional Agenda Setter', *The American Political Science Review*, 88, no. 1 (1994): 128–42.
20 Article 100 of the EEC Treaty stated, 'The Council shall, acting unanimously on a proposal from the Commission and after consulting the European Parliament and the Economic and Social Committee, issue directives for the approximation of such laws, regulations or administrative provisions of the member states as directly affect the establishment or functioning of the common market'.
21 HAEU, PE1-2796 Doc 1-84/1980, 14 April 1980 and PE1-4048 Doc. 1-545/82, 28 July 1982, respectively.
22 This attitude of conservative parties was consistent with the ideological reconceptualization of human rights along Cold War divisions of the previous decades.
23 See HAEU, PE2-7875 Motion for a resolution 2-374/84 31 July 1984; PE2-10441 Motion for a resolution B2-1064/85/rev 26 November 1985; PE2-13311 motion for a resolution Heinz Oskar Vetter 26 May 1987.

24 Parlement Européen, *Débats: Compte Rendu in extenso des séances du 9 au 12 mars 1987*.
25 HAEU, PE2-17992 A2-227/86/A and A2-227/86/B – motion for a resolution, explanatory statement and annexes, 23 February 1987.
26 HAEC, 337.1 1986 1164 EC Commission, General Secretariat SP(86)3807, 5 November 1986. Most discussions involved German representatives, because West Germany was the most sensitive member state to the issue at the time, but they were not limited to them.
27 Parlement Européen, *Débats: Compte Rendu in extenso des séances du 9 au 12 mars 1987*.
28 See, among others, European Communities, 'Declaration on European Identity', *Bulletin of the European Communities*, 12 (1973): 118–22, or the 'Adonnino Report' - Report to the European Council by the ad hoc committee 'On a People's Europe', https://www.cvce.eu/en/collections/unit-content/-/unit/02bb76df-d066-4c08-a58a-d4686a3e68ff/95a065c6-38e9-45da-8bbe-66f958a8b005/Resources#c853bbef-a767-4dde-b8ba-f575b738188f_en&overlay (accessed 2 May 2020).
29 The 1969 OAU Convention Governing the Specific Aspects of Refugee Problems in Africa moves from the definition of refugee given by the Geneva Convention ('a person who, owing to a well-founded fear of being persecuted for reasons of race, religion, nationality, membership of a particular social group or political opinion, is outside the country of his nationality and is unable or, owing to such fear, is unwilling to avail himself of the protection of that country'), enlarging it to 'every person who, owing to external aggression, occupation, foreign domination or events seriously disturbing public order in either part or the whole of his country of origin or nationality, is compelled to leave his place of habitual residence in order to seek refuge in another place outside his country of origin or nationality'.
30 The 'first entry principle' established that, in case of non-authorized arrival, the first country where asylum seekers entered had to be considered responsible for their application (no matter asylum seekers' intention). The 'clause en route' established that asylum seekers had to live a certain amount of time in a (transit) country for this country to be responsible for their application (the time spent there by asylum seekers was interpreted as an implicit expression of intention to stay there). The CAHAR promoted the 'clause en route' at the beginning, the Twelve also discussed the criterion, but they never implemented it. To deepen these points, see Gaia Lott, 'Dublin and the First Entry rule', under publication.
31 This is confirmed by many experts who worked in the asylum field at the time. See, for instance, David Martin, Interview by the author, 15 May 2020; and Christopher Hein, Interview by the author, 25 May 2020.
32 HAEC, BAC 41/1989 n.1047 Ad Hoc Group SN 2692/87 WGI, 11 September 1987.
33 Andrew Moravcsik, *The Choice for Europe: Social Purpose and State Power from Messina to Maastricht* (London: UCL Press, 1998), 371.
34 HAEU, BAC 41/1989 n.1046 de Lobkowicz (EC, General Direction Internal Market and Industrial Affairs, hereafter DG III) 'Meeting of EP Judicial Committee 29-31.10', 19 November 1986.
35 Parlement Européen, *Débats: Compte Rendu in extenso des séances du 20 au 24 Novembre 1989* and Annexe N.3-384 du 11 au 15 décembre 1989 and HAEU, PE3-24319 B3-1142/90 19 June 1990, PE3-24539 B3-1382/90 12 July 1990.
36 See, for instance, Joint Resolution replacing Docs B 2-1469, 1470, 1471 and 1473/88, OJ C 96, 17 April 1989.

37 The National Archives (hereafter TNA), HO 394/910, Pelham, 'Note of the Meeting of the Ad Hoc Group on Immigration 14-15.03.1989', 20 March 1989.
38 Article 16 of the Basic Law stated, 'persons persecuted on political grounds shall enjoy the right of asylum'. For an overview of the West Germany asylum policy, see Wolfgang Bosswick, 'Development of Asylum Policy in Germany', *Journal of Refugee Studies*, 43 (2000): 43–60.
39 AMAE, 1851INVA34 Renouard, 'Note', 5 November 1986. West Germany played a primary role at the start of the Dublin negotiations, consistent with Emmanuel Comte's thesis that Bonn was the most relevant actor in the establishment of a European migration system, see Comte, *European Migration Regime*.
40 According to de Lobkowicz, German support for community competence on asylum resulted from 'the pressure of events' and was shared by the Bundesrat. HAEC, BAC 224/1994 N.1177 De Lobkowicz 'Mission Report', 19 November 1988.
41 HAEC, BAC 224/1994 N.1178 de Lobkowicz, 'Right of Asylum, Position of the Minister of the Interior of West Germany', 24 December 1987. But such change would be only temporary and probably tactical: at the beginning of the 1990s, West Germany rearranged its posture, going back to its initial view and becoming the first promoter of community competence on asylum and migration.
42 See Decision 85/381 of 18 July 1985 (1985) OJ L217 and the judgement of the European Court of Justice in joint cases 281, 283, 284, 285 and 287/85 in https://eur-lex.europa.eu/legal-content/EN/TXT/PDF/?uri=OJ:L:1985:217:FULL&from=IT (accessed 2 May 2020). Richard Plender, 'European Community Law and Nationals of Non-member States', *The International and Comparative Law Quarterly*, 39(1990): 599–610.
43 Michelle Cini, *The European Commission: Leadership, Organisation, and Culture in the EU Administration* (Manchester: Manchester University Press, 1996), 104.
44 To deepen the discussions within the Legal Service, see HAEC, BDT-315.2014 1044 70.253.032. The point was whether there was or not a Community competence and, in positive case, whether to refer to article 100 (as suggested by DG III) or 235 (on concurrent competence, as defended by the Legal Service) of the EEC Treaty.
45 The directive allowed family unification with asylum seekers and third nationals with a permit of stay, whereas the Dublin (article 4) and Schengen Convention (article 35) admitted it just with refugees already recognized as such.
46 The only case where the asylum seeker's intention was not taken into account was for applications lodged after an irregular stay in a member state (article 10). Upon the insistence of Mediterranean States, the Commission added that after six months of stay in the country where the application was made, that country should be considered responsible (similarly to article 6.2 of the Dublin Convention). HAEC, BDT-315.2014 1044 70.253.032 Braun and Perissich (EC Commission, DG III), Note III/D/1, 28 January1988.
47 Article 20 was elicited after the UNHCR and member states' opposition. The UNHCR promoted approximation of national procedures, but since the directive made no attempt to approximate normal procedures, the institution contested that it did not make sense to foster it for abridged procedures. HAEC, BAC 41/1989 n.1047 Ivo Schwartz (EC Commission, DG III) 'Note to Perrisich', 25 July 1988.
48 The meeting between experts from the Twelve and the Commission on 17–18 March 1988 was a determinant for the withdrawal. HAEC, BDT-315.2014 1044 70.253.032 Williamson (EC Commission, General Secretariat), SG (88) 3312, 25 March 1988.

49 TNA, FCO 30/7571 Eaton (British permanent representative to the EC) – Durbin (HO) 23 February 1988.
50 TNA, FCO 30/7564 Durbin – Quidt, 'Report EC Working Group 04.03', 10 March 1988.
51 Anne Stevens, *Brussels Bureaucrats? The Administration of the European Union* (New York: Palgrave Macmillan, 2001), 140.
52 HAEC, BAC 408/1991 N.148 Sutton, 'Stavenheagen Meeting with Lord Cockfield', 9 September 1986.
53 On the subsidiarity principle, see Vincent Dujardin et al., eds, *The European Commission 1986-2000 History and Memories of An Institution* (Luxembourg: Publications Office of the European Union, 2019), 155–65.
54 HAEU, FL-627 EC Commission, Cabinet of the President, François Lamoureux 'Note for the President' 88/204, 15 July 1988.
55 HAEC, BAC 41/1989 n.1047 Fortescue, 'Note to Cockfield', 27 September 1988.
56 HAEU, JD-21 Statement of President Jacques Delors on the orientation of the Commission in front of the European Parliament, 14 Janury1985.
57 Comte, *European Migration Regime*, 178.
58 Asylum would be included in the Third Pillar by the Treaty on European Union, under article K1. OJ C 326, 26 October 2012. Kay Hailbronner and Claus Thiery, 'Schengen II and Dublin: Responsibility for Asylum Applications in Europe', *Common Market Law Review*, 34 (1997): 962.
59 See, among others, European Parliament News, 'EU Asylum Rules: Reform of the Dublin System', 24 July 2019, *europarl.europa*, https://www.europarl.europa.eu/news/en/headlines/priorities/refugees/20180615STO05927/eu-asylum-rules-reform-of-the-dublin-system (accessed September 2020).

Part III

Other Europes

9

Human rights NGOs in Western Europe and the intervention of the Council of Europe in the Nigerian Civil War

Oluchukwu Ignatus Onianwa

Western Europe's interest in human rights in the world emerged partly as consequence of the Nigerian Civil War. One of the largest humanitarian crises after the Second World War, the Nigerian Civil War introduced one of the most significant nucleuses upon which human rights debates developed over the following years, namely individuals' and unarmed civilians' rights to life, survival and access to basic needs. As such, the Nigerian Civil War transcended both its domestic nature and Euro–Nigerian relations. It assumed a global dimension, with a transnational movement in solidarity of the civilian population, which surpasses ethnic, ideological and political differences.

The consternation over the extent of human catastrophe in the fighting was beyond national frontiers. The head of the British Relief Mission to Nigeria and Biafra Lord Hunt puts it aptly:

> There was a deep concern and anxiety by people all over the world about the fate of innocent people who had been caught up, many of them not of their own free will, in the holocaust of the civil war. Even allowing for the fact that this human sympathy was allied in the minds of many with political aspirations and aims of one or the other side, the fact cannot be denied that this great welling up of feelings by people outside Nigeria was a major feature of the history of this war which will be seen in retrospect as one of its more redeeming characteristics. It was a revelation of the spiritual bonds which link people with people, irrespective of man-made frontier. As such it overrides the boundaries of national sovereignty.[1]

The concept of human rights is shared globally and as such forms a basis for the international community of states, international organizations and social movements, all of which regard themselves as members of international society. Human rights can also be a means which people can use as a tool for social transformation.[2] Human rights campaign during the Nigerian Civil War revolved round fundamentally 'the need for international efforts to relieve human sufferings. And if nothing was done to save lives many could die'.[3] Also, part of the issue posed during the civil war that had great impact on human rights campaign was why civilian population would be treated unjustly. It was this important perception which guided the activities of human rights NGOs and the reactions of Council of Europe (CoE) to the fighting. In short, without the human rights voices which spread across Western Europe and elsewhere the tragic death toll inside Biafra would have risen to astronomic proportions.

This chapter interrogates human rights non-governmental organizations (NGOs) in Western Europe and the response of the CoE to the Nigerian Civil War. The CoE was among the European supranational organizations such as the defunct Western European Union which reacted to the ongoing war, and in so doing, it paved the way for a stronger European interest in human rights abuses in the world, which was later embodied by the European Community.[4] Indeed, during the late 1960s, member states of the European Community were unable to elaborate a common position on the Nigerian Civil War, due to EC institutional limits and lack of political ambitions as well as divisions among national governments as evidenced in the British application to join the EC. Britain nearly lost its bid to join the EC because of its involvement in the civil war but that never happened, giving the vested interests of some European powers. However, the quest for the adoption of a more humanistic approach to matters like human rights and the need to achieve strong European unity and solidarity and to create greater cooperation between Europeans and the wider world left the CoE as one of the European supranational institutions able to assume a position vis-à-vis the humanitarian crisis occurring in Nigeria.

The perception of the civil war as a struggle for justice and human rights influenced the NGOs and human rights activists in Western Europe who believed that the struggle was not just the theoretical or legalistic question of secession from an established entity. It was also about the preservation of fundamental human rights. The chapter points out that human rights campaign that took place during the Nigerian Civil War were highly effective in Western Europe. The highly cherished liberal and democratic principles in Western Europe made it easier for the eruption of some kind of grass-roots consciousness and European human rights voices on the conflict. Campaign for human rights was not monolithic rather it was a collective and plural effort. The CoE considered its role in the conflict as within the 'rights and conscience of the people of Europe' as evident in a number of resolutions it adopted. The humanitarian concern of the CoE member states on the war lifted them above politics and entitled them to disregard the norms of international conduct between sovereign states in responding to the conflict. By the end of the conflict in 1970 global human rights discourse had expanded leading to the formation of laws to protect the right of civilians to live and survive in war.

The Nigerian Civil War and human rights NGOs in Western Europe

NGOs' efforts gave an important contribution to the progress made over decades in the promotion and protection of global human rights. While at national and international level, NGOs have performed significantly in campaigning for the protection of human rights, they have equally played a helpful role in informing and sustaining public opinion that has often paved the way and stimulated governmental humanitarian actions.[5]

The important place to begin with how human rights of that period evolved is Biafra, an example of the connection among the human rights breakthroughs of the 1970, humanitarianism and genocide. The Nigerian counterinsurgency in the late 1960s prompted widespread moral outrage across the West, including accusation of genocide.[6]

In the summer of 1968, media reports of human sufferings in the Nigerian Civil War began to disconcert the conscience of the world particularly in Western Europe. Readers around the world were shocked when they were confronted with photographs of starving children in the secessionist Republic of Biafra. Many were soon convinced that genocide against Biafra's Igbo was impending; the spectre of a West African Auschwitz loomed large on the postcolonial horizon. The war became the first postcolonial conflict to engender transnational and non-governmental organizations principally in the International Committee of Red Cross and a number of religious organizations under the umbrella of Joint Aid, which organized an airlift to bring food into Biafra.[7] As Lassen Heerten rightly argued:

> At least at first sight this episode seems to be a perfect fit for the new body of scholarship on the history of human rights. Historians have recently begun to shed new light on the 1970s, reinterpreting the decade as a period of global transformation. This is held to be connected to the rise of human rights as one of the lingua francas of the international politics in the age of audiovisual mass media.[8]

In Western Europe, opinion about the Nigerian Civil War spread wider and deeper, and crystallized in the appearance of well-built grass-roots networks of human right NGOs. Thousands of ordinary people popularly known as the 'man-on-the-street' were realistically mobilized to make a case for the rights of the war victims. Biafra attracted strong attention in Europe as long as human rights were concerned but within the context of generality of the war. European citizens created strong awareness about plight of the unarmed civilians in the warzone, while some even equated the Nigerian conflict as a violation of existing international humanitarian laws such as the Geneva Conventions of 1949.

Among the prominent European organizations that took part in the campaign for human rights protection of unarmed civilian population in the Nigeria–Biafra crisis was the Confèdèration Française Dèmocratique du Travail based in Paris (CFDT). The CFDT, usually known as the Catholic Workers Union was the largest trade union in France. It had three-quarters of a million workers as its members. On 14 August 1968 it issued a communiqué in Paris on the Nigerian–Biafran conflict which 'appealed to all workers for their solidarity in preventing the elimination of Biafran people through murder and starvation; called on the United Nations Secretary-General, U-Thant, to take all necessary measures to organize relief operations and the conclusion of a ceasefire and called upon countries supplying arms to cease deliveries and carry out an embargo'.[9]

Amnesty International, Bureau International-Catholique de L'Enfance (International Catholic Child Bureau) Caritas, Suisse, Commission Internationale de Juristes (CIJ) Conference des Eveques Suisses, Entraide Universitaire Mondiale (World University Service) Friends World Committee for Consultation (Quakers) and Ligue Suise Des Femmes Catholic (LSFC) were well-known human rights NGOs that brought the plight of the civilian population to the attention of the international community, particularly of the refugees and prisoners of war. On 26 August 1968, they jointly issued a text of appeal for a total end of the Nigeria–Biafra conflict. According to the communiqué released on behalf of the NGOs by the Sponsoring Committee based in Geneva:

> Whereas the Charter of the United Nations solemnly proclaimed the faith of the peoples of the UN in the dignity and worth of the human person; whereas this declaration of faith had been reaffirmed in the Universal Declaration of Human Rights, the twentieth anniversary of which was celebrated this year (1968); whereas the UN had affirmed in the Declaration of the Rights of the Child that mankind owed to the child the best it has to give; noted that the situation in Nigeria-Biafra as it presented itself was likely to develop into grave risk of leading to genocide as

Figure 9.1 Women and children receiving food at refugee camp during the Biafra war. European NGOs and the Council of Europe were deeply concerned at the fate of civilians during the Biafran war.

defined by the Convention on the Prevention and Suppression of Genocide of 9 December 1948.[10]

These NGOs urged the Secretary General of the United Nations, U-Thant, the United States and European governments; African governments and the Organization of African Unity (OAU) to take adequate and necessary measures to prevent the perpetration of genocide in any form whatsoever, directly or indirectly in the civil war.[11]

The International Union for Child Welfare (IUCW), an umbrella organization in Geneva NGO with 104 organizations in 52 countries in 5continents, including Europe, realized that irrespective of all considerations of its political, religious or military character, it was children that had suffered most acutely in the civil war. On 15 August 1968 the IUCW through its Secretary General, Pierre Zumbach, made a solemn appeal to the chairman of the OAU Consultative Committee Her Imperial Majesty Emperor Haile Selassie of Ethiopia to do all in his power to obtain from the two parties of the war the guarantee of access to basic needs of survival to the children who were the most affected. The IUCW felt most strongly that in the war the safety of children required the greatest urgent action.[12]

The Society for the Promotion of Arts and Sciences based in Berlin but with offices in Uganda's capital, Kampala, championed the cause of human rights during the civil war. The organization wrote a petition to the British government concerning the plight of civilian population in the conflict. Having investigated the political and international law aspects of the problem, they were of the conviction that the conflict between Nigeria and Biafra could only be solved on the basis of self-determination. The right of self-determination was one of the clear international political doctrines established by UN, and it was also a fundamental principle of modern international law by its being accepted as part of the Charter of the United Nations.[13]

The Socialist International was another prominent international player that canvassed heavily for the human rights of the civilian population and the need for urgent humanitarian action in the Nigerian–Biafran conflict. On 26August 1968, a resolution was collectively passed at the meeting of the Council of the organization. According to the resolution:

> The Socialist International, appalled by the bloodshed and loss of life involved in the conflict over Nigeria-Biafra, requests the combatants and other interested parties to abstain from all action which could prolong the armed conflict, calls for an international embargo on the supply of arms to either side in Nigeria, deplores the obstacles which prevent the ready access of relief to distressed civilian population, and calls for the removal of these obstacles and at the same time an amplification of the programme of international aid and urged the participants in the war to reach an early settlement with the assistance of the OAU and the UN.[14]

The National Executive at Labour Party Conference held in Blackpool on 3 October 1968 passed a resolution no. 356 that called the British government to stop the sale of arms to Nigeria and to intensify efforts to bring the two sides together for peaceful settlement.[15]

After the Labour Party's Conference in Blackpool passed its resolution, delivered to the British prime minister, on 9 November 1968 thirteen British citizens unanimously sent a letter to the British Secretary of State for Foreign and Commonwealth Affairs, Michael Stewart, at his Whitehall office in London. The group had in the name of humanity and on behalf of the majority of the British citizens insisted that the Foreign Secretary should immediately implement the unqualified demand of the Labour Party Conference as enshrined in the resolution 356. According to the group:

> We insist that you respond to the explicit wishes of the large majority of the British people. . We insist that current British policy which had helped to cause the death and starvation of millions of people be reversed, and an end put to the violations of the United Nations Declaration of Human Rights, Article 3; everyone has the right to life, liberty and security of person. We are individuals who have tried in many ways to bring the suffering and the war to end, by petitions, vigils, fasts, lobbying, fundraising, leafleting, articles and letters to the press. We have now come together for a non-violent direct campaign against the British contributions to this war. We will not rest until our government carries out its basic moral obligations. We urgently await their fulfillment.[16]

The Socialist Morality Council led by Bishop Butler, auxiliary bishop of Westminster, the British Humanist Association chaired by Peter Draper, the United Nations Association, and the British Committee for Peace in Nigeria played a prominent role in the conflict on human rights grounds. On 28 March 1969 these NGOs held a public meeting at the St. Pancras Town Hall in London to express concern over the fate of civilian victims and human rights protection in the fighting. Bishop Butler said at the meeting that:

> If conditions for a just war were ever fulfilled in the Nigerian conflict, they were no longer being fulfilled. The casualties there now equaled those sustained by Soviet Union during the whole of World War II. The British government and Foreign Office should get away from the rather conventional thinking about the situation, which was no longer adequate to the human realities. Pressure should be brought to bear on Russia through the UN. Why could not Britain and France in a joint action on an issue which could be important?[17]

Peter Draper said that 'ending the war campaign was not merely anti-Labour'. He stressed the moral basis of the campaign and suggested raising the issue at the UN.[18] As David Perman rightly argued European reactions to the Nigerian war and human rights concerns presented a remarkable picture of a continent deeply concerned with the fate of an African people. It could not be explained in terms of national interests in Nigeria of the political role of France or Portugal or the missionary interests of the Norwegian in West Africa. The concern of Europe and sympathy for Biafrans cut across political lines, with the exception of the Communists.[19] The Biafran cause was for many Europeans a clear issue of saving a people from destruction and human rights abuses, and for this reason European's reaction had not been clouded by the political complexities felt by Britain with its commitment to support another Commonwealth government.[20]

During the Nigerian Civil War, transnational human rights and humanitarian activists challenged the Cold War configuration of international relations. In its place they offered a new set of international priorities based not on a divide between political or economic ideologies but on a universal principle of human rights. In this universal configuration borders, frontiers and sovereignty took a backseat to the plight of humanity. Focusing on ideals, universality, and the interdependence of man, activists reacting to the conflict offered new human rights diplomacy. Human rights diplomacy was both a process, working through non-governmental and international organizations rather than nation-states, and an end goal, imposing a new set of rules and dynamics based on the principles and rights of humanity onto international politics.[21] These NGOs and activists challenged the traditional Cold War paradigm of interstate relations by offering an alternative, global framework best described as a new human rights diplomacy that focused on human interdependence and not sovereignty, territorial integrity of states or economic ideologies.[22]

NGOs and intervention of the Council of Europe

The activities and appeals of human rights NGOs in Western Europe fuelled the diplomatic window of discussions of the Nigerian conflict by the CoE. The intervention of this supranational institution was the height of the human rights campaign concerning the civil war. Its member states were convinced that there was no guarantee of human security in the conflict, for there was huge influx of refugees across the war-ravaged territory and many were exposed to live threatening situations such as military attacks, hunger, starvation, famine, malnutrition, disease, displacement and lack of healthcare.

The most important appeal that prompted the CoE to debate the civil war was made by United Nations Children Fund (UNICEF) and the Pax Christi Movement. In a telegram dated 26 July 1968, M.M.E. Gertrude Lutz, the acting director of UNICEF appealed to the President of the CoE to bring the plight of women and children in the conflict and the need to provide emergency relief to the war victims to the attention of the members of the Council whose support was considered crucial in order to obtain special attention from their national governments.[23]

On 5 August 1968, the Executive Committee of the Pax Christi Movement presided over by H.E. Cardinal Alfrink referred to the UN Year of Human Rights to issue an appeal to the CoE, all churches, European governments, statesmen, parliamentarians, political parties, trade unions and employers' organizations in Europe to do everything possible in their power to prevent the starvation of millions of people in Nigeria–Biafra. According to the communiqué issued by the Movement:

> Without delay it must be seen to that food and medicaments, sent from many different sides, can reach their destination in areas of distress unhindered, so that numerous people, threatened by death can be saved. Quick and effective action is a

duty of human solidarity. Moreover, an appeal is being made to all above mentioned persons, organizations and authorities to achieve the immediate abolition of arms supplies, in order to hasten at least, the end of bloodshed, after the awful events that have taken place.[24]

The Pax Christi Movement appeal was transmitted to the CoE headquarters in Strasbourg, France, on 29 August 1968. After due considerations, the Bureau of the Consultative Assembly of the CoE filed a case on behalf of the movement titled 'Assistance for the Inhabitants of Biafra' for further deliberations by the council ministers and deputies of the CoE.[25] Indeed, this was a triumphant victory for the European human rights agitators during the war. It brought more closely the attention of the European governments to the plight of the people on both sides and facilitated adequate time devotion to the civil war issue by the CoE.

The year 1968 as the International Human Rights Year (IHRY) offered a unique opportunity for the CoE member states to share their thoughts and pass resolutions on the conflict. While the IHRY had called for the review and assessment of activities in the field of global human rights since the end of Second World War, the outbreak of the civil war and its effect on the civilian population was a strict reminder that the world had not done enough in the protection of human rights.[26] According to Mommersteeg:

> This year 1968 is Human Rights Year, proclaimed by the United Nations. The events in . . . Biafra constitute some of the most eloquent proofs of the fact that we are still far from the full implementation of the universal declaration of human rights in the world, and even, in Europe, of the European Convention. In Biafra we are confronted with the most primary right that a human being has, the right to live.[27]

Brian McNeil argued that the Nigerian Civil War demonstrates the new challenges arising from the universal principle of human rights and the ways that states had to adjust and react to it. In addition, many of the central conflicts of the post-war era were overlapping and coming to a head during the war: the Cold War, decolonization, human rights and humanitarianism, state sovereignty and globalization.[28] Thus, the year 1968 created an opportunity for stronger debates for alternative programmes and supranational interventions for the protection of individual rights to safety in war.

The CoE intervention in the Nigerian conflict was equally inspired by the UN International Conference on Human Rights held in Tehran, Iran, from 22 April to 13 May 1968, in which the UN General Assembly convened the conference as part of the activities to mark the IHRY. The conference was organized for the purpose of reviewing the progress made in the field of human rights since the adoption of the Universal Declaration in 1948 and to formulate a programme of activities for the future.[29] In one of its passages, the Final Proclamation of Teheran clarified:

> Steps could be taken to secure the better application of existing humanitarian international conventions and rules in all arms conflict; and the need for additional humanitarian international conventions or for possible revision of

existing conventions to ensure the better protection of civilians, prisoners and combatants in all armed conflicts and the prohibition and limitation of the use of certain methods and means of warfare.[30]

The Nigerian–Biafran conflict played a role in the introduction of resolution on human rights in armed conflict, for there were already ongoing debates on how to protect war victims vulnerable to military attacks and the humanitarian aid workers in the warzone. A sturdy emphasis on this point was made by Sean MacBride in a letter sent to the Chairman of the Sub-Committee on Human Rights, Van der Stoel, regarding the resolution of the eleventh General Conference of the Non-Governmental Organizations in consultative status with UN Economic and Social Council (ECOSOC) regarding the protection of observers engaged in peaceful humanitarian, social or educational work adopted on 3 October 1969:

> This resolution was prompted by the fact that seven representatives of humanitarian organisations lost their lives in the Nigerian-Biafran conflict. In addition, observers from NGOs have also been arrested and imprisoned in the course of their missions. While the Conference appreciated that it would not be possible to obtain a special diplomatic status for observers of NGOs, they did feel that governments should be requested to ensure their safety and to extend facilities to them.[31]

While these efforts were made to secure better application of The Hague and Geneva conventions in armed conflict, it was believed that the CoE could better reinforce any steps necessary to strengthen the existing international conventions on human rights and could take steps to ensure that the minimum rules are applied.[32]

Meeting of the Council of Europe on the Nigerian–Biafran conflict, 1968–70

During the meeting of the Political Committee of the Consultative Assembly held on 30 March 1968 in Paris the delegate from the Federal Republic of Germany, Kliesing proposed the inclusion of 'a condemnation of genocide in Biafra' in the draft resolution of the Political Committee.[33] On 29 August 1968 the Nigerian–Biafran case was officially inscribed in the agenda of the CoE Consultative Assembly Committee on Population and Refugee for the meeting to be held on Friday 30 August 1968.[34]

The Nigeria–Biafra issue was widely discussed at the CoE headquarters in Strasbourg on 10 September 1968.[35] The meeting was opened by the Chairman Margue from Luxembourg. During the meeting, the chairman referred the Committee to the appeal made by the Pax Christi Movement. The question was referred to the Committee on Population and Refugees, as the competent committee to handle the matter. It was for this reason that the chairman was glad that the director of the International Committee of Red Cross (ICRC) Claude Pilloud was present at the meeting. Pilloud told the Committee about the situation in Biafra and what the ICRC had done to assist the victims of the civil war. He argued that 'despite appeals by the ICRC, the Geneva

Conventions for the treatment of civilians and prisoners of war were rarely respected. In addition, there was almost no legal basis for bringing aid to the territory'.[36]

The Norwegian representative Pohler expressed great admiration for the work of the Red Cross in tackling a problem where politics had failed. He then declared that 'the Council of Europe should urge member governments to increase aid and also to do all that was possible in the political field'.[37] The chairman referred to the motion for a recommendation, which was signed by all members present. In accordance with the motion the Committee could present a request for urgent procedure, for the question to be included during the September session. This was agreed. The chairman suggested the need for the Committee to appoint a rapporteur on the question. At the suggestion of the French delegate Zussy, the Committee decided to appoint Margue as the rapporteur.[38]

The meeting of the Consultative Assembly's Committee on Population and Refugees continued on 23 September 1968 in Strasbourg.[39] Chairman Margue from Luxembourg referred members of the Committee about the information communicated to governments on aid to the population in Nigeria–Biafra territories. The chairman welcomed Gaillard, deputy director of the ICRC to the meeting. Gaillard said his main intention was to supplement the information provided by Pilloud, director of the ICRC at its meeting in Paris, and to inform it of the recent development.[40]

Following this, the Committee decided to appoint George Margue, Luxembourg Social Christian, as rapporteur on 'assistance to the victims of the civil war in Nigeria'. The chairman suggested that the Committee could proceed to adopt the preliminary draft recommendation on this question. The Committee adopted its preliminary draft Recommendation 532 on the assistance to the victims of the civil war in Nigeria. According to the recommendation:

> The Assembly, expressing its grave concern at the development of the civil war in Nigeria and in particular at the many serious reported cases of starvation, illness and injuries among the civilian population of Biafra; considering that any further delay in the aid to the victims of the civil war in Nigeria will result in a catastrophe shameful to humanity; welcoming the efforts of the International Committee of the Red Cross with vigorous support from its National Societies as of other voluntary organizations to relieve the suffering of the population, in particular women and children, in the civil war areas; grateful for the contributions in cash and in materials which had been made by the governments of the Member-States of the Council of Europe in support of the first aid measures.[41]

Under Recommendation 532 the member governments of the Committee of Ministers were urged to continue to provide food and medical supplies for the victims of the civil war in Nigeria and to support the work of the ICRC with large financial contributions and to facilitate its initiatives and those of other voluntary organizations.[42] Consequently, the rapporteur, Margue, produced an explanatory memorandum in which he argued that 'it was a humanitarian duty of the governments of member-states of the CoE to support and also to use their influence to facilitate immediately all actions to rescue the victims of the civil war in Nigeria'.[43]

On 26 September 1968 the Assembly convened again to continue the discussion on assistance to the victims of the civil war. Before the debate started, Sir Geoffrey de Freitas, President of the Assembly, reminded members that the motion for urgent procedure which had asked for a debate on Nigeria had been confined to the humanitarian aspect of the war. The matter was referred to the Political Committee and the debate did not offer scope for political discussion. The delegate from the Federal Republic of Germany said that the political and humanitarian questions of the war could not be completely separated. The CoE should not only concern itself with sending foods and medicine to the starving people in Nigeria but it should also try to prevent military aid being sent there either directly or indirectly. Although some would argue that if European countries did not send arms to Nigeria, the Soviet Union would; this kind of intellectual argument should be overruled by humanitarian considerations. Europe should not descend to the level of the Soviet Union. The delegate from Switzerland, M. Reverdin, spoke of the sophisticated weapons which were made in Europe and supplied to people who were in less developed countries. European governments had followed different aims in Biafra and should have a common policy to give assistance to the victims of the war. The Assembly later adopted the text of the Recommendation 532 on the assistance to aid the civil war victims.[44]

The meeting of the Committee on Population and Refugees held on 17 December 1968 at the office of the CoE in Paris was attended by Chairman Margue from Luxembourg, Vice Chairman Firnberg from Austria and representatives from other member states.[45] The chairman informed the Committee that he expected the Committee of Ministers' reply to the Recommendation 532 on the victims of the civil war in Nigeria at the beginning of January 1969. Asscher from the Office of the UN High Commissioner for Refugees drew attention to the difficult position of the Biafran refugees that stayed in the Western African states. Thus, he argued that 'these countries were not sufficiently equipped to provide these refugees with the aid they needed. At a future meeting of the Committee, he would present more details on this question'.[46]

The meeting of the Committee continued at the Riverwalk House in London on 2–4 June 1969. Following an address by British journalist Auberon Waugh on Nigeria and Biafra the Committee instructed the chairman to put a question to the Committee of Ministers at the September session of the Assembly on the measures taken by the CoE member states on the victims of the civil war in Nigeria.[47] When the Committee held its meeting in Strasbourg on 30 September 1969, Margue reminded the Committee that he had put a Written Question No. 139 titled 'Assistance to Aid the Victims of Civil War in Nigeria' to the Committee of Ministers asking them which action had been taken by CoE member governments among those proposed in the previous recommendation.[48]

Consequently, at its 174thmeeting held on 28–30 October 1968 the deputies of the Committee of Ministers exchanged views on Assembly Recommendation 532. They agreed to transmit to respective European governments its paragraph 8(a) that was, 'to urge member governments to continue and extend food and medical supplies for the victims of the civil war in Nigeria and to support the work of the ICRC with large financial contributions, and to facilitate its initiatives and those of other voluntary organisation', whose humanitarian aspect they appreciated. They decided however to take no action, at least for the moment, on paragraph 8(b) being 'to urge the

Nigerian government to adopt immediately every appropriate means of permitting the rapid transport of food and medical supplies and also medical staff to Biafra', whose political aspects were likely to arouse misunderstanding among the African countries.[49]

The deputies agreed that they would decide at the present meeting on the terms of the reply by the Committee of Ministers to Assembly Recommendation 532, on the basis of a draft from the secretariat. The secretariat accordingly proposed the following text:

> The Committee of Ministers had considered Recommendation 532 on assistance to the victims of the civil war in Nigeria. Appreciating the humanitarian aims of the Recommendation as set out particularly in its paragraph 8(a), the Committee of Ministers had decided to transmit that part of the Recommendation to the governments of the member-States of the CoE. The Committee of Ministers had noted with satisfaction that financial aid, food and medical supplies have been contributed by member governments for the relief of suffering in Nigeria; impressive amounts of aid have likewise flowed from private and other charitable sources within the members States for this purpose.[50]

The issue of arms supplies which increased the tempo of military onslaught by the Nigerian Army and Biafran soldiers thereby endangered the human security in the conflict triggered a debate by the CoE on the need to halt purchase of arms in black markets in European countries. On 30 January 1969 the Consultative Assembly referred to the Political Affairs Committee a motion for a resolution presented by James Johnson, a British delegate, that the CoE should investigate the black market in arms and take action to end it. In the proposed resolution the Assembly noted with concern the continued and serious nature of the civil war in Nigeria. The motion condemned

> the sale of arms upon the international black market, supplied from European sources to both sides in the war. It also supported the action taken by the Swiss government to stop any dealing in this black market by its citizens and called upon the member states of the CoE to take action to suppress this infamous traffic in munitions of war Federal Government and Biafra.[51]

Since arms particularly from European sources were used to execute the civil war, thereby increasing human sufferings, the proposed resolution sought to admonish the member states of the CoE to avoid any action which prolonged or aggravated the conflict.

Kaj Bjork of Swedish Social Democrat was appointed as the rapporteur at the Political Affairs Committee meeting held on 18 March 1969 with a mandate to extend the terms of reference of the motion for a resolution, on the grounds that the traffic of arms from private sources into Nigeria was an important factor, but not the only cause for the continuance of the civil war. In surveying the military, political and humanitarian terms and attitudes of other countries and international organizations towards the civil war, Bjork argued:

The problem of Nigeria does not enter into the immediate responsibilities of the CoE and it is not the task of European organisations to intrude into African affairs. All the same, it is clear that European states have a certain responsibility and should avoid any action which might prolong or aggravate the conflict. In this connection, the problem of arms deliveries arises. The Federal Government received official arms deliveries from the Soviet Union and the United Kingdom. Biafrans were supplied by certain firms or interests from Europe.[52]

The eight Consultative Assembly's Political Affairs Committee meeting was held on 26 April 1969 at the Paris Office of the CoE.[53] Chairman Struye from Belgium asked Bjork to open the discussion. Bjork pointed out that the report was provisional and would be brought up to date for the May session of the meeting. It was decided at the last meeting of the Political Affairs Committee to extend the terms of reference of motion for a resolution, since the Assembly would not only express an opinion on the black-market traffic of arms. West German member Bruck doubted whether an appeal to stop arms deliveries would be very effective. Kliesing said that the President of the Assembly could be asked to transmit the Assembly's views to the member governments of the OAU.[54]

The Political Affairs Committee of the Consultative Assembly held its first meeting of the twenty-first session of the Assembly in Strasbourg on 12 May 1969 and resumed its discussions on the Biafra crisis.[55] Specifically it resumed the discussion of the question whether allusion should be made in the draft resolution to the danger of genocide in Biafra. Griffiths said he would prefer to see the draft maintained in its present form. The delegate from Italy, Badini Confalioneri, said he thought that mention should be made in the draft resolution of the danger of genocide that threatened the Biafran population. Bjork moved that the first paragraph of the draft resolution be amended by the addition of the following that represented a serious threat to the survival of the minority opposing the federal government. The amendment was adopted by twelve votes to nil, with one abstention.[56]

The Political Affairs Committee held another meeting on 15 May 1969 at Strasbourg. Chairman Kirk from the United Kingdom referred members to the amended version of the draft resolution and suggested that the Committee should proceed to the final adoption of the text. James Johnson who substituted Sir Geoffrey de Freitas from the UK said he would oppose the appeal for a general arms embargo made in paragraph 8 of the resolution. According to Johnson: 'Assembly's action should be limited to proposing a prevention of the black-market traffic in arms, as was stated in the motion for a resolution of which he was the author and which had brought this subject to the Committee. The sentiments expressed in the resolution were laudable but the text would have no effect.'[57]

According to the draft resolution the Assembly was deeply concerned at the large-scale human suffering caused by the civil war in Nigeria, which represented a serious threat to the survival of the minority opposing the federal government. It was aware that the Organization of African Unity had requested its member states and all member states of the United Nations to refrain from any action likely to impede the peace, unity and territorial integrity of Nigeria and it also recognized that the problem of Nigeria was essentially African:

Considered however that European nations have a common moral responsibilities to alleviate the sufferings caused by the conflict, to avoid any action which might increase the number of victims and to use all available means in order to help towards a peaceful solution; asked all European governments to increase their humanitarian aid to the victims of the conflict, to support the work of the ICRC and the voluntary relief organisations, and to facilitate and support the efforts of these organizations to coordinate and to give maximum effect to their relief activities; appealed to all governments whether Western or Eastern Europe, to establish joint a general arms embargo as a step towards a general agreement covering a ceasefire ... and urged African governments to do their utmost to achieve a rapid cessation of the hostilities and to lay the foundation of a peaceful settlement.[58]

The Committee later adopted the resolution by sixteen votes to zero with four abstentions. European states were urged to avoid any action that might prolong or aggravate the conflict. The European governments that were not directly involved in the conflict should exercise a severe control on the sale of arms on the international black market to both sides in the war.[59]

At its seventh sitting of the twenty-first Ordinary Session of the Consultative Assembly held on 16 May 1969 the report of the Political Affairs Committee on the suppression of traffic of arms and munitions of war into Nigeria was presented by Bjork. The Assembly considered the draft resolution. An amendment was proposed by Silkin to leave out the words 'to the survival of the minority opposing the Federal government' and to insert the words 'not only to fighting personnel but also to civilians'. A verbal sub-amendment to add at the end, the words 'whether they be on one side or the other' proposed by MacEntee was agreed on. Another amendment proposed by Silkin in paragraph 8 to insert the words 'to do anything within their power' was agreed to. Another amendment was proposed by Destermau at the end of paragraph 8 to leave out the word 'black-market'. The amendment was withdrawn. Thereafter, an agreement on what now became Resolution 413 was reached.[60]

The deputies discussed Resolution 413 on the suppression of the traffic of arms and munitions of war in Nigeria, in connection with the discussion at the forty-fourth session of the Committee of Ministers on transmission of CoE documents to the UN. The delegates at the meeting that included the United Kingdom, Sweden and Switzerland unanimously doubted the advisability of transmitting the resolution to the UN given African susceptibilities towards the Europeans passing resolutions on African questions. The Secretary General added that the Assembly considered that it had a role to play in the war as the conscience of the people of Europe and as was apparent from a number of the texts adopted.[61]

On 28 January 1970 the Committee on Population and Refugee held another meeting in Strasburg to assess the extent of response of European governments to the humanitarian needs of the civilian population in Nigeria–Biafra. Individuals who attended the meeting as observers were Walter Besterman, deputy director of the Intergovernmental Committee for European Migration; Schnelter, special representative of the Council of Europe for National Refugees and Over-Population; Rodie, counsellor of the Intergovernmental Committee for European Migration;

Granville Fletcher, officer of the United Nations in Geneva; Bouge, International Union of Family Organizations; Miss Des Gachons, World Union of Catholic Women's Organizations; and Van Mierlo-Mutsaers, European Union of Women. Chairman Margue from Luxembourg opened the meeting at 9 a.m. and welcomed to the meeting Besterman, deputy director of the Intergovernmental Committee for European Migration, and Schneiter, Special Representative of the CoE for National Refugees and Over-population.[62] During this meeting, an alternative draft recommendation and alternative draft resolution were presented which stated that:

> The Assembly ... expressing its confidence that the Nigerian government will in a spirit of humanity and mercy continue to take all necessary steps to bring about a lasting peace based on respect for human rights and to guarantee a return to normal life of all the people of this country who have been so cruelly stricken and urged its embers to make any suitable approach to their governments and to take any necessary steps in their parliaments to ensure speedy implementation of the measures above and in recommendation referred to. This new recommendation should not contain any of the point included in the original draft texts on which objections had been raised.[63]

The Committee members unanimously adopted the draft recommendation presented by the Committee on Population and Refugees which stated that the Assembly has taken note of the ceasefire of January 1970 in Nigeria. The Committee also expressed its gratitude to those CoE member states that had already assisted the population in distress. It recommended that the Committee of Ministers invite the government of member states to continue to make available the financial assistance, transportation, food, medical supplies, and equipment for those operations for persons in need in Nigeria.[64]

CoE regarded the Biafran issue as a humanitarian affair. Not only did it appealed to Western European member states to commit themselves to the humanitarian tasks posed by the conflict, but it also called on the belligerents to conform strictly to the provisions of international human rights laws by ensuring the safety and protection of civilian population. In doing so, the CoE had simply intensified efforts towards promoting human rights in armed conflict. President of the CoE Consultative Assembly, Geoffrey de Freitas, argued, 'This matter deals solely with the question of humanitarianism. Accordingly, it is not within the scope of our debate to deal with political aspects. It comes to us, under the urgent procedure on humanitarian grounds.'[65]

The pressures of public opinion in Western European countries forced CoE member states into active intervention on humanitarian grounds as a way of holding aloof from political involvement with one side or the other in the conflict. The consistent demands for action and sympathy for the war victims drew Western governments into the humanitarian issue. No government was willing or able to defend inactivity on the grounds that this was Nigeria's problem. Thus, to justify political inactivity they had to engage in tackling the humanitarian issue.[66]

The CoE saw no reason why the Nigerian government and Biafran authorities should obstruct and prevent humanitarian aid to the victims of the war. Also difficult to see was why people were still dying of starvation in Biafra already occupied for a long time by the Nigerian army. Also difficult to see was why they prevented transport aircraft from landing in the unoccupied zones of Biafra when they could control in advance what was on board those aircraft. Therefore, strong demands were made that Nigeria and Biafra leaders should make concessions for humanitarian action and that whoever prevented humanitarian aid for whatever political reasons cuts himself off from humanity and civilization for what might seem to be a momentary political advantage did not in the long run make up for the damage caused by loss of moral authority.[67]

The federal government of Nigeria became extremely bitter about the pressures to which they were subjected by CoE member states. It was torn between a genuine desire to allow the call by CoE for humanitarian aid to reach the war victims in Biafra and their resentment at the apparent determination of Western Europe to intervene in Nigeria's internal affairs, denigrate or infringe her sovereignty and give comfort and support to Biafra.[68]

As scholar Brian McNeil rightly argued, to Nigerians, perhaps justified in their suspicions of European motives, the right to interfere based on human rights was nothing more than imperialism rebranded: a way for ex-colonial powers to control the affairs of their former colonies. Gowon complained that proposals on relief had always been presented as 'moral obligations' without any consideration of Nigeria's national interest. He resented external attempts to run operations in Nigeria without full regard for Nigerian sovereignty and concluded that Europeans would never treat another European country in this way.[69] Nevertheless, the controversy and pressures did reflect a real, widespread and deeply felt concern with a genuine human disaster; it evoked generosity, disinterested hard work and bravery from individual viewpoint. It certainly saved many hundreds of thousands of lives. It caught the imagination and activated the idealism of people all over the world.

Conclusion

The human rights campaign related to the Nigerian Civil War that developed in Western Europe took the direction of the consciousness over the impeding humanitarian catastrophe and contextualization of the conflict as a struggle for justice and human rights. From activists' perspectives, the war was not just about the theoretical legitimacy of the right of secession; it was above all about protecting human rights. The prevalent liberal and democratic principles in Western Europe made it flexible for the eruption of some kind of grass-roots consciousness and human rights voices on the conflict. Human rights ideas were outsourced from public domain and prominent individuals concerned over the right of survival in the war. However, concern about slow response to humanitarian operations influenced Western European human rights activists to mount pressure on European member states and the CoE to intervene in the civil war. Due to deepening domestic pressures in their respective countries Western European governments agreed that action needed to be taken with the aim of saving lives threatened by the war. The international voluntary organizations tried to convince the

CoE member states on the necessity for effective collaboration on the facilitation of access and supply of basic needs of survival to the war victims. Their actions increased the level of commitment by Western Europeans to the conflict on humanitarian grounds. The result was the series of discussions of the conflict by CoE member state which provided greater opportunity for a proper understanding of the Nigerian situation and its human rights implications. With the recognition that the war victims must be assisted, the CoE became the forerunner of championing the campaign for the removal of obstacles that hampered humanitarian operations. This was done through constant reminder of the warring parties and their supporters to agree through negotiations on the acceptable ways of conducting efficient humanitarian delivery to the civilian population. Hence, the available option was that in the absence of cooperation, the CoE expressed readiness to join international efforts beyond national sovereignty to carry out humanitarian assistance to those in need. The CoE recognized that absence of arms in the hands of the combatants was the only way of weakening the military strength of both sides and straightforward technique of working towards termination of the war. Thus, it issued historic recommendations on the stoppage of arms sales in the international black market and halting of arms supplies to Nigeria and Biafra by European member states. Solidarity and sympathy with the civilian population were cardinal factors behind the actions of the CoE member states. The CoE considered its role in the conflict as within the 'rights and conscience of the people of Europe' as evident in a number of resolutions it adopted. By the same token, the generally less successful and almost powerless Council of Europe took a stronger position vis-à-vis the humanitarian crisis in Nigeria, and echoing European public opinion urged its member states to take a stronger action in the crisis. In doing that, it encouraged one of the first human right-based campaigns among Europe's citizens and paved the way for a stronger attention to human rights abuses in the world by European government and supranational institutions.

Notes

1 Lord Hunt, *Nigeria. The Problem of Relief in the Aftermath of the Nigerian Civil War: Report of Lord Hunt's Mission* (London: Government Printing Office, 1970).
2 Wolfgang Benedek, *Understanding Human Rights: Manual on Human Rights Education*, 2nd edn (Graz: European Training and Research Centre for Human Rights and Democracy ETC, 2006), 33. James Griffin, *On Human Rights*, 1st edn (London: Oxford University Press, 2009). K. Mills, *Human Rights in the Emerging Global Order: A New Sovereignty?* International Political Economy Series (New York: Palgrave Macmillan, 1998). Adam Etinson, *Human Rights: Moral or Political* (London: Oxford University Press, 2020). Hurst Hannum, *Rescuing Human Rights: A Radically Moderate Approach* (Cambridge: Cambridge University Press, 2019).
3 Roger Moody, 'Biafra: What Is to be Done?' *Peace News*, 19 July 1968, 1.
4 Oluchukwu Ignatus Onianwa, 'The Western European Union and European Politics in the Nigerian Civil War: The Italian Experience, 1967-1970', in *A Tight Embrace: Narratives and Dynamics of Euro-Africa Relations*, ed. Marco Zoppi (London and New York: Rowman & Littlefield International 2021), 99–118. Lasse Heerten, *The Biafran*

War and Postcolonial Humanitarianism: Spectacles of Suffering: Human Rights in History (Cambridge: Cambridge University Press, 2017).

5 Consultative Assembly Report on the Programme of action relating to Human Rights after the International Human Rights Year 1968, 22. Document No. 2505, 15 January 1969. The Council of Europe Digital Archives (hereinafter CEDA):http://rm.coe.int/0900001680977ba6 (accessed 20 October 2020).
6 Samuel Moyn, 'The Return of the Prodigal: The 1970s as a Turning Point in Human Rights History', in *The Breakthrough: Human Rights in the 1970s*, ed. Jan Eckel and Samuel Moyn (Philadelphia: University of Pennsylvania Press 2014), 5.
7 Lasse Heerten, 'The Dystopia of Postcolonial Catastrophe: Self-determination, the Biafran War of Secession, and the 1970s Human Rights Moment', in Ibid., 15–32.
8 Ibid.
9 The National Archives, London (hereinafter TNA), Foreign and Commonwealth Office (hereinafter FCO) 38/86, Minute on Statement on Biafra by CFDT. No N1/2 from Leslie Fielding (British Embassy in Paris) to FCO, 14 August 1968.
10 TNA, FCO 38/303, J.R.H. Evans (UK Mission to the UN) to FCO Appeal Drawn up by a Number of Non-Governmental Organizations and Individuals in Geneva Concerning the Nigeria-Biafra Dispute, 26 August 1968.
11 Ibid.
12 TNA, FCO 38/302, Telegram by the Secretary of the International Union for Children Welfare to His Imperial Majesty Haile Selassie First, 15 August 1968.
13 TNA, FCO 65/202, Petition from the Society for the Promotion of Arts and Science to Harold Wilson, 13 October 1968.
14 TNA, FCO 30/220, Resolution Passed by Socialist International on the Nigerian-Biafran Conflict from D.P.R. Mackilligin to the British Secretary of state for Foreign Affairs, 26 August 1968.
15 Frank Allaun, Biafra and Blackpool, *Labour Party Fellowship Newsletter: 1968 Labour Conference Issue*, September 1968, 1.
16 TNA, FCO 38/273, Letter Sent to the British foreign Secretary by thirteen British prominent citizens, 9 November 1968.
17 'Biafra Moving towards Vietnam Situation Says Bishop Butler', *Catholic Herald*, 28 March 1969, 1.
18 Ibid.
19 Ibid.
20 David Perman, 'Nigeria Costs Britain the Goodwill of Europe Heerten', *The Observer Foreign News Service*, No. 25677. 27 September 1968, 3–4.
21 Brian E. McNeil, 'Frontier of Need: Humanitarianism and the American Involvement in the Nigerian Civil War, 1967-1970' (PhD diss., University of Texas, 2014), 8.
22 Ibid.
23 TNA, FCO 38/298, Telegram on Helping the War Victims from M.M.E. Gertrude Lutz (Acting Director UNICEF) to the President of Council of Europe, 26 July 1968.
24 Appeal by the Pax Christi Movement on Assistance for the Victims of the Civil War in Nigeria, 5 August 1968. CEDA: http://rm.coe.int/090000168079cb3c/ (accessed 7 August 2020).
25 Proposal on Assistance for the Victims of the Civil War in Nigeria, 29 August 1968. CEDA: http://rm.coe.int/090000168079cb3c/ (accessed 7 August 2020).
26 Consultative Assembly Report and Exploratory Memorandum on the Programme of action relating to Human Rights after the International Human Rights Year 1968

by Martinsson, 8. Document No. 2505, 15 January 1969. CEDA: https://rm.coe.int/0900001680977ba6 (accessed 7 August 2020).
27 Parliamentary Assembly of the Council of Europe (hereinafter PACE) 048, Official Report of Debates Volume II Sitting 10 to 18, 303–605.
28 McNeil, 'Frontier of Need', 20.
29 International Conference on Human Rights at Tehran, Doc. H (68) 5/COE056215, Strasburg, 24 May 1968. CEDA: https://rm.coe.int/0900001680677 (accessed 7 August 2020).
30 Proclamation of the International Conference on Human Rights at Tehran, Appendix IV, 24 May 1968. CEDA: https://rm.coe.int/0900001680677dac (accessed 7 August 2020).
31 PACE, PACECOMO35917/As/Jur/(21) 39/, Letter on the 8th Meeting of International Organizations interested in questions relating to Human Rights Held in Strasburg on 3 October 1969 from Sean MacBride Secretary-General of the International Commission of Jurists to Van der Stoel Chairman of the Sub-Committee on Human Rights from Legal Affairs Committee Consultative Assembly of Council of Europe, Strasburg, 21 October 1969.
32 Ibid.
33 Minutes of the Twelfth Meeting of the Political Committee of the Consultative Assembly Held on 30 March 1968 in Paris, 2 April 1968. CEDA: http://rm.coe.int/090000168079a7ab (accessed 7 August 2020).
34 Revised Draft Agenda of the Bureau of the Consultative Assembly for the Meeting of to be Held on Friday 30 August 1968 at 3 p.m. at the Paris Office of the Council of Europe, 29 August 1968. CEDA: https://rm.coe.int/090000168079cb3c (accessed 7 August 2020).
35 Minutes of the Meeting of the Committee on Population and Refugees of Consultative Assembly held at 10 a.m. on Tuesday 10 September 1968. CEDA: http://rm.coe.int/090000168079a452 (accessed 7 August 2020).
36 Ibid.
37 Ibid.
38 Ibid.
39 Minutes of the Meeting of Committee on Population and Refugees of Consultative Assembly Held at 2 p.m. on Monday 23 September 1968. CEDA: https://rm.coe.int/090000168079a452 (accessed 7 August 2020).
40 Ibid.
41 Ibid.
42 Ibid.
43 Consultative Assembly Exploratory Memorandum on Assistance to the Victims of the Civil War in Nigeria by Georges Margue Document No. 2459, 3–6. CEDA: https://rm.coe.int/09000016807a9add (accessed 20 October 2020).
44 TNA, FCO 38/305, Telegram, Consultative Assembly Debate on Nigeria held on 26 September 1968 from United Kingdom Mission in Strasbourg to Foreign Office.
45 Minutes of the Meeting of the Consultative Assembly Committee on Population and Refugees Held at 10 a.m. on Tuesday 17 December 1968 at the Paris Office of the Council of Europe. CEDA: http://rm.coe.int/090000168079a450 (accessed 7 August 2020).
46 Ibid.
47 Minutes of the Meeting of the Consultative Assembly Committee on Population and Refugees Held from 2–4 June 1969 in London Riverwalk House No, 18 June 1969. CEDA: https://rm.coe.int/090000168079a7f (accessed 7 August 2020).

48 Minutes of the Meeting of Consultative Assembly Committee on Population and Refugees Held on 30 September 1969. CEDA: http://rm.coe.int/090000168079a7f0 (accessed 7 August 2020).
49 TNA, FCO 65/245, the 174th Meeting of the Deputies on the Assistance to the Victims of the Civil War in Nigeria: Recommendation 532.
50 Assistance to the Victims of the Civil War in Nigeria: Recommendation 532, 20 December 1968. CEDA: https://rm.coe.int/0900001680914623 (accessed 14 October 2020).
51 TNA, FCO 65/245, Council of Europe Consultative Assembly 21st Ordinary Session: Part One Held in Strasburg on 21–16 May 1969 on the Suppression of Traffic of Arms and Munitions of War into Nigeria No. CoE Guidance (69) 23.
52 Preliminary Draft Report of the Political Affairs Committee of the Consultative Assembly on the Suppression of Traffic of Arms and Munitions of War into Nigeria. CEDA: https://rm.coe.int/090000168079a62c (accessed 7 August 2020).
53 Minutes of the Eighth Meeting of Consultative Assembly Political Affairs Committee Held on 26 April 1969. CEDA: https://rm.coe.int/090000168079a49f (accessed 7 August 2020).
54 Ibid.
55 Minutes of the First Meeting of the 21st Session of the Political Affairs Committee of the Consultative Assembly Held in Strasbourg on 12 May 1969. CEDA: http://rm.coe.int/090000168079a49 (accessed 7 August, 2020).
56 Minute of the Eighth Meeting of Consultative Assembly Political Affairs Committee Held on 26 April 1969. CEDA: https://rm.coe.int/090000168079a49f (accessed 7 August 2020).
57 Minutes of the Second Meeting of the Consultative Assembly Political Affairs Committee Held on 15 May 1969. CEDA: https://rm.coe.int/09000016807b105 (accessed 7 August 2020).
58 Summary of Provisional Draft Resolution of the Political Affairs Committee Doc. 2553 on Suppression of Arms Traffic to Nigeria for the Debate in the Council of Europe's Assembly. Rapporteur Kaj Bjork Swedish Social Democrat, 16 May 1969. CEDA: https://rm.coe.int/09000016807b1005 (accessed 7 August 2020).
59 Ibid.
60 TNA, FCO 65/245, Report of the Political Affairs Committee, Debate and Vote on the Draft Resolution Doc. 2553 and Amendment of the Proposal of Suppression of Traffic of Arms and Munitions into Nigeria at the 21st Ordinary Session of the Consultative Assembly of the Council of Europe Held on 16 May 1969 in Strasbourg France.
61 TNA, FCO 65/245, Deputies of Committee of Ministers' Debate on Resolution 413 on the Suppression of Traffic of Arms and Munitions of War into Nigeria.
62 Minutes of the Meeting of Consultative Assembly Committee on Population and Refugees Held on 28 January 1970 in Strasbourg. CEDA: http://rm.coe.int/090000168079a7ec (accessed 7 August 2020).
63 Alternative Preliminary Draft Resolution of the Consultative Assembly Committee on Population and Refugees Proposed by Mr Silkin on Relief Measures for Victims of the Civil War in Nigeria following the Ceasefire of 11 January 1970. CEDA: https://rm.coe.int/090000168079cd54 (accessed 7 August 2020).
64 PACE, AS/PR (21) PV 6/Pacecomo36351, Minutes of the Meeting of Consultative Assembly Committee on Population and Refugees Held on 28 January 1970 in Strasburg, 10 February 1970.

65 PACE 048, Council of Europe Consultative Assembly Twentieth Ordinary Session Second Part Held on 23–7 September 1968 in Strasburg Official Report of Debates Volume II Sitting 10 to 18, 303–605.
66 *Politics of Relief: Some Reflections on the Aspect of the Nigerian Civil War* (London: Foreign and Commonwealth Office, 1970), 1.
67 Official Report of Thirteenth Sitting of the Twentieth Ordinary Session of Consultative Assembly of the Council of Europe Held on Tuesday 24 September 1968. CEDA: https://rm.coe.int/090000168079a476 (accessed 20 August 2020).
68 *Politics of Relief*, 10.
69 McNeil, 'Frontier of Need', 18.

Beyond victims of communism?

Austria and the human rights question in the 1970s

Maximilian Graf

On 13 September 1973, the International Council Meeting of Amnesty International (AI) convened in Vienna. Austrian chancellor Bruno Kreisky gave a welcome address in which he wholeheartedly identified with the aims and intentions of the organization. His own biography made him a perfect advocate for the cause of AI. In the interwar period, Kreisky had been persecuted by the Austrian dictatorship. After the annexation of Austria by Nazi Germany in 1938 he had to flee and found refuge in Sweden. Since the 1950s, he had decisively shaped Austrian foreign policy. Kreisky served as state secretary (1953–9) and foreign minister (1959–66). After years in opposition he was elected chancellor and further developed his profile as an experienced expert on international affairs (1970–83). During the heyday of détente in Cold War Europe, his personal approach to humanitarian engagement was dialogue and discretion rather than public polemics. Kreisky exemplified this in his address to the AI meeting by mentioning the dissident scientist Andrei Sakharov and the need to uncomplainingly explain to Soviet leaders that human rights violations constitute obstacles to increasing East–West exchanges and cooperation in the fields of science and culture. Towards the end of his speech, the chancellor remarked 'that one cannot remain silent on events in Chile and the death of Allende, for many reasons and not least because otherwise one would lose the moral right to stand up for Sakharov and his fellow combatants'.[1]

Of course, it was a coincidence that the AI meeting took place shortly after the coup against Chilean president Salvador Allende. Nevertheless, Kreisky's speech and the time it was given reveal a lot about the Austrian government's dealing with the question of human rights on an international scale and the changes the country's human rights policy underwent. It shows the anti-communist Cold War origins and the degree of universality human rights had reached at the time. Until the 1960s, Austria's engagement for the enforcement of human rights primarily focused on neighbouring communist regimes. Thereafter, despite this manifestly geographical focus a more global approach evolved.

Reviewing Austria's post-1945 foreign policy, diplomats Franz Cede and Christian Prosl claim an outstanding record in human rights politics. They substantiate this view by highlighting the country's engagement on human rights within international organizations and the deserving role of Austrian individuals (politicians and experts) in this field. Both aspects cannot be detailed in this chapter. Unfortunately, this self-assessment of the Austrian human rights record is flawed by reproducing myths already revealed as such by historical research. A crucial example is the entirely unfounded claim that Kreisky played a decisive role in shaping the Helsinki Final Act and especially its humanitarian provisions in Basket III. Despite such exaggerations, Cede and Prosl concede that Vienna's human rights policy was not pursued in a vacuum and naturally conflicted with the country's political and economic interests.[2]

This chapter provides, first, a brief overview on Austria's ambitions as a Western Cold War humanitarian power until the end of the 1960s. Secondly, it proceeds by addressing the country's engagement vis-à-vis the European socialist states in the 1970s on the bilateral and multilateral level, with a focus on dissidents in the Soviet Union and Czechoslovakia. Consequently, the analysis also focusses on Kreisky's positioning and understanding of détente. Special attention is paid to the Austrian communication of its position on human rights in its dialogue with the East and West. Third, the potential impact of the global is discussed in the example of Chile after the coup of 1973. The conclusion compares the case studies and puts the developments of the 1970s into a broader historical context. The focus on Austria allows us to comprehend how the EC's approach to human rights was not the only European initiative on human rights during the 1970s. On the contrary, the EC had to cope with a variety of European actions on human rights. Being a neutral country, Austria was quite effective in advancing its own agenda for human rights in the world. Similarly, in developing its own action, Austria was determined to know and understand actions undertaken by EC member states in European Political Cooperation (EPC).

Humanitarian power? Neutral Austria and human rights in Cold War Europe

In 1955, Austria regained its sovereignty with the conclusion of the State Treaty and adopted a neutrality law.[3] It did not take long until Austria's new status was put to a test when the Soviet Union violently suppressed the Hungarian uprising. On 28 October 1956, Austrian chancellor Julius Raab appealed to the Soviet Union to end the bloodshed and declared: 'Based upon Austria's freedom and independence which are ensured by its neutrality, the Austrian government favours a normalisation of conditions in Hungary with the goal that through the reestablishment of liberty in accordance with human rights, European peace will be strengthened and ensured.'[4] Austria's commitment to human rights in the Western Cold War fashion did not influence Soviet decision-making. A second military intervention ended the revolution and caused the flight of up to 180,000 Hungarians to Austria. All of them were granted political asylum; however, only a maximum of 20,000 to 30,000 stayed in Austria permanently. International anti-communist solidarity secured a fast onwards movement for most of the refugees. Serving as state secretary, Kreisky was conscious of the international reputation Austria had earned in the West and advocated claiming a new role in the world. He opined that as Switzerland was associated with the Red Cross, Austria could prove itself to the world as a country granting asylum.[5] Recent research has challenged the persistently commemorated welcoming Austrian attitude towards refugees from communist countries. The initial humanitarian efforts in 1956 and on later occasions were without a doubt remarkable and indispensable. However, an analysis beyond the first weeks reveals that public and political attitudes towards refugees took a negative turn: a pattern that continued to shape Austrian reactions to refugees until today and has become more visible since the early 1980s.[6]

Unlike Switzerland (initially serving as model for Austrian neutrality), Austria joined the United Nations in 1955 and the Council of Europe in 1956. Both steps were in line with the country's Western orientation and resulted in a commitment to Western human rights standards. The European Human Rights Convention of 1958 perfectly fitted the Austrian positioning as a humanitarian actor along the Cold War divide. Austria's relations to Spain, Portugal and Greece exemplified that the country was firmly embedded in the Western Cold War consensus. Vienna did not pursue a particular human rights policy vis-à-vis the Southern European dictatorships on the Iberian Peninsula and in the Aegean. Due to increasing public attention, the situation changed gradually from the mid-1960s. In the case of the Greek junta several humanitarian interventions calling for amnesty were undertaken.[7]

Despite some ambivalences, the Alpine Republic cultivated its image as a country of first asylum for refugees from countries under communist rule. Until 1968 the annual influx amounted to approximately 4,000 people only, of whom a large majority were granted political asylum.[8] Following the crushing of the 'Prague Spring', at least 162,000 people came to Austria. In total, merely 12,000 Czechs and Slovaks applied for political asylum in Austria and it is estimated that only 2,000 to 3,000 stayed permanently. For most refugees, Austria only served as a temporary haven. Many returned to Czechoslovakia or migrated to other Western countries in need of a skilled workforce.[9] Austria regarded itself primarily as a country of refugee transit and it served as such by facilitating Jewish emigration from Eastern Europe.

By the early 1950s, the post-war Jewish exodus through Austria was largely prevented by the Iron Curtain;[10] however, it never ceased entirely and resumed on an even greater scale with the emigration of Soviet Jews through Austria from the mid-1960s until the collapse of the USSR. More than 250,000 people migrated, mostly to Israel and the United States. Up to 7,000–8,000 decided to stay or re-migrated to Austria.[11] In September 1973, Jewish emigration from the Soviet Union turned into a target of Middle Eastern terrorism on Austrian soil. Suddenly, one pillar of the country's rather discrete humanitarian engagement was under attack and subject to international discussion. Chancellor Kreisky reacted by closing the targeted transit camp Schönau (which had been under the sole authority of the 'Jewish agency') but secured uninterrupted emigration via other camps administrated by the Red Cross. This step caused severe conflict with Israel and temporary outrage in the United States that receded once it had become clear that in practice nothing had changed.[12] By the end of the decade (in which Jewish emigration from the USSR had a strong influence on Washington's policy towards Moscow not least regarding human rights) Kreisky was once again lauded for his role in facilitating this migration movement when paying a visit to the United States in 1979.[13]

Despite Austria's Western orientation and its role as a refuge and country of transmigration, relations to socialist Eastern Europe developed constantly. The Soviet Union aimed at shaping Austrian neutrality within its foreign policy concept of 'peaceful coexistence' and encouraged Vienna to develop relations with the socialist countries.[14] This enabled Austria to pursue its own 'Ostpolitik' quite successfully. Vienna maintained good relations with the Soviet Union and managed to improve relations with almost all the socialist bloc countries throughout the 1960s. Only relations to Czechoslovakia remained burdened; and East Germany was excluded from this policy until 1972. One of the characteristics of Austrian Ostpolitik was a strictly bilateral approach, pronouncing the diversity of the socialist bloc.[15] Even the crushing of the 'Prague Spring' in 1968 marked only a short setback to the development of détente. In contrast to its sharp reaction to the 1956 crackdown on the Hungarian revolution, Austria abstained from an official condemnation. This marked a certain shift in the Austrian interpretation of its neutrality. Wolfgang Mueller identified a 'mental neutralisation' of leading Austrian politicians.[16] In the end there was 'no damage done to Austrian–Soviet relations'.[17] However, despite consideration of Soviet sensitivities in favour of good relations, Austria's Western orientation was never in question. Limitations in the sphere of participation in West European integration remained until the Cold War drew to a close.

Unsurprisingly, the Soviets tried to win over Austria to promote their goal of a Conference on Security in Europe. But the Austrian government refused to fulfil the Soviet desire, and finally Finland launched the idea.[18] Austria welcomed the initiative and constructively participated in what developed into the Conference on Security and Cooperation in Europe (CSCE). However, Austrian politicians had certain reservations with regard to the inclusion of human rights questions in the CSCE negotiations.[19] In contrast, Austrian diplomats quickly realized the importance of Basket III and as 'a Western actor in neutral clothes' contributed within the N+N (Neutral and Non-aligned) group to making the Helsinki Final Act possible.[20] The main reason for the initial Austrian reservation concerning the inclusion of human rights in the CSCE agenda was the expectation that negotiations on that matter would lead to nothing. Leading politicians had learned that in humanitarian hardship cases, 'silent diplomacy' was usually more successful.[21]

Silent diplomacy and public statements: Dissidents and the CSCE process

The Austrian case shows that some aspects of the Helsinki Final Act already had been implemented in bilateral East–West relations and therefore constituted elements of a genuine European détente. Austria's pre-Helsinki achievements with Eastern Europe comprised the safety and permeability of its borders at the Iron Curtain and the solution of humanitarian hardship cases with a direct connection to Austria (i.e.

emigration, marriage and travel permits). In these fields Austria regularly intervened on the sidelines of bilateral encounters. Dissidents were not on the top of Austria's human rights agenda. When the CSCE negotiations commenced, hardly any humanitarian issues between Austria and Poland or Hungary existed. On the contrary, with Poland even a treaty on the abolition of mutual visa requirements was signed in 1972 and Austrian–Hungarian relations had started to turn into a 'masterpiece of European détente'.[22] When Austrian foreign minister Rudolf Kirchschläger and his Hungarian counterpart Frigyes Puja met in Vienna in 1974 they looked back at an impressive collaboration. After severe incidents in the mid-1960s, the common border had been demilitarized and demined by the early 1970s. As a consequence, cross-border contacts and cooperation increased by leaps and bounds. Kirchschläger enthusiastically highlighted that solutions for almost every humanitarian concern were found. He did not expect the CSCE negotiations to get close to what Austria and Hungary already had achieved. Puja expressed his hope that Austria would exert some 'positive' influence among the Western countries. Although Austria insisted on progress in Basket III, Kirchschläger claimed to have told his Western colleagues that it could not be seen as a 'crusade against communism'.[23]

The situation in relation to Czechoslovakia and its post-1968 'normalisation' regime was more difficult. Austrian–Czechoslovakian relations, despite some occasionally occurring gleams of hope, were constantly heavily burdened from 1945 until the early 1970s. The expulsion of the German-speaking minority, the communist takeover in 1948 and the implementation of the Iron Curtain drew a dividing line between the historically 'begrudging neighbours'.[24] Traditional cross-border contacts intensified again with the liberalization in Czechoslovakia in the 1960s. East–West tourism increased and even boomed during the 'Prague Spring'.[25] In contrast, political relations remained highly strained throughout the 1950s and 1960s. No top-level visits took place and diplomatic relations were not normalized until the 1970s. After the conclusion of the treaty on proprietary rights in 1974 (securing Austrians at least a symbolic compensation), relations improved, diplomatic representations were raised to the level of embassies in 1975 and mutual state visits by foreign ministers and heads of government became possible.[26] Finally, it seemed that even with Czechoslovakia some sort of honeymoon was achieved. Shortly before the Helsinki Summit, Austria reminded Czechoslovakia that it would continue to bring forward humanitarian interventions (i.e. family reunifications and emigration permits) by referring to the CSCE consensus about facilitating human contacts. Czechoslovakia seemed to acknowledge that progress in these fields would be Austria's indicator when evaluating the success of the CSCE.[27]

Kreisky's personal position towards the CSCE was ambiguous. He did not believe in changes within the socialist countries through conferences. Instead, Kreisky hoped for an inclusion of the conflict in the Middle East on the agenda. Another aim of the Austrian chancellor gaining importance by the mid-1970s was a closer cooperation in the fields of economics and energy supplies between East and West within the framework of the CSCE. This was paramount to a similar shift in his bilateral Ostpolitik, which had primarily domestic political reasons: against the background of global economic changes since the beginning of the 1970s, Austria's nationalized industries were facing a severe crisis. Loan-financed, large-scale orders from Eastern Europe constituted a welcome relief.[28] Since his personal ambitions all came to naught, Kreisky never warmed to the seemingly endless conference of diplomats, the CSCE represented to him. However, on the occasion of the signing of the Helsinki Final Act he made the most distinct statements by a Western politician regarding the Third Basket, stressing readiness for a continued ideological argument with communism. This very statement led to an overrating of Kreisky's role in Austria's CSCE politics. Jokingly, one Soviet diplomat even called it a 'declaration of war'.[29]

Post-Helsinki diplomatic exchanges with Hungary and East Germany showed that both countries were ready for concessions towards Austria as long as humanitarian interventions were a bilateral concern. However, it became equally clear that none of the socialist states intended to let the provisions of Basket III undermine their societal system.[30] Nevertheless, the effects of the Final Act soon became visible. Now the citizens of socialist countries had a document signed by 'their' leaderships they could refer to when demanding their rights. The same holds true for the Western countries when bi- and multilaterally dealing with those regimes on humanitarian issues. Austria still pursued a bilateral 'silent diplomacy' approach; however, the publicity of the fate of dissidents increased.

Not least because of the experience with the Soviet occupation of Austria after the Second World War, the image of the Soviet Union was negative and had fostered the national anti-communist consensus. Nikita Khrushchev's secret speech had revealed some of Stalin's worst crimes, and the 'thaw' he initiated created new hopes. When Soviet cultural politics hardened once again in the early 1960s and dissidents were put on trial again, this was even publicly discussed by the tiny Austrian Communist Party[31] and reflected a growing Western public interest in the fate of Soviet dissidents. In the 1970s, Austrian intellectuals and politicians frequently appealed to Soviet leaders in favour of Soviet dissidents, albeit with limited success. Many of the Austrian interventions faced outright rejection. Others provoked Soviet complaints and counteractions to the point of retaliation. At times, Moscow regarded Austrian media coverage of the dissidents' fate as the most severe burden on bilateral relations. Although Austrian diplomats held the view that interventions by the neutral country were received with more tolerance than those by others, there is hardly any evidence for this claim. Nevertheless, despite overall disappointing results, Kreisky continued to appeal to the Soviet prime ministers throughout and beyond the decade.[32]

AI and several other organizations requested Kreisky to intervene in many human rights matters. The scope of requests to the chancellor ranged from petitions on behalf of persecuted individuals to the restoration of human rights in Ukraine. The Foreign Ministry carefully weighed in which cases action by Kreisky seemed reasonable. According to the Viennese experience, Moscow differentiated between cases with direct relation to Austria (like marriage permits) and interventions for Soviet citizens. While the former were usually accepted (but not necessarily solved), the latter were regarded as interference in domestic affairs. Still, sometimes there were unexpected successes like the emigration permit for the artist Ernst Neizvestny.[33]

When minister of justice Christian Broda paid a visit to the Soviet Union in September 1976, he used a private conversation with his counterpart Vladimir Terebilov to petition the amnesty and release of the writer Vladimir Bukovsky for humanitarian reasons. To stress the solely humanitarian motives of his petition, Broda mentioned that Austria was granting asylum to politicians of the Left from Chile, Argentina and Uruguay (see later). Terebilov promised to inform the responsible Soviet authorities, voiced his disregard for Bukovsky and stated: 'There would be another wagonload of such people that probably should be deported to Austria.' Despite the Soviet stance of rejecting any interference in internal affairs, Austrian diplomacy had the impression that the Kremlin felt uncomfortable with interventions by Western statesmen and media campaigns, especially in view of the Helsinki Final Act and with the follow-up meeting in Belgrade approaching. Aiming at a more human image, Western campaigns (to which Austria had contributed) had some success.[34] In late 1976, Bukovsky and Leonid Plyushch (for whom Austria had also intervened) were expatriated and emigrated to the West. Kreisky was far from welcoming to this approach to getting rid of dissent. However, before and after the Helsinki Final Act, he compared this practice with the fate of dissidents in the Stalin era. Taking this perspective, one could in fact speak of an improved situation and Kreisky regarded it as an achievement of the CSCE.[35]

In 1976 Kreisky had spoken out in favour of dissidents several times. When the East German singer-songwriter Wolf Biermann was expatriated while touring West Germany, he publicly offered for him to continue his work in Austria. However, in comparison to Czechoslovakia, dissidents played a minor role in Austrian–East German relations.[36] After Kreisky had visited Czechoslovakia in February 1976, it seemed that relations had finally fully normalized. Yet, this rare phase of Austrian–Czechoslovakian honeymoon was not destined to last long. In fact, relations remained at least cyclically burdened and became a minefield when it came to humanitarian questions and dissent.[37]

The first scandal resulted from denying Václav Havel (who was awarded the Austrian State Prize for European Literature in 1968) the right to travel to Austria in autumn 1976. Inspired by this and the Biermann expatriation, Kreisky offered all East European dissidents asylum. After the publication of Charter 77 that criticized the government for failing to implement human rights provisions it had signed for example in the Helsinki Final Act, many of the responsible Czechoslovak dissidents were traced and state repression was decried in the West. Kreisky unconditionally stood up for the dissidents and renewed his offer for asylum in Austria. Not all dissidents were happy about Kreisky's offer since it was suitable for abetting their expatriation. However, some, like Zdeněk Mlynář, had already accepted the offer and claimed asylum in Austria in the course of the year 1977. Relations between Prague and Vienna once again worsened.[38] This pattern of ups and downs continued in the following years and remained closely linked to dissent.

While the dissident question was mostly an issue in relations between Prague and Moscow, progress on bilateral humanitarian concerns varied from country to country. Still, the concessions made by the socialist regimes depended on progress in other fields of relations.[39] In times of international tensions, high-level state visits and large-scale economic agreements could do wonders. Hence, despite his engagement for East European dissidents, Kreisky warned not to reduce the Belgrade CSCE follow-up to this aspect and continued to lobby for economic cooperation. How did Austria interact with the West in the view of Belgrade? The most intimate exchange was conducted with Switzerland. When Austrian foreign minister Willibald Pahr met with his Swiss counterpart Pierre Graber, both worried about the climate in which the meeting in Belgrade would take place. Convinced that the CSCE already had caused problems for the Soviet Union and its allies, the new US rhetoric on human rights was regarded as potentially damaging for the process. There was consensus that the two neutrals were facing a challenge: on the one hand, they felt obliged to do everything possible to prevent an 'éclat'; on the other hand, they worried about public opinion at home.[40]

When Kreisky paid a visit to the United States in March 1977 he told the *New York Times* 'that he found the Carter administration's emphasis on human rights issues "very impressive," but he expressed concern that the campaign might damage quieter forms of helping individuals in authoritarian societies'. Concerning dissidents in the Soviet bloc, he remarked that 'there are two kinds of issues – the highly visible and audible, which are important, but also those daily contacts, diplomatic and by other means, which don't ever get publicised'. However, Kreisky also said that 'he did not see any fundamental danger for the policy of East–West détente in the Carter administration's human rights program' and once again called for ideological competition.[41] Two months later Carter stated in a letter to Kreisky: 'I admire your moral courage in speaking out against serious violations of human rights wherever they occur and providing by your deeds that Austria adheres firmly to the human values that both our societies cherish.'[42] Despite different approaches Carter regarded Kreisky as an ally.

As feared by the East and West alike, the meeting in Belgrade commenced with a clash in the implementation debate. In contact with Eastern Europe, Austria opined that the US position would go beyond propaganda against the socialist states and also apply to the rest of the world.[43] Talking with Western representatives, Austrian diplomats expressed their hopes that the EC Nine would find a common position and keep contact with the neutrals.[44] West German officials showed understanding for the neutral desire not be excluded from the conversations of the Nine, which were even described as a bit too 'inward looking'. Time and again the Council of Europe surfaced as a potential platform for increased West European exchange beyond the EC. However, despite the Council's merits and vocal commitments to its persisting importance, there was some sort of consensus about its actually declining relevance in European politics.[45] This is somewhat surprising since two Austrians served as the Council of Europe's general secretaries at the beginning and the end of the decade.[46]

In March 1979, the meeting in Belgrade ended with a minimal consensus that secured the continuation of the CSCE process. Throughout the meeting and thereafter, repression of dissidents had not subsided. Already in early 1978, Austrian ambassador to Prague Johann Pasch warned that the award of the Austrian State Prize for European Literature to the 'dissident-author' Pavel Kohout could harm the 'spring in Austrian–Czechoslovakian relations'.[47] Shortly after the visit by President Rudolf Kirchschläger in 1979, rounding out the formal normalization process of diplomatic relations, Czechoslovakian authorities expatriated Kohout who at the time worked in Austria. Kreisky publicly spoke out in the case of Kohout and claimed it to be a violation of the Helsinki principles.[48] The CSCE had constituted a challenge for the regime in Prague and its effects were yet another severe burden for Austrian–Czechoslovakian relations.

Nine months after the end of the meeting in Belgrade, the international situation had deteriorated further. The Austrian government cautiously but unequivocally condemned the Soviet invasion of Afghanistan in late 1979, and Austria did not boycott the Moscow 1980 Summer Olympics as requested by Carter.[49] While being a discrete ally in promoting human rights, neutral Austria was not when it came to sanctions. In a conversation with East German leader Erich Honecker in November 1980, Kreisky stated that Afghanistan was not central for the Austrian public, but developments in Poland really moved the people.[50]

Public protest in Poland started in August 1980 and soon the independent trade union Solidarność turned into a political faction. Austria reacted with sympathy and caution. With the increasing escalation, Kreisky became more and more reserved and the inner-Austrian debate turned more controversial. The reasons for that were twofold: (1) the economic dimension and the crisis-related absence of Polish coal deliveries. Within this context, Kreisky made inconsiderate statements (calling the Polish workers back to the mines and criticizing the role of the Catholic Church in Poland) that caused domestic political conflict with the opposition (intensifying its contacts to dissidents) as well as the church. (2) Already before the imposition of martial law in December 1981, up to 40,000 Poles had travelled to Austria as tourists and many of them subsequently claimed asylum. Supposedly, large parts of the Austrian population showed hardly any sympathy for Polish refugees, and the yellow press put pressure on the Kreisky government. Only a few days before the imposition of martial law, Austria unilaterally suspended the treaty on visa-free travel. However, after the first bloodshed, Austria granted asylum to all potentially persecuted Poles. Again, Austria aimed at being a transit country only; it intensively sought third countries to accommodate refugees and requested financial aid from the international community. The response was minimal and slow compared to previous occasions. Within a few years Poland, once regarded as a role model in the socialist bloc, had become the most severe cause of violations against human rights. To Kreisky the CSCE had made the appearance of Solidarność possible and at the same time the regime's treatment of the independent trade union was a violation of the principles agreed upon in Helsinki. For Kreisky (and many other Western politicians), sustaining détente and not risking a Soviet intervention dominated over supporting Solidarność. Despite his consistent advocacy for an end to martial law and the release of all political detainees, Warsaw was grateful for his rejection of a boycott of the Polish regime.[51] Dialogue had to continue regardless of all problems that needed to be addressed unpolemically in international fora.[52]

Against the backdrop of imminent US elections, Austria expected another heated implementation debate at the CSCE follow-up in Madrid commencing in November 1980. Talking to the Dutch foreign minister, who stressed his country's interest in the dissident question, Pahr stated that unequivocal but unpolemical 'statements on Afghanistan and the dissidents are necessary and also for Austria inevitable because of domestic political reasons'. In view of international developments he insisted: 'An isolation of the East European countries must be avoided, because otherwise the human rights situation would deteriorate further.'[53] Once again, there was an Austrian desire for joint West European coordination in the Council of Europe.[54] Additionally,

Austria expressed its wish to be informed about 'the results or at least the trends' of debates (preparing the EC's CSCE strategy) in EPC.⁵⁵

In Madrid, the Austrian delegation, an integral part of the N+N group, was decisive in finding a way to a conclusion of the meeting, despite the fact that it took place during the last peak of the Cold War. After the implementation of martial law in Poland, the solution was an adjournment for several months, proposed and negotiated by the Austrian and French delegations. Hence, Madrid can be regarded as a success for Austrian diplomacy, not only because Austria additionally managed to get the next CSCE follow-up to Vienna, but also because in the end a substantial document was signed. German historian Benjamin Gilde even spoke of a 'moment of glory' for Austrian diplomacy. Yet, the role of the N+N states, despite their merits, should not be overestimated. The main reason why a substantial document was signed resulted from the Soviet aim to receive a mandate for the Conference on Confidence and Security Building Measures and Disarmament in Europe. Therefore, Moscow made substantial concessions in the Third Basket. In the final phases of Madrid, the West and Austria had stood as one.⁵⁶ Austria acknowledged the role played by the EC and was keen to stress the importance of the neutrals. In exchange with Belgian colleagues, leading Austrian diplomat Friedrich Bauer said: 'In Madrid, we have seen that only a firm position of the [EC] Ten can influence Washington. Furthermore, there must be close contacts with the N+N. Indeed, they are the only ones who can induce the East to a maximum of concessions.' His interlocutors did not comment on the Austrian self-perception but indicated a certain slackening of EPC's 'confidentiality principle' to enable closer cooperation as desired by Vienna.⁵⁷

The Austrian assessment of the state of affairs in the field of human rights shows that, in spite of growing activism and media attention, the handling of humanitarian issues in relation to Eastern Europe had not changed much since the beginning of the CSCE process. Still Austrian interventions were almost exclusively pursued on the bilateral level with success varying from country to country. In case of the USSR, Austria had opted to react to only marginal progress by presenting the most pressing unresolved cases directly but not publicly to the Soviet delegation at the Madrid follow-up. In relations with Czechoslovakia and the USSR, Austria additionally continued to intervene in favour of amnesty, travel and emigration permits for Catholic and Orthodox priests, scientists, dissidents (signatories of Charter 77), religious minorities and other individual hardship cases by referencing the Final Act – with some, but limited success.⁵⁸

The impact of the Global: Chile and its consequences

Kreisky was personally interested in the North–South dimension of global politics and received a lot of international attention for his policy in the Middle East. This resulted in a diversification and internationalization of Austria's foreign policy. Engagement on development policy (proposing a new 'Marshall Plan') also increased his interest in Latin America towards the end of the 1970s.⁵⁹ In the first half of the decade the region was not central in exchanges with foreign politicians. Of course, parts of the Austrian left had engaged in solidarity with Algeria during decolonization and, naturally, humanitarian disasters like Biafra surfaced in the media but in general, the Global South had not taken centre stage in the Austrian public sphere of the 1960s. In comparison to other Western countries (most notably neutral Sweden), protest against the Vietnam War was small. Despite advocating peace in Indochina, Austrian politicians refrained from criticizing the United States. Washington was glad that Kreisky did his best to keep that way.[60]

In late summer 1973, a coup by the Chilean military violently ended civilian rule by President Salvador Allende and his Unidad Popular government. Although Austrian public opinion was divided in its interpretation of events in Chile, the voices opposing the junta led by General Augusto Pinochet were strong. Soon reports about human rights violations in Chile shaped the news. The Kreisky government condemned the military takeover. As a matter of diplomatic principle Austria recognized only states and not governments (that changed permanently anyway), but the Foreign Ministry stressed that any impression of recognizing the junta should be avoided by all means. At the same time, contacts with the Chilean authorities were maintained to secure Austrian interests[61] and to conduct humanitarian interventions.

Since the Austrian ambassador in Santiago de Chile (who held a very negative view of Allende and his politics) was reluctant to grant asylum on his premises, he was immediately replaced. His successor opened the Austrian embassy for those who feared persecution and the government decided to welcome 200 refugees from Chile. The life-long anti-communist Kreisky personally appealed to Pinochet to prevent the expected execution of the incarcerated leader of the Chilean Communist Party Luis Corvalán (who was subsequently exchanged for the Soviet dissident Bukovsky in 1976). Many more interventions in favour of imprisoned (mostly socialist) politicians by Kreisky and other Austrian politicians followed. Austria offered asylum in case of their release and expatriation by the junta.[62] Regardless of public hostility towards contact with the junta, a continuation of humanitarian efforts could not be endangered by refraining from the necessary minimum.[63] Despite many appeals from society, Austria did not sever diplomatic relations with Chile. Instead, it became the protecting power for Hungary and Bulgaria whose embassies in Santiago also hosted refugees. Allende's widow toured Austria in 1974 and was received by Kreisky. Nevertheless, Austria refrained from any condemning statement on the first anniversary of the coup, not least because it took for granted that any such move would impair the country's discreet humanitarian engagement. To its critics, the government highlighted its merits regarding refugees and the possibility of claiming asylum in the Austrian embassy in Santiago de Chile.[64]

Until the 1970s, whenever Austria was approached by the international community, it did not receive refugees from the Global South. The Austrian excuse usually read that the country was itself overburdened with hosting refugees and for the same reason Vienna's financial contributions never reached the level of similar states. Thereafter, Austria received Indians from Uganda (expelled by Idi Amin), Chileans and later Vietnamese 'boat people'. Because of the rather assimilatory Austrian understanding of integration, refugees from the Global South were primarily regarded as a problem.[65] The acceptance of Chilean refugees representing a varied sample of the country's left reversed the predominant pattern of welcoming refugees from countries under communist rule. Their reception in Austria was at best a misunderstanding. Interpretations clash between activists and officials. Activists of the Austrian 'Chile Solidarity Front' blamed the Austrian authorities for their dealing with the refugees.[66] Former officials claim to have done everything according to national and international standards of the time and saw no reason for privileging refugees who in their view predominantly behaved like exiled politicians.[67]

While the refugees' hopes for a quick return to Chile faded over the years, the 'Chile Solidarity Front' stayed active and kept criticizing the Austrian government for its relations to Chile and similar regimes.[68] Echoing AI's request to the World Bank to deny the junta fresh loans, the 'Chile Solidarity Front' complained about the increasing trade volume between Austria and Chile. The Foreign Ministry opposed sanctions, not only because oppositional voices from Chile held the view that an economic boycott would primarily harm the population but also because it would impair Austrian economic interests.[69] Orders placed with the Austrian nationalized industries seemingly reassured the Foreign Ministry that developing relations to a regime criticized for its human rights violations was the right decision. Furthermore, no state comparable to Austria had severed relations with Chile.[70]

Also, in dialogue with Latin American politicians, Austria emphasized that it did not regard human rights as a means of politics but as a tool to help individuals, referring to the many humanitarian cases solved in Eastern Europe and Chile. Paying a visit to Mexico in 1978, Pahr admitted that despite strong European criticism of the military dictatorships in Latin America, Austria aimed at an intensification of relations.[71] Visiting Argentina (also ruled by a military dictatorship) in 1979, Pahr handed over a list of eleven human rights cases on which Austria had been engaged for a while. As in the case of dialogue with Eastern European politicians he declared that Austria did not intend to interfere in internal affairs of Argentina but had a humanitarian interest in the emigration of these individuals to Austria.[72] By the late 1970s, Austrian human rights politics towards Latin America did not differ from the approach towards Eastern Europe. 'Silent diplomacy' prevailed. As in the case of Eastern Europe, Austria opposed any isolation of regimes, whether it was Chile or Cuba and in spite of the criticism it had to face for its foreign policy views. How much the Austrian attitude towards Latin America had changed and to what degree interest had increased throughout the 1970s became visible in the example of Nicaragua. Already in 1978, a 'solidarity committee' was formed and chaired by Kreisky himself. Austrian support aimed at assisting a desired democratic 'third way', serving as a counterexample to military and communist dictatorships.[73] However, idealistic foreign policy aims continued to conflict with economic interests (most notably of the Austrian nationalized industries that had secured full employment for most of the 1970s).

In the aftermath of the coup, Kreisky had decided against the selling of machine guns to Chile;[74] however, this stance on the export of weaponry had already weakened by the mid-1970s.[75] In 1980, a weapon manufacturing enterprise of Austria's nationalized industries concluded a 162 million USD deal to export tanks and machine guns to Chile. This happened with full backing of the government and Kreisky justified his approval by referring to a contract clause 'guaranteeing' that the delivered 'machines' would be used for defence purposes only. The insignificance of such a guarantee by Pinochet's regime caused public outrage – not least because tanks manufactured in Austria were used during the coup in Bolivia in July 1980. After heated debates, in which the significance of such exports for the Austrian job market surfaced prominently, a broadening protest coalition filing petitions, organizing demonstrations and even conducting hunger strikes finally achieved a reversal of the course and the export deal was called off in August.[76] This concluding episode serves as a reminder of the fact that human rights policies conflicted with other, often economic interests and undermined Austria's reputation in the field domestically and internationally.

Conclusion

Neutral Austria achieved international recognition as a humanitarian actor for its handling of the 1956 refugee crisis and successfully cultivated its role as a place of first asylum and refugee transit. Despite a certain 'mental neutralisation' becoming visible in 1968 and in consideration of Soviet sensibilities, Austria achieved something quite significant and perfectly suited the Western Cold War consensus. The achievements at the bilateral level were remarkable. Especially in relations with Hungary, transformative processes were already set in motion before the CSCE started. Armed with two decades of experience in dealing with socialist regimes and despite some initial reservations, Austria became a constructive protagonist of the CSCE, indeed, a 'Western actor in neutral clothes'. While aiming at closer cooperation with the EC members, Austria did its best to find compromises with the East. Growing engagement in favour of dissidents was a reflection of increasing public attention towards their fate. Both, Chile and dissidents show that organizations like AI and activists for a certain cause had increased their leverage on politics.

In times of international tensions, Austria advocated sustaining détente over change with incalculable outcomes. This became evident in the country's attitude during the 'Polish crisis' and the CSCE follow-up in Madrid. Dialogue had to continue, and Austria acted accordingly. The aim of keeping good relations with the USSR and the other Warsaw Pact states and profiting from economic dealings with them was certainly important for the Austrian attempt to balance between silent humanitarian engagement and public statements on human rights. Public shaming of human rights violations was considered to be likely to threaten détente by provoking the USSR. Additionally, any such hardening was regarded as potentially harming the successes achieved on the bilateral level. This might be considered a somewhat egoist-national approach to human rights, but it worked with all socialist states to varying degrees as soon as overall bilateral relations had reached a certain level in which Austria was also interested not least for economic reasons.

This Austrian attitude so characteristic for the country's Ostpolitik was not only applied to Eastern Europe but increasingly also on a global scale as the case of Chile shows. In the 1970s, the Austrian humanitarian engagement went beyond the socialist states. The country's opening up for asylum seekers from the Global South is one of the indicators for this development. Growing reluctance towards accepting refugees in general surfaced in the early 1980s and thus impaired the founding pillar of Austria's humanitarian engagement in the Cold War.

Vienna's policy towards Latin American military dictatorships followed the lines established in dealing with Eastern Europe. Dialogue was continued and aimed at improving the situation. While the much desired loan-financed exports and other big deals of Austria's nationalized industries with the socialist states generally contributed to improving relations and as a side effect also facilitated the country's humanitarian efforts vis-à-vis these countries, the planned arms export to Chile had to be prevented by an activist campaign against an Austrian contribution to the junta's dark record. Austria's humanitarian engagement of the 1970s went beyond the victims of communism (who had shaped its development most), however, as the case of Chile shows, it was easily flawed when it conflicted with other national interests.

Notes

1 'Tagung des Internationalen Rates von Amnesty International, 13 September 1973', in *Kreisky Reden*, vol. II (Vienna: Verlag der Österreichischen Staatsdruckerei, 1981), 330-2. On Kreisky's biography, see Wolfgang Petritsch, *Bruno Kreisky. Die Biografie* (Sankt Pölten: Residenz Verlag, 2010).
2 Franz Cede and Christian Prosl, *Anspruch und Wirklichkeit. Österreichs Außenpolitik seit 1945* (Innsbruck: StudienVerlag, 2015), 59-65.
3 Gerald Stourzh and Wolfgang Mueller, *A Cold War over Austria: The Struggle for the State Treaty, Neutrality, and the End of East-West Occupation, 1945-1955* (Lanham: Lexington Books, 2018).
4 Quoted from Andreas Gémes, *Austria and the 1956 Hungarian Revolution: Between Solidarity and Neutrality* (Pisa: University Press, 2008), 26.
5 Bruno Kreisky, *Im Strom der Politik. Erfahrungen eines Europäers* (Berlin: Goldmann, 1988), 231; Patrik-Paul Volf, 'Der politische Flüchtling als Symbol der Zweiten Republik: Zur Asyl- und Flüchtlingspolitik seit 1945', *zeitgeschichte*, 22 (1995): 415-36.
6 For a critical reassessment, see Maximilian Graf and Sarah Knoll, 'In Transit or Asylum Seekers? Austria and the Cold War Refugees from the Communist Bloc', in *Migration in Austria*, ed. Günter Bischof and Dirk Rupnow (New Orleans: UNO Press, 2017), 91-111.
7 Stefan A. Müller, David Schriffl and Adamantios T. Skordos, *Heimliche Freunde. Die Beziehungen Österreichs zu den Diktaturen Südosteuropas nach 1945: Spanien, Portugal, Griechenland* (Vienna: Böhlau, 2016).
8 Eduard Stanek, *Verfolgt Verjagt Vertrieben. Flüchtlinge in Österreich von 1945-1984* (Vienna: Europaverlag, 1985), 82-6.
9 Silke Stern, 'Die tschechoslowakische Emigration: Österreich als Erstaufnahme- und Asylland', in *Prager Frühling: Das internationale Krisenjahr 1968*, ed. Stefan Karner et al., 2 vols (Vienna: Böhlau, 2008), 1025-43.
10 Thomas Albrich, ed., *Flucht nach Eretz Israel: Die Bricha und der jüdischer Exodus durch Österreich nach 1945* (Innsbruck: StudienVerlag, 1998); Thomas Albrich and Ronald W. Zweig, eds, *Escape Through Austria: Jewish Refugees and the Austrian Route to Palestine* (London: Routledge, 2002).

11 Hannes Leidinger, 'Jüdische Emigration aus der Sowjetunion', in *Migration. Flucht – Vertreibung – Integration*, ed. Stefan Karner and Barbara Stelzl-Marx (Graz: Leykam, 2019), 137–46; Gabriele Anderl and Viktor Iščenko, 'Die jüdische Emigration aus der Sowjetunion via Österreich', in *Österreich – Russland. Stationen gemeinsamer Geschichte*, ed. Stefan Karner and Alexander Tschubarjan (Graz: Leykam, 2018), 241–51.
12 Thomas Riegler, *Im Fadenkreuz: Österreich und der Nahost-Terrorismus 1973–1985* (Göttingen: V&R unipress, 2011).
13 Österreichisches Staatsarchiv (hereinafter) ÖStA, AdR, BMAA, II-Pol 1979, GZ. 518.01.08/31-II.1/79, Ambassador Schober to Austrian Foreign Ministry (AFM), Washington, 5 November 1979.
14 Wolfgang Mueller, *A Good Example of Peaceful Coexistence: The Soviet Union, Austria, and Neutrality, 1955–1991* (Vienna: ÖAW, 2011), 16–20.
15 Arnold Suppan and Wolfgang Mueller, eds, *Peaceful Coexistence or Iron Curtain? Austria, Neutrality, and Eastern Europe in the Cold War and Détente, 1955–1989* (Vienna: Lit 2009).
16 Mueller, *A Good Example*, 179.
17 Stefan Karner and Peter Ruggenthaler, 'Austria and the End of the Prague Spring: Neutrality in the Crucible?' in *The Prague Spring and the Warsaw Pact Invasion of Czechoslovakia in 1968*, ed. Günter Bischof, Stefan Karner and Peter Ruggenthaler (Lanham: Lexington Books, 2010), 419–39.
18 Thomas Fischer, '"A Mustard Seed Grew Into a Bushy Tree": The Finnish CSCE-Initiative of 5 May 1969', *Cold War History*, 9 (2009): 177–201.
19 Benjamin Gilde, '"Kein Vorreiter". Österreich und die humanitäre Dimension der KSZE 1969–1973', in *Der KSZE-Prozess. Vom Kalten Krieg zu einem neuen Europa 1975 bis 1990*, ed. Helmut Altrichter and Hermann Wentker (Munich: Oldenburg, 2011), 41–50.
20 Benjamin Gilde, *Österreich im KSZE-Prozess 1969–1983. Neutraler Vermittler in humanitärer Mission* (Munich: Oldenbourg, 2013), 439.
21 For my assessment of Austria's CSCE policies regarding Basket III and its implementation in relations with the Socialist states, see Maximilian Graf, 'European Détente and the CSCE: Austria and the East-Central European Theatre in the 1970s and 1980s', in *The CSCE and the End of the Cold War: Diplomacy, Societies and Human Rights, 1972–1990*, ed. Nicolas Badalassi and Sarah B. Snyder (New York: Berghahn Books, 2019), 249–74.
22 Ibid.
23 ÖStA, AdR, BMAA, II-Pol 1974, GZ. 222.18.02/19-6/74, Memcon Kirchschläger – Puja, Vienna, 15 February 1974.
24 Arnold Suppan, *Missgünstige Nachbarn. Geschichte und Perspektiven der nachbarschaftlichen Beziehungen zwischen Tschechien und Österreich* (Heidenreichstein: Club Niederösterreich, 2005).
25 David Schriffl, 'Der "Prager Frühling" 1968 und die österreichisch-slowakischen Beziehungen', in *Osteuropa vom Weltkrieg bis zur Wende*, ed. Wolfgang Mueller and Michael Portmann (Vienna: ÖAW, 2007), 299–311, here 306–8.
26 Paul Ullmann, *Eine schwierige Nachbarschaft. Die Geschichte der diplomatischen Beziehungen zwischen Österreich und der Tschechoslowakei 1945–1968* (Vienna: Lit, 2006).
27 ÖStA, AdR, BMAA, II-Pol, GZ. 502.01.07/29-II.3/75, Ambassador Pasch to AFM, Prague, 23 June 1975.

28 I have shown this in detailed case studies on economic relations between Austria and the GDR as well as on Austria and Poland. Maximilian Graf, *Österreich und die DDR 1949–1990. Politik und Wirtschaft im Schatten der deutschen Teilung* (Vienna: ÖAW, 2016), 381–404, 425–33, 459–70, 497–528, 535–47; Id., 'Kreisky und Polen. Schlaglichter auf einen vernachlässigten Aspekt der österreichischen "Ostpolitik"', in *Bananen, Cola, Zeitgeschichte. Oliver Rathkolb und das lange 20. Jahrhundert*, 2 vols, ed. Lucile Dreidemy et al. (Vienna: Böhlau, 2015), 692–706, 700–4. On Austria's economic relations to Eastern Europe in general, see Andreas Resch, 'Der österreichische Osthandel im Spannungsfeld der Blöcke', in *Zwischen den Blöcken. NATO, Warschauer Pakt und Österreich*, ed. Manfried Rauchensteiner (Vienna: Böhlau, 2010), 497–556; Gertrude Enderle-Burcel et al., eds, *Gaps in the Iron Curtain: Economic Relations between Neutral and Socialist Countries in Cold War Europe* (Kraków: Jagiellonian University Press, 2009).
29 Gilde, *Österreich im KSZE-Prozess*, 248–55, 445–6.
30 ÖStA, AdR. BMAA, II-Pol, GZ. 502.16.00/10-II.3/75, Memorandum 'Bilateraler Meinungsaustausch mit Ungarn und der DDR, Zusammenfassung', Vienna, 14 October 1975.
31 Maximilian Graf, 'Franz Marek – Stalinist, Kritiker, Reformer, Ausgeschlossener', in *Dissidente Kommunisten. Das sowjetische Modell und seine Kritiker*, ed. Knud Andresen, Mario Keßler and Axel Schildt (Berlin: Metropol, 2018), 107–34, here 123–5. On Soviet dissidents and their treatment by the regime, see Vladislav Zubok, *Zhivago's Children: The Last Russian Intelligentsia* (Cambridge, MA: Harvard University Press, 2009).
32 For the best summary, see Mueller, *A Good Example*, 225–30.
33 ÖStA, AdR, BMAA, II-Pol, GZ. 517.00.00/14-II.3/76, Information for the Minister, 'Sowjetische Bemerkungen zu den Interventionen des Herrn Bundeskanzlers an sowjetischen Persönlichkeiten in humanitären Fällen: Übersicht über österr. Interventionen', Wien, 7 May 1976.
34 ÖStA, AdR, BMAA, II-Pol, GZ. 518.03.12/3-II.3/77, Ambassador Standenat to AFM, Moscow, 20 September 1976.
35 'Globale Koexistenz – Illusion oder reale Chance, Wiesbaden, 23. Oktober 1974' and 'Freiheit und Diktatur, Alpbach, 3. September 1976', in *Kreisky Reden*, vol. II, 444–51, 450; 616–28, 625.
36 Graf, *Österreich und die DDR*.
37 Ullmann, *Eine schwierige Nachbarschaft*, 223–34.
38 Gilde, *Österreich im KSZE-Prozess*, 289–97.
39 ÖStA, AdR, BMAA, II-Pol, GZ. 500.26.01/40-IV.2/77, Memorandum 'Humanitäre Härtefälle Stand: 1. September 1977 (Arbeitsunterlage für Belgrad)'.
40 ÖStA, AdR, BMAA, II-Pol, GZ. 518.02.03/15-II.1/77, Memcon Pahr – Graber, Berne, 9/10 February 1977.
41 ÖStA, AdR, BMAA, II-Pol, GZ. 518.01.03/13-II.1/77, Telex Austrian consulate to AFM, New York, 15 March 1977; ÖStA, AdR, BMAA, II-Pol, GZ. 518.01.03/14-II.1/77, Telex Austrian consulate to AFM, New York, 17 March 1977.
42 ÖStA, AdR, BMAA, II-Pol, GZ. 517.00.23/2-II.1/77, Carter to Kreisky, 11 May 1977.
43 ÖStA, AdR, BMAA, II-Pol, GZ. 518.02.00/27-II.3/77, Memcon Pahr – Puja, Budapest, 25 October 1977.
44 ÖStA, AdR, BMAA, II-Pol, GZ. 518.02.14/26-II.1/77, Memorandum 'Offizieller Besuch von Bundesminister Pahr in Paris (28 October 1977) Gesonderte Erörterung der KSZE-Folgekonferenz in Belgrad'. On the EC and Belgrade, see Angela Romano,

'The European Community and the Belgrade CSCE', in *From Helsinki to Belgrade. The First CSCE Follow-up Meeting and the Crisis of Détente*, ed. Vladimir Bilandžić, Dittmar Dahlmann and Milan Kosanović (Bonn: University Press, 2012), 205–24.

45 ÖStA, AdR, BMAA, II-Pol, GZ. 518.02.05/30-II.1/77, Memcon: exchange with the West German Foreign Office, Bonn, 2 November 1977.

46 Probably this was due to the fact that both secretary generals Lujo Tončić-Sorinj (1969–1974) and Franz Karasek (1979–1984) belonged to the oppositional conservative Austrian People's Party.

47 ÖStA, AdR, BMAA, II-Pol, GZ. 35.02.02/1-II.3/78, Ambassador Pasch to AFM, Prague, 24 January 1978.

48 Gilde, *Österreich im KSZE-Prozess*, 297–304.

49 Agnes Meisinger, 'Die österreichische Haltung zum Boykott der Olympischen Sommerspiel in Moskau 1980 unter besonderer Berücksichtigung der Rolle Bruno Kreiskys' (MA-thesis University of Vienna, Vienna, 2012).

50 SAPMO-BArch, DY 30/J IV 2/2/1866, Bl. 36–47, Memcon Honecker – Kreisky, Vienna, 10 November 1980.

51 Maximilian Graf, 'Österreich und die 'polnische Krise' im Kontext 1980–1983', in *Österreich – Polen. Stationen gemeinsamer Geschichte im 20. Jahrhundert*, ed. Peter Ruggenthaler and Wanda Jarząbek (Graz: Leykam, 2021, in print); Oliver Rathkolb, 'Austria: An Ambivalent Attitude of Trade Unions and Political Parties', in *Solidarity with Solidarity: Western European Trade Unions and the Polish Crisis, 1980–1982*, ed. Idesbald Goddeeris (Lanham: Lexington Books, 2010), 269–88.

52 ÖStA, AdR, BMAA, II-Pol, GZ. 502.16.07/13-II.3/83, Memcon Bauer – Olechowski, Vienna, 14/15 April 1983.

53 ÖStA, AdR, BMAA, II-Pol, GZ. 518.02.02/27-II.1/80, Memcon Pahr – Van der Klaauw, 11 June 1980.

54 ÖStA, AdR, BMAA, II-Pol, GZ. 518.02.00/41-II.1/79, Memcon Pahr – Simonet, 24 October 1979.

55 ÖStA, AdR, BMAA, II-Pol, GZ. 518.01.15/13-II.1/80, Memcon Bauer – Dyvig, Copenhagen, 15 October 1980. Angela Romano, 'The Main Task of the European Political Cooperation: Fostering Détente in Europe', in *Perforating the Iron Curtain: European Détente, Transatlantic Relations, and the Cold War, 1965–1985*, ed. Puol Villaume and Odd Arne Westad (Copenhagen: Museum Tusculanum Press, 2010), 123–41.

56 Gilde, *Österreich im KSZE-Prozess*, 397–431; Thomas Fischer, 'Bridging the Gap between East and West: The N+N as Catalysts of the CSCE Process, 1972–1983', in *Perforating the Iron Curtain*, ed. Villaume and Westad, 143–78, here 159–66.

57 ÖStA, AdR, BMAA, II-Pol, GZ. 502.16.12/56-II.8/83, Memcon Bauer – Belgian diplomats, Vienna, 6/7 October 1983.

58 ÖStA, AdR, BMAA, II-Pol, GZ. 502.12.00/25-II.2/83, Regarding bilateral problems, Hungary and Poland (despite the growing number of cases as a result of the Polish crisis) were regarded the model pupils, the GDR continued to have its specifics, the USSR, Bulgaria and Romania had the worst record of solving pending humanitarian hardship cases. Memorandum 'Geplante Abhaltung einer Pressekonferenz durch den Herrn Bundesminister anläßlich des Abschlusses der Madrider KSZE-Folgekonferenz; humanitäre Anliegen', Vienna, 18 July 1983.

59 Elisabeth Röhrlich, *Kreiskys Außenpolitik. Zwischen österreichischer Identität und internationalem Programm* (Göttingen: V&R unipress, 2009), 301–42.

60 Wolfgang Mueller and Maximilian Graf, 'An Austrian Mediation in Vietnam? The Superpowers, Neutrality, and Kurt Waldheim's Good Offices', in *Neutrality and Neutralism in the Global Cold War: Between or Within the Blocs?*, ed. Sandra Bott, Jussi Hanhimaki, Janick Schaufelbuehl and Marco Wyss (London: Routledge, 2016), 127–43.

61 ÖStA, AdR, BMAA, II-Pol, Chile 3, GZl. 30.482/7/73, GZ. 44.993-7(Pol)/73, Memorandum 'Chilenischer Staatsstreich; Möglichkeit der Notifizierung der Regierungsübernahme durch die Junta', Vienna, 14 September 1973.

62 ÖStA, AdR, BMAA, II-Pol, GZ. 31.03.01/70-7/74, Memorandum 'Erich Schnacke, ex-Senator der PS; allfällige Intervention', Vienna, 13 November 1974.

63 ÖStA, AdR, BMAA, II-Pol, GZ. 31.03.01/51-7/74, Information for the Minister 'Frage der Teilnahme des öst. Geschäftsträgers in Santiago de Chile an einem Festakt', Vienna, 11 September 1974.

64 ÖStA, AdR, BMAA, II-Pol, GZ. 31.03.01/52-7/74, Memorandum, Vienna, 13 November 1974.

65 Homayoun Alizadeh, 'Österreichische Flüchtlingspolitik der 70er Jahre', in *Asylland wider Willen*, ed. Gernot Heiss and Oliver Rathkolb (Vienna: Dachs, 1995), 188–94, which is little more than a summary of Stanek, *Verfolgt Verjagt Vertrieben*, 155–67.

66 Sigrun and Herbert Berger, ed., *Zerstörte Hoffnung, gerettetes Leben. Chilenische Flüchtlige und Österreich* (Vienna: Mandelbaum, 2002).

67 Stanek, *Verfolgt Verjagt Vertrieben*, 112–32.

68 Herbert Berger, *Solidarität mit Chile. Die österreichische Chile-Solidaritätsfront 1973-1990* (Vienna: Edition Volkshochschule, 2003).

69 ÖStA, AdR, BMAA, II-Pol, GZ. 31.20.01/1-II.1/76, Memorandum 'Wirtschaftssanktionen gegen Chile?' Vienna, 23 February 1976.

70 ÖStA, AdR, BMAA, II-Pol, GZ. 31.20.01/2-II.1/77, Memorandum 'Chile-Beilage der Tageszeitung "Die Presse" vom 28.1.1977; Beschwerde der Chile-Solidaritätsfront wegen Beitrags des österreichischen Handelsdelegierten Dr. Wiederwald', Vienna, 17 February 1977.

71 ÖStA, AdR, BMAA, II-Pol, GZ. 518.02.03/75-II.1/78, Memcon Pahr – Roel, Mexico, 2 May 1978.

72 ÖStA, AdR, BMAA, II-Pol, GZ. 518.02.02/106-II.1/79, Memcon Pahr – Pastor, 11 September 1979.

73 ÖStA, AdR, BMAA, II-Pol, GZ. 518.02.02/27-II.1/80, Memcon Pahr – Van der Klaauw, 11 June 1980. On Austria and Nicaragua, see Laurin Blecha, 'Von Ottakring nach Cuatro Esquinas. Beziehungen und Kooperationen zwischen Nicaragua und Österreich von 1979 bis 1990', in *Kleinstaaten und sekundäre Akteure im Kalten Krieg. Politische, wirtschaftliche, militärische und kulturelle Wechselbeziehungen zwischen Europa und Lateinamerika*, ed. Albert Manke and Kateřina Březinová (Bielefeld: transcript, 2016), 275–302.

74 ÖStA, AdR, BMAA, II-Pol, GZ. 505.02.00/165-II.1/75, Memorandum 'Ausfuhr von Maschinenpistolen nach Chile', Vienna, 9 September 1975.

75 ÖStA, AdR, BMAA, II-Pol, GZ. 31.05.80/1-II.1/76, Memorandum 'Fa. Hirtenberger; Antrag auf Ausfuhr von 10 Mio. Zündhütchen für Militärpatronen nach Chile', Vienna, 13 April 1976.

76 Berger, *Solidarität mit Chile*, 89–95; Thomas Riegler, '"Macht's es unter der Tuchent". Die Waffengeschäfte der österreichischen Verstaatlichten Industrie und der Noricum-Skandal', *Vierteljahrshefte für Zeitgeschichte*, 64 (2016): 99–137.

Part IV

After the breakthrough
The European Union and human rights

11

The Twelve and the 1993 World Conference on Human Rights

Elena Calandri

As is often the case when it comes to human rights, judgements on the 1993 Vienna Conference and its meaning for the international human rights regime have been polarized. Some have belittled and even ridiculed the results of this gigantic meeting, attended by representatives of 171 states, with around 7,000 participants in total and representatives of over 800 non-governmental organizations – which allegedly produced a collection of rhetorical statements just a few hundred kilometres from Bosnia–Herzegovina where atrocious ethnic cleansing was underway.[1] According to others, the conference was an unexpected success in that it confirmed principles such as the universality and indivisibility of human rights, advanced women's rights, recognized the role of NGOs and laid the groundwork for the UNGA resolution that in December 1993 established the High Commissioner for Human Rights.[2] There is little doubt however that, first proposed in 1988 and advanced through contested preparatory work for the next four years, it unveils less-known aspects of the UN-EU evolving relation and is revealing of the changing attitude of the EC and its member states towards the international human rights debate. From the latter part of the Cold War,[3] through the unexpected end of the East–West conflict and into the first arduous years of the post-bipolar system, human rights were increasingly seen as a key ethical and political anchorage. The Twelve hammered out a more assertive vision of the role they wanted human rights to play in EU foreign policy and as a founding principle of the European Union, with an eye on enlargement. This vision also directed the role they wanted the EU to play in the international community, in front of both non-Western cultural assertiveness and the emerging American unipolarism.

To demonstrate the contrasted, yet founding, nature of this moment, this chapter first observes the response of the Twelve to the proposed conference in light of the last decade of international debate on human rights. Arguing that the Twelve feared the United Nations could become a theater of polarization of North-South positions, the chapter will then argue that the fall of the Berlin Wall triggered an impulse to incorporate more firmly human rights into EC foreign policy, and that the conference preparatory works were instrumental in pushing the Twelve to increase coordination and to project a dynamic and effective image of the new EU. It will be explained how the Twelve managed to sort out internal disagreements and wove a compromise with a majority of non-Western countries around the development-democracy-human rights triad. Finally, we will look at the final phase of the conference preparation and at the Twelve commitment to prevent a North-South faultline to consolidate, while reasserting European leadership in human rights.

The sources, drawn from the French Foreign Ministry archives, include both Coreu (Correspondance Européenne, the EPC-ECSP communication network) and French diplomatic correspondence. It is considered important to focus on the paradigm shift and the exchange of ideas prompted by the Conference, as well as to evaluate how, in the transition from the EC to the EU, the adaptation of the intergovernmental mechanism to the new common foreign policy had in the United Nations an area that was both crucial and particularly difficult, with the French point of view considered particularly significant given the specific influence of France on the common foreign policy and their self-appointed 'peculiar role' in the field of human rights.

The international human rights debate at the end of the Cold War

The reaction of the EC governments to the proposal to hold, on the twenty-fifth anniversary of the 1968 Tehran conference, a second international conference on human rights is a useful vantage point from which to read their assessments and attitudes on human rights developments in the last decade of the Cold War. The proposal met with critical reactions, first of all because it came from Morocco, an autocratic regime whose goals of economic development had not improved the living standards of the population and in which political opponents and ethnic and religious minorities were repressed. While complaining that the country was aiming to 'clean up' its image in a historical phase in which democracy seemed to be becoming an internationally recognized norm, these reactions by the Twelve implied that the human rights international debate was flawed and politicized. It is a useful starting point for this analysis, however; because Morocco was a pro-Western regime, its proposal enlightened how Western countries were themselves aware of their own contradictions, as Morocco had enjoyed Western support in the Western Sahara conflict, and was isolated in its continent after leaving, along with Mobutu's Zaire, the Organization for African Unity following the Organization's recognition of the Saharawi Republic. Its leadership gave no guarantee of success and it put into focus the European's own ambiguities.

Much more than reveiling Europe's bad conscience, however, the proposal evoked a Western political and diplomatic defeat and the inauguration of an attempt of what has been defined a 'post-colonial redefinition of human rights'.[4] In Western memories of the Teheran meeting developing countries, starting with the Shah in his inaugural address, called for an adjustment of human rights as defined in 1948. They denounced the Universal Declaration as reflecting a purely Western vision, at best obsolete, at worst 'colonial', the result of a historical phase in which developing countries had no voice in the definition of the common rules of the international community. This meant, against the prioritization of political and civil rights, a prioritization of economic and social rights in the context of underdevelopment and poverty, a step forward after the twin negotiations of the 1966 conventions on political and civil rights and on economic, social and cultural rights. The G77's next totem was the intangibility of national sovereignty that precluded any interference, including that of the international community, into internal affairs. What the West considered the 'attack' on Western values continued in the opposition between individual and collective rights. This superposed the political division between the capitalist West and the socialist East to the civilizational division between Western individualism and religious and political cultures in which the social group mattered more than the individual, thus incorporating the opposition between the G77 and the Communist bloc and the West into the Cold War human rights debate.

Even if over time the political battles had been frequently overcome thanks to equivocal interpretations of terms such as 'indivisibility', 'interdependence' and so on, a divide had grown in the United Nations, during the years in which the 'North' and 'South' had been separated by the New Economic International Order, the debt crisis and the SAPs, deliberately. The contestation of 'Western' human rights united pro-Western, neutralist and pro-socialist regimes under the roof of developmentalism. Indeed, development was put forward as a new paradigm, and later as a human right in itself.

After the 1974 Charter of Economic Rights and Duties of States, by 1977 the 'right to development' had become a fixed item in the agenda of the Commission on Human Rights and the Third Committee of the General Assembly until in 1986 the General Assembly adopted the Declaration on the Right to Development. Years of negotiations had failed to produce agreements on most issues, so that the Declaration defined development as a human right assigned interchangeably to individuals, peoples and states and embracing conflicting and often competing versions. It had also marked a division in the West, with the United States voting against, France and the Netherlands along with Australia, Canada and New Zealand voting in favour, and eight abstaining, mainly Western European countries.[5] Among the abstainers, the Nordic countries warned against confusing collective rights with human rights.

At the end of the 1980s, negotiations were still open and the right to development remained a contrasted theme. Those who feared that the confusion between collective rights and human rights could undermine the guarantees of the individual against oppression and abuse of power by state authorities had worked to bring the individual back to the centre and to link together development and democracy. The final report of the 'Global Consultation on the Right to Development' held in January 1990 stressed that 'the human person is the central subject rather than merely an object of the right to development. This means that the concept of participation is of central importance in the realization of the right to development. Democracy at all levels (local, national and international) and in all spheres is essential for true development'.[6] Yet, the 'development issue' tended not only to generate a North–South divide, which the EC was eager to avoid, but also to split the European community, thwarting efforts to speak with one voice and increase unanimous votes of the member states that was perhaps the main objective the EC set itself with respect to the UN. This was also the case when the UN bodies discussed a set of particularly problematic themes such as the Republic of South Africa, apartheid, racism, the Israeli occupation of Palestinian territories and Iran.[7] At the time of the fall of the Wall, human rights were more an area of North–South divide than an issue of East–West conflict, but Westerners who saw relations at the UN as part of a tripolar scheme attributed the political force of the arguments of the developing countries to their ability to play within the bipolar system.

The human rights debate in the United Nations, as well as the debates in the context of the Lomé Conventions and in the economic cooperation relations between the EC and Asian and Latin American countries, was as rigid and ideological in principle as it was political and pragmatic in substance. The set of working groups, special envoys and rapporteurs that had been built over time seemed quite effective, if lacking in coordination. It had the advantage of 'the pluriformity of efforts and separate power bases in separate mandates'. In each UN session, through the different bodies with competences in the human rights field – Assembly, III Commission, Commission on Human Rights, Geneva Centre for Human Rights, rapporteurs, investigations – the Western governments conducted politically well-geared initiatives which led to satisfactory results. And almost every European country had networks within the G77 that responded to broader national strategies well adapted to the predictable Cold War array.

The Human Rights conference was to be the second in a series of major meetings that, from Rio in 1992 to Beijing in 1995, would attempt to restore the UN's role as a global assembly and to agree on a common ground of ideas and principles for the future world order, a goal shared by the Twelve. Although multilateralism had not yet been conceptualized as a fundamental reference for European practice in international politics, the Twelve were in favour of a return to the UN as a multilateral assembly and the proposed global conferences in the UN context promoted in the first half of the 1990s. In the case of human rights however, EC countries were alarmed by the prospect of a meeting in which the rhetoric and politicization would be amplified by the international limelight and the West might find itself in the minority in a new stage of a long attrition. It was feared that the conference could corroborate the emergence of a 'post-colonial' vision of human rights and the 'writing of new rights'. The end of the bipolar system did not seem to help, since the developing countries, seeing that the manoeuvring space that the bipolar system had offered them was vanishing, were expected to close in a position of all-out defence of national sovereignty and of their most radical positions, leading the conference to a failure or to some negative trade-off. This would end up weakening the tools of enquiry, control and human rights promotion built in the previous years. Apart from the politicization around the issues and countries that were submitted to the examination of the UN bodies, which the United States tended to read in an East–West key, and the Europeans in a North–South key, Westerners shared the concern about a creeping revision. A major international assembly on human rights risked showing the weakness of the Western bloc and the challenge facing the EC in asserting its international identity as member states would easily split and fail to vote unanimously.

The European stand on the conference was therefore to ban any discussion on new rights and the examination of specific national cases and to put on the agenda the consolidation of existing norms and the strengthening of the tools for the implementation: 'A long preparation by UN agencies, the regional groups, NGOs, an agenda centered on the application of norms'.[8] The Twelve also believed it useful to avoid too open a Western leading role. In 1990 they sponsored the UNGA resolution that conservatively defined the goals of the conference,[9] a footnote during an assembly focused on the Iraqi invasion of Kuwait and on the drafting of the resolutions calling for international intervention to restore Kuwaiti sovereignty.[10] When in March 1991 the Human Rights Commission, overshadowed by the ongoing Persian Gulf War, wrote instructions for the Preparatory Committee, the Twelve consolidated the framework defined by the UNGA resolution and promoted a Preparatory Committee in which all member states would be represented.[11] The Committee would work by geographic groups in accordance with UN working practices. It was a European success, the role recognized by the UN bodies with expertise in human rights, first of all the Geneva Centre for Human Rights, then led by the French diplomat Antoine Blanca. Even more, it was a Western success that NGOs were admitted to have a role both in the preparations and in the conference itself, even if the details would remain the matter for heated debate until the very eve of the conference. 'Many consider the Conference to come at a time of major transition in the focus of international human rights work, from standard setting to implementation. There is a concern, however, that the preparatory steps to date have not been significant enough to ensure that the Conference will be a productive forum for discussing and resolving current human rights problems'.[12] In late 1991 the Twelve still required themselves to keep a low profile, arguing that any overt Western initiative would elicit adverse reactions.

Strategy shift or paradigm shift?

The mid-1980s have been seen as the time when the 1970s breakthrough in human rights started to bear fruit in EC policies,[13] starting from the 21 July 1986 declaration of Foreign Ministers of the Community on Human Rights. The picture remained fragmented however. The United Nations continued to be the preferred arena of the developing countries for discussing human rights in often acrimonious tones, as in the case of the 1986 Resolution on the rights to development. In the meantime, EC and ACP countries moved closer for example on apartheid and conflict in Southern Africa. A litmus test was, of course, the Lomé Convention. Reference to human rights and conditionality had been vetoed by the ACP countries in Lomé II, but after the adoption of the African Charter on Human and People's Rights a reference to the principles of the United Nations Charter and fundamental rights was entered in the preamble to the Lomé III Convention, even if with a degree of deliberate equivocality.[14] In Lomé IV, in 1989, the human rights clause gained the dignity of a programmatic principle. Although in practice the Commission applied conditionality,[15] formally the agreement remained at a minimum. Besides the opposition of the ACP countries, the slow advancement of human rights stemmed from internal intergovernmental disagreements, with countries like the Netherlands and the UK in favour of suspension of aid and negative conditionality, and France, Italy and Belgium prone to promote compliance with human rights rules via incentives.

The end of the Cold War sent shocks that revitalized the debate on human rights. In August 1990 the Conference of Islamic Foreign Ministers adopted the Cairo Declaration on Human rights in Islam, subsequently transmitted to the Secretariat of the World Conference. As it has been observed, this specific, Islamic, position on the international human rights debate pertains both to the position of what constitutes a 'right', and its derivation from divine, instead than human or natural, law bases, and to a number of more specific issues within the rights field, deriving from Muslim law and practice;[16] a pronouncement that aroused immediate scholarly and political interest.[17] During the Conference Islamic states joined with East Asian states in criticizing UN and Western double standards, its violation of sovereignty, its neglect of economic rights and its imposition of 'Western' values. In November 1990 the Charter of Paris for a New Europe was a pan-European attempt to agree rules and values for the continent's post-Communist era. As we'll see, the preparatory works for the 1993 World Conference was the occasion for attempts to define the 'Asian values', that remained a topic in the international debate until the Asian economic crash of 1998 challenged one of its basic tenets, the link between economic miracle, strong state and social discipline.

Within the EC context, when political conditionality became associated with making the fall of communist regimes irreversible, a meeting point was found within the Twelve and human rights became part of the legal basis and policy-making of the Community. In the meantime, with the end of the trilateral structure of Cold War diplomacy, the developing countries had lost the room for manoeuvre that had strengthened their hand against EC requests.

Between 1990 and 1992, the Twelve incorporated human rights into the two main branches of the community's foreign policy. In truth, the EC moved first on the issue of racism and xenophobia, an internal preoccupation with a clear foreign policy dimension. After racism and xenophobia became a widespread emergency, so that it appeared for the first time in a Eurobarometer survey carried out in November 1988,[18] in the European Parliament the socialist and moderate parties created a committee to map the situation in both Western and Eastern Europe, to counter the rise of right-wing forces that politicized the issue of immigration and the acts of violence against immigrants and anti-Semitism. In the Ford Report presented in February, the risk was looming that the impending single market would foster the rise of xenophobia, because the easier movement of people and the impact of economic liberalization on the labour market would fuel social conflict.[19] The Report also shows concern about the xenophobia and anti-Semitism that had appeared in Eastern Europe as soon as political control had been loosened, and about the combination of political liberalization and economic crisis in the former communist countries. In its resolution of 22 November 1990 on the impending intergovernmental conferences on EMU and political union, Parliament called for the inclusion in the new treaty of fundamental rights and freedoms designed for the protection of every individual who was subject to Community law. In December 1990, the Parliament adopted the second report of the Ford Commission.[20] In May–June 1990, the Council issued declarations on racism and xenophobia and in Maastricht in December 1990 it emitted a new declaration on anti-Semitism, racism and xenophobia.[21]

These balanced statements had a foreign policy dimension, as they responded to criticism of the plight of immigrants at the very moment the EC pushed forward with incorporating human rights into its policy towards both the developing countries and those East European countries that were receiving massive economic assistance, as well as those created by the breaking up of Yugoslavia. In these measures, the strategy to use the appeal and conditionality on democracy and human rights to dismantle socialist regimes through the dyad of market economy and liberal democracy was evident. Economic assistance, in some cases even humanitarian assistance, was tied to political as well as economic conditionality. After the European Council in Luxembourg in June 1991, a session fraught with burning international crises, issued a declaration on human rights, on 16 December guidelines were issued on the recognition of new states in Central and Eastern Europe and in the Soviet Union and Yugoslavia in which respect for democracy, rule of law, human rights and the rights of ethnic and national groups and minorities were included.[22] Where the agreements were actually heading was clear from the (non-public) declaration informing the Commission that respect for human rights as defined in the Helsinki Act and the Charter of Paris, as well as the principles of the market economy, should be 'essential elements' of the cooperation agreements with the Central and Eastern European partners (11 May 1992).[23] Thus, unlike in the 1990 Phare agreements with Poland and Hungary, conditionality was included in those with the Baltic countries and Albania in May 1992 and later with Romania and Bulgaria. In contemplating the breakup of Yugoslavia, the EC would hold onto conditionality. In 1993 the Copenhagen Principles provided for respect for democracy, rule of law and human rights for the future accession of the Central and Eastern European states.

These declaratory acts intertwined with the intergovernmental conference for political union. In its first contribution to the works of the conference, the Commission proposed EU recognition of the European Convention for the Protection of Human Rights and the right to invoke it as the first privilege of the nascent European citizenship. Within the framework of the common foreign and security policy, the EU 'shall seek to promote democracy, the rule of law and respect for human rights', an objective and a wish.[24] Some member countries also included human rights in their memoranda on political union.[25] With a leap forward from the Single Act, where human rights appeared only in the preamble, in the Maastricht Treaty signed in February 1992 they appeared in the preamble, in the common provisions and in the specific provisions on citizenship, development assistance, common foreign and security policy, and cooperation in justice and home affairs.

In the meantime, the link between development, democracy and human rights had been also formalized. A few weeks after, at the first meeting of the Preparatory Committee of the World Conference on Human Rights, conflict had broken out between regional groups, and the Dutch presidency had declared the indivisibility of human rights.[26]

On 28 November 1991 the Council and the member states meeting in the European Council adopted the resolution on human rights, democracy and development. The link between the three dimensions had been anticipated in a communication from the Commission (25 March 1991) and reaffirmed by the Parliament (22 November 1991). It had also emerged in working meeting with the US delegation as a formula able to soften US opposition to discussing development in human rights context.

So in the 1990–1 'acceleration of history', the Twelve reacted by incorporating human rights, democracy and the rule of law into foreign policy towards Eastern Europe and the developing countries, and denounced racism, xenophobia and anti-Semitism with one eye on the internal level and one on the external one. On the latter issue, made more relevant by the anti-Muslim ethnic cleansing in former Yugoslavia for which Europe was blamed by the international Muslim community, the EC initiatives had an obvious diplomatic scope. The shaping of the new EU policy would culminate in the Mauritius revision of the 4th Lomé Convention of November 1995 and the March 1996 Commission communication 'The European Union and the issue of conflicts in Africa: Peace-building, conflict prevention and beyond'.[27] Here the new concept of 'good governance' entered in political conditionality.

A leap forward, after all

On the eve of the opening of the Vienna Conference, the French diplomat in charge observed that 'attacks on Western views during regional preparatory conferences have justified the fears'.[28] Even the limited goal of the Conference's approval of a final declaration did not seem within the reach, and the Undersecretary's draft was still punctuated with brackets, variants and gaps. The task entrusted to Ibrahima Fall in November 1992, to draw up a draft starting from the European text, seemed far from success. The work through regional groups appeared to have turned regionalism into a group discipline led by the hardliners and a call for radicalization.

By that time however a majority among the Twelve had come to see the conference, and its possible failure, not only as a test case for Western capacity to defend its vision of human rights but also as a test for the credibility of the new EU and its common foreign policy. It seems clear that the signing of Maastricht had led to a reappraisal, inspired by the need for the UE to show leadership, authority and cohesion. After being adopted as a feature of EU foreign policy, positive militancy for a more effective implementation of human rights international rules and for a blunt reaffirmation of basic principles like universalism became a feature of its global outlook.

The 'concrete and anti-rhetorical' declaration statement presented in March 1992 by the Portuguese presidency at the second meeting of the Preparatory Committee stated the EC's 'indispensable' objectives: the conference was

> A unique opportunity to review the progress made and what remains to be done to ensure universal respect for and full realisation of human rights. It is important to strengthen regional and national institutions as well as UN mechanisms to

promote a universal culture of human rights. The Community attaches great importance to the links between human rights, democracy and development.[29]

As the meeting ended in failure – 'the 2nd session of the committee was marked only by the demobilisation of NGOs, regional polarisation, pessimism among delegations and officials, which were evoking the postponement or even the cancellation of the world conference'[30] – the Twelve detected the basis for a breakthrough: 'only the last hours of the debate [. . .] finally saw the resumption of dialogue between the groups, and highlighted Westerners'cohesion, Latin Americans' division, the growing reservations of Africa in the face of Asians' diktat'.[31] The change of heart appeared in a rejection of WEOG discipline, a more independent approach with respect to the United States, a negotiations strategy addressed to members of other regional groups and a new assertiveness concerning the agenda and the final document.[32] These different paths sometimes clashed, yet they seem to have been instrumental in determining the positive outcome of the conference around balanced and acceptable formulas. The Twelve relinquished the deliberately passive attitude they had chosen in the early phase of the preparatory works and moved autonomously from other WEOG members, for example Canada and Australia, whose insistence on 'special rights' – native people, women, children – was considered a possible way out for those willing to deny universalism.

More importantly, the Twelve distanced themselves from the Bush administration, whose position they saw as exceedingly maximalist and affected by a 'financial obsession'.[33] In the 1992 General Assembly, the United States advocated refusal of financial assistance and a ban on access to international loans for countries (with a list that included China, Mauritania, Iran, Sudan, Equatorial Guinea and Afghanistan), defined development 'a goal to be achieved, not a right in itself', and argued that 'development, democracy, [and] human rights should be discussed together' and 'an agreed position on the development issue within WEOG was essential'. They aimed at a 'depolicization of human rights issues' as a premise for cooperation with Eastern European countries and others. Perhaps more importantly, while Washington was taking an increasingly active role in the crises that were souring at the end of the East–West conflict, in the Middle East, South-East Asia, and Africa, it wanted the UN to acknowledge a link between human rights and international peace and security, according with their reading of the Mazowiecki Report on the former Yugoslavia. The Bush administration goals for the conference included a call for the elimination of torture by the year 2000, a reduction in the gap between de jure and de facto compliance with human rights instruments through education, publicity and pressure, further technical assistance programmes for the promotion of human rights, human rights programmes aimed at police and military forces, strong UN electoral assistance mechanism, and 'elections as a basic right' should figure in declarations.[34] In Spring 1993 the Clinton administration revived the traditional US proposal for the creation of a High Commissioner for Human Rights, based in Geneva. The role was conceived as exceedingly important, as it would coordinate all the services of the Secretariat relevant to human rights: in addition to the Geneva Human Rights Centre, the Secretariat of the Commission on the Status of Women, the Electoral Assistance Unit, the Center against

Apartheid and the Division for Palestinian Rights. It was expected to be the 'champion' of human rights, implement the decisions of the United Nations, send missions to critical areas, and ensure coordination with other elements of the UN system including those responsible for peacekeeping missions. The new presidency was in favour of increasing the percentage of the UN budget dedicated to human rights from 1 per cent to 2.5 per cent, but was also willing to increase the payments of the voluntary quota to the human rights fund. Clinton confirmed Bush's linking of human rights to international peace and security in the very months in which US forces deployed to Somalia under the Restore Hope mission, refusing the authority of the United Nations and the coordination by the chief of the UN mission, Kofi Annan.

In summary since the key months of summer 1992 the EU worked out its own strategy, in particular trying to undo the opposed fronts that they considered a consequence of working through the regional groups. France was probably the most outspoken supporter of a more independent EU initiative, as in July 1992 it proposed to create a broader European group through the Council of Europe, to refuse convening a meeting of the WEOG mirroring the regional assemblies of Tunis (2–6 November 1992), San José de Costa Rica (18–22 January 1993) and Bangkok (29 March–2 April 1993). This aimed at defusing the wall-to-wall opposition between regional groups that was blocking the conference. The Twelve organized instead, in January 1993, a meeting of world experts and NGOs under the aegis of the Council of Europe, to reaffirm the universality of the discourse on human rights, bring it back to a global level and make Strasbourg the capital of human rights. The same attempt to break the front created by the hardliners was made, once again following a French proposal, by addressing countries in the other regional groups.[35]

The French proposal aimed at reaching out to a select group of governments, namely Morocco, Senegal, Bangladesh, India, the Philippines, Mexico, Venezuela, Ukraine and Poland, raising issues of their particular interest, for example, drugs and debt with Latin Americans, and former refugees with Bangladesh. This episode was a clear test of the difficult rearrangement of the intergovernmental machinery in the passage from the EC to the EU. The French idea that the governments of non-European countries should be approached by a single European government on the basis of the closest relations was, in fact, rejected by all the other member countries, including the Commission, in favour of the idea that a semi-official mission to the chosen countries should be carried out by the troika. The outcry was unanimous and showed both a high degree of suspicion of French protagonism and the desire to project the image of the new EU. The only alternative proposal, put forward by the British, that the presidency would act, appeared completely self-serving, given that UK held the turning presidency. The French judgements on the formula adopted were later scathing, and certainly fuelled the determination with which the Quai d'Orsay in the final phase of the negotiations instructed its representative to act independently and to activate the network of francophony. In the end the troika visits to twenty-two countries certainly emphasized the new EU willingness to play a role in international negotiations, but it also demonstrated the persistent tension between national roles and common initiative.

The Twelve's assertiveness grew at the third meeting of the Preparatory Committee, 14–18 September 1992. The statement by the British presidency indicated as major concerns 'universal adherence to existing human rights instruments' and the strengthening of implementation measures, mechanisms and bodies at all levels. In the key paragraph the right to development, political conditionality and indivisibility of priorities among different categories of rights were tackled. The Twelve overturned the argument that development was a precondition for human rights and affirmed on the one hand that 'the individual is at the center of both the development process and the human rights protection system', and on the other hand that 'development cannot be sustained without economic, social and cultural rights, as well as civil and political rights'. A call for NGO participation was also emphasized.

Yet again the meeting failed to reach an agreement on the agenda of the conference, Europe – now the West and the East together – continued campaigning for universalism. From others came a variety of priorities – development, racism, self-determination, national sovereignty and cultural differences. France was the most outspoken in arguing that the Western countries had to be pushed to accept some compromise on the points dear to developing countries, namely the right to development, non-selectivity, objectivity, self-determination and racism. The right to development and the fight against racism could not be ignored and 'only bother a few Westerners'. Also for the first time an evolutionary attitude appeared, where it was observed that 'the topic human rights and development, treated in a dynamic way, notably by introducing the concept of democracy and the reminder that people must be the beneficiaries of development, can prove to be very promising'.[36] Opposition was more and more identified as 'Asian', no matter if countries like Cuba often played a leading role and flexibility appeared among a group of Arab countries, that gave up their demand that the conference make recommendations 'respecting cultural and religious particularities' and only remembered 'the diversity of contexts'.[37] In fact, it was a group composed of Iran, Iraq, Yemen, China, Pakistan and Libya that proposed a denial of the universal value of human rights, that appeared to have the support of some fifteen other mainly Southeast Asian countries. Once again, the French observed: 'If we were to finally opt for a postponement or cancellation, then ideally the 'hardliners' in the Asian group (Syria, Yemen, Pakistan, China more discreetly) should be held responsible'.[38]

In October 1992 the third committee of the UNGA managed to overcome the opposition and adopted the agenda of the conference.[39] In the spring of 1993, the Bangkok meeting of the Asian Group seemed to put any agreement back on the high seas. Remaining in history as the most comprehensive and formal definition of so-called Asian values and of the idea that civil and political rights were culturally specific and could not be applied universally, the 'Bangkok Declaration' stated that civil and political rights had to be understood in the context of the states in which they were practised, affirmed the right to self-determination and emphasized non-interference and national sovereignty. Section 8 stated that 'while human rights are universal in nature, they must be considered in the context of a dynamic and evolving process of international norm-setting, bearing in mind the significance of national and regional particularities and various historical, cultural and religious backgrounds'. It stressed that human rights should not be linked to development assistance, and that only states are responsible for overseeing human rights within borders. The show of unity was made by Asian countries that claimed their economic success was due to its basis in the cultural specificity of community societies.[40]

The same issues came up again in the discussion of the final document of the conference at the fourth Preparatory meeting. The EU was able to have its text adopted as the starting draft by Ibrahima Fall, the Senegalese new Assistant Secretary-General for Human Rights appointed by the new General Secretary Boutros Boutros-Ghali in 1992. According with European views the final document included a declaration and a programme of action.

> The longest debate arose from the insistence by Asians and some Latin Americans on introducing the idea of a fair and balanced approach to human rights issues and on focusing on the issue of obstacles, particularly economic ones, to the realisation of human rights. There was no agreement on the preambular paragraph on the place of the individual: the controversy is about the respective place of collective and individual rights.[41]

The last months of the preparation witnessed a faltering cohesion among member states both on negotiation strategy and contents.[42] The Fall document had been drafted on the basis of the idea of hammering the nail of universalism and opposing the treatment of specific and 'special' rights that risked calling into question precisely the idea of universalism. France however worked for example both within the framework of the Western Group and the Twelve, but also 'and if necessary separately', in the direction of the other groups and in particular in an informal meeting of French-speaking countries to search an agreement on women's rights, children's rights, the right to development, the rights of indigenous peoples and technical assistance on human rights. It was precisely with the support of the Africans that France obtained an extension of the negotiations in Geneva, instead of the interruption that Holland, Great Britain and Austria would have preferred in order to start from scratch. In the next step, the creation of a select committee, again France managed to participate as a representative of the West together with the United States and Denmark as EU's rotating president, while the Netherlands was excluded and replied with a negative opinion on a number of the action plan's points. Including also Pakistan, India, China, Syria, Cuba, Mexico, Chile, Brazil, Poland, Russia, Tunisia, Kenya, Nigeria and Senegal, the group was asked to negotiate in parallel on the most sensitive issues: universalism/particularism, development/democracy/human rights, human rights and sovereignty, obstacles to enjoyment of human rights, implementation and an integrated action programme. The restricted group seemed to push the hardliners to be less intransigent.[43] In the 'Fall Committee', the United Kingdom and the United States on one side and Pakistan, Syria, Mexico and Cuba on the other side were the hardliners. France played an important role of Fall's suggestion and promotion of the compromise, but this split the Twelve. Another classic item of intra-European tensions at the UN appeared when France and the UK requested that the permanent members of the Security Council have seats in the bureau of the Vienna Conference.

In Vienna, once again problems arose on well-known sticking points and new formulas for old issues. Even if the preamble to the draft document contained a tribute to the universal declaration, the opposition between universality and particularism reappeared. Thus, at the end a formula was agreed that reaffirmed universalism, acknowledged 'the importance of national and regional particularities and historical, cultural and religious diversity', and reaffirmed the centrality of the states in the protection and promotion of human rights. A lively debate concerned the so-called obstacles to the realization of human rights, with several attempts by a group of African states to listing these obstacles, that alternatively included unjust international order, terrorism, debt burden, threat to peace and security, racism, international economic climate, poverty, intolerance or environmental dangers. The relationship between the development of democracy and human rights and the problems of conditionality continued to generate the most animated discussions. The Westerners proposed to make no explicit reference in the text to the idea of economic pressures on countries that did not respect human rights and to focus on the necessary strengthening of technical assistance. The G77 in particular under the influence of Cuba continued to demand an explicit prohibition of all conditions that linked to economic assistance. And on institutional issues, the countries of the South advocated the 'rationalization' of the existing system and rejected even the most tenuous link between human rights and the maintenance of peace and security, all the more so the American model of a High Commissioner. Westerners were increasingly wary of this rationalization, which tended to be confused with the idea of limiting the responsibilities of existing mechanisms, and had largely advocated for a High Commissioner without, however, insisting on allocating an ambitious mandate. And as feared, a privileged place was given to certain important themes in the programme of action such as the rights of women, children and the disabled; but this choice underlined the fact that the strengthening of mechanisms for the surveillance and protection of general human rights was very far from being treated in the same way.

Conclusion

The end of the Cold War opened a window of opportunity that the Twelve gradually recognized. They were able to exert a considerable influence on the conference that they had initially tried to circumvent. In the Vienna Declaration they accomplished the reassertion of the universality of human rights that they considered the quintessential Western way of defining human rights, as well as a blunt affirmation of the centrality of the individual in the human rights regime,[44] winning what they thought to be a clear victory by isolating those who advocated cultural diversity as a substitute for the previous North–South and East–West differentiations. Measures and resources for enhanced implementation and incentives, the role of NGOs and the link established between development, democracy and human rights represented a mediation between the Western 'radicals' and the G77, in which the Twelve had a key role. The institution of the High Commissioner was due above all to the American support, and among EU countries remained a debated idea, that only Germany had always sponsored with conviction.

The role of the European Commission in the conference, in spite of Jacques Delors's attention to human rights and the activism of the Commission's delegation in New York, remained limited due to lack of legal competence. In contrast to the opinion of the Legal Office of the General Secretariat, of some partners including the United States, and of some member states, the New York delegation was then arguing that the UN should grant the EU a sui generis status, certifying the legal uniqueness of the European institutions, the first and only experiment of supranational integration and shared sovereignty, with the value of a universal model. The Commission took the opportunity at subsequent major conferences to ask for an 'enhanced status' in all areas in which it had powers, even non-exclusive. They obtained it for the Cairo conference on population in 1994, for the Copenhagen summit on social development in 1995 and for the Beijing conference on women.[45]

Paradoxically the United Nations, considered one of the fundamental scenarios for the affirmation of the EC first and then the EU as an influential global actor, proved to be the most difficult context in which to achieve unity of action. The premise of abstention from national action in favour of common action was unpalatable in the very core of the international community, in particular in the moment in which a new attempt was underway to make it the pivot of the new international governance.

Notes

1 Susan Marks, 'Nightmare and Noble Dream: The 1993 World Conference on Human Rights', *Cambridge Law Journal*, 53 (1994): 54–62.
2 Kevin Boyle, 'Stock-taking on Human Rights: The World Conference on Human Rights, Vienna 1993', *Political Studies*, XLIII (1995): 79–95; Donna J. Sullivan, 'Women's Human Rights and the 1993 World Conference on Human Rights', *American Journal of International Law*, 88 (1994): 152–67; Theo Van Boven, 'The United Nations High Commissioner for Human Rights: The History of a Contested Project', *Leiden Journal of International Law*, 20 (2007): 767–84.
3 Rosemary Foot, 'The Cold War and Human Rights', in *The Cambridge History of the Cold War*, Vol. III, ed. Melvyn Leffler and Odd Arne Westad (Cambridge: Cambridge University Press, 2010), 445–65.
4 Roland Burke, 'From Individual Rights to National Development: The First UN International Conference on Human Rights, Tehran, 1968', *Journal of World History*, 19 (2008): 275–96.
5 Denmark, Finland, Iceland, Sweden, Israel, Japan, Great Britain, Federal Republic of German. See Ragnar Hallgren, 'The UN and the Right to Development', *Peace Research*, 22/23 (1990–1): 31–41.
6 United Nations, *Global Consultation on the Realization of the Right to Development as a Human Right*, Geneva, 8–12 January 1990, https://digitallibrary.un.org/record/634189 (accessed 18 October 2020). See also R. L. Barsh, 'The Right to Development as a Human Right: Results of the Global Consultation', *Human Rights Quarterly*, 13(1991): 332–8.
7 E. Fierro, *The EU's Approach to Human Rights: Conditionality in Practise* (Leiden: Martinus Nijoff, 2013); M. Holland, *The European Community and South Africa: European Political Co-operation under Strain* (London and New York: Pinter, 1985).

8 Archives du Ministère des Affaires Étrangères (hereinafter AMAE) série Nations Unies et Organisations Internationales Dossiers 1991-1995 (hereinafter NUOI), b. 3730, Direction des Nations Unies et des organisations internationales, Sous-direction des droits de l'homme et des questions humanitaires, budgétaires et sociales, Note, a.s. Conférence mondiale sur les droits de l'homme, no. 184/NUOI/s, 27 June 1991.
9 The six objectives laid down for the World Conference were (1) to review and assess progress in the field of human rights since 1948 and to identify obstacles and ways to overcome these; (2) to evaluate the effectiveness of the UN's methods and mechanisms in the field of human rights; (3) to formulate concrete recommendations for improving the UN human rights activities and mechanisms; (4) to make recommendations to ensure the necessary resources for UN human rights activities; (5) to examine the relationship between development and all human rights and (6) to examine ways and means to improve the implementation of existing human rights standards and instruments. General Assembly Resolution 45/155 of 18 December 1990.
10 See the speech on 25 September 1990 at the General Assembly by Italian foreign minister Gianni De Michelis on behalf of the EC, which made no reference to the human rights conference, http://undocs.org/en/A/45/PV.6 (accessed October 2020).
11 https://undocs.org/pdf?symbol=en/E/1991/22(Supp) (accessed October 2020).
12 Penny Parker and David Weissbrodt, 'Major Developments at the UN Commission on Human Rights in 1991', *Human Rights Quarterly*, 13 (1991): 573–613.
13 Lorenzo Ferrari, *Sometimes Speaking with a Single Voice: The European Community as an International Actor* (Brussels: Peter Lang, 2016).
14 Lomé III: the Preamble, Article 4(t) and the joint declaration on Article 4. See Guia Migani, 'EEC/EU and Development Aid from Lomé to Cotonou', https://ehne.fr/en/encyclopedia/themes/europe-europeans-and-world/international-action-and-external-policies-european-union/eeceu-and-development-aid-lom%C3%A9-cotonou (accessed 19 October 2020); Lorenzo Ferrari, 'The European Community as a Promoter of Human Rights in Africa and Latin America, 1970-80', *Journal of European Integration History*, 21 (2015): 217–30.
15 Dieter Frisch, interview, https://archives.eui.eu/en/oral_history/INT162 (accessed 19 October 2020).
16 Fred Halliday, 'Relativism and Universalism in Human Rights: The Case of the Islamic Middle East', *Political Studies*, XLIII (1995): 152–67; Kevin Dwyer, *Arab Voices: The Human Rights Debate in the Middle East* (London: Routledge, 1991); Id., 'Universal Visions. Communal Visions: Human Rights and Traditions', *Peuples Mediterranéens*, 58–9 (1991): 205–20.
17 Ann Mayer, *Islam and Human Rights* (London: Westview, 1991).
18 Eurobarometer, Racism and xenophobia October–November 1988, https://ec.europa.eu/commfrontoffice/publicopinion/index.cfm/Survey/getSurveyDetail/yearFrom/1988/yearTo/2019/search/racisme/surveyKy/99 (later access October 2020).
19 Report drawn on behalf of the Committee of Enquiry on Racism and Xenophobia, rapporteur Glyn Ford A3.195-90, 23 February 1990, www.statewatch.org/media/documents/news/2015/jun/ep-racism-ford-report-1991.pdf (later access October 2020).
20 European Commission Press Release Database, http://europa.eu/rapid/press-release_IP-88-182_fr.htm (accessed October 2020).
21 The Council and the Member States Resolution on racism and xenophobia, 29 May 1990 (Official Journal C 157, 27/06/1990 P. 0001–0003), and the European Council

Meeting in Dublin, 25–26 June 1990, https://www.consilium.europa.eu/media/20562/1990_june_-_dublin__eng_.pdf (accessed 30 October 2020).

22 Declaration on the 'Guidelines on the Recognition of New States in Eastern Europe and in the Soviet Union', 16 December 1991, https://www.dipublico.org/100636/declaration-on-the-guidelines-on-the-recognition-of-new-states-in-eastern-europe-and-in-the-soviet-union-16-december-1991/ (accessed 20 October 2020).
23 AMAE NUOI, b. 4092 TDFRA Bruxelles 851, 13 May 1992.
24 SEC(91) 500, 15 May 1991, *Initial Contributions by the Commission to the Intergovernmental Conference on Political Union*, http://aei-dev.library.pitt.edu/4679/ (accessed October 2020). Every Union citizen shall be entitled to invoke the rights guaranteed by the European Convention for the Protection of Human Rights and Fundamental Freedoms, which the Union accepts. The common external policy shall cover common foreign and security policy, external economic policy and development cooperation policy as well as external relations in the other areas falling under Union responsibility. In the conduct of this policy, the Union shall seek to promote democracy, the rule of law and respect for human rights.
25 Finn Laursen and Sophie Vanhoonacker, *The Intergovernmental Conference on the Political Union* (Maastricht: Martinus Nijhoff, 1992).
26 AMAE NUOI, b. 3729 United Nations, Communiqué de presse HR 2880, 10 September 1991.
27 Article 5 states that 'development policy and co-operation shall be closely linked to respect for and enjoyment of fundamental human rights and to the recognition and application of democratic principles, the consolidation of the rule of law and good governance'. See also COM(95) 567 final, 'The European Union and the External Dimension of Human Rights Policy: From Rome to Maastricht and Beyond', 22 November 1995, http://aei.pitt.edu/5140/ (accessed 18 October 2020) and 'The European Union and the Issue of Conflicts in Africa: Peace-building, Conflict Prevention and Beyond', March 1996, http://aei.pitt.edu/4280/ (accessed 11 October 2020).
28 AMAE, NUOI 3729, Direction des Nations Unies et des organisations internationales, Sous-direction des droits de l'homme, des questions humanitaires et sociales, Jean-Pierre Lafon, *Note pour le ministre a/s. Conférence mondiale des droits de l'homme*, 17 June 1993.
29 AMAE, NUOI b. 3729, United Nations Communiqué de presse, HR/3072, 6 April 1992.
30 AMAE, NUOI, b. 3729, DLFRA Geneva, 732, 15 April 1992.
31 Ibid.
32 AMAE, NUOI, b. 3730, Conférence des droits de l'homme. Bilan de la deuxième session du comité préparatoire. Actions et mesures à prendre pour la réussite de la conférence, Genève 4, 26 May 1992.
33 Michael Ignatieff, ed., *American Exceptionalism and Human Rights* (Princeton: Princeton University Press, 2005).
34 AMAE, NUOI, b. 4092 COREU Arrivée 19667, Meeting of the Troika of Expert with the US on Human rights, Brussels 4 September 1992.
35 AMAE, NUOI, 3730, TA Coreu Départ 17072, 22 June 1992.
36 AMRE, NUOI 3730, Direction des Nations Unies et des organisations internationales, Sous-direction des droits de l'homme et des questions humanitaires, budgétaires et sociales, Note, a.s. Conférence mondiale sur les droits de l'homme, no. 152/NUOI/s, 1 June 1992.

37 Halliday, 'Relativism and Universalism'.
38 AMAE, NUOI, b.3730, Direction des Nations Unies et des organisations internationales, Sous-direction des droits de l'homme et des questions humanitaires, budgétaires et sociales, Note (Minute), a.s. Conférence mondiale sur les droits de l'homme, no 263/NUOI/s, 25 September 1992.
39 The Moroccan presidency proposed a draft resolution co-sponsored by ninety-six countries, of which thirty-three Africans, twenty-four Westerners, sixteen Latin Americans, fourteen Eastern Europeans and nine Asians. After lengthy negotiations and some cosmetic amendments, the resolution was cosponsored by 103 countries including Philippines, Thailand, Singapore, Indonesia and also the hardliners China, Syria and Iran.
40 Final Declaration of the Regional meeting for Asia of the World Conference on Human Rights. On 'Asian Values' and their parabola from the 1980s to the East Asian financial crisis of 1997–8, see Daniel Kingsbury and Leena Avonius, eds, *Human Rights in Asia: A Reassessment of the Asian Values Debate* (Basingstoke: Palgrave Macmillan, 2008).
41 AMAE, NUOI b. 3729, TD DFRA Genève 1027 Miyet, 28 April 1993.
42 AMAE NUOI b. 3729, Direction des Nations Unies et des organisations internationales, Sous-direction des droits de l'homme, des questions humanitaires et sociales, Nicolas Mettra, Note a/s Conference mondiale ddh, 8-4-1993, no. 51/NUOI/s
43 AMAE NUOI b. 3729, TD DFRA Genève 1066, 5 May 1993.
44 https://www.ohchr.org/en/professionalinterest/pages/vienna.aspx (accessed 18 October 2020).
45 Elena Calandri, 'Unione europea, Onu e diritti umani: una via al 'ruolo globale', in *L'Europa adulta. Attori, ragioni e sfide dall'Atto Unico alla Brexit*, ed. Elena Calandri, Giuliana Laschi and Simone Paoli (Bologna: il Mulino, 2020), 320–40.

12

The European Union's influence on the Dutch position in the United Nations Human Rights Commission, 1995–2003[1]

Peter Malcontent

In the 1970s the Netherlands emerged as one of the frontrunners in the field of international human rights by making human rights an integral part of its foreign policy.[2] In the field of standard setting the Netherlands, together with like-minded country Sweden, took on a guiding role in the negotiations on the United Nations Declaration and the UN Convention against Torture.[3] Moreover, with respect to concrete situations of gross violations of fundamental human rights, the Dutch government became increasingly active. Criticism of the South African Apartheid regime grew louder.[4] Development aid to crown colony Indonesia was increasingly used as an instrument to force General Suharto's regime to release political prisoners. In the case of Chile, Dutch development aid was even reduced to zero after General Augusto Pinochet's bloody military coup against the democratically elected President Salvador Allende in 1973.[5] Within NATO, the Netherlands not only questioned the NATO membership of the military dictatorships of Greece and Portugal, but also vigorously opposed a proposal by the United States to strengthen NATO's ties with Franco's Spain.[6] And in Helsinki, during the 1975 Conference on Peace and Security in Europe (CSCE), the Netherlands emerged as one of the Soviet Union's sharpest criticasters concerning the lack of human rights in the communist East bloc.[7]

The Dutch government's increasing human rights activism in the 1970s seems to fit seamlessly into Samuel Moyn's revisionist view on the history of human rights. He states that human rights had to await this decade before they would really start to conquer the world as a universally celebrated concept. Both in *The Last Utopia* (2010) and its sequel *Not Enough* (2018), Moyn at the same time warns against the danger of expecting too much from human rights as the last remaining utopia. By transforming the idea of human rights into a universal remedy for all evil and misery in the world, it may easily become just as disappointing and overly politicized as the previous utopias of socialism, communism and liberal-capitalism.[8]

Moyn's pessimism regarding the longevity of what he calls the international human rights revolution of the 1970s seems to be justified in the case of the Netherlands. In their landmark publication *Human Rights in the Foreign Policy of the Netherlands*

(2002), Peter Baehr, Monique Castermans-Holleman and Fred Grünfeld – on the basis of case studies concerning Dutch responses to human rights violations in Argentina, Chile, Central America, Turkey, the Soviet Union, China, Indonesia and South Africa – conclude that the role of the Netherlands as an international guiding country started to pale in the 1980s and 1990s when the government became increasingly 'less outspoken' on the subject of human rights. To explain this development, Baehr et al. refer, among others, to the increased foreign policy cooperation at the European level, marked by the establishment of the Common Foreign Security Policy (CFSP) as part of the 1992 Maastricht Treaty on the European Union.[9] As the successor of the less formal European Political Cooperation (EPC) framework, the CFSP demanded that the EU partners strengthen their willingness to harmonize their national foreign policies by increasingly adopting common positions and starting joint actions. But as the intergovernmental CFSP's decision-making model continued to be based on the principle of unanimity, each common position or joint action would always be the product of a political compromise based on the lowest common denominator. In other words, the CFSP's compulsory character, combined with the preservation of the EPC's consensus decision-making model, made the Dutch position on human rights increasingly vulnerable to becoming 'less outspoken'.

However, the absence of a further conceptualization of the phrase 'less outspoken' in Baehr et al. makes it quite difficult to assess this conclusion. Is 'less outspoken' about declining efforts, decreasing effectiveness, a combination of both, or maybe a declining visibility of both efforts and effectiveness? Apart from that, the book is mainly based on case studies dealing with Dutch policies on country issues. Issues concerning the Dutch position on the proliferation of norms and the establishment of supervisory mechanisms have not been taken into account. Moreover, the authors' conclusions are not supported by the results of interviews held in 2005 with diplomats from ten EU and non-EU missions in Geneva.[10] On questions concerning their experiences with their Dutch colleagues in the Geneva-based United Nations Commission on Human Rights (CHR), they all endorsed the visible importance the Netherlands continued to attach to the promotion of international human rights. Thus, further research concerning the CFSP's influence on the Dutch policy efforts in the field of human rights and their effectiveness therefore continues to be welcome. Moreover, such research may also contribute to the discussion on to what extent it is still possible for smaller EU member states to establish foreign policies reflecting their own political and cultural traditions.

The discussion on the so-called Europeanization of national foreign policies of smaller EU member states really took off with the appearance of Ben Tonra's *The Europeanisation of National Foreign Policy* in 2001.[11] A steady number of case studies have been published since, but their number remains small and their range restricted. The CFSP's influence on Greek foreign policy, for example, has already been the topic of several articles and book chapters.[12] Studies on EU founding fathers like Belgium and the Netherlands are, however, hardly available or of disputable quality. Tonra himself is responsible for the only case study on the Europeanization of Dutch foreign policy. Unfortunately, his findings are based on a small bibliography of outdated sources. Therefore, his conclusion that the process of EU foreign policy cooperation has rather enhanced than decreased the abilities of smaller member states to make an impact upon the international environment needs further testing.[13]

In this chapter the CFSP's influence on Dutch human rights policy will be analysed by focusing on the Dutch position in the UN Commission on Human Rights. This multilateral forum, composed of fifty-three member states each serving for a three-year period, used to be the UN's human rights flagship until it was replaced by the Human Rights Council in 2006. The results presented in this chapter are confined to the Dutch conduct in the CHR during the first decade after the CFSP's entry into force in November 1993. Central are the periods 1995–8 and 2001–3 in which the Netherlands first as a full member and subsequently as an observer state without voting rights (1998–2003) was expected to intensify its cooperation with the other EU member states under the flag of the new CFSP.

In order to analyse the Dutch position in the CHR, a distinction will be made between efforts and their effectiveness. 'Efforts' refer to steps taken to transform policy principles into concrete deeds. With respect to country issues, this could be the pursuit of the adoption of condemning resolutions, CHR Chairperson's statements[14] or the critical mentioning of serious human rights violations in the EU country speech read by the European Union Presidency on behalf of all member states. With respect to thematic issues, one could think of participating in the drafting of relevant declarations, treaties and additional protocols on standards and supervisory procedures, including mandates concerning the establishment of special thematic rapporteurs. 'Effectiveness' refers to whether the Netherlands' efforts to transform policy principles into concrete deeds have actually resulted in visible outcomes. Whether the international protection of human rights has benefited from these outcomes is a different matter which is beyond the scope of this analysis.

In order to present a more profound picture of the CFSP's influence on the Netherlands' position in the CHR, two country and two thematic cases have been investigated on the basis of interviews and new research in the archives of the Foreign Ministry and the Permanent Representation (PR) of the Netherlands in Geneva. The selected country issues deal with the Dutch position towards human rights violations in China and Indonesia, including Indonesian violations in East Timor. Both cases cover the period of 1995–7 as well as the period of 2001–3. The selected thematic issues concern the Dutch position towards the establishment of a threesome of new international human rights instruments: the two Optional Protocols to the UN Convention on the Rights of the Child (adopted in 2000) and the Optional Protocol to the UN Convention against Torture and other Cruel, Inhuman or Degrading Treatment or Punishment (adopted in 2002). The first two Protocols concern the improvement of existing norms laid down in the Children's Convention on the involvement of children in armed conflicts, and the sale of children, child prostitution and child pornography. The latter Protocol intends to strengthen the supervision of the compliance with the Anti-Torture Convention through the establishment of national and international mechanisms for the inspection of detention centres. The analysis of the Dutch contribution to the establishment of the Protocols to the Children's Convention covers the period 1995–7. The Dutch position towards the Anti-Torture Protocol has been studied for both research periods.

Efforts concerning thematic issues

In spite of the fact that children's rights were regarded as a priority of Dutch human rights policy since the beginning of the 1990s, the Dutch efforts concerning the establishment of the Optional Protocol on the Sale of Children, Child Prostitution and Child Pornography in the period 1995-7 were undeniably restrained. Referring to the general policy principles of what could be called its 'human rights policy bible', the 1979 'Human rights in foreign policy' memorandum,[15] the government defended its position by stating that it would not support the adoption of human rights instruments if these had no additional value to already existing ones. The government therefore immediately rejected a first preparatory document that, according to the Foreign Ministry, included so many legal flaws that it was hard to imagine how a Protocol based on this document would allow for a more effective curtailment of child abuse.[16] A French proposal obliging states to establish universal jurisdiction for the offences the Protocol would cover did receive equal opposition. If adopted, this obligation would require the Dutch authorities to prosecute or extradite nationals for activities that were legal in the Netherlands but constituted criminal offences in the country where they had taken place. According to the Dutch government this infringement of the so-called double criminality rule would imply a serious attack on the principle of legal certainty for citizens and was therefore regarded as unacceptable.[17]

In an attempt to shield the foundations of its legal system from undesired international obligations, the Dutch government also fiercely resisted any effort to establish consensus definitions on the four determining concepts central in the Protocol: the sale of children, child prostitution, child pornography and child sex tourism. According to the government, the major differences between national laws and the limited knowledge of legislative techniques in the field of criminal law among several delegations constituted complicating factors. Therefore, efforts to establish palatable definitions would only degenerate into endless discussions producing nothing more than unworkable draft texts.[18] The possible negative consequences for the Dutch legal practice were elucidated with a reference to the working definition of child sex tourism. According to the Dutch, the concept of sex tourism had to be incorporated in the definition of child prostitution because otherwise it would remain so all-encompassing that it would open the doors for the prosecution of tourist agencies even when their direct complicity in the abuse of children could not be demonstrated.[19]

Furthermore, with respect to the establishment of the Optional Protocol on the Involvement of Children in Armed Conflicts, the Netherlands clashed with its EU partners. The basic attitude of the Netherlands concerning this instrument was noticeably more positive, but that did not prevent the government from vehemently resisting the adoption of the so-called straight eighteen rule. This rule prohibited any kind of recruitment or involvement in military conflicts of persons younger than eighteen years. The straight eighteen rule constituted the core element of a text proposal prepared by the Committee on the Rights of the Child that served as the basis for the negotiations in the CHR working group on the Protocol.

In spite of the fact that the Netherlands was not the only EU country opposing the straight eighteen principle, other EU partners were strongly in favour of it. In the first half of 1996, the existing differences came to a head when a compromise text, submitted by Belgium, France and Sweden, to raise the minimum age for voluntary recruitment to seventeen years, was returned with a counter proposal from the Netherlands, Denmark and the United Kingdom, firmly holding on to the lower standard of sixteen years.[20] One year later, in an effort to reinvigorate the deadlocked negotiations, the Netherlands, together with Australia and EU countries Austria and France, finally gave in by accepting seventeen years as a minimum age. This gesture, however, came too late, because in the meantime Belgium, Finland, Sweden and a number of non-EU countries had again raised the minimum age for voluntary recruitment to eighteen years.[21]

The clashes between the Netherlands and its EU partners on the content of the two Protocols to the Convention on the Rights of the Child were facilitated by the absence of any structural form of CFSP cooperation on thematic issues. According to the Permanent Representation (PR) of the Netherlands in Geneva, one of the causes underlying this lack of cooperation was a lack of interest among EU member states in participating in ongoing negotiations on the establishment of new thematic human rights. In 1996, in a memo to the Foreign Ministry in The Hague, the Dutch PR wrote that besides the Netherlands only Denmark, Germany and the United Kingdom were prepared to make available the necessary human resources to offer substantial contributions to the discussions in several CHR working groups.[22] Therefore, the Belgian initiative at the end of 1996 to reach a common EU position concerning the content of the Child Abuse Protocol met with quite a reserved response from the Dutch PR. As from January 1997, the Netherlands would hold the position of EU Presidency, it was all too obvious that the Belgians wanted to make their neighbours responsible for the implementation of their own initiative. The Dutch PR did not particularly fancy this idea, because even if the Netherlands would succeed in uniting all EU partners on a common position, Belgium would receive all the praise. If the Netherlands failed, which was not unlikely, the Dutch government would have to bear the blame.[23]

Only during the negotiations on the Optional Protocol to the Anti-Torture Convention did the EU partners finally succeed in operating as one bloc, though this did happen automatically.[24] The negotiations in the CHR centred around a Costa Rican proposal to strengthen the implementation of the UN Anti-Torture Convention with an international supervision mechanism that would have unrestricted access to detention facilities in all states party to the Protocol. Although the Netherlands feared the extra financial costs the new control mechanism would entail for the UN's Human Rights Division, it soon emerged as one of the draft proposal's main proponents, together with Denmark, France, Spain, the United Kingdom, Sweden and some non-EU Western countries. These so-called friends of the Protocol functioned as the Western group's frontline against continuing attacks from a group of Southern hardliners with a not particularly blank record in the field of torture, including China, Cuba, India, Mexico, Nigeria and Syria. After eight years of fruitless deliberations, the Protocol's friends started to lose ground to this Southern collective when Mexico tabled a counter draft Protocol that proposed to regulate the monitoring primarily at the national level.[25] It was only then that the European friends of the Protocol managed to get the other EU countries behind a concerted effort to prevent the future Protocol from becoming an empty shell.[26]

Efforts concerning country issues

The EU partners managed to cooperate more intensely on country issues, as is illustrated by the fact that from 1995, the speech on country issues delivered by the EU Presidency replaced individual member states' oral interventions on gross violations of human rights. Against this background, the deviant position of the Netherlands within the framework of the CFSP on China and Indonesia in the period 2001–3 was actually more remarkable than its obstinate attitude during the negotiations on the Protocols to the Children's and Anti-Torture Conventions.

China definitely became a priority on the Dutch human rights agenda after the violent crackdown on the pro-democracy movement in June 1989 at Tiananmen Square in 1989 and the proclamation of martial law in Tibet shortly before. The Netherlands became one of the driving forces behind the annual introduction of a condemning draft resolution in the UN Human Rights Commission. However, time and again China managed to neutralize these draft resolutions even before they were put to the vote by gathering sufficient support among its non-Western allies to successfully table a so-called 'no-action' motion. These no-action motions did not prevent the Netherlands from continuing to induce the EU to keep on introducing or at least co-sponsoring new draft resolutions even though the EU's willingness to bring this instrument against China gradually declined.[27] As a result, the Netherlands after 1997 shifted its attention from the Human Rights Commission to a revived EU human rights dialogue, hoping that this less adversarial approach would bear more fruits than the strategy of public condemnation.[28]

In 2001 the Dutch Foreign Ministry nevertheless had to admit that the results of this dialogue had so far been marginal. Continuing acts of repression, like the mass persecution of adherents of the religious sect 'Falun Gong', showed that China was still a country characterized by grave violations of political and civil human rights.[29] Therefore, the Dutch government persistently started to persuade its European partners that the EU should give up its passive attitude by not only voting in favour, but also by co-sponsoring a US draft resolution against China, provided that such a draft resolution would survive a Chinese no-action motion.[30] A number of EU countries, including Denmark, Germany and the United Kingdom, initially advocated in favour of the Dutch proposal. However, because it was clear in advance that not all EU partners were prepared to do this, they one by one withdrew their support.[31]

Therefore, it was quite remarkable to see how the Netherlands in 2002 even went another step further. When the submission of a new American draft resolution became increasingly uncertain after the United States was not re-elected as a member of the CHR, the Foreign Ministry suggested that the EU take the lead. Not surprisingly, the support among the other EU partners for this initiative was even smaller. Many of them referred to the negative consequences the submission of an EU draft resolution might have for the continuation of the EU diplomatic human rights dialogue with China, while others also feared a deterioration of the general political and economic relations with the rising super power.[32]

In the period 1995–7, the efforts of the Netherlands in the CHR concerning the human rights situation in Indonesia and especially the Indonesian army's repressive conduct in East Timor broadly corresponded to its own policy principles as stated in the 1979 Human Rights Memorandum and subsequent progress memoranda. These not only recommend the Dutch government limit its actions to those that are expected to have a positive effect on the country issue at stake, but also underline that there may be extra cause for action when these concern violations in countries with which the Netherlands 'for historical or other reasons maintains special relations'.[33] On the basis of these criteria, the Netherlands could be expected to take serious action against Indonesia, which used to be its most important colony until 1948. In practice, this commitment was translated into the pursuit of statements by the CHR Chair in 1995 and 1996, the tabling of a draft resolution in 1997 and the inclusion of a passage on the East Timor issue in the annual EU country speech on the theme 'Violations of human rights and fundamental freedoms anywhere in the world'.

In 1995 and 1996, the Netherlands only pushed for a Chairperson's statement because the human rights situation in East Timor showed positive signs, such as the Indonesian government's cooperation in a visit to the island by the special UN rapporteur on extrajudicial and summary executions. Against this background, the Netherlands and its EU partners considered a Chairperson's statement, written in collaboration with the Indonesian government to be more effective than a confrontational resolution that possibly could not count on a majority vote in the Human Rights Commission.[34]

However, when the regime of President Suharto turned out to be increasingly uncooperative in implementing the recommendations from the Chairperson's statements, the EU, in 1997, eventually fell back on the submission of a condemning draft resolution. The initiative for this was taken by Portugal, as East Timor's former colonizer still felt a moral responsibility for its population's well-being. Feeling increasingly frustrated by the lack of progress in the UN-led negotiations with Indonesia on East Timor's future, Portugal, backed by the Netherlands and the other EU member states, hoped that a condemning resolution would force Suharto to become more lenient in recognizing the Timorese people's right to self-determination.[35]

After Suharto's fall in 1998, his immediate successor B. J. Habibie finally gave in and granted the East Timorese a referendum to speak out about their future. However, when in August 1999 an overwhelming majority voted for full independence, the Indonesian army with the help of pro-Indonesian militias orchestrated a campaign of terror during which at least 1,000 people were killed and hundreds of thousands were deported to prison camps in Indonesian West Timor.

When Indonesia's new democratic government showed no willingness to bring the perpetrators to justice, the Netherlands and its EU partners from 2000 started to focus their efforts in the Human Rights Commission on establishing a Chairperson's statement calling on the Indonesian government to face up to its responsibilities. In 2001 the Netherlands also pushed for a second Chairperson's statement calling attention to grave violations of human rights in other corners of the Indonesian Archipelago, such as the Moluccas, Aceh and Irian Jaya. This initiative hardly garnered any support from the other EU partners who discarded it as unrealistic. A second Chairperson's statement would not only damage the negotiations with Indonesia on the realization of a new CHR Chairperson's statement concerning East Timor, but would also weaken the position of Indonesia's democratic reformers against hardliners from the military establishment.[36]

Motives

Although an analysis of four case studies only offers a small basis for drawing definitive conclusions, it is nevertheless striking to see that all of them show that the CFSP's influence on the Dutch policy efforts' content remained relatively small. In all cases, the Netherlands dared to take independent and deviating positions from other EU countries, which foreign diplomats and NGO observers stationed in Geneva tended to describe as somewhat 'arrogant', 'dogged' and 'inflexible'.[37] In the case of the two Children's Protocols, the Netherlands opted for a more restrained position than larger EU partner countries such as France and Germany. In the case of the Anti-Torture Protocol, it emerged as one of the leading countries in protecting the central idea of an international inspection mechanism. In the case of China, the Netherlands became one of the leading forces behind the annual submission of an EU draft resolution. Finally, in the case of Indonesia, it turned out to be the only EU country favouring a second Chairperson's statement.

The Netherlands' independent position within the CFSP framework was first of all determined by a strong belief in the fundamental principles underlying its own human rights policy. This was particularly visible in the Dutch policy efforts concerning China. In spite of Chinese threats of economic repercussions, the Netherlands year after year continued to aim for the submission of a condemning resolution against this country, even though it was hardly realistic to expect that the CHR would ever adopt such a resolution. During negotiations with his EU colleagues in Geneva, the Dutch Permanent Representative underlined that non-submission would undermine the credibility of the EU human rights foreign policy and would make the EU susceptible to the reproach of selectivity. In addition, the PR pointed out that a weakened EU stance in the CHR would undermine the efforts of Chinese political dissidents to induce the government in Beijing to serious reforms.[38] Even the Netherlands' negative stance with respect to the Child Abuse Protocol was largely inspired by principled arguments. Apart from concerns about the draft text's added value, the government feared that the Protocol would seriously harm Dutch citizens' legal certainty by infringing upon the so-called double criminality rule.[39]

Secondly, the Dutch policy efforts were fuelled by political motives. Sometimes the latter tended to overshadow the former, but in many cases they complemented each other. In the case of China, the principled argument that the seriousness of the human rights situation left no other choice than to submit a draft resolution was reinforced by the political awareness that going for less would damage the international image of the Netherlands as a champion of human rights.[40] In the case of the Child Abuse

Protocol, the Netherlands' principled resistance against this Cuban initiative was reinforced by political motives related to the rising North–South divide in the CHR. In the eyes of the Netherlands, the increasing polarization between the industrialized North and the developing countries from the South was nourished by ad hoc coalitions of like-minded Southern countries seizing every opportunity to criticize the Western group's alleged political misuse of the CHR as an instrument to name and shame Southern governments.[41] According to the Netherlands, the establishment of a CHR working group with the task of drafting a Protocol specifically dealing with the sexual exploitation of children was nothing less than a disguised political attack by the South against the North. This initiative was not directed at improving the protection of children's rights, but at highlighting a sensitive issue that was particularly fit to embarrass Western governments.[42] By magnifying the role of Western sex tourism operators or by referring to the use of modern technology in the sex industry, the sexual exploitation of children could easily be presented as a problem predominantly caused by Western countries. For the Netherlands, this was unacceptable. Already suffering from a disputable international reputation concerning issues of child abuse,[43] the Dutch government felt no urge to make things even worse by contributing to the establishment of a human rights instrument that was based on a rather one-sided representation of reality.[44]

In only one of the four case studies presented here, the government's international human rights objectives were completely overshadowed by other interests. This concerned the Dutch position on the inclusion of the so-called straight eighteen rule in the Children in Armed Conflicts Protocol. Although the government had elevated children's rights to a priority on its human rights agenda, the straight eighteen rule was regarded as too harmful. This had everything to do with the suspension of compulsory recruitment from 1996. Confronted with an impending shortage of personnel, the Ministry of Defence saw no other solution than increasing its efforts to convince sixteen-year-old school-leavers and drop-outs to opt for a military career. Therefore, the government thought it was not in the national interest to support a principle that, when accepted, would prohibit any kind of recruitment of children below the age of eighteen, including voluntary recruitment.[45]

Effectiveness with respect to country issues

As mentioned earlier, foreign diplomats and NGO representatives stationed in Geneva characterized the Dutch behaviour in the CHR as 'arrogant', 'dogged' and 'inflexible'. Even more interesting is the fact that these same external observers believed that it was not *in spite of* but *due to* this tenacious diplomatic style that the conduct of the Dutch was also quite effective.[46] The question remains: 'How effective was it'?

As far as the Netherlands was successful in translating its efforts concerning Indonesia into satisfactory results, this is restricted to the issue of East Timor. In 1997 the Netherlands, in its role as EU Presidency, played an important role in the drafting and submission of a condemning European draft resolution, which was adopted by twenty votes to fourteen, with eighteen abstentions.[47] In other years, the

Netherlands contributed to the realization of a CHR Chairperson's statement stemming from political negotiations with the Indonesian government on the basis of a draft text prepared by the EU. However, especially in 2001 and 2002, the Indonesian delegation succeeded in delaying these negotiations to the very end with feeble and therefore hardly satisfying final texts as the end result.[48] Only the Chairperson's statement of 2003, which clearly expressed the CHR's disappointment with Indonesia's failure to bring to justice those responsible for the terror campaign in East Timor in 1999, satisfactorily corresponded with the contents of the instructions for the Dutch delegation to the CHR. However, this success was actually a Pyrrhic victory because already during the course of the negotiations on this Chairperson's statement Indonesia hinted that this would be the last one it would be willing to cooperate with.[49]

The effectiveness of the Dutch efforts concerning China was limited too. After the bloodbath on Tiananmen Square in 1989, the EU became one of the driving forces behind the annual introduction of a condemning draft resolution against China. However, time and again the voting on these draft resolutions was blocked by the adoption of a Chinese no-action motion. Only in 1995 did China fail to mobilize enough support to launch another successful no-action motion, as a result of which a European draft resolution was put to the vote, which was only narrowly defeated by twenty-one votes to twenty, with twelve abstentions.[50]

The EU countries' frustrations with their narrow loss in 1995 did not help to increase their enthusiasm to launch another draft resolution in 1996. France in particular started to express serious objections against what it called a ritual dance that invariably turned out to be negative for the EU. Apart from that, France's opposition was also fed by the importance attached to its flourishing economic relations with China.[51] Although France in 1996 finally decided to submit to a still prevailing EU consensus on introducing another draft resolution, its reluctant attitude during the CFSP negotiations made it impossible for the EU to reach a timely decision. Only one week after the start of the CHR's annual session, the European Council of Ministers was able to announce that the EU would confront China with a new draft resolution.[52] However, because it had taken so long to secure France's support, hardly any time was left to start a proper lobby campaign in order to make this initiative a success.

The increasing cracks in the EU front against China did not discourage the Netherlands from initiating a new EU draft resolution in 1997. In spite of the Netherlands EU Presidency in 1997, however, Dutch foreign minister Hans van Mierlo did not succeed in maintaining the previously existing consensus. After two weeks of CHR deliberations in Geneva, France, followed by Germany, Italy and Spain, announced that they were not prepared to support the introduction of a new draft resolution against China.[53] Not prepared to resign himself to this fait accompli, Van Mierlo wrote to his European colleagues that if it was impossible for all EU member states to side with initiatives directed against major powers like China, it was better not to take common initiatives against specific violators of human rights at all. Van Mierlo explained that when representing the EU in the CHR he did not wish to invite the reproach that the European Union's indignation was selective.[54]

Even though the other EU partners did not welcome this move,[55] Van Mierlo persisted in his position. As a result, he was able to force the most influential dissenters,

Germany and France, to make two important concessions. First, they promised to cease their resistance against the establishment of a critically disposed China paragraph in the EU speech on country issues. Secondly, they both expressed their readiness to vote against a Chinese no-action motion in case other EU partners would decide to continue their efforts to table a Euro-tinted draft resolution against China.[56] When Denmark on behalf of nine other EU member states indeed submitted a new draft resolution,[57] France and Germany kept their promise. This, however, could not thwart the adoption of another no-action motion, as a result of which the Danish draft resolution was not considered by the CHR.[58]

What can be seen from the China case is that CFSP cooperation offered the Netherlands greater opportunities to effectuate its efforts than pursuing these alone. Although the 1995 draft resolution was not adopted, it was at least voted upon. An achievement the Netherlands would probably not have been able to accomplish if it would have tabled a draft resolution unilaterally. A hampering factor was however the CFSP's laborious and time-consuming consensus decision-making model.[59] Other members of the Western group blamed the EU countries for only occupying themselves with internal consultations, thereby forgetting to take into account what happened outside the EU's conference rooms. The Dutch PR in Geneva subscribed to this critique and admitted that, as a result of endless internal negotiations, the EU only involved its partners in the preparation of draft resolutions when there was hardly any time left for further consultations.[60]

The success of these consultations was also dependent on the quality of the EU Presidency's leadership. China's failure to block the voting on a European draft resolution in 1995 was, according to the Dutch PR in Geneva, not attributable to the disputable quality of the French EU Presidency, but to a well-organized lobby campaign of the United States.[61] When in 1996 the Italian EU Presidency blamed the EU's failure to prevent the adoption of another Chinese no-action motion on the increasing North–South divide in the Commission, the Dutch PR stated that the Italian government also had to take a good look at itself. If it had acted more firmly, it could have prevented Ukrainian and Belarusian support for the Chinese no-action motion and an abstaining vote from the Russian Federation.[62]

It was not only the CFSP's decision model that limited the effectiveness of Dutch efforts concerning China. A second major barrier was created by the increasing political antagonism between the North and the South and the limited voting powers of the Western group in the CHR.[63] Southern frustrations with Western naming and shaming practices were each year skilfully used by the Chinese government to raise sufficient support to block the submission of an EU draft resolution.[64] In the case of Indonesia, the rising North–South divide negatively affected the Netherlands' opportunities to influence the content of new Chairperson's statements concerning the issue of East Timor in 2001 and 2002. Indonesia knew that the Commission's changing atmosphere would not allow the EU to be successful again if it would revert to submitting a condemning draft resolution, as it had done in 1997. Therefore, the EU no longer had any real alternatives to force the Indonesian government to constructively cooperate when the latter seriously started to obstruct and delay the negotiations on new Chairperson's statements in 2001 and 2002.[65]

Effectiveness with respect to thematic issues

The North–South divide also obstructed the effectiveness of the Dutch policy efforts with respect to thematic issues. For example, the Netherlands could not prevent the CHR's adoption of the Child Abuse Protocol. This was a Protocol that the Netherlands had never wanted in the first place because it would only serve notorious Southern human rights violators like Cuba and Iran in their efforts to divert attention from their own human rights problems by using the CHR's limited time and means to address an issue that was embarrassing to the industrialized North.[66] The fear of a Protocol presenting the sexual abuse of children as a problem caused by the North, however, did not turn out to be completely warranted. The definitive text no longer included an Iranian text proposal referring to the 'consumer market that nurtures the increase in the sale of children'. However, by considering underdevelopment and poverty to be the main causes of child trafficking, prostitution and pornography, the text still allowed Southern countries to exonerate themselves from their own responsibilities in the field of the sexual exploitation of children.[67]

North–South tensions furthermore heavily frustrated the Dutch efforts to establish a strong Anti-Torture Protocol based on the establishment of an independent international inspection mechanism. These efforts almost started to become meaningless when, after the terrorist attacks on 11 September 2001, the United States joined an influential bloc of Southern countries in their resistance against an international inspection mechanism out of fear that such a mechanism might also demand access to suspects of terrorism held in Guantanamo Bay.[68] In a concerted effort to save what still could be saved, the Netherlands and its EU partners decided to table their own draft Protocol that met the requirements of the Southern proposal to establish national inspection mechanisms but opposed it by continuing to stress the importance of a dominant international mechanism.[69] As the Chair of the intersessional working group coordinating the negotiations on the Protocol, Costa Rica succeeded in merging both draft Protocols into one that received a majority vote in the CHR's fifty-eighth session in 2002.[70]

Although the Costa Rican proposal mainly reflected the views of the Netherlands and the EU, their victory came at a price. Accepting the inclusion of mandatory national inspection mechanisms to maintain the establishment of a dominant international mechanism implied that all EU countries now became subject to no less than three different inspection mechanisms, as they had already accepted a regional inspection mechanism under the European Convention for the Prevention of Torture.[71] The Dutch government and especially the Ministry of Justice did not particularly welcome the extra organizational and administrative burden two extra inspection mechanisms would bring. This explains why after the Protocol's adoption by the UN General Assembly in December 2002 it would take more than two years before the government sent it for ratification to Parliament, which approved the Protocol in 2005.[72]

The foregoing discussion shows that the growing gap between the North and the South also made the effectiveness of the Dutch conduct regarding thematic issues increasingly dependent on the willingness of all EU partners to cooperate within the framework of the CFSP. The problem was that the EU partners were less inclined to take joint action with respect to issues of standard setting and supervision than with respect to gross violations of human rights in specific countries. A concerted effort to maintain a strong and independent international inspection mechanism as the central part of the Anti-Torture Protocol was only developed when it was almost too late. Moreover, with respect to the drafting of the Child Abuse Protocol, it turned out to be impossible to develop a common EU approach. Because not all EU partners shared the Dutch lack of enthusiasm for the Cuban initiative, in 1995 negotiations were started on a text proposal that was abhorred by the Netherlands, but ironically was nothing less than an adapted version of a text originally drafted by EU partner France.[73]

An advantage of the non-structural character of the CFSP cooperation in the field of thematic issues was that it lowered the threshold for individual member states to join other coalitions that were pursuing comparable policy aims. Such coalitions were not always available, but if they were available they could make a difference. The course of the negotiations on the Children in Armed Conflicts Protocol serves as an example. In spite of the internal discord among the EU partners regarding the so-called straight eighteen rule, the Netherlands' efforts directed against the inclusion of this principle turned out to be successful because they were shared by a powerful ad hoc coalition of countries that, among others, included the United States, China and influential EU countries like France and Germany. As a result, the Protocol's final text does not set a minimum age for indirect participation in hostilities and, corresponding with the Dutch government's wishes, only raised the minimum age for voluntary recruitment to sixteen years.[74]

Conclusion

How and to what extent was the Dutch conduct in the CHR influenced by the increasing institutionalization of the foreign policy cooperation among the EU partners after the establishment of the CFSP in the beginning of the 1990s? In order to answer this question, two aspects of the Dutch conduct have been analysed: on the one hand the government's efforts to translate its policy principles into concrete deeds, and on the other hand their effectiveness, which refers to the extent to which the government's efforts actually resulted in visible outcomes in the framework of the CHR.

With regard to the Dutch efforts, the four case studies do not suggest that the CFSP reduced the Dutch government's 'outspokenness' in the field of human rights, as Baehr et al. suggest. First, the Netherlands' efforts were mostly in line with its policy principles in the field of human rights. Only in the case of the Children in Armed Conflicts Protocol did a serious gap arise between principles and practice. The Dutch unwillingness to support the so-called straight eighteen rule was, however, not related to the CFSP but caused by the government's fear that adopting this principle would seriously impede the armed forces' ability to recruit enough soldiers. Secondly, the Netherlands did not easily compromise on positions taken and held to these as long as possible. This not only happened with respect to thematic issues on which the level of CFSP cooperation was rather weak, but also with respect to country issues on which the cooperation between the EU partners was much tighter and demanding.

Also with respect to the effectiveness of the Dutch conduct, the findings of this study do not support the conclusions of Baehr et al. The CFSP offered the Netherlands opportunities which it would not have otherwise had. Even though EU cooperation in the CHR concerning thematic issues was rather weak, it was strong enough to save the inclusion of an international inspection mechanism as the main part of the Optional Protocol to the Anti-Torture Convention. CFSP cooperation also facilitated the Dutch efforts to establish a draft resolution against China and Chairperson's statements on Indonesia's human rights violations in East Timor.

All of these findings provide further support for Tonra's conclusion that the process of EU foreign policy cooperation enhanced rather than decreased the ability of smaller states like the Netherlands to implement their foreign policy goals. Yet, there remained much to be desired. Successfully launching common initiatives within the CFSP framework is one thing, but getting them adopted in the CHR is another. Especially with regard to the latter, the Dutch efforts were rarely successful. The definitive texts of the Chairperson's statements on East Timor that the EU agreed upon with Indonesia seldom reflected the original position of the Netherlands and the EU's draft resolutions against China were either prematurely blocked by the adoption of a no-action motion or defeated by a majority vote. Partly this was due to the laborious and time-consuming nature of the CFSP's consensus decision-making model. By making itself a prisoner of endless internal consultations, the EU increasingly became inward-looking. Hardly any time was reserved for coordinating its initiatives with other potential supporters, which did not help to bring about their successful submission in the CHR. The increasing gap between the North and the South in the CHR was not helpful either. On the one hand, the rising political tensions with the Southern bloc forced the EU countries to cooperate in order to effectuate their policy goals. However, at the same time, Western bloc formation also invited the Southern countries to strengthen their mutual cooperation. Moreover, because the Southern countries comprised a majority in the CHR, getting Western initiatives to be adopted became increasingly difficult. This problem did not diminish with the replacement of the CHR by the Human Rights Council in 2006. As a result, the EU increasingly aimed for consensus, which meant avoiding a vote on resolutions it proposed, which in turn meant avoiding the inclusion of language that would generate opposition.[75] The impact of the EU's consensus-seeking behaviour on the Dutch efforts and their effectiveness in the Human Rights Council is a question to be dealt with at another time.

Notes

1 This chapter is an improved and completely rewritten version of an earlier essay I wrote: Peter Malcontent, 'The European Union's Influence on the Character and Effectiveness of the Dutch Conduct in the UN Commission on Human Rights', in *Liber Amicorum Cees Flinterman; Changing Perceptions of Sovereignty and Human*

Rights; Essays in Honour of Cees Flinterman, ed. Ineke Boerefijn and Jenny E. Goldschmidt (Antwerp etc.: Intersentia, 2008), 199–231.

2 Alison Brysk, *Global Good Samaritans: Human Rights as Foreign Policy* (Oxford: Oxford University Press, 2009); Jan Eckel, *Die Ambivalenz des Guten. Menschenrechte in der internationalen Politik seit den 1940ern* (Göttingen: VandenHoeck & Ruprecht, 2014), 441–62.

3 Hilde Reiding, *The Netherlands and the Development of International Human Rights Instruments* (Antwerp: Intersentia, 2007), 53.

4 Stefan de Boer, *Van Sharpeville tot Soweto. Nederlands regeringsbeleid ten aanzien van apartheid, 1960-1977* (Den Haag: Sdu Uitgevers, 1999).

5 Peter Malcontent, 'Myth or Reality? The Dutch Crusade Against Human Rights Violations in the Third World, 1973-1981', in *Human Rights in Europe since 1945*, ed. Antoine Fleury, Carole Fink and Lubor Jilek (Bern etc.: Peter Lang, 2003), 229–57. See also Peter Malcontent, *Op kruistocht in de Derde Wereld. De reacties van de Nederlandse regering op ernstige en stelselmatige schendingen van fundamentele mensenrechten in ontwikkelingslanden, 1973-1981* (Hilversum: Verloren, 1998).

6 Stefanie Massink, 'The Dutch will give you problems' (Nederland en Spanje in transitie van dictatuur naar democratie, PhD-diss., 2020); Tinco de Goede, 'De mensenrechten in het Nederlandse buitenlands beleid ten aanzien van Spanje, Portugal en Griekenland', in *Geschiedenis van de mensenrechten*, ed. Maarten Kuitenbrouwer and Marij Leenders (Hilversum: Verloren, 1996), 227–58.

7 Floribert Baudet, *'Het heeft onze aandacht'. Nederland en de rechten van de mens in Oost-Europa en Joegoslavië, 1972-1989* (Amsterdam: Boom, 2001).

8 Samuel Moyn, *The Last Utopia. Human Rights in History* (Cambridge, MA: Harvard University Press, 2010); Samuel Moyn, *Not Enough: Human Rights in an Unequal World* (Cambridge, MA: Harvard University Press, 2018).

9 Peter Baehr, Monique Castermans-Holleman and Fred Grünfeld, *Human Rights in the Foreign Policy of the Netherlands* (Antwerp: Intersentia, 2002), 224–5, 233–5.

10 The author would like to thank Hans Thoolen for conducting these interviews. The interviewed diplomats came from China, Canada, Greece, Cuba, Norway, East Timor, Spain, Switzerland, the United States and Sweden. All interviewed persons have been promised anonymity.

11 Ben Tonra, *The Europeanisation of National Foreign Policy: Dutch, Danish and Irish Foreign Policy in the European Union* (Aldershot: Ashgate, 2001).

12 See for example Dimitrios Kavakas, *Greece and Spain in European Foreign Policy. The Influence of Southern Member States in Common Foreign and Security Policy* (Aldershot: Ashgate, 2001); Spyros Economides, 'The Europeanization of Greek Foreign Policy', *West European Politics*, 28 (2005): 471–91; Charalambos Tsardanidis and Stelios Stavridis, 'From Special Case to Limited Europeanization', in *National and European Foreign Policies: Towards Europeanization*, ed. Reuben Wong and Christopher Hill (London and New York: Routledge, 2011), 111–30.

13 Tonra, *The Europeanisation of National Foreign Policy*, 287.

14 Statements on specific country issues read out by the Chair of the CHR are being regarded as less confronting and condemning than resolutions because they are based on a political compromise with the target country.

15 Dutch House of Representatives (hereinafter DHR), 1978-1979, 15571, nos 1–2.

16 Dutch Archive Foreign Ministry (DAFM), Foreign Ministry's Department of International Organisations (DIO) to Foreign Minister, with draft instructions for the Dutch delegation to the 51st CHR in 1995, 17 January 1995.

17 DHR, 2003-2004, 29451, no. 1; DAFM, Permanent Representation (PR) Geneva to Foreign Ministry's Human Rights, Good Governance and Democratisation Department (DMD), 24 October 1996, Report 1st session CHR working group on the Child Abuse Protocol, 10 February 1995, paragraphs 83, 85, UN document E/CN.4/1995/95.
18 Report 2nd session CHR working group on the Child Abuse Protocol, 25 March 1996, paragraph 27, UN document E/CN.4/1996/101; Report 3rd session CHR working group on the Child Abuse Protocol, 2 April 1997, paragraph 32, UN document E/CN.4/1997/97.
19 Ibid; DAFM, PR Geneva to DMD, 3 March 1997.
20 Report 2nd session CHR working group on the Children in Armed Conflicts Protocol, 21 March 1996, paragraphs 115-16, UN document E/CN.4/1996/102.
21 Report 3rd session CHR working group on the Children in Armed Conflicts Protocol, 13 March 1997, paragraph 87, UN document E/CN.4/1997/96.
22 DAFM, PR Geneva to DMD, 24 October 1996.
23 Ibid.
24 PR Geneva to Foreign Ministry, 10 November 1995, DAFM. In this memo the PR informed that from all EU member states only the Netherlands, Finland and the UK were actively contributing to the negotiations on the Anti-Torture Protocol during the third session of the CHR open-ended working group on the Anti-Torture Protocol.
25 Reiding, *The Netherlands*, 65-71.
26 DAFM, PR Geneva to Foreign Ministry, 23 February 2001.
27 Ann Kent, 'China and the International Human Rights Regime: A Case Study of Multilateral Monitoring, 1989-1994', *Human Rights Quarterly*, 17 (1995): 1-47; Baehr, Castermans-Holleman and Grünfeld, *Human Rights in the Foreign Policy of the Netherlands*, 149-72.
28 Ibid., 158-9. See also DAFM, instructions for the Dutch delegation to the 55th CHR in 1999.
29 DAFM, Instructions for the Dutch delegation to the 57th CHR in 2001.
30 DAFM, Foreign Ministry's Human Rights and Peace Building Department (DMV) (successor of DMD) to Foreign Minister, 22 February 2001; Instructions DMV for the meeting of the Political Committee (COPO) of the EU Council of Ministers on 26 February 2001, AFM; Minutes meeting of the Working Group on Human Rights (COHOM) of the EU Council of Ministers on 28 February 2001.
31 DAFM, DMV to PR Geneva, 5 March 2001.
32 DAFM, DMV to PR Geneva, 27 November 2001, DMV to PR Geneva, 7 December 2001; DMV to embassy Beijing, 15 February 2002; Dutch Human Right Ambassador to embassy Beijing, 19 February 2002; Human Rights Ambassador to Foreign Minister, 6 March 2002; Unaddressed and undated memo to Foreign Minister concerning the Dutch position in the EU Council of Ministers on General Affairs and External Relations, 11 March 2002.
33 DHR, 1978-1979, 15571, no. 1-2; DHR, 2001-2002, 27742, no. 2.
34 DAFM, Draft instructions for the Dutch delegation to the 51st CHR, 17 January 1995.
35 DAFM, PR Geneva to Foreign Ministry, 1 November 1996; Foreign Ministry to embassy Lisbon, 14 January 1997; PR Geneva to Foreign Ministry, 16 April 1997.
36 DAFM, DMV to Foreign Minister, 7 March 2001; Minutes meeting EU Council of Ministers on General Affairs and External Relations on 19-20 March 2001; PR Geneva to Foreign Ministry, 21 March 2001.
37 Interviews by Hans Thoolen.

38 DAFM, PR Geneva to Foreign Ministry, 11 March 1996; DIO to Foreign Minister, undated, 1996; Foreign Ministry to PR Geneva, 12 March 1996.
39 Even though the government would remove this rule from the Dutch criminal law code in 2001, as far as it concerned sexual offences.
40 DAFM, DMD to Foreign Minister, 11 November 1996.
41 DAFM, DIO to Foreign Minister, with draft instructions for the Dutch delegation to the 51st CHR in 1995, 17 January 1995; PR Geneva to Foreign Minister, 23 March 1995; Minutes evaluation meeting at the PR in Geneva concerning the 52nd CHR in 1996, 26 April 1996.
42 DAFM, PR Geneva to DMD, 24 October 1996; interviews by Hans Thoolen.
43 For example, in the early 1980s the Netherlands was embarrassed by the so-called Spartacus affair, which was about a Dutch operator organizing tours for homosexuals and its brochures mentioned the possibility of paedophile contacts in the countries of destination. International indignation arose when this organization could not be prosecuted because of a lack of evidence. In 1984, the Dutch international reputation was again subjected to pressure when an American report depicted the Netherlands as a major source of child pornography. Additionally, in 1994 and 1998 the Netherlands was visited by the UN Special Rapporteur on the sale of children, child prostitution and pornography, both times resulting in rather critical reports: Reiding, *The Netherlands*, 237-8.
44 DAFM, Report 1st session CHR working group on the Child Abuse Protocol, paragraph 15; Report 2nd session CHR working group on the Child Abuse Protocol, paragraph 14; DIO to PR Geneva, 13 March 1996. See also footnote 41.
45 Interviews by Hans Thoolen.
46 Interviews by Hans Thoolen.
47 Commission on Human Rights, Report on the 53rd session, 10 March-18 April 1997. Supplement no. 3, E/CN.4/1997/150 - E/1997/23, 211.
48 DAFM, PR Geneva to Foreign Ministry, 4 April 2002; DMV and the Foreign Ministry's Asia and Oceania Department (DAO) to PR Geneva, 5 April 2002; PR Geneva to Foreign Ministry, 8 April 2002; PR Geneva to Foreign Ministry, 10 April 2001; PR Geneva to Foreign Ministry, 25 April 2002; PR Geneva to Foreign Ministry, 1 May 2001; EU Presidency assessment 58th CHR, 8 May 2002; Interviews by Hans Thoolen; DHR, 2001-2002, buza 000353; Commission on Human Rights, Report on the 57th session, 19 March-27 April 2001. Supplement no. 3, E/CN.4/2001/167 - E/2001/23, 400-2; Commission on Human Rights, Report on the 58th session, 18 March-26 April 2002. Supplement no. 3, E/CN.4/2002/200 - E/2002/23, 461-3.
49 DAFM, PR Geneva to Foreign Ministry, 17 April 2003; PR Geneva to Foreign Ministry, 2 May 2003; Interviews by Hans Thoolen; Commission on Human Rights, Report on the 58th session, 383-5.
50 DAFM, DIO to Foreign Minister with draft instructions for the Dutch delegation to the 51st CHR in 1995; Instructions for the Dutch delegation to the 59th CHR in 2003; Text proposal Foreign Ministry to Italian EU Presidency, 16 February 1996; Commission on Human Rights, Report on the 51st session, 30 January-10 March 1995. Supplement no. 4, E/CN.4/1995/176 - E/1995/23, 389-392; Commission on Human Rights, Report on the 52nd session, 18 March-26 April 1996. Supplement no. 3, E/CN.4/1996/177 - E/1996/23, 352-5.
51 DAFM, Foreign Ministry to PR Geneva, 12 March 1996; PR Geneva to Foreign Ministry, 8 May 1996; Interviews by Hans Thoolen; Human Rights Watch, *Chinese*

Diplomacy, Western Hypocrisy and the U.N. Human Rights Commission, March 1997, http://www.hrw.org/reports/1997/china2/ (accessed 4 October 2020).
52 DAFM, PR Geneva to Foreign Ministry, 4 April 1996.
53 DHR, 1996-1997, 25000 V, no. 76.
54 DAFM, Dutch Foreign Minister to his EU colleagues, 31 March 1997.
55 DAFM, DHR, 1996-1997, 25000 V, no. 76; PR Geneva to Foreign Ministry, 2 April 1997; Danish Foreign Minister to his Dutch colleague, undated; British Foreign Minister to his Dutch colleague, 3 April 1997.
56 DAFM, PR Geneva to Foreign Ministry, 4 April 1997; DHR, 1996-1997, 25000 V, no. 76. See also Baehr, Castermans-Holleman and Grünfeld, *Human Rights in the Foreign Policy of the Netherlands*, 156–7.
57 Although the Netherlands firmly supported the submission of this draft resolution, it left the introduction to Denmark. As the Netherlands held the EU Presidency in 1997, taking the lead in submitting a draft resolution would give the impression that it still was about an EU initiative. However, this was no longer the case because of the dissenting opinions of France, Germany, Italy and Spain.
58 DAFM, PR Geneva to Foreign Ministry, 21 April 1997; Commission on Human Rights, Report on the 53rd session, 355–7.
59 See also Karen E. Smith, 'Speaking with One Voice? European Union Co-ordination on Human Rights Issues at the United Nations', *Journal of Common Market Studies*, 44 (2006): 113–37.
60 DAFM, PR Geneva to Foreign Ministry, 23 March 1995; PR Geneva to Foreign Ministry, 15 April 1996; Interviews by Hans Thoolen.
61 DAFM, PR Geneva to Foreign Ministry, 23 March 1995; Embassy Washington to Foreign Ministry, 2 December 1996; Embassy Washington to Foreign Ministry, 19 December 1996.
62 DAFM, PR Geneva to Foreign Ministry, 2 May 1996; PR Geneva to Foreign Ministry, 8 May 1996.
63 The Western Europe and Others Group occupied ten out of fifty-three seats. After the end of the Cold War the Western Group increasingly started to cooperate with the Eastern European Group (five seats). However, this cooperation was not always a given fact.
64 China's no-action motions were principally supported by Asian and African states.
65 DAFM, DHR, 2002-2003, buza 020294; PR Geneva to Foreign Ministry, 4 April 2002; DMV and DAO to PR Geneva, 5 April 2002; PR Geneva to Foreign Ministry, 8 April 2002; PR Geneva to Foreign Ministry, 25 April 2002; EU Presidency assessment 58th CHR, 8 May 2002.
66 DAFM, PR Geneva to DMD, 24 October 1996.
67 Report 1st session CHR working group on the Child Abuse Protocol, paragraphs 108 and 115; Report 6th session CHR working group on the Child Abuse Protocol, 28 March 2000, Annex: Optional Protocol, UN document E/CN.4/2000/75.
68 DAFM, PR Geneva to Foreign Ministry, 18 January 2002.
69 Report 9th session CHR working group on the Anti-Torture Protocol, 13 March 2001, Annex II, UN document E/CN.4/2001/67.
70 Ibid; Commission on Human Rights, Report on the 58th session, 476–8.
71 DAFM, PR Geneva to Foreign Ministry, 23 January 2002; Report 10th session CHR working group on the Anti-Torture Protocol, 20 February 2002, paragraph 84, UN document E/CN.4/2002/78.
72 Reiding, *The Netherlands*, 70–1.

73 DAFM, Report 1st session CHR working group on the Child Abuse Protocol, paragraphs 31–4; DIO to Foreign Minister with draft instructions for the Dutch delegation to the 51st CHR in 1995, 17 January 1995.
74 Commission on Human Rights, Report on 56th session, 20 March–28 April 2000. Supplement no. 3, E/CN.4/2000/167 – E/2000/23, 254–61.
75 Karen E. Smith, 'The European Union at the Human Rights Council: Speaking with One Voice but Having Little Influence', *Journal of European Public Policy*, 17 (2010): 224–41.

References

Introduction

Primary sources

'Declaration on European Identity', *Bulletin of the European Communities*, 12 (1973): 118–22.
Official Journal of the European Communities, no. C 172/36, 2 July 84.

Secondary sources

Arts, Karin. *Integrating Human Rights into Development Cooperation: The Case of the Lomé Convention*. The Hague: Kluwer Law International, 2000.
Ayso, Anna. 'La relación euro-latinoamericana a través del proceso de integración Regional Europea', *Afers Internacionals* 32 (1996): 147–64.
Bonino, Pauline. 'France against Human Rights? The Difficult Ratification of the European Convention on Human Rights (1950–1974)', *Relations Internationals* 174 (2018): 91–108.
Buchanan, Tom. 'Human Rights, the Memory of War and the Making of a "European" Identity, 1945–1975', in *Europeanization in the Twentieth Century: Historical Approaches*, ed. Martin Conway and Kiran K. Patel, 157–71. Basingstoke: Palgrave Macmillan, 2010.
De Angelis, Emma, and Eirini Karamouzi. 'Enlargment and the Historical Origins of the European Community's Democratic Identity', *Contemporary European History* 25 (2016): 439–58.
Del Pero, Mario, Víctor Gavín, Fernando Guirao, and Antonio Varsori. *Democrazie. L'Europa meridionale e la fine delle dittature*. Florence: Le Monnier, 2010.
Duchêne, François. 'Europe's Role in World Peace', in *Europe Tomorrow: Sixteen Europeans Look Ahead*, ed. R. Mayne, 32–47. London: Fontana, 1972.
Duchêne, François. 'The European Community and the Uncertainties of Interdependence', in *A Nation Writ Large? Foreign-Policy Problems before the European Community*, ed. M. Kohnstamm and W. Hager, 1–21. London: Macmillan, 1973.
Duranti, Marco. *The Conservative Human Rights Revolution: European Identity, Transnational Politics, and the Origins of the European Convention*. Oxford and New York: Oxford University Press, 2016.
Eckel, Jan, and Samuel Moyn, ed. *The Breakthrough: Human Rights in the 1970s*. Philadelphia: University of Pennsylvania Press, 2014.
Ferguson, Niall, Charles S. Maier, Erez Manela, and Daniel J. Sargent, ed. *The Shock of the Global: The 1970s in Perspective*. Cambridge, MA: Harvard University Press, 2010.
Ferrari, Lorenzo. *Sometimes Speaking with a Single Voice: The European Community as an International Actor*. Brussels: Peter Lang, 2016.
Gfeller, Aurélie É. 'Champion of Human Rights: The European Parliament and the Helsinki Process', *Journal of Contemporary History* 49 (2014): 390–409.

Iriye, Akira, Petra Goedde, and William Hitchcock, ed. *The Human Rights Revolutions. An International History*. Oxford and New York: Oxford University Press, 2012.

Keys, Barbara. *Reclaiming American Virtue. The Human Rights Revolution of the 1970s*. Cambridge, MA: Harvard University Press, 2014.

Madsen, Mikael R. *La genèse de l'Europe des droits de l'Homme. Enjeux juridiques et stratégies d'État*. Strasbourg: Press Universitaires de Strasbourg, 2010.

Mariager, Rasmus, Karl Molin, and Kjersti Brathagen, ed. *Human Rights in Europe during the Cold War*. London and New York: Routledge, 2014.

Migani, Guia. 'Lomé and the North-South Relations (1975–1984): From the 'New International Economic Order' to a New Conditionality', in *Europe in a Globalising World. Global Challenges and European Responses in the 'long' 1970s*, ed. Claudia Hiepel, 123–46. Baden-Baden: Nomos, 2014.

Moyn, Samuel. *The Last Utopia: Human Rights in History*. Cambridge, MA: Harvard University Press, 2010.

Palayret, Jean-Marie. 'Da Lomé I a Catonou: Morte e trasfigurazione della Convenzione Cee/Acp', in *Il primato sfuggente. L'Europa e l'intervento per lo sviluppo (1957–2007)*, ed. Elena Calandri, 35–51. Milan: FrancoAngeli, 2009.

Soriano, Víctor F. *Le fusil et l'olivier. Les droits de l'Homme en Europe face aux dictatures méditerranéennes (1949–1977)*. Brussels: Éditions de l'Universitéde Bruxelles, 2015.

Thomas, Daniel C. 'Constitutionalization Through Enlargement: The Contested Origins of the EU's Democratic Identity', *Journal of European Public Policy* 13 (2006): 1190–210.

Varsori, Antonio. 'Crisis and Stabilization in Southern Europe during the 1970s: Western Strategy, European Instruments', *Journal of European Integration History* 15 (2009): 5–14.

Varsori, Antonio, and Guia Migani, ed. *Europe in the International Arena during the 1970s. Entering a Different World*. Brussels: Peter Lang, 2011.

Zamburlini, Ilaria. 'Diritti umani e politica di sviluppo. Il caso della Comunità Europea', PhD diss., University of Trieste, 2018.

Chapter 1. Soriano, Knocking on Europe's doors: Community Europe and human rights after dictatorial rule in Southern Europe (1974–7)

Archival collections

AEI – Archives of European Integration, University of Pittsburgh.
CVCE – Centre virtuel de la connaissance sur l'Europe, Luxemburg.
HAEU – Historical Archives of the European Union, Florence.
PACE – Parliamentary Assembly of the Council of Europe, Strasbourg.

Other primary sources

'Commission Opinion on Greek Application for Membership, 29 January 1976', *Bulletin of the European Communities Supplement* 2, February 1976.

'Declaration on European Identity', *Bulletin of the European Communities* 12 (1973): 118–22.

EP, *Débats, 1975–1976*, 15 October 1975.
EP, 'Resolution on the Situation in Spain (12 May 1976)', *Official Journal of the European Communities* C125 (1976).
'Résolution sur la Situation en Espagne', *Journal officiel des Communautés européennes* C 239/41, 20 October 1975.
Tindemans, Leo. 'Report on European Union', *Bulletin of the European Communities* Supplement 1 (1976): 11–35.

Secondary sources

'Commission Calls on EEC Nations to Break off Trade Talks with Madrid', *The Times*, 2 October 1975.
'Dix Gouvernements ont Appelés en Consultation leur représentant'. *Le Monde*, 30 September 1975.
'Eurocrats Join Protest against Spain', *Financial Times*, 30 September 1975.
'La CEE est diposée à reprendre les contacts avec l'Espagne dans les limites des anciennes orientations - Aucune évolution n'est pour le moment prévue vers d'autres liens', *Europe* 1901, 21 January 1976.
'La Commission européenne s'est prononcée pour la suspension des négociations avec l'Espagne, et elle invite le Conseil à faire sienne cette position', *Europe* 1830, 2 October 1975.
'Le Conseil constate que les négociations entre la CEE et l'Espagne ne peuvent pas être reprises et les ministres reprouvent les récents évènements en Espagne', *Europe* 1834, 8 October 1975.
'Le pape fait appel à la clémence du général Franco', *Le Monde*, 23 September 1975.
'Les évènements d'Espagne: Le boycott s'étend', *Europe* 1830, 2 October 1975.
'Les Neufs tentent toujours de s'accorder pour agir en faveur des condamnés espagnols', *Le Soir*, 26 September 1975.
'Pays-Bas: Quinze mille personnes derrière le premier ministre', *Le Monde*, 30 September 1975.
'Trois coups frappés à la porte des Neuf', *Vision. Le Magazine économique européen* 76 (March 1977).
Andresen-Leitão, Nicolau. *Estado Novo: Democracia e Europa, 1947–1986*. Lisbon: Impresa de Ciências Sociais, 2007.
Andresen-Leitão, Nicolau. 'Portugal's European Integration Policy, 1947–1972', *Journal of European Integration History* 7 (2001): 25–35.
Andresen-Leitão, Nicolau. 'The Reluctant European: A Survey of the Literature on Portugal and European Integration', *e-Journal of Portuguese History* 3 (2005): 1–12.
Balios, Sethelos Isidoros Balios. *Grecia y España de las dictaduras a la CEE: Procesos de democratización, representaciones y relaciones bilaterales*. PhD diss., Universidad Complutense, Madrid, 2019.
Bassols Jaca, Raimundo. *Veinte años de España en Europa*. Madrid: Política Exterior, 2007.
Brier, Robert. 'Beyond the Quest for a Breakthrough: Reflections on the Recent Historiography on Human Rights', *European History Yearbook* 16 (2015): 155–73.
Castaño, David. 'A practical test in the détente: International support for the Socialist Party in the Portuguese Revolution (1974–1975)', *Cold War History* 15 (2015): 1–26.
Castaño, David. 'Mário Soares e o sucesso da transição democrática', *Ler História* 63 (2012): 9–31.

Conway, Martin. 'Democracy in Postwar Western Europe: The Triumph of a Political Model', *European History Quarterly* 32 (2002): 59–84.

Conway, Martin, and Volker Depkat, 'Towards a European History of the Discourse of Democracy: Discussing Democracy in Western Europe 1945–1960', in *Europeanisation in the Twentieth Century: Historical Approaches*, ed. M. Conway and Kiran Klaus Patel, 132–55. Basingstoke: Palgrave Macmillan, 2010.

Costa Pinto, António, and Nuno Severiano Teixeira, ed. *Southern Europe and the Making of the European Union*. New York: Columbia University Press, 2002.

Crespo MacLennan, Julio. *Spain and the Process of European Integration, 1957–1985*. Basingstoke and New York: Palgrave Macmillan, 2000.

Cunha, Alice. 'Underwriting Democracy: Portugal and European Economic Community's Accession', *Cahiers de la Méditerranée* 90 (2015): 47–58.

De Angelis, Emma, and Eirini Karamouzi, 'Enlargement and the Historical Origins of the European Community's Democratic Identity, 1961–1978', *Contemporary European History* 25 (2016): 439–58.

Del Pero, Mario, Víctor Gavín, Fernando Guirao, and Antonio Varsori. *Democrazie. L'Europa meridionale e la fine delle dittature*. Florence: Le Monnier, 2010.

Eckel, Jan, and Samuel Moyn, ed. *The Breakthrough: Human Rights in the 1970s*. Philadelphia: University of Pennsylvania Press, 2014.

Gateva, Eli. *European Union Enlargement Conditionality*. Basingstoke: Palgrave Macmillan, 2015.

Gfeller, Aurélie É. 'Champion of Human Rights: The European Parliament and the Helsinki Process', *Journal of Contemporary History* 49 (2014): 390–409.

Hebel, Kai, and Tobias Lenz. 'The Identity/Policy Nexus in European Foreign Policy', *Journal of European Public Policy*, 23 (2016): 473–91.

Hoffmann, Stefan-Ludwig. 'Human Rights and History', *Past & Present* 232 (2016): 279–310.

Hronesova, Jessie, Petra Guasti, and Zdenka Mansfeldová. *The Nexus between Democracy, Collective Identity Formation, and EU Enlargement*. Prague: Academy of Sciences of the Czech Republic, 2011.

Karamouzi, Eirini. 'A Strategy for Greece: Democratization and European Integration, 1974–1975', *Cahiers de la Méditerranée* 90 (2015): 11–24.

Karamouzi, Eirini. *Greece, the EEC and the Cold War, 1974–1979: The Second Enlargement*. Basingstoke: Palgrave Macmillan, 2014.

Laschi, Giuliana. *L'Europa e gli altri. Le relazioni esterne della Comunità dalle origini al dialogo Nord-Sud*. Bologna: Il Mulino, 2015.

López Gómez, Carlos. 'Europe as a symbol: The Struggle for Democracy and the Meaning of European Integration in Post-Franco Spain', *Journal of European Contemporary Research* 10 (2014): 74–89.

Melhausen, Thomas. *European Union Enlargement: Material Interests, Community Norms and Anomie*. London and New York: Routledge, 2016.

Moreno Juste, Antonio. 'The European Economic Community and the End of the Franco Regime: The September 1975 Crisis', *Cahiers de la Méditerranée* 90 (2015): 25–45.

Moyn, Samuel. *The Last Utopia. Human Rights in History*. Cambridge, MA: Harvard University Press, 2010.

Pardo Sanz, Rosa. 'La politique extérieure espagnole de la fin du franquisme et son héritage sur la transition démocratique', *Histoire@Politique* 29 (2016): 125–40.

Patel, Kiran K. 'Who Was Saving Whom? The European Community and the Cold War, 1960s–1970s', *The British Journal of Politics and International Relations*, 19 (2017): 29–47.

Ponte e Sousa, Pedro. 'Portugal and the EEC Accession: Informal Practices and Arrangements', *e-International Relations*, 14 May 2017.

Rittberger, Berthold, and Frank Schimmelfenning, ed. *The Constitutionalization of the European Union*. London and New York: Routledge, 2007.

Sajdik, Martin, and Michael Schwarzinger. *European Union Enlargement: Background, Developments, Facts*. New Brunswick and London: Transaction, 2008.

Soriano, Víctor F. 'Facing the Greek Junta (1967–1974): The Council of Europe, the European Community, and the Rise of Human Rights Politics', *European Review of History* 24 (2017): 358–76.

Soriano, Víctor F. *Le fusil et l'olivier: Les droits de l'Homme en Europe face aux dictatures méditerranéennes*. Brussels: Éditions de l'Université de Bruxelles, 2015.

Soriano, Víctor F. '"Quel Pays Plus que la Grèce?" La Place de la Grèce dans la Construction de l'Europe : Une mise en Perspective Historique', *Histoire@Politique* 29 (2016): 141–57.

Telo, António José. 'Portugal y la integración europea (1945–1974)', *Ayer* 37, *Portugal y España contemporáneos* (2000): 287–319.

Thomas, Daniel C. 'Constitutionalization through Enlargement: The Contested Origins of the EU's Democratic Identity', *Journal of European Public Policy* 13 (2006): 1190–210.

Trouvé, Matthieu. *L'Espagne et l'Europe: De la dictature de Franco à l'Union européenne*. Brussels: Peter Lang, 2008.

Tulli, Umberto. 'Challenging Intergovernmentalism and EPC: The European Parliament and its Actions in International Relations, 1970–1979', *Journal of Contemporary European Research* 13 (2017): 1076–89.

Varsori, Antonio. 'Crisis and Stabilization in Southern Europe during the 1970s: Western Strategy, European Instruments', *Journal of European Integration History* 15 (2009): 5–14.

Verney, Susannah. 'Justifying the Second Enlargement: Promoting Interests, Consolidating Democracy or Returning to the Roots?', in *Questioning EU Enlargement: Europe in Search of Identity*, ed. Helene Sjursen, 19–43. London and New York: Routledge, 2006.

Wassenberg, Birte. *History of the Council of Europe*. Strasbourg: Council of Europe Publishing, 2013.

Chapter 2. Zamburlini, Introducing human rights within development cooperation policies: The European Community between the United States and the Soviet Union (1968–79)

Archival collections

CVCE - Centre virtuel de la connaissance sur l'Europe, Luxemburg.
HAEC – Historical Archives of the European Commission, Brussels.
HAEP – Historical Archives of the European Parliament, Luxemburg.
HAEU – Historical Archives of the European Union, Florence.

Other primary sources

'Declaration on European Identity', *Bulletin of the European Communities*, 12 (1973): 118–22.

First Report of the Foreign Ministers to the Heads of State and Government of the Member States of the European Community. Luxembourg: European Communities, 1970.

United Nations, *International Development Strategy for the Second United Nations Development Decade*, no. 2626 (XXV), 10 December 1970.

United Nations, *United Nations Development Decade. A Programme for International Economic Cooperation (I)*, no. 1710 (XVI), 19 December 1961.

Secondary sources

Allen, David, Reinhardt Rummel, and Wolfgang Wessels, ed. *European Political Cooperation: Towards a Foreign Policy for Western Europe*. London: Butterworth Scientific, 1982.

Arts, Karin. *Integrating Human Rights into Development Cooperation: The Case of the Lomé Convention*. The Hague: Kluwer Law International, 2000.

Arts, Karin, and Anna K. Dickinson, ed. *EU Development Cooperation: From Model to Symbol*, Manchester: Manchester University Press, 2004.

Barratt, Bethany. *Human Rights and Foreign Aid. For Love or for Money?* Abingdon: Routledge, 2008.

Bartels, Lorand. *Human Rights Conditionality in the EU's International Agreements*. Oxford: Oxford University Press, 2005.

Betts, Raymond F. *Decolonization*. London: Routledge, 1998.

Bindi, Federiga. *The Foreign Policy of the European Union: Asserting Europe's Role in the World*. Washington: Brookings Institution Press, 2012.

Calandri, Elena. *Prima della globalizzazione: l'Italia, la cooperazione allo sviluppo e la guerra fredda 1955–1995*. Padova: Cedam, 2013.

Cooper, Frederick. *Colonialism in Question: Theory, Knowledge, History*. Berkeley and Los Angeles: University of California Press, 2005.

Del Pero, Mario, and Federico Romero, ed. *Le crisi transatlantiche. Continuità e trasformazioni*. Roma: Edizioni di storia e letteratura, 2007.

Dietrich, Simone, and Amanda Murdie, 'Human Rights Shaming through INGOs and Foreign Aid Delivery', *The Review of International Organizations* 12 (2016): 1–26.

Eckel, Jan, and Samuel Moyn, ed. *The Breakthrough. Human Rights in the 1970s*. Philadelphia: University of Pennsylvania Press, 2014.

Ferrari, Lorenzo. 'The European Community as a Promoter of Human Rights in Africa and Latin America, 1970–1980', *Journal of European Integration History* 21 (2015): 217–30.

Ferrari, Lorenzo. *Sometimes Speaking with a Single Voice. The European Community as an International Actor*. Brussels: Peter Lang, 2016.

Flores, Marcello, and Giovanni Gozzini. *1968. Un anno spartiacque*. Bologna: il Mulino, 2018.

Garavini, Giuliano. 'Il confronto Nord-Sud allo specchio: l'impatto del Terzo mondo sull'Europa occidentale (1968-1975)', in *Alle origini del presente. L'Europa occidentale nella crisi degli anni Settanta*, ed. Antonio Varsori, 67–95. Milano: Franco Angeli, 2007.

Gfeller, Aurélie É., 'Champion of Human Rights: The European Parliament and the Helsinki Process', *Journal of Contemporary History* 49 (2014): 390–409.

Gordon Lauren, Paul. *The Evolution of International Human Rights. Visions Seen*. Philadelphia: University of Pennsylvania Press, 2011.

Hobsbawm, Eric J. *Age of Extremes. The Short Twentieth Century, 1914–1991*. London: Random House, 1994.

Hoffmann, Stefan-Ludwig. *Human Rights in the Twentieth Century*. New York: Cambridge University Press, 2010.

Holland, Martin. *The European Union and the Third World*. Houndmills: Palgrave, 2002.

Hurwitz, Leon. *The European Community and the Management of International Cooperation*. Santa Barbara: Greenwood Press, 1987.

Ignatieff, Michael. *Human Rights as Politics and Idolatry*. Princeton: Princeton University Press, 2001.

Judt, Tony. *Postwar. A History of Europe since 1945*. New York: The Penguin Press, 2005.

Keys, Barbara. *Reclaiming American Virtue. The Human Rights Revolution of the 1970s*. Cambridge, MA: Harvard University Press, 2014.

King, Toby. 'Human Rights in the Development Policy of the European Community: Towards a European World Order?', *Netherlands Yearbook of International Law* 28 (December 1997): 51–99.

Laschi, Giuliana. *L'Europa e gli altri. Le relazioni esterne della Comunità dalle origini al dialogo Nord-Sud*. Bologna: il Mulino, 2015.

Lister, Marjorie. *The European Community and the Developing World: The Role of the Lomé Convention*. Aldershot: Avebury, 1988.

Lorenzini, Sara. *Una strana guerra fredda. Lo sviluppo e le relazioni Nord-Sud*. Bologna: il Mulino, 2017.

Manners, Ian. 'The Constitutive Nature of Values, Images and Principles in the European Union', in *Values and Principles in European Union Foreign Policy*, ed. Sonia Lucarelli, and Ian Manners, 19–41. Abingdon: Routledge, 2006.

Migani, Guia. 'Strategie nazionali ed istituzionali alle origini dell'assistenza comunitaria allo sviluppo: la Cee, la Francia e l'Africa negli anni sessanta', in *Il primato sfuggente. L'Europa e l'intervento per lo sviluppo (1957–2007)*, ed. Elena Calandri, 17–34. Milano: Franco Angeli, 2009.

Moyn, Samuel. *The Last Utopia: Human Rights in History*. Cambridge, MA: Harvard University Press, 2010.

Overseas Development Institute, 'Briefing Paper', *ODI Briefing Papers*, 1 (1980).

Ravenhill, John. *Collective Clientelism: The Lomé Conventions and North-South Relations*. New York: Columbia University Press, 1985.

Romano, Angela. *From Détente in Europe to European Détente. How the West Shaped the Helsinki CSCE*. Brussels: Peter Lang, 2009.

Romero, Federico. *Storia internazionale dell'età contemporanea*. Roma: Carocci, 2012.

Simma, Bruno, Jo Beatrix Aschenbrenner, and Constanze Schulte, 'Human Rights Considerations in the Development Co-operation Activities of the EC', in *The EU and Human Rights*, ed. Philip Alston, Mara Bustelo, and James Heenan, 571–626. Oxford: Oxford University Press, 1999.

Tulli, Umberto. 'Challenging Intergovermentalism and EPC: The European Parliament and its actions in International Relations, 1970–1979', *Journal of Contemporary European Research* 13 (2017): 1076–89.

Villaume, Poul, Rasmus Mariager, and Helle Porsdam, ed. *The 'Long 1970s'. Human Rights, East- West Détente and Transnational Relations*. Copenhagen: Museum Tusculanum Press, 2010.

Zamburlini, Ilaria. 'Human Rights and Foreign Aid: Three NGOs Influencing the European Community (1974–1979)', in *The Informal Construction of Europe*, ed. Lennaert Van Heumen, and Mechthild Roos, 129–42. Abingdon: Routledge, 2019.

Chapter 3. Tulli, A reluctant promoter: The EC, CSCE and human rights in East–West relations

Archival collections

ADSA – Andrei D. Sakharov Archives, Harvard University.
AMAE – Archives du Ministère des Affaires Etrangères, Paris.
CVCE – Centre virtuel de la connaissance sur l'Europe, Luxemburg.
HAEP – Historical Archives of the European Parliament, Luxemburg.
HAEU – Historical Archives of the European Union, Florence.
JCPL – Jimmy Carter Presidential Library, Atlanta.
TNA – The National Archives, London.

Other primary sources

'Declaration on European Identity', *Bulletin of the European Communities* 12 (1973): 118–22.
'Resolution on Human Rights in Poland', *OJEC*, no. C265, 13 October 1980.
'Resolution on Human Rights in the Soviet Union', *OJEC*, no. C61, 20 June 1983.
'Resolution on the Respect for Human Rights in Czechoslovakia', *OJEC*, no. C117, 12 April 1980.
'Resolution on the Situation of the Jewish Community in the Soviet Union', *OJEC*, , no. C296, 11 December 1978.
'United States and Allied Approaches to the Current Issues of European Security', 31 October 1969; http://history.state.gov/historicaldocuments/frus1969-76v39/d10.
Chronicle of Human Rights in the Soviet Union, March 1977.
Documents on British Policy Overseas, Series III, Vol. II, London: The Stationery Office, 1987.
Memorandum, Cabinet Meeting, 8 August 1975, http://cdn.geraldrfordfoundation.org/memcons/1553206.pdf.
Parlement Européen. *Débats*, 15 October 1980.

Secondary sources

'Brezhnev at Helsinki'. *New York Times*, 1 August 1975.
'Giscard, Schmidt on Détente', *Washington Post*, 19 July 1977.
Aunesluoma, Juhana. 'Finlandisation in Reverse: The CSCE and the Rise and Fall of Economic Détente, 1968–1975', in *Helsinki 1975 and the Transformation of Europe*, ed. Oliver Bange, Gottfried Niedhart, 98–113. New York: Berghahn Books, 2008.
Badalassi, Nicolas, and Sarah Snyder, ed. *The CSCE and the End of the Cold War: Diplomacy, Societies and Human Rights, 1972–1990*. New York: Berghahn Books, 2019.
Baudet, Floribert. 'It Was Cold War and We Wanted to Win': Human Rights, Détente, and the CSCE', in *Origins of the European Security System: The Helsinki Process Revisited, 1965–1975*, ed. Andreas Wenger, Vojtech Mastny, and Christian Nuenlist, 184–91. London: Routledge 2008.
Bilandžić, Vladimir, Dittmar Dahlmnn, and Milan Kosanović, *From Helsinki to Belgrade: The First CSCE Follow-Up Meeting in Belgrade*. Bonn: Bonn University Press, 2012.

Boel, Bent. 'Western Journalism in the Soviet Bloc during the Cold War: Themes, Approaches, Theses', *Cold War History* 19 (2019): 593-614.

Bradley, Mark Ph. *The World Reimagined: Americans and Human Rights in the Twentieth Century*. New York: Cambridge University Press, 2016.

Buwalda, Piet. *They Did Not Dwell Alone: Jewish Emigration from the Soviet Union 1967-1990*. Baltimore and London: Johns Hopkins University Press, 1997.

CDU/CSU Group in the Bundestag. *White Paper on the Human Rights Situation in Germany and of the German in Eastern Europe*. Bonn, October 1977.

Davy, Richard. 'Helsinki Myths: Setting the Record Straight on the Final Act of the CSCE', *Cold War History* 9 (2009): 1-22.

Eckel, Jan, and Samuel Moyn, ed. *The Breakthrough: Human Rights in the 1970s*. Philadelphia: University of Pennsylvania Press, 2014.

Garthoff, Raymond L. *Detente and Confrontation: American-Soviet Relations from Nixon to Reagan*. Washington: The Brookings Institution, 1985.

Gfeller, Aurélie É. 'Champion of Human Rights: The European Parliament and the Helsinki Process', *Journal of Contemporary History*, 2 (2014): 390-409.

Hanhimäki, Jussi. '"They Can Write It in Swahili". Kissinger, the Soviets and the Helsinki Accords', *Journal of Transatlantic Studies* 1 (2003): 37-58.

Lamberti-Moneta, Sara. 'Helsinki Disentangled (1973-1975): West Germany, the Netherlands, the EPC and the Principle of the Protection of Human Rights', PhD Diss., University of Trento, Trento, 2012.

Lomellini, Valentine. *L'appuntamento mancato. La sinistra italiana e il dissenso nei regimi comunisti, 1968-1989*. Florence: Le Monnier, 2010.

Maresca, John. *To Helsinki. The Conference on Security and Cooperation in Europe, 1973-1975*. Durham: Duke University Press, 1987.

Moyn, Samuel. *The Last Utopia: Human Rights in History*. Cambridge, MA: Harvard University Press, 2010.

Renouard, Joe. 'No Relief for a Troubled Alliance: Human Rights and Transatlantic Relations in the 1970s)', in *Transatlantic Conflict and Consensus: Culture, History and Politics*, ed. R. Haar and N. Wynn, 145-62. Cambridge: Cambridge Academic, 2009.

Romano, Angela. 'The EC and the Socialist World', in *Europe's Cold War Relations. The EC Towards a Global Role* ed. Ulrich Krotz, Kiran Klaus Patel, and Federico Romero, 51-71. London: Bloomsbury, 2019.

Romano, Angela. *From Détente in Europe to European Détente. How the West Shaped the Helsinki CSCE*. Brussels: Peter Lang, 2009.

Romano, Angela. 'G7 Summits, European Councils and East-West Economic Relations (1975-1982)', in *International Summitry and Global Governance: The Rise of the G7 and the European Council*, ed. Emmanuel Mourlon Druol, and Federico Romero, 198-222. London and New York: Routledge, 2014.

Schmidt, Helmut. *Men and Power: A Political Retrospective*. New York: Random House, 1989.

Schulz, Matthias, and Thomas A. Schwartz, ed. *The Strained Alliance: U.S.- European Relations from Nixon to Carter*. Cambridge: Cambridge University Press, 2010.

Snyder, Sarah. *Human Rights Activism and the End of the Cold War*. New York and Cambridge: Cambridge University Press, 2012.

Suri, Jeremi. 'Détente and Human Rights: American and West European Perspectives on International Change', *Cold War History* 8 (2008): 527-45.

Thomas, Daniel C. *The Helsinki Effect. International Norms, Human Rights and the Demise of Communism* Princeton: Princeton University Press, 2001.

Tulli, Umberto. *A Precarious Equilibrium. Human Rights and Détente in Jimmy Carter's Soviet Policy*. Manchester: Manchester University Press, 2020.

Varsori, Antonio, and Guia Migani, ed. *Europe in the International Arena during the 1970s*, ed. Antonio Varsori, and Guia Migani. Brussels: Peter Lang, 2011.

Chapter 4. Ferrari, EC member states' stance on human rights issues: The perspective from the UN General Assembly, 1970-9

Archival collections

AMAE – Archives du Ministère des Affaires Etrangères, Paris.
TNA – The National Archives, London.

Other primary sources

'Statement from the Paris Summit', Bulletin of the European Communities 10, 21 October 1972.

Secondary sources

Birnberg, Gabriele. 'The Voting Behaviour of the European Union Member States in the United Nations General Assembly', PhD diss., LSE, London, 2009.

Bot, Bernard R. 'Cooperation between the Diplomatic Missions of the Ten in Third Countries and International Organisations', *Legal Issues of Economic Integration*, 11 (1984): 1.

Brückner, Paul. 'The European Community and the United Nations', *European Journal of International Law* 1 (1990): 174-92.

Ferrari, Lorenzo. 'The European Community as a Promoter of Human Rights in Africa and Latin America, 1970-1980', *Journal of European Integration History* 21 (2015): 217-30.

Ferrari, Lorenzo. 'How the European Community Entered the United Nations, 1969-1976, and What It Meant for European Political Integration', *Diplomacy & Statecraft* 29 (2018): 237-54.

Foot, Rosemary. 'The EC's Voting Behaviour at the UN General Assembly', *Journal of Common Market Studies* 17 (1979): 350-60.

Gainar, Maria. *Aux origines de la diplomatie européenne: Les Neuf et la Coopération politique européenne de 1973 à 1980*. Brussels: Peter Lang, 2012.

Gillissen, Christophe. 'Her Place among the Nations of the Earth: Irish Votes at the UN General Assembly, 1955-2005', *Estudios Irlandeses* 2 (2007): 68-77.

Holland, Martin *The European Community and South Africa. European Political Cooperation under Strain*. London and New York: Pinter, 1985.

Hosli, Madeleine O., Evelyn van Kampen, Frits Meijerink, and Tennis, Kathrine. 'Voting Cohesion in the United Nations General Assembly: The Case of the European Union', Paper presented at the 5th ECPR Pan-European Conference, 24-26 June 2010.

Hurwitz, Leon. 'The EEC in the United Nations: The Voting Behaviour of Eight Countries, 1948-1973', *Journal of Common Market Studies* 13 (1975): 224-43.
Johansson-Nogués, Elizabeth. 'The Voting Practice of the Fifteen in the UN General Assembly: Convergence and Divergence', Working Papers OBS no. 54. Institut Universitari d'Estudis Europeus, 2004.
Lindemann, Beate. 'Europe and the Third World: The Nine at the United Nations', *World Today* 32 (1976): 262-3.
Lindemann, Beate. 'European Political Cooperation at the UN: A Challenge for the Nine', in *European Political Cooperation*, ed. David Allen, Reinhardt Rummel, and Wolfgang Wessels, 110-33. London: Butterworth Scientific, 1982.
Luif, Paul. 'EU Cohesion in the UN General Assembly', Occasional paper no. 49. European Union Institute for Security Studies, Paris, 2003.
Maes, Albert C. 'The European Community and the United Nations General Assembly', *Journal of European Integration* 3 (1979): 73-83.
Owen, David. *Human Rights*. London: Jonathan Cape, 1978.
Smith, Karen E. 'Speaking with One Voice? European Union Co-ordination on Human Rights Issues at the United Nations', *Journal of Common Market Studies* 44 (2006): 113-37.
Svenbalrud, H. Kvale. 'Apartheid and NATO: Britain, Scandinavia, and the Southern Africa Question in the 1970s', *Diplomacy & Statecraft* 23 (2012): 746-62.
Tosi, Luciano. 'Europe, the United Nations and Dialogue with the Third World', in *Europe in the International Arena during the 1970s. Entering a Different World*, ed. Antonio Varsori and Guia Migani, 161-91. Brussels: Peter Lang, 2011.
Tosi, Luciano. 'L'Europa all'Assemblea Generale delle Nazioni Unite (1974-1991). Non solo parole', in *L'Europa nel sistema internazionale. Sfide, ostacoli e dilemmi nello sviluppo di una potenza civile*, ed. Giuliana Laschi and Mario Telò, 184-203. Bologna: il Mulino, 2009.

Chapter 5. Sergio, The European Union of Christian Democrats and the controversy regarding the Spanish accession to the EC in the 1970s: The human rights problem

Archival collections

ACS – Archivio Centrale dello Stato, Rome.
ASSR – Archivio Storico del Senato della Repubblica.
NARA – National Archives and Records Administration, Washington DC.

Other primary sources

'Decreto-ley 10/1975', *Boletín Oficial del Estado*, 26 August 1975.
Bulletin des Communautés européennes, 9 (1975).
Bulletin of the European Communities, 10 (1975).
Gehler, Michael, Marcus Gonschor, Hinnerk Meyer, and Hannes Schönner, ed. *Transnationale Parteienkooperation der europäischen Christdemokraten und Konservativen. Dokumente 1965-1979*, I. Berlin and Boston: de Gruyter GmbH, 2018.

Parliamentary Assembly of the Council of Europe, *Resolution on the Situation in Spain*, 14 January1976. Doc. 3714.

Secondary sources

'Kreuth International', *Der Spiegel*, 21 March 1977.

Aguilar Fernández, Paloma. *Memoria y olvido de la Guerra Civil española*. Madrid: Alianza, 1996.

Aguilera Barchet, Bruno. 'España y Europa veinte años después', in *Veinte años de España en Europa: actas de las Jornadas de Conmemoración del XX Aniversario de la Adhesión de España a la Unión Europea*, ed. Cristina J. Gortázar Rotaeche, and María José Castaño Reyero, 91–107. Madrid: Universidad Pontificia Comillas, 2008.

Allen, David, Reinhardt Rummel, and Wolfgang Wessels, ed. *European Political Cooperation: Towards a Foreign Policy for Western Europe*. Boston: Butterworth Scientific, 1982.

Amnesty International, *The Amnesty International Annual Report 1977*. London: Amnesty International Publications, 1977.

André-Bazzana, Bénédicte. *Mitos y mentiras de la transición*. Barcelona: El Viejo Topo, 2006.

Aschmann, Birgit. 'Die deutsch-spanische Kooperation in der Europapolitik nach 1945', in *Zeiten im Wandel: Deutschland im Europa des 20. Jahrhunderts*, ed. Jürgen Elvert, and Syvain Schirmann, 103–17. Bern: Peter Lang, 2008.

Aschmann, Birgit. 'Partner in der Protektion: Die deutsch-französische Kooperation zugunsten einer EWG-Integration Spaniens in den 60er Jahren', *Historische Mitteilungen der Ranke-Gesellschaft* 2 (1999): 262–74.

Aschmann, Birgit. 'The Reliable Ally: Germany Supports Spain´s European Integration Efforts, 1957–1967', *Journal of European Integration History* 7 (2001): 37–51.

Baby, Sophie. *Le mythe de la transition pacifique: Violence et politique en Espagne (1975–1982)*. Madrid: Casa de Velázquez, 2013.

Barbé, Eshter. 'Spain: The Uses of Foreign Policy Cooperation', in *The Actors in Europe's Foreign Policy* ed. Christopher Hill, 108–129. London: Routledge, 1996.

Bassols, Raimundo. *España en Europa, historia de la adhesión a la CE, 1957–1985*. Madrid: Política Exterior, 1992.

Camacho, Marcelino. *Memorias: confieso que he luchado*. Madrid: Temas de Hoy, 1993.

Crespo MacLennan, Julio. *Spain and the Process of European Integration, 1957–1985*. Basingstoke and New York: Palgrave Macmillan, 2000.

Cuesta Bustillo, Josefina. *La Odisea de la memoria, Historia de la memoria en España Siglo XX*. Madrid: Alianza, 2008.

de la Guardia, Martín. 'In Search of Lost Europe: Spain', in *European Union Enlargement. A Comparative History*, ed. Wolfram Kaiser, and Jurgen Elvert, 70–91. London : Routledge, 2004.

Dentice, Fabrizio. 'Il tempo del bastone e della garrota', *La tortura dopo Franco: L'Espresso Documenti*, 25 April 1976.

Dobry, Michel. 'Les voies incertaines de la transitologie. Choix stratégique, séquences historiques, bifurcations et processus de path dependence', *Revue française de science politique* 50 (2000): 585–613.

Eberwein, Wolf-Dieter and Karl Kaiser, eds. *Deutschlands neue Außenpolitik, IV, Institutionen und Ressourcen*. München: Oldenbourg, 1994.

Freia Niehus, Gerlinde. *Außenpolitik im Wandel. Die Außenpolitik Spaniens von der Diktatur Francos zur parlamentarischen Demokratie*. Frankfurt am Main: Vervuert, 1989.
Gallego, Ferran. *El mito de la Transición*. Barcelona: Crítica, 2008.
Gambino, Antonio. 'Madrid: dopo Franco come Franco', *L'Espresso*, 18 April 1976.
García Delgado, José Luis. 'La economía', in *Franquismo. El juicio de la historia*, ed. José Luis García Delgado, 115-70. Madrid: Temas de Hoy, 2000.
Gilmour, David. *The Transformation of Spain from Franco to the Constitutional Monarchy*. London: Quartet Books, 1985.
Guirao, Fernando. 'The European Community's Role in Promoting Democracy in Franco's Spain, 1970-1975', in *Beyond the Customs Union. The European Community's Quest for Deepening, Widening and Completion, 1969-1975*, ed. Jan van der Harst, 163-93. Baden Baden and Brussels: Nomos Verlag - Bruylant, 2007.
Hempel, Yvonne. 'Die Staatskanzlei als heimliche Parteizentrale?', in *Die CSU: Strukturwandel, Modernisierung und Herausforderungen einer Volkspartei*, ed. Gerhard Hopp, Martin Sebaldt, and Benjamin Zeitler, 287-308. Wiesbaden: Springer-Verlag, 2010.
Hermet, Guy. 'Espagne: Changement de la société, Modernisation autoritaire et démocratie octroyée', *Revue française de science politique* 27 (1977): 582-600.
Jansen, Thomas. 'The Dilemma for Christian Democracy. Historical Identity and/or the Political Expediency: Opening the Door at the Conservatism', in *Christian Democracy in the European Union 1945/1995*, ed E. Lamberts, 459-72. Leuven: Leuven University Press, 1997.
Juliá, Santos. 'Presencia de la guerra y combate por la amnistía en la transición a la democracia', in *Identidades y memoria imaginada*, ed. Justo Beramendi, Maria J. Baz Vicente, 85-107. Valencia: Universitat de València, 2008.
Juliá, Santos, and José Carlos Mainer. *El aprendizaje de la libertad. 1973-1986: la cultura de la transición*. Madrid: Alianza, 2000.
Kaiser, Wolfram, and Christian Salm. 'Transition und Europäisierung in Spanien und Portugal Sozial- und christdemokratische Netzwerke im Übergang von der Diktatur zur parlamentarischen Demokratie', *Archiv für Sozialgeschichte* 49 (2009): 259-82.
Linz, Juan J., and Alfred Stepan. *Problems of Democratic Transition and Consolidation. Southern Europe, South America and Post-communist Europe*. Baltimore and London: Johns Hopkins University Press, 1996.
Molinero, Carme. *La Transición, treinta años después*. Barcelona: Península, 2006.
Montero, Feliciano. 'Las derechas y el catolicismo español: Del integrismo al socialcristianismo', *Historia y Política* 18 (2007), 101-28.
Montero Díaz, Julio. 'El franquismo: del *esplendor* a la Crisis Final (1959-1975)', in *Historia contemporánea de España, II, Siglo XX*, ed. Javier Paredes, 720-1. Barcelona: Editorial Ariel, 2004.
Moreno Juste, Antonio. 'The European Economic Community and the End of the Franco Regime: The September 1975 Crisis', *Cahiers de la Méditerranée* 90 (2015): 25-45.
Nuttall, Simon. *European Political Cooperation*. Oxford: Clarendon, 1990.
Orella Martínez, José L., and José Díaz Nieva, 'La derecha franquista en la transición', in *Actas del III Simposio de Historia Actual. Logroño, 26-28 de octubre de 2000*, in ed. Carlos Navajas Zubeldía, 549-66. Logroño: Instituto de Estudios Riojanos, 2002.
Orizo, Francisco A. *España, entre la apatía y el cambio social. Una encuesta sobre el sistema europeo de valores: el caso español*. Madrid: Mapfre, 1983.
Powell, Charles. *El piloto del cambio: el rey, la monarquía y la transición a la democracia*. Barcelona: Planeta, 1991.

Preston, Paul. *The Triumph of Democracy in Spain*. London: Routledge, 2004.
Sánchez Sánchez, Esther M. *Rumbo Al Sur: Francia y la España Del Desarrollo, 1958–1969*. Madrid: CSIC, 2006.
Santos, Julià. 'Orígenes sociales de la democracia en España', *Ayer*, 15 (1994): 165–88.
Sastre García, J. Cayo. *Transición y desmovilización política en España (1975–1982)*. Valladolid: Universidad de Valladolid, 1997.
Sergio, Marialuisa L. '"Abbiamo la responsabilità del dire certi sì e certi no". Aldo Moro e le transizioni democratiche nell'Europa Mediterranea (Grecia, Spagna, Portogallo)', in *Una vita, un Paese: Aldo Moro e l'Italia del Novecento*, ed. R. Moro, and D. Mezzana, 559–82. Soveria Mannelli: Rubbettino, 2014.
Sergio, Marialuisa L. 'Détente and its Effects on Italian and German Political Systems (1963–1972)', *Rivista di Studi Politici Internazionali* 82 (2015): 411–30.
Sergio, Marialuisa L. *La diplomazia delle due sponde del Tevere: Aggiornamento conciliare e democrazia nelle transizioni internazionali (1965–1975)*. Rome: Studium, 2018.
Soriano, Jacinto. *Diccionario de la España franquista (1936–1975), ad vocem (Amnistía, ley de)*. Paris: L'Harmattan, 2018.
Spadafora, Pasqualino. *La Democrazia cristiana per una Spagna democratica*. Roma: Cinque lune, 1976.
Vidal-Beneyto, José. *Memoria democrática*. Madrid: Foca, 2007.

Chapter 6. Salm, The Socialist Group of the European Parliament and human rights in the second half of the 1970s

Archival collections

DLMLA – The Danish Labour Movement's Library and Archives, Copenhagen
HAEP – Historical Archives of the European Parliament, Luxemburg
HAEU – Historical Archives of the European Union, Florence
IISH – International Institute for Social History, Amsterdam.

Other primary sources

EP, Subcommittee on Human Rights. 'Hearing on Sport and Human Rights Focusing on the Situation of Migrant Workers in Qatar', https://www.europarl.europa.eu/cmsdata/64622/att_20140211ATT79166-3535033103333604899.pdf.
'Resolution on the Negotiations for the Renewal of the Convention of Lomé', *OJEC*, C 6/56. 8 January 1979.
'Resolution on the Outcome of the Belgrade Meeting as Provided for by the Final Act of the Helsinki Conference on Security and Cooperation in Europe', *OJEC*, C 131/46. 5 June 1978.
'Resolution on Violations of Human Rights in Argentina and on the Procedure to be Followed in the European Parliament to Combat Such Violations Throughout the World', *OJEC*, C 182/42. 31 July 1978.

Secondary sources

'Europe's Football Hooligans Can Expect Heavy Penalties in Argentina, Labour MP Advices', *The Times*, 23 May 1978.

'Fußball-WM im Land eines Terror-Regimes. Hearing in Brüssel: In Argentinien wird gefoldert - Käsemann beschuldigt deutsche Behörden', *Süddeutsche Zeitung*, 26 May 1978.

Arts, Karin. *Integrating Human Rights into Development Cooperation: The Case of the Lomé Convention*. The Hague: Kluwer Law International, 2000.

Badalassi, Nicolas, and Sarah Snyder, ed. *The CSCE and the End of the Cold War, Diplomacy, Societies and Human Rights, 1972-1990*. New York: Berghahn, 2019.

Drieghe, Lotte, and Jan Orbie. 'Revolution in Time of Eurosclerosis. The Case of the First Lomé Convention', *L' Europe en Formation* 50 (2009): 167-81.

Eckel, Jan. 'The Rebirth of Politics from the Spirit of Morality: Explaining the Human Rights Revolution of the 1970s', in *The Breakthrough. Human Rights in the 1970s*, ed. Jan Eckel and Samuel Moyn, 226-59. Philadelphia: University of Philadelphia Press, 2014.

Ferrari, Lorenzo. *Sometimes Speaking with a Single Voice. The European Community as an International Actor*. Brussels: Peter Lang, 2016.

Gfeller, Aurélie É. 'Champion of Human Rights: The European Parliament and the Helsinki Process', *Journal of Contemporary History*, 49 (2014): 390-409.

Havemann, Nils. *Samstags um halb 4 Die Geschichte der Fußballbundesliga*. Munich: Sielder, 2014.

Hoffmann, Stefan-Ludwig. *Geschichte der Menschenrechte - ein Rückblick*. Berlin: Suhrkamp, 2020.

Ismar, Georg. 'Der Ballsport im Dienst der eigenen Sache. Politisierung des Fußballs in Südamerika', in *Das Spiel mit dem Fußball. Interessen, Projektionen und Vereinnahmung*, ed. Jürgen Mittag, and Jörg-Uwe Nieland, 237-61. Essen: Klartext, 2007.

Kamminga, Meno. 'Human Rights and the Lomé Conventions', *Netherlands Quarterly of Human Rights* 7 (1989): 28-35, here 28.

Laaser, Erich. *Die Fußballweltmeisterschaft 1978 in der Tagespresse der Bundesrepublik Deutschland*. Berlin: Volker Spies, 1980.

Moyn, Samuel. *The Last Utopia: Human Rights in History*. Cambridge, MA: Harvard University Press, 2010.

Patel, Kiran K., and Christian Salm, 'The European Parliament during the 1970s and 1980s. An Institution on the Rise?' *Journal of European Integration History* 27 (2021): 5-20.

Rother, Berndt, and Wolfgang Schmidt, 'Einleitung. Über Europa hinaus. Dritte Welt und Sozialistische Internationale', in *Willy Brandt, Berliner Ausgabe*, vol. 8, ed. Helga Grebing, Gregor Schöllgen, and Heinrich A. Winkler, 15-107. Bonn: Dietz, 2006.

Salm, Christian. 'Major Sporting Events Versus Human Rights: Parliament's Position on the 1978 FIFA World Cup in Argentina and the 1980 Moscow Olympics', *EPRS Briefing - European Parliament History Series* PE 563.519 (2018): 1-8.

Salm, Christian. *Transnational Socialist Networks in the 1970s, European Community Development Aid and Southern Enlargement*. Basingstoke: Palgrave Macmillan, 2016.

Snyder, Sarah. 'Bringing the Transnational In: Writing Human Rights into the International History of the Cold War', *Diplomacy & Statecraft* 24 (2013): 100-16.

Soriano, Víctor F. 'Facing the Greek Junta (1967-1974): The Council of Europe, the European Community, and the Rise of Human Rights Politics', *European Review of History* 24 (2017): 358-76.

Tulli, Umberto. 'Bringing Human Rights In: The Campaign Against the 1980 Moscow Olympic Games and the Origins of the Nexus Between Human Rights and the Olympic Games', *The International Journal of the History of Sports* 33 (2017): 2026–45.

Tulli, Umberto. 'The European Parliament, the Single European Act and the (partial) Institutionalization of EPC', *Journal of European Integration History* 27 (2021): 121–38.

Twitchett, Cosgrove. *Europe and Africa: From Association to Partnership*. Farnborough: Saxon House, 1978.

Varsori, Antonio, and Guia Migani, 'Introduction', in *Europe in the International Arena during the 1970s. Entering a Different World*, ed. Antonio Varsori and Guia Migani, 15–26. Brussels: Peter Lang, 2011.

von Gehlen, Andreas. 'Europäische Parteiendemokratie? Institutionelle Voraussetzungen und Funktionsbedingungen der europäischen Parteien zur Minderung des Legitimationsdefizits der EU', PhD diss., Berlin: Free University Berlin, 2005.

Wilkens, Andreas. 'Der «Andere Deutsche» im Blick von außen. Zur Perzeption Willy Brandts zu seiner Zeit und in der heutigen Erinnerungskultur', in *Willy Brandt. Neue Fragen, neue Erkenntnisse*, ed. Berndt Rother, 54–84. Bonn: Dietz, 2011.

Young-Anawaty, Amy. 'Human Rights and the ACP-EEC Lomé II Convention: Business as Usual at the EEC'. *New York University Journal of International Politics* 13 (1980): 63–100.

Chapter 7. Grealy, An awkward partner?: Britain's human rights policy and EC relations, 1977–9

Archival collections

CVCE – Centre virtuel de la connaissance sur l'Europe, Luxemburg.
DOP – University of Liverpool Special Collections & Archives, David Owen Papers, Liverpool.
NARA – National Archives and Records Administration, Washington DC.
TNA – The National Archives, London.

Other primary sources

Documents on British Policy Overseas, Series III, Volume II. London: The Stationary Office, 1997.

Foreign Relations of the United States, 1977–1980, Volume I, Foundations of Foreign Policy, 1974–1980. Washington, DC: Government Printing Office, 2014.

Hansard: House of Commons.

Kimball, John W. interview with Charles Stuart Kennedy, Association for Diplomatic Studies and Training, Foreign Affairs Oral History Project, 24 May 1999, https://www.adst.org/OH%20TOCs/Kimball,%20John%20W.toc.pdf.

Public Papers of the Presidents of the United States, Jimmy Carter, 1977, Book I. Washington, DC: United States Government Printing Office, 1977.

Secondary sources

'A Bismarckian Critique', *The Times*, 19 July 1977.
'Handling Human Rights', *The Times*, 11 March 1977.
Alston, Philip, Mara Bustelo, and James Heenan, ed. *The EU and Human Rights*. Oxford: Oxford University Press, 1999.
Bartlett, C. J. *The Special Relationship: A Political History of Anglo-American Relations since 1945*. Harlow: Longman, 1992.
Broad, Roger. *Labour's European Dilemmas: From Bevin to Blair*. Basingstoke: Palgrave Macmillan, 2001.
Brown, Martin D. 'A Very British Vision of Détente: The United Kingdom's Foreign Policy During the Helsinki Process, 1969-1975', in *Visions of the End of the Cold War in Europe, 1945-1990*, ed. Frédéric Bozo, Marie-Pierre Rey, and N. Piers Ludlow, 139-56. New York and Oxford: Berghahn, 2012.
Buchanan, Tom. 'Human Rights, the Memory of War and the Making of a 'European' Identity, 1945-1975', in *Europeanization in the Twentieth Century: Historical Approaches*, ed. Martin Conway and Kiran K. Patel. Basingstoke: Palgrave Macmillan, 2010.
Cronin, James E. *Global Rules: America, Britain and a Disordered World*. New Haven, Connecticut & London: Yale University Press, 2014.
Dickie, John. *'Special' No More, Anglo-American Relations: Rhetoric and Reality*. London: Weidenfeld & Nicolson, 1994.
Dimbleby, David, and David Reynolds, *An Ocean Apart: The Relationship Between Britain and America in the Twentieth Century*. London: Hodder & Stoughton, 1988.
Dobson, Alan P. *Anglo-American Relations in the Twentieth Century: Of Friendship, Conflict and the Rise and Decline of Superpowers*. New York: Routledge, 1995.
Donoughue, Bernard. *Downing Street Diary, Volume II: With James Callaghan in No. 10*. London: Jonathan Cape, 2008.
Dumbrell, John. *A Special Relationship: Anglo-American Relations from the Cold War to Iraq*. Basingstoke: Palgrave Macmillan, 2006.
Eckel, Jan. *The Ambivalence of Good: Human Rights and International Politics since the 1940s*. Oxford: Oxford University Press, 2019.
Eckel, Jan, and Samuel Moyn, ed. *The Breakthrough: Human Rights in the 1970s*. Philadelphia: University of Pennsylvania Press, 2014.
Geddes, Andrew. *The European Union and British Politics*. Basingstoke: Palgrave Macmillan, 2004.
George, Stephen. *'An Awkward Partner': Britain in the European Community*. New York: Oxford University Press, 1990.
Gowland, David, and Arthur Turner. *Reluctant Europeans: Britain and European Integration, 1945-1998*. Harlow: Longman, 2000.
Grealy, David. 'Human Rights and British Foreign Policy, c. 1977-1997: An Intellectual Biography of David Owen', PhD diss., University of Liverpool, September 2020.
Greenwood, Sean. *Britain and the Cold War, 1945-1991*. Basingstoke: Macmillan, 2000.
Hill, Christopher, ed. *National Foreign Policies and European Political Cooperation*. London: George Allen & Unwin, 1983.
Hill, Christopher, and William Wallace, 'Introduction: Actors and Actions', in *The Actors in Europe's Foreign Policy*, ed. Christopher Hill, 1-17. London: Routledge, 1996.
Hyde-Price, Adrian. 'Interests, Institutions and Identities in the Study of European Foreign Policy', in *Rethinking European Foreign Policy*, ed. Ben Tonra, and Thomas Christiansen, 99-113. Manchester: Manchester University Press, 2004.

Jenkins, Peter. 'Delicate Balance', *Guardian*, 4 March 1977.
Keys, Barbara. '"Something to Boast About": Western Enthusiasm for Carter's Human Rights Diplomacy', in *Reasserting America in the 1970s: U.S. Public Diplomacy and the Rebuilding of America's Image Abroad*, ed. Hallvard Notaker, Giles Scott-Smith, and David J. Snyder, 229–44. Manchester: Manchester University Press, 2016.
Livingstone, Grace. *Britain and the Dictatorships of Argentina and Chile, 1973–1982: Foreign Policy, Corporations and Social Movements*. Basingstoke: Palgrave Macmillan, 2018.
Martin, Jurek. 'U.S. Welcomes Owen's Human Rights Speech', *Financial Times*, 5 March 1977.
Montana, Ismael Musah. 'The Lomé Convention from Inception to the Dynamics of the Post-Cold War, 1957–1990s', *African and Asian Studies* 2, no. 1 (2003): 63–97.
Morphet, Sally. 'British Foreign Policy and Human Rights: From Low to High Politics', in *Human Rights and Comparative Foreign Policy: Foundations of Peace*, ed. David P. Forsythe, 87–141. New York: UN University, 2000.
Moyn, Samuel. *The Last Utopia: Human Rights in History*. Cambridge, MA: Harvard University Press, 2010.
Murray, Ian. 'Carter Policy Attacked by President Giscard', *The Times*, 18 July 1977.
Nossiter, Bernard D. 'Britain Supports Carter Stand on Human Rights: Britain Backs Carter's View on Human Rights Question', *Washington Post*, 4 March 1977.
Overseas Development Institute, 'Lome II', Briefing Paper, no. 1, February 1980, https://www.odi.org/sites/odi.org.uk/files/odi-assets/publications-opinion-files/6636.pdf.
Owen, David. 'James Callaghan', in *Half In, Half Out: Prime Ministers on Europe*, ed. Andrew Adonis, 129–30. London: Biteback, 2018.
Pendas, Devin O. 'Towards a New Politics? On the Recent Historiography of Human Rights', *Contemporary European History* 21 (2012): 95–111.
Rist, Gilbert. *The History of Development: From Western Origins to Global Faith*. London: Zed Books, 2008.
Robb, Thomas K. *Jimmy Carter and the Anglo-American 'Special Relationship'*. Edinburgh: Edinburgh University Press, 2017: 44–8.
Romano, Angela. 'British Policy Towards Socialist Countries in the 1970s: Trade as a Cornerstone of Détente', in *The Foreign Office, Commerce and British Foreign Policy in the Twentieth Century*, ed. John Fisher, Effie Pedaliu, and Richard Smith. Basingstoke: Palgrave Macmillan, 2016.
Rummell, Reinhardt, and Jörg Wiedemann. 'Identifying Institutional Paradoxes of CFSP', in *Paradoxes of European Foreign Policy*, ed. Jan Zielonka, 53–66. The Hague: Kluwer Law International, 1998.
Ryder, Vincent. 'Human Rights Basic to Foreign Policy, Says Owen', *Daily Telegraph*, 4 March 1977.
Sanders, David. *Losing an Empire, Finding a Role: British Foreign Policy since 1945*. Basingstoke: Palgrave Macmillan, 1990.
Sington, Anne. 'Giscard "go-it-alone" Policy Winning Support in Europe', *Daily Telegraph*, 20 July 1977.
Suri, Jeremi. 'Détente and Human Rights: American and West European Perspectives on International Change', *Cold War History* 8 (2008): 527–45.
Van Hatten, Margaret. 'Owen Gives Strong Support to Carter's Human Rights Stand', *Financial Times*, 4 March 1977.
Vickers, Rhiannon. *The Labour Party and the World, Volume II: Labour's Foreign Policy since 1951*. Manchester: Manchester University Press, 2011.

Wall, Stephen. *A Stranger in Europe: Britain and the EU from Thatcher to Blair*. Oxford: Oxford University Press, 2008.
White, Brian. *Britain, Détente and Changing East-West Relations*. London: Routledge, 1992.
Williams, Philip. 'Britain, Détente and the Conference on Security and Cooperation in Europe', in *European Détente: Case Studies of the Politics of East-West Relations*, ed. Kenneth Dyson, 221–36. London: Frances Pinter, 1986.

Chapter 8. Lott, Between restrictiveness and humanitarianism: EC institutions and the asylum policies of the 1980s

Archival collection

AMAE – Archives du Ministère des Affaires Étrangères, Paris.
CVCE – Centre virtuel de la connaissance sur l'Europe, Luxemburg.
HACEU – Historical Archives of the Council of the European Union, Brussels.
HAEU – Historical Archives of the European Union, Florence.
TNA – The National Archives, London.

Interviews

Hein, Christopher. 25 May 2020.
Martin, David. 15 May 2020.

Other primary sources

'Declaration on European Identity', *Bulletin of the European Communities* 12 (1973): 118–22.
Convention Determining the State Responsible for Examining Applications for Asylum Lodged in one of the Member States of the European Communities, *Official Journal of the European Communities*, C 254, 19 August 1997.
European Parliament News, 'EU Asylum Rules: Reform of the Dublin System', 24 July 2019, *europarl.europa*, https://www.europarl.europa.eu/news/en/headlines/priorities/refugees/20180615STO05927/eu-asylum-rules-reform-of-the-dublin-system.
Judgement of the European Court of Justice in joint cases 281, 283, 284, 285 and 287/85 in https://eur-lex.europa.eu/legal-content/EN/TXT/PDF/?uri=OJ:L:1985:217:FULL&from=IT.
Parlement Européen. *Débats*, 9–12 March 1987.
Parlement Européen. *Débats*, 13–16 March 1991.
Parlement Européen. *Débats*, 20–24 November 1989.
Parliamentary Assembly of the Council of Europe, Recommendation 1236 (1994), http://assembly.coe.int/nw/xml/XRef/Xref-XML2HTML-en.asp?fileid=15270&lang=en.
UNHCR Executive Committee, Conclusion n.15 (1979), https://www.unhcr.org/excom/exconc/3ae68c960/refugees-asylum-country.html.

Secondary sources

Bosswick, Wolfgang. 'Development of Asylum Policy in Germany', *Journal of Refugee Studies*, 43 (2000): 43–60.

Cini, Michelle. *The European Commission: Leadership, Organisation, and Culture in the EU Administration*. Manchester: Manchester University Press, 1996.
Colloquy on European Law, *The Law of Asylum and Refugees. Present Tendencies and Future Perspectives: Proceedings of the Sixteenth Colloquy on European Law*. Strasbourg: Council of Europe, 1987.
Comte, Emmanuel. *The History of the European Migration Regime: Germany's Strategic Hegemony*. New York: Routledge, 2018.
Dujardin, Vincent, et al., ed. *The European Commission 1986-2000 History and Memories of An Institution*. Luxembourg: Publications Office of the European Union, 2019.
Hailbronner, Kay, and Claus Thiery, 'Schengen II and Dublin: Responsibility for Asylum Applications in Europe', *Common Market Law Review* 34 (1997): 957–89.
Joly, Danièle, and Robin Cohen, ed. *Reluctant Hosts: Europe and Its Refugees*. Aldershot: Hants, 1989.
Kritzman-Amir, Tally. 'Not In My Backyard: On the Morality of Responsibility Sharing in Refugee Law', *Brooklyn Journal of International Law* 2 (2009): 355–94.
Loescher, Gil. *Beyond Charity: International Cooperation and the Global Refugee Crisis*. Oxford: Oxford University Press, 1993.
Martin, David A, ed. *The New Asylum Seekers: Refugee Law in the 1980's: The Ninth Sokol Colloquium on International Law*. Boston: Dordrecht, 1988.
Moravcsik, Andrew. *The Choice for Europe: Social Purpose and State Power from Messina to Maastricht*. London: UCL Press, 1998.
Paoli, Simone. *Frontiera Sud: l'Italia e la nascita dell'Europa di Schengen*. Milano: Mondadori, 2018.
Plender, Richard. 'European Community Law and Nationals of Non-Member States', *The International and Comparative Law Quarterly* 39(1990): 599–610.
Salt, John. *Current Trends in International Migration in Europe*, Council of Europe Working Paper, November 2001, https://www.coe.int/t/dg3/migration/archives/Documentation/Migration%20management/2001_Salt_report_en.pdf.
Tsebelis, George. 'The Power of the European Parliament as a Conditional Agenda Setter', *The American Political Science Review* 88, no. 1 (1994): 128–42.

Chapter 9. Onianwa, Human rights NGOs in Western Europe and the intervention of the Council of Europe in the Nigerian Civil War

Archival collections

CEDA – Council of Europe Digital Archive.
PACE – Parliamentary Assembly of the Council of Europe, Strasbourg.
TNA – The National Archives, London.

Secondary sources

'Biafra Moving Towards Vietnam Situation Says Bishop Butler', *Catholic Herald*, 28 March 1969.
Allaun, Frank. 'Biafra and Blackpool'. *Labour Party Fellowship Newsletter: 1968 Labour Conference Issue*, September 1968.

Benedek, Wolfgang. *Understanding Human Rights: Manual on Human Rights Education*. Graz: European Training and Research Centre for Human Rights and Democracy ETC, 2006.
Eckel, Jan, and Samuel Moyn, ed. *The Breakthrough: Human Rights in the 1970s*. Philadelphia: University of Pennsylvania Press, 2014.
Etinson, Adam. *Human Rights: Moral or Political*. London: Oxford University Press, 2020.
Goodhart, Michael. *Human Rights: Politics and Practice*. London: Oxford University Press, 2016.
Griffin, James. *On Human Rights*. London: Oxford University Press, 2009.
Hannum, Hurst. *Rescuing Human Rights: A Radically Moderate Approach*. Cambridge: Cambridge University Press, 2019.
Heerten, Lasse. *The Biafran War and Postcolonial Humanitarianism: Spectacles of Suffering: Human Rights in History*. Cambridge: Cambridge University Press, 2017.
Hunt, John [Lord Hunt]. *Nigeria: The Problem of Relief in the Aftermath of the Nigerian Civil War: Report of Lord Hunt's Mission*. London: Government Printing Office, 1970.
McNeil, Brian E. 'Frontier of Need: Humanitarianism and the American Involvement in the Nigerian Civil War, 1967–1970', PhD diss., University of Texas, 2014.
Mills, Kurt. *Human Rights in the Emerging Global Order: A New Sovereignty?* New York: Palgrave Macmillan, 1998.
Moody, Roger. 'Biafra: What is to be Done?'. *Peace News*, 19 July 1968.
Oluchukwu Ignatus Onianwa. 'The Western European Union and European Politics in the Nigerian Civil War: The Italian Experience, 1967–1970', in *A Tight Embrace: Narratives and Dynamics of Euro-Africa Relations*, ed. Marco Zoppi. 99–118. London and New York: Rowman & Littlefield International 2021.
Perman, David. 'Nigeria Costs Britain the Goodwill of Europe', *The Observer Foreign News Service*, 27 September 1968.
Politics of Relief: Some Reflections on the Aspect of the Nigerian Civil War. London: Foreign and Commonwealth Office, 1970.

Chapter 10. Graf, Beyond victims of communism?: Austria and the human rights question in the 1970s

Archival collections

ÖStA – Österreichisches Staatsarchiv, Wien.
SAPMO – Stiftung Archiv der Parteien und Massenorganisationen der DDR im Bundesarchiv, Berlin.

Secondary sources

Albrich, Thomas, ed. *Flucht nach Eretz Israel: Die Bricha und der jüdische Exodus durch Österreich nach 1945*. Innsbruck: StudienVerlag, 1998.
Albrich, Thomas, and Ronald W. Zweig, ed. *Escape Through Austria. Jewish Refugees and the Austrian Route to Palestine*. London: Routledge, 2002.
Alizadeh, Homayoun. 'Österreichische Flüchtlingspolitik der 70er Jahre', in *Asylland wider Willen*, ed. Gernot Heiss and Oliver Rathkolb, 188–94. Vienna: Dachs, 1995.

Anderl, Gabriele, and Viktor Iščenko, 'Die jüdische Emigration aus der Sowjetunion via Österreich', in *Österreich – Russland. Stationen gemeinsamer Geschichte*, ed. Stefan Karner and Alexander Tschubarjan, 241–51. Graz: Leykam, 2018.

Berger, Herbert. *Solidarität mit Chile. Die österreichische Chile-Solidaritätsfront 1973–1990*. Vienna: Edition Volkshochschule, 2003.

Blecha, Laurin. 'Von Ottakring nach Cuatro Esquinas. Beziehungen und Kooperationen zwischen Nicaragua und Österreich von 1979 bis 1990', in *Kleinstaaten und sekundäre Akteure im Kalten Krieg. Politische, wirtschaftliche, militärische und kulturelle Wechselbeziehungen zwischen Europa und Lateinamerika*, ed. Albert Manke and Kateřina Březinová, 275–302. Bielefeld: transcript, 2016.

Cede, Franz, and Christian Prosl. *Anspruch und Wirklichkeit. Österreichs Außenpolitik seit 1945*. Innsbruck: StudienVerlag, 2015.

Enderle-Burcel, Gertrude, et al., ed. *Gaps in the Iron Curtain. Economic Relations between Neutral and Socialist Countries in Cold War Europe*. Kraków: Jagiellonian University Press, 2009.

Fischer, Thomas. '"A Mustard Seed Grew Into a Bushy Tree": The Finnish CSCE-Initiative of 5 May 1969', *Cold War History* 9 (2009): 177–201.

Gémes, Andreas. *Austria and the 1956 Hungarian Revolution: Between Solidarity and Neutrality*. Pisa: Univ. Press, 2008.

Gilde, Benjamin. '"Kein Vorreiter". Österreich und die Humanitäre Dimension der KSZE 1969–1973', in *Der KSZE-Prozess. Vom Kalten Krieg zu einem neuen Europa 1975 bis 1990*, ed. Helmut Altrichter and Hermann Wentker, 41–50. Munich: Oldenburg, 2011.

Gilde, Benjamin. *Österreich im KSZE-Prozess 1969–1983. Neutraler Vermittler in humanitärer Mission*. Munich: Oldenbourg, 2013.

Graf, Maximilian. 'European Détente and the CSCE. Austria and the East-Central European Theatre in the 1970s and 1980s', in *The CSCE and the End of the Cold War. Diplomacy, Societies and Human Rights, 1972–1990*, ed. Nicolas Badalassi and Sarah Snyder, 249–74. New York: Berghahn Books, 2019.

Graf, Maximilian. 'Franz Marek – Stalinist, Kritiker, Reformer, Ausgeschlossener', in *Dissidente Kommunisten. Das sowjetische Modell und seine Kritiker*, ed. Knud Andresen, Mario Keßler, and Axel Schildt, 107–34. Berlin: Metropol, 2018.

Graf, Maximilian. 'Kreisky und Polen. Schlaglichter auf einen vernachlässigten Aspekt der österreichischen "Ostpolitik"', in *Bananen, Cola, Zeitgeschichte. Oliver Rathkolb und das lange 20. Jahrhundert*, 2 vols., ed. Lucile Dreidemy et al., 692–706. Vienna: Böhlau, 2015.

Graf, Maximilian. *Österreich und die DDR 1949–1990. Politik und Wirtschaft im Schatten der deutschen Teilung*. Vienna: ÖAW, 2016.

Graf, Maximilian. 'Österreich und die "polnische Krise" im Kontext 1980–1983', in *Österreich – Polen. Stationen gemeinsamer Geschichte im 20. Jahrhundert*, ed. Peter Ruggenthaler and Wanda Jarząbek. Graz: Leykam, 2020, in print.

Graf, Maximilian, and Sarah Knoll. 'In Transit or Asylum Seekers? Austria and the Cold War Refugees from the Communist Bloc', in *Migration in Austria*, ed. Günter Bischof and Dirk Rupnow, 91–111. New Orleans: UNO Press, 2017.

Karner, Stefan, and Peter Ruggenthaler, 'Austria and the End of the Prague Spring: Neutrality in the Crucible?', in *The Prague Spring and the Warsaw Pact Invasion of Czechoslovakia in 1968*, ed. Günter Bischof, Stefan Karner, and Peter Ruggenthaler, 419–39. Lanham: Lexington Books, 2010.

Kreisky, Bruno. *Im Strom der Politik. Erfahrungen eines Europäers*. Berlin: Goldmann, 1988.

Kreisky, Bruno. *Reden*, vol. II. Vienna: Verlag der Österreichischen Staatsdruckerei, 1981.
Leidinger, Hannes. 'Jüdische Emigration aus der Sowjetunion', in *Migration. Flucht – Vertreibung – Integration*, ed. Stefan Karner and Barbara Stelzl-Marx, 137–46. Graz: Leykam, 2019.
Meisinger, Agnes. 'Die österreichische Haltung zum Boykott der Olympischen Sommerspiel in Moskau 1980 unter besonderer Berücksichtigung der Rolle Bruno Kreiskys', MA Thesis, University of Vienna, Vienna, 2012.
Mueller, Wolfgang. *A Good Example of Peaceful Coexistence. The Soviet Union, Austria, and Neutrality, 1955–1991*. Vienna: ÖAW, 2011.
Mueller, Wolfgang, and Maximilian Graf, 'An Austrian Mediation in Vietnam? The Superpowers, Neutrality, and Kurt Waldheim's Good Offices', in *Neutrality and Neutralism in the Global Cold War. Between or within the blocs?*, ed. Sandra Bott, Jussi Hanhimaki, Janick Schaufelbuehl, and Marco Wyss, 127–43. London: Routledge, 2016.
Müller, Stefan A., David Schriffl, and Adamantios T. Skordos, *Heimliche Freunde. Die Beziehungen Österreichs zu den Diktaturen Südosteuropas nach 1945: Spanien, Portugal, Griechenland*. Vienna: Böhlau, 2016.
Petritsch, Wolfgang. *Bruno Kreisky. Die Biografie*. Sankt Pölten: Residenz Verlag, 2010.
Rathkolb, Oliver. 'Austria: An Ambivalent Attitude of Trade Unions and Political Parties,' in *Solidarity with Solidarity. Western European Trade Unions and the Polish Crisis, 1980–1982*, ed. Idesbald Goddeeris, 269–88. Lanham: Lexington Books, 2010.
Resch, Andreas. 'Der österreichische Osthandel im Spannungsfeld der Blöcke', in *Zwischen den Blöcken. NATO, Warschauer Pakt und Österreich*, ed. Manfried Rauchensteiner, 497–556. Vienna: Böhlau, 2010.
Riegler, Thomas. *Im Fadenkreuz: Österreich und der Nahost-Terrorismus 1973–1985*. Göttingen: V&R unipress, 2011.
Riegler, Thomas. '"Macht's es unter der Tuchent". Die Waffengeschäfte der österreichischen Verstaatlichten Industrie und der Noricum-Skandal', *Vierteljahrshefte für Zeitgeschichte* 64 (2016): 99–137.
Röhrlich, Elizabeth. *Kreiskys Außenpolitik. Zwischen österreichischer Identität und internationalem Programm*. Göttingen: V&R unipress, 2009.
Romano, Angela. 'The European Community and the Belgrade CSCE', in *From Helsinki to Belgrade. The First CSCE Follow-up Meeting and the Crisis of Détente*, ed. Vladimir Bilandžić, Dittmar Dahlmann, and Milan Kosanović, 105–224. Bonn: University Press, 2012.
Schriffl, David. 'Der 'Prager Frühling' 1968 und die österreichisch-slowakischen Beziehungen', in *Osteuropa vom Weltkrieg bis zur Wende*, ed. Wolfgang Mueller and Michael Portmann, 299–311. Vienna: ÖAW, 2007.
Sigrun and Herbert Berger, ed., *Zerstörte Hoffnung, gerettetes Leben. Chilenische Flüchtlige und Österreich*. Vienna: Mandelbaum, 2002.
Stanek, Eduard. *Verfolgt Verjagt Vertrieben. Flüchtlinge in Österreich von 1945–1984*. Vienna: Europaverlag, 1985.
Stern, Silke. 'Die tschechoslowakische Emigration: Österreich als Erstaufnahme- und Asylland', in Stefan Karner et al., ed., *Prager Frühling: Das internationale Krisenjahr 1968*, 2 vols., 1025–43. Vienna: Böhlau, 2008.
Stourzh, Gerald, and Wolfgang Mueller, *A Cold War over Austria. The Struggle for the State Treaty, Neutrality, and the End of East-West Occupation, 1945–1955*. Lanham, MD: Lexington Books, 2018.

Suppan, Arnold. *Missgünstige Nachbarn. Geschichte und Perspektiven der nachbarschaftlichen Beziehungen zwischen Tschechien und Österreich*. Heidenreichstein: Club Niederösterreich, 2005.

Suppan, Arnold, and Wolfgang Mueller, ed., *Peaceful Coexistence or Iron Curtain? Austria, Neutrality, and Eastern Europe in the Cold War and Détente, 1955–1989*. Vienna: Lit 2009.

Ullmann, Paul. *Eine schwierige Nachbarschaft. Die Geschichte der diplomatischen Beziehungen zwischen Österreich und der Tschechoslowakei 1945–1968*. Vienna: Lit, 2006.

Villaume, Poul, and Odd Arne Westad, ed. *Perforating the Iron Curtain: European Détente, Transatlantic Relations, and the Cold War, 1965–1985*. Copenhagen: Museum Tusculanum Press, 2010.

Volf, Patrik-Paul. 'Der politische Flüchtling als Symbol der Zweiten Republik: Zur Asyl- und Flüchtlingspolitik seit 1945', *Zeitgeschichte* 22 (1995): 415–36.

Zubok, Vladislav. *Zhivago's Children. The Last Russian Intelligentsia*. Cambridge, MA: Harvard University Press, 2009.

Chapter 11. Calandri, The Twelve and the 1993 World Conference on Human Rights

Archival collections

AEI – Archives of European Integration, University of Pittsburgh.
AMAE – Archives du Ministère des Affaires Étrangères, Paris.

Other primary sources

De Michelis, Gianni, Speech at the General Assembly, http://undocs.org/en/A/45/PV.6.
Declaration on the 'Guidelines on the Recognition of New States in Eastern Europe and in the Soviet Union', 16 December 1991, https://www.dipublico.org/100636/declaration-on-the-guidelines-on-the-recognition-of-new-states-in-eastern-europe-and-in-the-soviet-union-16-december-1991/.
Eurobarometer, Racism and xenophobia. October–November 1988 https://ec.europa.eu/commfrontoffice/publicopinion/index.cfm/Survey/getSurveyDetail/yearFrom/1988/yearTo/2019/search/racisme/surveyKy/99.
European Commission Press Release Database, http://europa.eu/rapid/press-release_IP-88-182_fr.htm.
Report drawn on behalf of the Committee of Enquiry on Racism and Xenophobia, rapporteur Glyn Ford A3.195–90, 23 February 1990, www.statewatch.org/media/documents/news/2015/jun/ep-racism-ford-report-1991.pdf.
Resolution on racism and xenophobia, 29 May 1990. *OJEC* C 157, 27 June 1990.
United Nations, *Global Consultation on the Realization of the Right to Development as a Human Right*. Geneva, 8–12 January 1990, https://digitallibrary.un.org/record/634189.

Secondary sources

Barsh, R. L. 'The Right to Development as a Human Right: Results of the Global Consultation', *Human Rights Quarterly* 13 (1991): 332–38.

Boyle, Kevin. 'Stock-taking on Human Rights: The World Conference on Human Rights, Vienna 1993', *Political Studies* XLIII (1995): 79–95.

Burke, Roland. 'From Individual Rights to National Development: The First UN International Conference on Human Rights, Tehran, 1968', *Journal of World History* 19 (2008): 275–96.

Calandri, Elena. 'Unione europea, Onu e diritti umani: una via al "ruolo globale"', in *L'Europa adulta. Attori, ragioni e sfide dall'Atto Unico alla Brexit*, ed. Elena Calandri, Giuliana Laschi, and Simone Paoli, 320–40. Bologna: il Mulino, 2020.

Dwyer, Kevin. *Arab Voices. The Human Rights Debate in the Middle East*. London: Routledge, 1991.

Dwyer, Kevin. 'Universal Visions. Communal Visions: Human Rights and Traditions', *Peuples Mediterranéens* 58–59 (1991): 205–20.

Ferrari, Lorenzo. 'The European Community as a Promoter of Human Rights in Africa and Latin America', 1970–1980, *Journal of European Integration History*, 21 (2015): 217–30.

Ferrari, Lorenzo. *Sometimes Speaking with a Single Voice. The European Community as an International Actor*. Brussels: Peter Lang, 2016.

Fierro, Elena. *The EU's Approach to Human Rights. Conditionality in Practise*. Leiden: Martinus Nijoff, 2013.

Foot, Rosemary. 'The Cold War and Human Rights', in *The Cambridge History of the Cold War* vol. III, ed. Melvyn Leffler, and Odd Arne Westad, 445–65. Cambridge: Cambridge University Press, 2010.

Hallgren, Ragnar. 'The UN and the Right to Development', *Peace Research* 22/23 (1990–1991): 31–41.

Halliday, Fred. 'Relativism and Universalism in Human Rights: The Case of the Islamic Middle East', *Political Studies* XLIII (1995): 152–67.

Holland, Martin. *The European Community and South Africa: European Political Co-operation under Strain*. London and New York: Pinter, 1985.

Kingsbury, Daniel, and Leena Avonius ed. *Human Rights in Asia: A Reassessment of the Asian Values Debate*. Basingstoke: Palgrave Macmillan 2008.

Laursen, Finn, and Sophie Vanhoonacker. *The Intergovernmental Conference on the Political Union*. Maastricht: Martinus Nijhoff, 1992.

Marks, Susan. 'Nightmare and Noble Dream: The 1993 World Conference on Human Rights', *Cambridge Law Journal* 53 (1994): 54–62.

Mayer, Ann. *Islam and Human Rights*. London: Westview, 1991.

Migani, Guia. 'EEC/EU and Development Aid from Lomé to Cotonou', https://ehne.fr/en/encyclopedia/themes/europe-europeans-and-world/international-action-and-external-policies-european-union/eeceu-and-development-aid-lom%C3%A9-cotonou.

Parker, Penny, and David Weissbrodt, 'Major Developments at the UN Commission on Human Rights in 1991', *Human Rights Quarterly* 13 (1991): 573–613.

Sullivan, Donna J. 'Women's Human Rights and the 1993 World Conference on Human Rights', American *Journal of International Law* 88 (1994): 152–67.

Van Boven, Theo. 'The United Nations High Commissioner for Human Rights: The History of a Contested Project', *Leiden Journal of International Law* 20 (2007): 767–84.

Chapter 12. Malcontent, The European Union's influence on the Dutch position in the United Nations Human Rights Commission, 1995-2003

Archival collections

DAFM – Dutch Archive Foreign Ministry, The Hague.
DHR – Dutch House of Representatives, The Hague.

Secondary sources

Baehr, Peter, Monique Castermans-Holleman, and Fred Grünfeld, *Human Rights in the Foreign Policy of the Netherlands*. Antwerp: Intersentia, 2002.
Baudet, Floribert. *'Het heeft onze aandacht'. Nederland en de rechten van de mens in Oost-Europa en Joegoslavië, 1972-1989*. Amsterdam: Boom, 2001.
Brysk, Alison. *Global Good Samaritans. Human Rights as Foreign Policy*. Oxford: Oxford University Press, 2009.
de Boer, Stefan. *Van Sharpeville tot Soweto. Nederlands Regeringsbeleid ten aanzien van apartheid, 1960-1977*. Den Haag: Sdu Uitgevers, 1999.
de Goede, Tinco. 'De mensenrechten in het Nederlandse buitenlands beleid ten aanzien van Spanje, Portugal en Griekenland', in *Geschiedenis van de mensenrechten*, ed. Maarten Kuitenbrouwer and Marij Leenders, 227-58. Hilversum: Verloren, 1996.
Eckel, Jan. *Die Ambivalenz des Guten. Menschenrechte in der internationalen Politik seit den 1940ern*. Göttingen: VandenHoeck & Ruprecht, 2014.
Economides, Spyros. 'The Europeanization of Greek Foreign Policy', *West European Politics* 28 (2005): 471-91.
Human Rights Watch. *Chinese Diplomacy, Western Hypocrisy and the U.N. Human Rights Commission*, March 1997, http://www.hrw.org/reports/1997/china2/.
Kavakas, Dimitrios. *Greece and Spain in European Foreign Policy. The Influence of Southern Member States in Common Foreign and Security Policy*. Aldershot: Ashgate, 2001.
Kent, Ann. 'China and the International Human Rights Regime: A Case Study of Multilateral Monitoring, 1989-1994', *Human Rights Quarterly* 17 (1995): 1-47.
Malcontent, Peter. 'The European Union's Influence on the Character and Effectiveness of the Dutch Conduct in the UN Commission on Human Rights', in *Liber Amicorum Cees Flinterman; Changing Perceptions of Sovereignty and Human Rights; Essays in Honour of Cees Flinterman*, ed. Ineke Boerefijn and Jenny E. Goldschmidt, 199-231. Antwerp etc.: Intersentia, 2008.
Malcontent, Peter. 'Myth or Reality? The Dutch Crusade Against Human Rights Violations in the Third World, 1973-1981', in *Human Rights in Europe since 1945*, ed. Antoine Fleury, Carole Fink and Lubor Jilek, 229-57. Bern etc.: Peter Lang, 2003.
Malcontent, Peter. *Op kruistocht in de Derde Wereld. De reacties van de Nederlandse regering op ernstige en stelselmatige schendingen van fundamentele mensenrechten in ontwikkelingslanden, 1973-1981*. Hilversum: Verloren, 1998.
Massink, Stefanie. 'The Dutch Will Give You Problems'. Nederland en Spanje in transitie van dictatuur naar democratie, PhD diss., University of Utrecht, 2020.
Moyn, Samuel. *The Last Utopia. Human Rights in History*. Cambridge, MA: Harvard University Press, 2010.

Moyn, Samuel. *Not Enough. Human Rights in an Unequal World*. Cambridge, MA: Harvard University Press, 2018.
Reiding, Hilde. *The Netherlands and the Development of International Human Rights Instruments*. Antwerp: Intersentia, 2007.
Smith, Karen E. 'The European Union at the Human Rights Council: Speaking with One Voice But Having Little Influence', *Journal of European Public Policy* 17 (2010), 224–41.
Smith, Karen E. 'Speaking with One Voice? European Union Co-ordination on Human Rights Issues at the United Nations', *Journal of Common Market Studies* 44 (2006): 113–37.
Tonra, Ben. *The Europeanisation of National Foreign Policy: Dutch, Danish and Irish Foreign Policy in the European Union*. Aldershot: Ashgate, 2001.
Tsardanidis, Charalambos, and Stelios Stavridis, 'From Special Case to Limited Europeanization', in *National and European Foreign Policies. Towards Europeanization*, ed. Reuben Wong and Christopher Hill, 111–30. London and New York: Routledge, 2011.

Index

Ad Hoc Committee of Experts on the Legal Aspect of Territorial Asylum, Refugees, and Stateless Persons (CAHAR)   139–41, 150, 152
Alfrink, Bernard Jan   163
Allende, Salvador   178, 188, 216. *See also* Chile
Álvarez de Miranda, Fernando   92–3
Amalrik, Andrei   51. *See also* Conference on Security and Cooperation in Europe
Amin, Idi   105, 128, 188. *See also* Uganda
Amnesty International   3, 35, 50, 90, 97, 111–12, 160, 178, 180, 190
Annan, Kofi   208
Argentina   6, 102, 109–14, 184, 189, 217
Arias Navarro, Carlos   85, 90
Aronstein, Georges   85
Asian values   7, 204, 209
asylum   7, 139–48

Badini Confalonieri, Vittorio   169
Baehr, Peter   217, 228–9
Baena Alonso, José Humberto   86
Bahro, Rudolf   57
Bangkok Declaration   209. *See also* Asian values
Bauer, Friedrich   187
Begun, Josif   57
Belgrade CSCE Meeting   45, 50–8, 122–3, 184–6. *See also* Conference on Security and Cooperation in Europe
Benenson, Peter   3. *See also* Amnesty International
Bertrand, Alfred   35, 94
Besterman, Walter   170–1
Bethell, Nicholas   35
Birkelbach Report   2, 15, 82
Bjork, Kaj A.   168–70
Blanca, Antoine   203

Blüm, Norbert   92
Bouge, Donald J.   171
Boutros, Boutros-Ghali   210
Bradley, Mark Ph.   34
Brandt, Willy   47–8, 100–1, 114
Brewster, Kingman   123, 125
Broda, Christian   183–4
Broeksz, Johannes   106–8
Brown, Martin D.   121
Buchanan, Tom   121, 126
Bush, George H.W.   207–8
Butler, Paul   162

CAHAR. *See* Ad Hoc Committee of Experts on the Legal Aspect of Territorial Asylum, Refugees, and Stateless Persons
Calandri, Elena   7
Callaghan, James   120, 123–9, 131
Camacho, Marcellino   85
Carrero Blanco, Luis   85
Carter, James E.   39, 50–1, 106, 120–7, 131, 185–6
Castermans-Holleman, Monique   217
Cede, Franz   78–9
CFSP. *See* Common Foreign and Security Policy
Charter 77   17, 84
Cheysson, Claude   105–6, 128
children's rights   207, 210–11, 218–24, 227–8
Biafra   159–61, 163
Chile   6, 64, 69, 72, 104, 122, 143, 178–9, 187–91, 210, 216–17. *See also* Pinochet, Augusto
China   207–10, 217–18, 220–9
Cifarelli, Michele   55
Clinton, William   207–8
Cockfield, Arthur   146–7
Common Foreign and Security Policy (CFSP)   217–18, 220, 223–9
Comte, Emmanuel   140, 149

Conference on Security and Cooperation
    in Europe (CSCE) 1, 4–6
    Austria 181–7, 190
    EC 45–58
    European Socialists 45–58
    United Kingdom 121–5, 131
Council of Europe 1, 2, 6, 7, 14–16, 37, 102, 180, 185, 208
    Greece 17–18
    Nigerian Civil War 158–68, 170–3
    Portugal 19–21
CSCE. *See* Conference on Security and Cooperation in Europe

Dankert, Piet 5
Davy, Richard 46
De Angelis, Emma 15
De Areilza, José María 90
de Freitas, Geoffrey 35, 167, 169, 171
De Gucht, Karel 144
Dehousse, Fernand 2
de Lobkowicz, Wenceslas 143, 147
Delors, Jacques 144, 147–8, 212
De Martino, Francesco 89
den Uyl, Joop 21, 100, 103
Derian, Patricia 124
Des Gachons, Solange 171
Destermau, Bernard 170
Détente 5–6, 13, 32, 40, 100, 120, 179, 190
    Austria 181–6
    CSCE 46–58
    United Kingdom 121–31
Draper, Peter 162
Duchêne, François 4

ECHR. *See* European Convention on Human Rights
Eckel, Jan 101
EPC. *See* European Political Cooperation
Espersen, Ole 104
European Commission 1–4, 7, 16, 64, 69, 72, 84–5, 89, 104–6, 112, 125, 128
    asylum policies 139–49
    CSCE negotiations 48–52
    democratic transition in Greece 17–19
    democratic transition in Portugal 19–21

democratic transition in Spain 21–3
development aid 31–8
World conference on human rights 203–8, 212
European Convention on Human rights (ECHR) 1–4, 13–17, 101, 104, 121, 164
European Council 20, 48, 90, 125, 205–6, 225
    asylum policies 139–45
    CSCE 46, 50, 55–8
    Socialists in the EP 101–14
European Identity 1, 4, 15, 34–5, 48, 55, 71, 88, 121, 131, 143–4, 148–9
European Parliament 1–2, 5–7, 14–15, 35–6, 64, 94
European Political Cooperation (EPC) 4, 15, 22, 34, 47, 63, 87, 122, 127, 130–1, 145, 179, 187, 200, 217
European Union of Christian Democrats (EUCD) 81–90, 93

Fall, Ibrahima 210
Falun Gong 221
Fellermaier, Ludwig 104, 110–11
Ferrari, Lorenzo 6
Filatov, Ivan 56
Fischer, Per 53
FitzHerbert, Giles E. 130
Fletcher, Granville 171
Fontaine, Nicole 144
Fortescue, Adrian 147–8
Fraga Iribarne, Manuel 90, 92
Franco, Francisco 7, 21–3, 35–7. *See also* Spain

Gaillard, Philippe 166
Galván, Enrique Tierno 85
García Sanz, Ramón 1
General Assembly of the United Nations (UNGA) 63–75, 87, 164, 199, 201–9, 227
genocide 159–61, 165, 169
Genscher, Hans-Dietrich 24, 129
Gfeller, Aurélie É. 30, 101
Gilde, Benjamin 187
Ginzburg, Aleksandr 56
Giscard d'Estaing, Valéry 51, 125

Glouzman, Semion 57
Goldberg, Arthur 52
Gowon, Yakubu 172
Graber, Pierre 185
Graf, Maximilian 7
Greece 3–6, 13–21, 62, 101, 145, 180, 216
Grünfeld, Fred 217

Habibie, Jusuf 222
Hahn, Karl Josef 85
Harmel, Pierre 84
Hart, Judith 128
Havel, Václav 184. *See also* Charter 77
Heath, Edward 123
Hebel, Kai 15
Heck, Bruno 92
Heerten, Lessen 159
Hibbert, Reg 125, 127
High Commissioner for Human Rights 69, 199, 207, 211
High Commissioner for Refugees 167
Hill, Christopher 127
Hobsbawm, Eric 32
Honecker, Erich 186
Hunt, David 157
Hurd, Douglas 130

Ignatieff, Michael 34

Jackson, Robert 31
Jenkins, Roy 13
Johnson, James 168–9
Juan Carlos I de Borbón 89–90
Judt, Tony 32

Karamanlis, Konstantinos 17
Karamouzi, Eirini 15
Khruschchev, Nikita 183
Kimball, John W. 124
Kirchschläger, Rudolf 185
Kirk, Peter 169
Kissinger, Henry A. 4, 38, 47–8
Kliesing, Georg 165, 169
Kohl, Helmut 91–2
Kohout, Pavel 185
Kooijmans, Peter Hendrik 85
Krachmalnikowa, Sonja 57
Kreisky, Bruno 178–91

Lamberti-Moneta, Sara 49
Laschi, Giuliana 15
Laser, Erich 109
Lauren, Paul Gordon 34
Lenz, Tobias 15
Lizin, Anne-Marie 143
Lomé Conventions 5, 30, 33–6, 40, 101, 103–8, 121, 128–31
López-Bravo, Gregorio 82, 84
Lorenzini, Sara 31
Lott, Gaia 7
Luard, Evan 127
Luis Corvalán 188
Luns, Joseph 33
Lutz, Gertrude 163

MacBride, Sean 165
MacEntee, Sean 170
McNeil, Brian 164, 172
Madrid CSCE Meeting 56–8. *See also* Conference on Security and Cooperation in Europe
Malcontent, Peter 7
Malfatti, Franco M. 37
Mansholt, Sicco 85
Margue, George 165–8
Mitterand, François 5, 105–6
Mlynář, Zdeněk 184
Mobutu Sese Seko 200
Mommersteeg, Joep 164
Monnet, Jean 3
Montini, Giovanni Battista (Pope Paul VI) 88
Moro, Aldo 48, 82–3, 92
Moyn, Samuel 34, 216
Mueller, Wolfgang 181

Neizvestny, Ernst 183
Nixon, Richard M. 4, 32, 47, 121
Noël, Émile 36
Nudel, Ida 56

Olivi, Bino 22
Onianwa, Oluchukwu Ignatus 7
Orlov, Yuri 57
Ortoli, François-Xavier 1, 22–3
Osorio, Alfonso 90
Otaegui, Ángel 86
Owen, David 120–32

Pahr, Willibald 185–6, 189
Paoli, Simone 140
Paredes Manot, Juan 86
Paritsky, Alexander 57
Pasch, Johann 185
Patijn, Schelto 105
Paul VI. *See* Montini, Giovanni Battista
Perman, David 162
Perrisich, Riccardo 146
Pflüger, Friedbert 92
Pilloud, Claude 165–6
Pinochet, Augusto 64, 72, 104, 188, 190. *See also* Chile
Pisani, Edgar 107
Pohler, Heinz 166
Poland 24, 47, 56, 182, 186–7, 205, 208, 210
Pompidou, Georges 48
Portugal 3–6, 13–21, 24, 64, 70, 87, 145, 162, 180, 216, 220
Prescott, John 103–12
Prosl, Christian 178–9
Puja, Frigyes 182

Raab, Julius 179
Radoux, Lucien 50, 104
Ramsbotham, Peter 123
Rey, Jean 84
Rivierez, Hector 35
Rodò, Lòpez 82
Romano, Angela 30, 46
Romero, Federico 31
Rousset, David 3
Ruiz-Giménez, Joaquín 83–5, 91–2
Rumor, Mariano 56, 82–9

Sakharov, Andrei D. 57, 178
Salm, Christian 7
Sánchez Bravo, José Luis 85
Saragat, Giuseppe 82
Schmidt, Helmut 51, 125, 129
Schneiter, Pierre 171
Schröder, Gerard 82
Selassie, Haile 161
Sergio, Marialuisa L. 6
Sharansky, Nathan 56–7
SI. *See* Socialist International
Sieglerschmidt, Helmut 104

Silkin, Samuel 170
Silva Muñoz, Federico 83, 90–2
Slepak, Vladimir 56
Soames, Christopher 20
Soares, Mário 19–20
Socialist International (SI) 100, 161
Solzhenitsyn, Aleksandr 49
Sommer, Theo 38
Soriano, Víctor Fernández 6
South Africa 64, 68, 70, 73–5, 122, 202, 216, 217
Soviet Union (USSR) 4, 30–2, 36–9, 47–53, 56–7, 162, 167, 179–83, 190, 205, 217
Spain 1–6, 13–16, 21–4, 70, 81–94, 216, 220, 225
Stabler, Wells 91
Staderini, Ettore 89
Stalin Joseph 82, 183–4
Stewart, Michael 162
Strauß, Franz Josef 91–2
Struye, Paul 169
Suárez, Alfonso 92–3
Suharto, Haji Mohammad 216, 222
Suri, Jeremi 121

Taschner, Martin 147
Teitgen, Pierre Henri 2
Terebilov, Vladimir 183
Thant, U- 159
Thomas, Daniel C. 15, 46
Tibet 221
Tindemans, Leo 14, 92
Tonra, Ben 217, 229
torture 90, 111–12, 207, 220
    UN Convention against 216, 218, 220–3, 227–9
Tulli, Umberto 6, 15, 30, 35

Uganda guidelines 5
USSR. *See* Soviet Union

Vance, Cyrus 122–5
Van Mierlo, Hans 171, 225
Van Mierlo-Mutsaers, Catharina Maria 171
Van Raay, Janseen 144
Veil, Simone 5, 57

Vetter, Heinz Oskar   143–5, 148–9
Vinci, Piero   88
von Hassel, Kai-Uwe   83, 90, 92

Williamson, David   147
Wilson, Harold   123

World Conference on Human Rights   199–212

Zamburlini, Ilaria   6
Zumbach, Pierre   161
Zussy, Modeste   166

www.ingramcontent.com/pod-product-compliance
Lightning Source LLC
Chambersburg PA
CBHW052219300426
44115CB00011B/1754